SAGE was founded in 1965 by Sara Miller McCune to support the dissemination of usable knowledge by publishing innovative and high-quality research and teaching content. Today, we publish over 900 journals, including those of more than 400 learned societies, more than 800 new books per year, and a growing range of library products including archives, data, case studies, reports, and video. SAGE remains majority-owned by our founder, and after Sara's lifetime will become owned by a charitable trust that secures our continued independence.

Los Angeles | London | New Delhi | Singapore | Washington DC | Melbourne

THE THREE TAGORES, DWARKANATH, DEBENDRANATH & RABINDRANATH

THE THREE TAGORES, DWARKANATH, DEBENDRANATH & RABINDRANATH

India in Transition

Bidyut Chakrabarty

Los Angeles | London | New Delhi
Singapore | Washington DC | Melbourne

Copyright © Bidyut Chakrabarty, 2022

All rights reserved. No part of this book may be reproduced or utilized in any form or by any means, electronic or mechanical, including photocopying, recording or by any information storage or retrieval system, without permission in writing from the publisher.

First published in 2022 by

SAGE Publications India Pvt Ltd
B1/I-1 Mohan Cooperative Industrial Area
Mathura Road, New Delhi 110 044, India
www.sagepub.in

SAGE Publications Inc
2455 Teller Road
Thousand Oaks, California 91320, USA

SAGE Publications Ltd
1 Oliver's Yard, 55 City Road
London EC1Y 1SP, United Kingdom

SAGE Publications Asia-Pacific Pte Ltd
18 Cross Street #10-10/11/12
China Square Central
Singapore 048423

Published by Vivek Mehra for SAGE Publications India Pvt Ltd. Typeset in 10.5/13 pt Adobe Caslon Pro by Zaza Eunice, Hosur, Tamil Nadu, India.

Library of Congress Cataloging-in-Publication Data

Names: Chakrabarty, Bidyut, 1958- author.
Title: The three Tagores, Dwarkanath, Debendranath and Rabindranath: India in transition/Bidyut Chakrabarty.
Description: New Delhi; Thousand Oaks, California: SAGE Publications India Pvt Ltd, 2022. | Includes bibliographical references and index. |
Identifiers: LCCN 2022004365 | ISBN 9789354793837 (hardback) | ISBN 9789354793950 (epub) | ISBN 9789354793967 (ebook other)
Subjects: LCSH: Tagore, Dwarkanath, 1794–1846. | Ṭhākura, Debendranātha, 1817–1905. | Tagore, Rabindranath, 1861–1941. | India—History—British occupation, 1765–1947. | India—Civilization—1765–1947. | Great Britain—Colonies—Asia.
Classification: LCC DS464 .C44 2022 | DDC 954.03—dc23/eng/20220218
LC record available at https://lccn.loc.gov/2022004365

ISBN: 978-93-5479-383-7 (HB)

SAGE Team: Rajesh Dey, Syed Husain Mendhdi Naqvi
Photographs used on the cover: Courtesy - Rabindra-Bhavana, Visva-Bharati, Santiniketan

To

*those battling hard to sustain
the humanistic sociocultural values.*

Thank you for choosing a SAGE product!
If you have any comment, observation or feedback,
I would like to personally hear from you.

Please write to me at **contactceo@sagepub.in**

Vivek Mehra, Managing Director and CEO, SAGE India.

Bulk Sales

SAGE India offers special discounts
for purchase of books in bulk.
We also make available special imprints
and excerpts from our books on demand.

For orders and enquiries, write to us at

Marketing Department
SAGE Publications India Pvt Ltd
B1/I-1, Mohan Cooperative Industrial Area
Mathura Road, Post Bag 7
New Delhi 110044, India

E-mail us at **marketing@sagepub.in**

Subscribe to our mailing list
Write to **marketing@sagepub.in**

This book is also available as an e-book.

Contents

Preface ix

Introduction 1

Part A: Dwarkanath Tagore

1 A New Ideational World 47
2 A Successful Entrepreneur 77

Part B: Debendranath Tagore

3 Continuity with the Past 127
4 Breaking with the Past 160

Part C: Rabindranath Tagore

5 Intermingling of Ideas 209
6 Deriding 'Nationalism' 251
 Conclusion 292

Select Bibliography 321
About the Author 329
Index 330

Preface

The Three Tagores, Dwarkanath, Debendranath and Rabindranath emerged out of my studies that I undertook while working on my earlier book on Rabindranath Tagore's social and political thoughts, entitled *Sociopolitical Thought of Rabindranath Tagore* (New Delhi: SAGE Publications, 2020). Conceptually and also empirically, this book is a sequel to the one that was published in 2020. I have also drawn, rather indiscriminately, on my other works on the intellectual history of sociopolitical ideas that became prominent in our conceptualization of the past mode of thinking. Being a student of sociopolitical processes, I also hold the view that the prevalent socio-economic and politico-ideological visions remain critical to the shaping of one's views and preferences. For instance, Bankim Chandra Chattopadhyay (1838–1894) was one of the prominent ideologues of the 19th century, who propounded views which did not match with what Gandhi in the 20th century held while leading perhaps the most gigantic nationalist struggle against perhaps the mightiest colonial power of the 20th century. It also confirms that the 19th century was an era when both derivative and indigenous ideas figured prominently in the contemporary discourses. It was a unique endeavour for, on the one hand, the prominent Indian thinkers who were persuaded by the Enlightenment philosophy since it contained within itself the seeds of the universal well-being; despite being loyalist in their political commitment to colonialism, they also felt the need, on the other hand, of exploring India's own intellectual heritage. It was not surprising that both Rammohun and his colleague Dwarkanath of the Brahmo Sabha drew on the major Western texts which were complemented with their search for knowledge and wisdom in the indigenous discourses, especially from the Vedas and Upanishads. At one level, they were nurturing the spirit of renaissance; at another level, they were also practitioners since they undertook many concrete steps to pursue their sociocultural mission, couched in uniquely textured politico-ideological preferences. *The Three Tagores, Dwarkanath, Debendranath and Rabindranath* is just a modest endeavour seeking to clearly articulate the new texture of sociocultural visions that gradually gained momentum as the campaign against colonialism spread out from towns to the villages.

The book is basically an argument to defend the point that the three Tagores represented in a concerted effort to shape a specific sociocultural design based on their ideas of how to bring about radical sociocultural changes. It was an effort which was thus a powerful statement against the prevalent power relationships governing interpersonal and also intercommunity interactive existences. At one level, they were pioneers in many respects; at another level, they, by being appreciative of the contributions of their predecessors in this regard, carried forward a sociocultural template which started unfolding by the initiatives of both the indigenous ideologues and their British colleagues of the Asiatic Society of Bengal in opposition to the Anglicists who hardly paid attention to the indigenous intellectual traditions.

The idea of this book was broached by my academic mentor at the London School of Economics and Political Science, Professor (Lord) Meghnad Desai. Over lunch in one of the South London pubs in 2017, Professor Desai bestowed the responsibility of putting together the significant contributions of three Tagores. I remember that in the discussion, he talked at length about the meteoric rise of Dwarkanath, the grandfather of Rabindranath, in trade and commerce in the Empire and also the liquidation of the business empire soon after his demise in 1846. Similarly, he was also fascinated by the saintly lifestyle of his son, Debendranath, despite being born and nurtured in an atmosphere of affluence. Through his experiment of Visva-Bharati which came into being in 1921, Rabindranath had shown different kinds of capabilities which did not exactly match with those of his grandfather or father.

By drawing on the discussion that we had in the pub, I began working on this aspect of Bengal's sociocultural history once I joined Visva-Bharati as its vice chancellor in 2018. First, I focused on the unique sociopolitical priorities that Rabindranath evinced in his creative texts and also manifold activities that he undertook at the aegis of the university. My book entitled *Sociopolitical Thought of Rabindranath Tagore* (New Delhi: SAGE Publications, 2020) is an outcome of my effort. As a sequel to this text, I prepared the present text, which, by encapsulating the intellectual endeavour complemented by their activities, is an initiative to explore further relatively unknown areas of India's sociocultural rejuvenation in the wake of colonialism.

I am indebted to many while completing the book during the most uncertain phase of human history due to the outbreak of COVID-19 and our inability to contain its virulence across the globe. I must have received best wishes from my well-wishers, besides verbal appreciation by many who remain emotionally connected with me regardless of the circumstances. I express my heartfelt gratitude to them. I specifically mention their contribution to my creativity since they sustained my academic zeal by always emotionally charging me whenever I seem to have lost directions. By supplying books and other published materials as quickly as possible, Visva-Bharati librarian Dr Nimai Saha extended yeoman services to an author who never suffered 'writers' block' as he never had to wait for the texts which were indispensable for developing and also supporting the argument. I am thankful to Dr Nilanjan Bandyopadhyay of Rabindra Bhavan for drawing my attention to and collecting the relevant archival resources for the book. The support that I received from Professor Amrit Sen of the Department of English, Visva-Bharati, was most invaluable. I also put on record my appreciation for him. Without the help of the SAGE team, led by Sri Vivek Mehra, it would not have been possible for me to put this academic text in the public domain. I am personally thankful to the SAGE acquisition editor, Sri Rajesh Dey, who, by being author-friendly, considerably eased my task.

Being the vice chancellor of a public university who is always embroiled in works which are distantly connected with academics, it is difficult to carry on what one likes for emotional gratification unless one is supported by a set of team members who are both reliable and appreciative of academic creativity. I thank my stars and also the invisible providential power that I am highly privileged to have a team of that sort. Visva-Bharati's vice chancellor secretariat has no dearth of people who are both committed to Visva-Bharati's well-being and are always there to help me pursue my academic zeal. I express my gratitude to all of them. Of them, Dr Tanmoy Nag has been of extreme help since he eased my task by thoroughly decoding the bureaucratic languages in which most of the official notes are scribbled. Gopal, by providing umpteen cups of tea and coffee, sustained my energy in the office; he also indirectly helped in fulfilling my academic prowess by helping me to retain my energy by making cups of tea and coffee available to me as and when they were needed. By not simply providing me with his service as a university driver, Toofan is also of great support to my creativity by being so humane and punctual—the two qualities that I always privilege since they are at the root of human success.

The purpose of this book is to not merely recreate the past by focusing on the significant contributions of the principal actors in history but also develop a methodology to comprehend the complex sociocultural processes of the period and politico-ideological preferences of those who steered them. It is an attempt to understand the broad trends of human history in a wider canvas. If *The Three Tagores, Dwarkanath, Debendranath and Rabindranath* serves that purpose well, I shall have achieved the objective for which I undertook the endeavour while discharging my role as Visva-Bharati's vice chancellor.

Introduction

The title of the book, *The Three Tagores, Dwarkanath, Debendranath and Rabindranath*, is illustrative of the principal theme that develops in the discussion that follows. It is not, at all, a biographical study, but one that helps us understand the noticeable socio-economic and cultural changes in India in the wake of colonial rule. The Tagore patriarchs epitomized the transformation of their writings and deeds. By seeking to grasp their activities with reference to the prevalent context, the study is an endeavour to capture the complex unfolding of India's socio-economic and cultural milieu during the onset, high noon and decline of colonial rule in India. Dwarkanath represented a quest for an identity by drawing, rather zealously, on the principles of Enlightenment tradition which he accepted as critical to generate enthusiasm for radical social, economic and cultural metamorphosis in India. While he was, on the one hand, a harbinger of significant changes, by being involved in commercial ventures, he also proved, on the other hand, his mantle for activities which, so far, remained an exclusive domain for the British. Aided by his colleagues, including Rammohun Roy, Dwarkanath carved a definite space for the Indians in the fields of literature, trade and commerce in colonial India which was perhaps easier since he stood out as a loyalist. His son, Debendranath, pursued the path a little differently. Unlike Dwarkanath, who largely drew his politico-ideological inspiration from the Western intellectual discourses, Debendranath built his conceptual perspective by creatively blending both the Western and indigenous sources of wisdom. For him, the Vedas and Vedantic texts[1] were equally critical to view humanity. It was a unique attempt though, the roots of which can be

---

[1] Vedas are four in numbers (Rig Veda, Yajur Veda, Sama Veda and Atharva Veda: Of these, the Rig Veda is the oldest). Upanishads are commonly referred to as Vedanta, which is interpreted as 'the last chapters or part of the Vedas', also containing the commentaries on the Vedas.

traced back to Rammohun who brought our attention to the ideas of Vedas and Upanishads to defy Brahminical claim of sati custom being justified by the ancient Hindu texts. Debendranath went a little further by seeking to evolve a mindset by drawing on the 'lost' intellectual treatises which were both intellectually persuasive and directional to mankind. Being fiercely critical of Hindu orthodoxy, he was drawn to the religion, Brahmoism, which was founded by his mentor, Rammohun Roy, along with his like-minded people. Questioning the idolatry, he was persuaded to believe that the Almighty had no form. Not only was he one of the oldest members of the Brahmo Samaj but his devotion for institutionalizing the new religion was also admirable. In fact, it will not be an exaggeration that without his inspiration, the renewed interests among the educated Bengalis in the Vedas and Vedantic texts would have been inconceivable. By holding regular discussion on these ancient texts, Debendranath can be said to have kindled a fire of imagination among his contemporaries and his followers. Inspired by Isha Upanishad's idea of God being omnipresent in all human activities, Debendranath argued that this was a universal truth which he defended by drawing attention to the poetic texts of the Egyptian poet Hafez Ibrahim (1872–1932). That he drew on the humanitarian ideas of Francois Fenelon (1651–1715) was evident when he appreciated the French archbishop because he scathingly criticized the king for violating human rights which was articulated when he suggested that 'to abandon the sentiment of humanity is not merely to renounce civilization and relapse into barbarism, it is to share in the blindness of the most brutish brigands and savages; it is to be a man no longer, but a cannibal'.[2]

Critical to Debendranath's viewpoints was Fenelon's emphatic declaration which was manifested in many of his writings and activities. One is thus persuaded to argue that the second patriarch of the Tagore family evolved an eclectic mode of thinking by creatively blending ideas from various ideologues with identical sociopolitical priorities.

---

[2] Francois Fenelon, *Socrate et Alicibiade: dialogue des morts* (1898), cited in Paul Hazard, ed., *The European Mind, 1680–1715* (New York: Meridian Books, 1967), 282–283.

The campaign that he had launched was a serious threat to the Derozians who, by being scathingly critical to Hindu orthodox practices, created a strong support base among the newly English-educated Bengalis. In tune with his philosophical disposition, Debendranath Tagore however found the Vedas and Vedantic texts as sources of knowledge which were useful to understand India, presumably given their indigenous intellectual roots. Here is a powerful argument to defend the knowledge system that had emerged in India unlike his detractors who blindly accepted the Western discourses as the roots of greater wisdom. Rabindranath Tagore, son of Debendranath, pursued his father's dream with elan and confidence. Seeking to accomplish the tasks that Debendranath left incomplete, the last of the Tagore mavericks set out his mission accordingly. It is true that by the time Debendranath passed away (in 1905), Brahmo Samaj became popular among a sizeable section of the elite Bengalis despite the internecine feud among the followers which divided the Samaj primarily because of personality clashes among its leaders. Nonetheless, Rabindranath continued with the tradition that his father initiated in 1843. Like his father, who established a Brahmo School in 1861 in Santiniketan, he founded Patha Bhavana in 1901 which was a continuity of the school founded by Debendranath. In 1921, Visva-Bharati came into being as an alternative centre of pedagogy and learning at the behest of Rabindranath. Ideologically akin to his father, the youngest son of Debendranath developed his politico-ideological priorities with the aid of an eclectic fusion of not only the core tenets of the central Hindu texts but also the pressing contextual inputs emerging out of contemporary nationalist fervour. Rabindranath stands out in two clear ways: On the one hand, while his grandfather and father were largely social reformers, nationalism which blossomed in full form later did not appear to have been critical in their thinking presumably because of the sociopolitical circumstances in which they articulated their voices. The scene had undergone a sea change when Rabindranath appeared. Aside from his scathing critique of social orthodoxy which he developed in his literary texts, he hardly wavered, on the other hand, while championing his nationalist vision. By supporting Gandhi's anti-British campaign and also by expressing his solidarity with Subhas Chandra Bose when he was ousted from the Congress in 1939, he sent a clear nationalist message to inspire the participants in the campaign. Basic here is the argument that presumably because of the changes in the prevalent politico-ideological circumstances and also his personal nationalist inclination, it was possible for Rabindranath to generate ideas in support of the attack on the British. One should add a caveat here: Unlike Gandhi, Tagore did not directly participate in the nationalist campaign, though in his many writings, including novels and short stories and other critical essays, he expressed his disenchantment with the government.

I

The three generations of the Tagores, beginning with Dwarkanath born in 1794 and ending with his grandson Rabindranath who died in 1941, cover the history of the modern (British) period of undivided Bengal. Dwarkanath's son and Rabindranath's father, Debendranath also carved a space in history by initiating a new religious faith, the Brahmo religion, which was powerful against orthodox Hinduism. It was he who can be said to have consolidated a new intellectual trend by not ignoring India's rich sociocultural heritage. In other words, unlike the first patriarch of the Tagore family, Dwarkanath (1794–1846), Debendranath (1817–1905) created an era in which the derivative Western mode of thinking was simultaneously appreciated along with its indigenous counterpart. It was a remarkable shift in the prevalent intellectual discourse. It was also a watershed moment for colonial India since it also witnessed a powerful critique of Western philosophical discourses which no longer remained axiomatic to the Indians. The Tagores had a critical role in the entire process: On the one hand, Dwarkanath, by being involved in many business ventures, became a tough competitor to the British entrepreneurs which helped him build and consolidate his reputation as a successful Indian among the elites in the British society. With his remarkable success in business, he reversed the image of Indians from being incapable and servile to the ones who were well equipped to excel in any field of human intervention. By demonstrating that intellectually Indians were equally innovative, his son, Debendranath, created, on the other hand, circumstances in which an alternative voice was articulated by drawing on the ancient Indian texts, especially Vedas and Vedantic texts (Upanishads).

In his conceptual mould, the Western philosophical discourses were creatively mingled with their Indian counterparts which led to the rise of a new mode of conceptualization of the unfolding of human life and its constantly changing texture. Rabindranath Tagore (1861–1941) carried the tradition forward and played a significant role in reinforcing the sociocultural traditions that his father had built in collaboration with his equally talented colleagues who felt alike.

II

There is no denying that the three Tagores evolved a new sociocultural vision which was based on a creative blending of the derivative Western discourses with what had emerged out of the Vedas and Vedantic texts, or, for want of a better expression, indigenous discourses. It was relatively easier for them to espouse their distinct approaches to humanity presumably because of the increasing importance of a voice of protest against Hindu orthodoxy and also their exposure to the principles of Western Enlightenment. In other words, a perusal of how they pursued their ideas rather successfully reveals that they were supported by a group of their like-minded colleagues who also had the same vision which the Tagores epitomized. One cannot however undermine the critical role that Rammohun Roy played in the early part of the 19th century in favour of deistic religious ideas which can be said to have triggered momentous sociocultural metamorphosis in Bengal. In view of the available historical accounts, it can be persuasively argued that Rammohun's idea of God was seriously deistic since he questioned prayer in front of the Hindu deities as illogical. As argued by Farquhar, Rammohun was heavily influenced by deism which was very popular among the European rationalists in the 18th century; he readily accepted deism presumably because 'it harmonized well both with what he found in the Upanishads and with what he had learned from Muhammadan rationalists'.[3] Persuaded by Rammohun, Dwarkanath, the senior most of the Tagore patriarchs, joined hands with Rammohun who also accepted him as a compatriot in his mission for purging Hindu

[3] J. N. Farquhar, *Modern Religious Movements in India* (New York: The Macmillan Company, 1915), 37.

society of superstitious beliefs. There is no doubt that Dwarkanath infused new life into the activities that Rammohun undertook by being integrally connected with the endeavour. Before Dwarkanath became active, the prayer for the 'Nirakar Brahma' (shapeless almighty) was conducted in English which needed to be conducted in mother tongue, urged Dwarkanath, to popularize the deistic ideas of religion among their Bengali colleagues and compatriots. With support from Tarachand Chakrabarti and Chandrasekhar Deb who were associated with Rammohun, it was easier for Dwarkanath to defend his claim which was immediately accepted. The effort was successful when both Dwarkanath and Kalinath Munshi agreed to bear the expenses for renting out a hall in Calcutta for regular prayers. A big hall belonging to Kamallochon Bose was taken as the prayer hall on rent. For the first time in 1829, the Brahmo Samaj bought a piece of land in Calcutta to build a prayer hall in the name of, besides Dwarkanath, Kalinath Roy, Prasanna Tagore, Ramchandra Vidyabagish and Rammohun Roy; later on in 1830, new members, Ramanath Tagore, Radhaprasad Roy and Baikunthanath Roy, were also made trustees of the property that their colleagues bought in 1829 for constructing a place for prayer for those believing in deism.[4]

That the Brahmo Samaj was an outcome of collective effort is beyond doubt though the role of Dwarkanath was critical since, given his continuous financial support, the Samaj's activities continued unabated. There are two reasons to account for this: On the one hand, the ideological appeal for deism remained as powerful as before and, on the other hand, the second of the Tagore patriarchs, Debendranath, who after his father's untimely demise in London in 1846, carried the baton to the next generation. Persuaded by Rammohun's conceptual view that 'original Hinduism was a pure spiritual theism ... articulated in the Vedas and Vedantic treatises',[5] Debendranath devoted wholeheartedly to the cause that his father along with his compatriots pursued in adverse sociocultural milieu in Bengal. Like his father, he was

[4] These inputs are drawn from Kshitindranath Tagore, *Dwarkanath Thakurer Jibani* (In Bangla; Biography of Dwarkanath Tagore; Kolkata: Rabindra Bharati Viswavidalaya, 2009; reprint), 64–66.
[5] Farquhar, *Modern Religious Movements in India*, 39.

fortunate to have had a group of colleagues who held identical views against Hindu orthodoxy. Of them, Keshab Sen was most prominent simply because he not only was a vocal critique of superstitious Hindu sociocultural beliefs in the public domain but also had a tremendous capacity to attract 'young students to him'.[6] Very soon, he fell out with Debendranath because he was alleged to have been drawn initially to Christianity which was contrary to the religious faith that the Brahmo Samaj was committed to uphold; later on, his insistence on accepting some of the Hindu sociocultural practices created an unbridgeable gulf with Debendranath and other members of the Samaj, which was culminated in the bifurcation of the Samaj into Adi Brahmo Samaj and Brahmo Samaj of India in 1866.[7] Nonetheless, there were many prominent individuals who joined the Brahmo Samaj when Debendranath took charge of the organization in 1848. He was joined by Vidyasagar, Rajendralal Mitra, Rajnarayan Bose, Sridhar Nayaratna, Radhaprasad Roy and Shyamacharan Mukhopadhyay. Besides conforming to the Rammohun's deistic religion, they also started a school to spread their distinct views on Hinduism which was headed by Akshay Dutta who was known for his prowess in Mathematics and other core disciplines in Science.[8] As per the contemporary historical account, with the joining of Anandachandra Vedantavagish in 1849, the Samaj had one who was an expert in Vedas. Like his father, Debendranath also collected a galaxy of illustrious individual around him for a common cause, although it was an exclusive association since the *Sudras* (or untouchables in common parlance) were not allowed to listen to the chanting from the Vedas and also commentaries offered by experts. In view of his concern for gender equality, it was also reported that Debendranath requested 'his colleague, Sridhar Nayaratna to visit many of the personal residences of the members of Samaj to spread the ideas of Vedas among the women there'.[9] His efforts yielded results and the Brahmo Samaj gained momentum to a significant

[6] Ibid., 41.
[7] Ibid., 41–45.
[8] The discussion is based on Ajit Kumar Chakraborti, *Maharshi Debendranath Thakur* (In Bangla; Biography of Maharshi Debendranath Tagore; Kolkata: Paschimbanga Bangla Akademi, 2013; reprint), 129–131.
[9] Ibid., 153.

extent which also meant that the orthodox forces, especially those led by Dharma Samaj, considerably lost their appeal. Unlike his father who did not seem to have been involved in the activities of the Samaj to the extent he was expected presumably because of his manifold preoccupations, Debendranath sustained the unity of the collectivity except the cessation of Keshab in 1866.

The last of the Tagore patriarchs, Rabindranath, did not appear to have devoted much attention to the Brahmo Samaj; in fact, he attended a programme, organized by his father's detractor, Keshab, presumably because he was persuaded by the latter's 'recognition of the unity underlying religious diversity'.[10] He appears to have been impressed by not Keshab's spirituality but his universality that became part and parcel of Rabindranath's conceptual universe, as history demonstrates. One of the outcomes of the coming together of the poet and Keshab was the dissolution of the organization that was formed by the latter in 1866 in protest against the ideological inclination of the Brahmo Samaj which was later known as Adi Brahmo Samaj. In 1911, the bard took over the leadership of the Adi Brahmo Samaj which he ran quite successfully with the support of his equally competent colleagues, Troylokya Nath Sanyal and Ramananda Chatterjee, the editor of the *Modern Review* and *Prabashi*; he also brought another bright young scholar, Prasanta Mahalanobis, to the Samaj. One of the critical factors that partly explain the growing importance of the Adi Brahmo Samaj was certainly the revival of *Tattwabodhini Patrika* which was discontinued in 1905 after the death of his father, Debendranath. By emphasizing universal humanism in opposition to national egoism and rivalry, his written treatises in the *Patrika* attracted many readers and helped build a milieu in which Adi Brahma Samaj gained popularity. Opposed to caste segregation, the bard invited K. K. Mitra, a non-Brahmin but a Kayastha, to sit at the altar which annoyed the orthodox members of the Samaj since it was an anathema to them. A strong believer of humanism, Rabindranath condemned the effort of his colleagues in the Samaj by saying that Brahmos, in the last analysis, 'instead of worshipping God, worshipped *dol* or

---

[10] David Kopf, *The Brahmo Samaj and the Shaping of the Modern Mind* (New Delhi: Archives Publishers, 1988), 298.

faction'.[11] His primary concern, which was evident in his written texts in *Tattwabodhini Patrika*, was to establish universal humanism. As he believed, 'Brahmo religion … is without dogma and [draws] all people together' regardless of class, caste and ethnicity.[12] Despite his admiration of Russia when he visited the country in 1930, he did not mince words while condemning the totalitarian system of governance that emerged following the 1917 Russian revolution. His main point of critique was based on the argument that

> The Russian ruler forget that by enfeebling the individual, the collective being cannot be strengthened. If the individual is in shackles, society cannot be free. They have here the dictatorship of the strong man. The rule of the many by one may perchance produce good results for a time but not for ever.[13]

Being a priest of humanism, he reiterated the view in his letters to the young members of Adi Brahmo Samaj, including Promotholal Sen, Ajit Chakrabarti, Ramananda Chatterjee and Prasanta Mahalanobis, among others. Inspired by the poet's vision of humanity, one of the younger members, Sukumar Ray, also argued that 'Brahmos were neither Hindus nor non-Hindus, but constituted a society of progressive-minded men and women'.[14] Primary to Rabindranath's mental universe was his heartfelt concern for universal humanism, an idea which he propounded throughout his active life in the tumultuous days of the nationalist struggle for political freedom. The point required to be emphasized here is that the desire to serve humanity that his grandfather, Dwarkanath, evinced continued to remain relevant to the poet who also succeeded in gathering a group of highly energetic and progressive-minded youths around him. So it was also a collective venture in which Rabindranath remained the nucleus.

---

[11] Rabindranath Tagore, 'Adi Brahmo Samajer Vedi', 363, cited in ibid., 300.
[12] Kopf, *The Brahmo Samaj*, 303.
[13] Rabindranath Tagore, *Letters from Russia* (Kolkata: Visva-Bharati, 1984; reprint), 92.
[14] Kopf, *The Brahmo Samaj*, 304.

There are three core points that need attention to argue that it was possible for the Tagore patriarchs to champion the cause that Brahmo Samaj represented primarily because they had, around them, a galaxy of young and vibrant individuals with identical politico-ideological views. First, there is no doubt that the tradition of questioning the Hindu orthodoxy had begun with Rammohun Roy who, by creatively blending the derivative Western with indigenous intellectual discourses, created a new genre of thinking which immediately attracted some of the prominent Hindus in Bengal in opposition to those supportive of the archaic and also superstitious religious beliefs. The point needs to be made with a caveat since besides having internalized some of the core values of Western discourses, he also drew on some of the fundamental tenets of Islamic philosophy. His idea of 'Nirakar Brahma' (shapeless almighty) can be said to have been inspired from there. To illustrate my point, I have referred to Rammohun's pamphlet in Persian, *Tuhfatul Muwahhiddin: A Gift to Deists*. Furthermore, between 1816 and 1819, he published, in both Bangla and English, some important segments of four Upanishads to argue, in an Islamist strain, that Upanishads taught 'pure theism', uncontaminated by idolatry. Rammohun also drew on the Bible, in fact, to substantiate his claim that the doctrines of Christ were supportive of his belief in those principles that justified equality among human beings in absolute terms. Second, it was relatively easier for him to inspire the youth of Calcutta primarily because he, by challenging the well-established superstitious Hindu beliefs, triggered a sociocultural revolution against the proponents of orthodox Hinduism. Furthermore, with the association of Dwarkanath and his compatriots who upheld identical politico-ideological views, the voice that Rammohun had articulated gained momentum. For them, it was not an attempt of Hindu revivalism but an endeavour towards purging Hinduism of superstitions and archaic values, being justified as fundamental to Hinduism. Apart from pursuing Rammohun's mission, the newly inspired group of young men was easily drawn to the campaign given their social commitment to alter the ruling primordial mindset that flourished at the behest of Dharma Sabha, steered by Radhakanta Deb and his blind followers. As mentioned above, with their critical understanding of Vedas and Vedantic texts, the followers of Brahmo Samaj succeeded in demonstrating that by clinging to orthodox ideas of Hinduism, the Dharma Sabha was just an impediment to sociocultural transformation in Bengal. Finally, what Rammohun started, followed by Dwarkanath and his colleagues, continued with Debendranath, the second of the Tagore patriarchs. For the Brahmos, the Vedas were recognized as the sole source of their inspiration and the absence of authentic translation was a constraint. So Debendranath sent four of the Brahmo Samaj members to Varanasi to study and copy the original version of Vedas, which was not of much help as they also justified segregations among human beings based on the accident of birth. In other words, those believing in deism did not appreciate the artificial division based on mere birth. Being drawn to Upanishads which were commentaries and also critical assessments of some of the fundamental ethos and also tenets of the Vedas, Debendranath and his compatriots appeared to have found an intellectual tool to firmly establish the ideas of undivided humanity that their predecessors espoused. Accordingly, he compiled a series of extracts from Hindu literature, the bulk of them from Upanishads, for use in public worship and private devotion, which later was published with the title, *Brahma Dharma*. Fundamental here is the argument that what guided Brahmo Samaj was rationalism or deism in religion. It was not an easy task because (a) the Brahmos were limited in number and (b) the tentacles of orthodox Dharma Sabha were widely spread not only in Calcutta but also in the *mufassil*. Nonetheless, by being steadfastly committed to their cause, the Brahmos not only articulated a powerful voice of protest against Hindu orthodoxy but also successfully steered their mission to fruition since their campaign helped develop a persuasive critique against those obscurantist Hindu beliefs defending partisan interests.

III

The three Tagores represented different eras of British colonialism in India. Dwarkanath saw the era in which the most ruthless and expansionist East India Company spread its tentacles in India by forcibly occupying the areas which remained outside its administrative control. Also, this was the phase when the Bengali intellectuals appear to have favoured the ideas of the Enlightenment as perhaps the only acceptable mode of radical socio-economic and cultural metamorphosis; these ideas were considered to be revolutionary and were thus uncritically acclaimed as instruments of change which were most desirable in circumstances when human beings were governed more by well-entrenched archaic beliefs and less by humane values. The memory of Muslim rule being an epitome of torture for the Hindus remained an important part of the then intellectual psyche. It was therefore not perplexing to find out that the litterateur Bankim Chandra Chattopadhyay (1838–1894) focused on how the sustained Muslim administration by deliberately nurturing anti-Hindu sentiments while governing the areas in which it reigned supreme. His novel, *Anandamath*, published in 1882, is illustrative here. The endeavour that Bhavananda Swami, a Hindu monk, undertook to organize his disciples for liberating the enslaved country which was envisioned as Mother India was the main theme of the novel. For Bankim, the arrival of the British was a source of joy in such a context when Hindus were subject to torture since they held onto a different religious faith other than that of the rulers. Bankim was not an exception, as many of the leading personalities subscribed to this point of view. The growing acceptance of the principles of Enlightenment was thus attributed to the past memory of the majority of the population of Muslims being opposed to Hindu faith and also the 'progressive' values that evolved in India in the wake of the East India Company governance. It can thus be fairly argued that the British rule confronted less opposition in Bengal presumably because it supposedly drew its sustenance from those humanitarian philosophical ideas which were likely to thrive with the consolidation of alien administration. In other words, that the British rule in Bengal was a harbinger of hope was critical to the formation of a mindset in its favour. One has to however accept the claim with a caveat since there were alternative voices which did not tally with the derivative views in support of the British rule. Nonetheless, as history demonstrates, the opposition to the foreign domination gradually lost steam, to a significant extent, at least at the outset, largely due to favourable sociocultural circumstances in which the East India Company relatively easily established its authority.

Socioculturally and in economic terms, India was passing through massive transformation with the ascendancy of the British. Once the

1793 Permanent Settlement was legalized whereby the landlords were made to pay a regular sum to the government, especially following the execution of the Sunset Law, they had no option but to accept the decision for the sake of retaining their landed properties, the only source of income then. After the British settlement in Calcutta which later became the capital of India, the city rose as a hub of all kinds of economic activities; it radically altered the Bengal's socio-economic milieu especially in two major ways: First, with the influx of the landlords and their families from villages to Calcutta, the villages saw the rise of middle men or those who took care of the responsibilities, including cultivation, which broke the emotional chord that evolved between the zamindars and their subjects; it was primarily a symbiotic network, as shown in the available researches, that protected the latter in case of difficulties confronting them.[15] With landlords' departure for Calcutta, this set of people, known as *jotedar*, became prominent in rural Bengal and alienated the cultivators to a significant extent by being indifferent to them even during their sufferings which were generally mitigated earlier by the kind-hearted landlords. Second, once Calcutta became British India's capital, not only it became the centre of governance but also the city provided all kinds of new opportunities which also attracted people from other parts of India, besides Bengal. People found new vocations which were highly limited in the past; once English was introduced in place of Persian as the official mode of communication with the acceptance of the 1835 Macaulay Minutes, many schools were founded for imparting training in English. Bengalis accepted this readily, since it allowed them to be absorbed in government jobs for which the knowledge of English was one of the primary requisites.

The massive economic transformations brought about radical social changes; the class balance which was tilted in favour of the landlords so far was no longer the same because of the creation of many other professions to make money. Besides government jobs and legal professions, Bengalis were found to have been drawn to trade and commerce. Also striking was the flow of ideas from the West to India and, with

---

[15] Sugata Bose elaborated the theme in his *Agrarian Bengal* (Cambridge: Cambridge University Press, 1986).

the consolidation of English as a medium in many places of learning, it was easier for the intellectuals to have access to the Western literature and other politico-ideological discourses. The regular intellectual contacts with the West not only allowed the transfer of knowledge but also created a group of intellectuals who, by being inspired by the derivative ideas, helped develop an ambience in which Western discourses emerged as organic to the indigenous system of thinking. It was an era of hope, promise and change. Implicit here are two major arguments which are directed to understand the comprehensive sociocultural changes in Bengal that spread to the rest of India in due course. On the one hand, the free flow of ideas in the wake of the consolidation of British rule in India contributed immensely to the evolution of new discourses that heavily drew upon the Western ideas of Enlightenment. As the colonial rule became invincible presumably, largely because it developed organic roots in India, the indigenous sources of knowledge lost the importance that it had in the earlier days. Despite efforts by the Asiatic Society of Bengal, founded in 1784, at the behest of William Jones for conserving the indigenous languages, the spread of the English language was unhampered, since it had the full backing of the colonial authorities.

The slavish imitation of European culture saw its peak in the late 18th and early 19th centuries. The first of the Tagore patriarchs, Dwarkanath, was an exemplar of this; he found liberatory potential in the cultural values of the English civilization and thus preferred the English language and lifestyle to the traditions he had been raised in. He thus declared that

> It was England who sent out Clive and Cornwallis to benefit India by their counsels and arms. It was England that sent out of that distant nation the great man who succeeded in establishing peace in the world, and who was the first man that introduced a power and permanent order of things in the East. It was the country which ... protected his countrymen from the tyranny and villainy of the Mohamedans.[16]

[16] Dwarkanath to the Queen Victoria, 29 July 1842, cited in Kissory Chand Mittra, *Memoir of Dwarkanath Tagore* (Calcutta: Thacker & Spink and Co., 1870), 17.

Illustrative here is how Dwarkanath viewed the Company rule which was a relief from the despotic Muslim rule. Here he held the same perception that Bankim did in his writings. The point that deserves to be noted is that the elite Hindus did not seem to have been opposed by the Muslim rulers simply because they were Muslims but because they unleashed a reign of terror that alienated the Hindus. History is a testimony here. For instance, the series of decrees against the Hindus by the Mughal emperors were largely driven by their stiff opposition to Hinduism which was one of the major factors why Hindus welcomed the East India Company in opposition to the prevalent Muslim rulers. For most of the elite Hindus, the arrival of the East India Company was fresh air because it brought with them a design of governance in which Hindus were purportedly not to be discriminated against. It was evident when Dwarkanath hailed the Company rule for being 'impartial and generous' which was further expanded by stating that

> Firm conviction that the happiness of India is best secured by her connection with [this] great and glorious country … whose noble solitude for the welfare and improvement of the millions committed by Providence to its charge, may challenge the admiration of the whole world.[17]

Such an uncritical admiration did not seem to be an exception; instead, it will not be an exaggeration that Hindu elites became a firm loyalist presumably because they were persuaded to believe that alien government was less prejudiced than what they confronted so far during the Muslim rule. A reality check also confirms that while it was easier for Vidyasagar to legalize widow remarriage, Rammohun's endeavour towards abolishing cruel Sati custom would have been futile had the British authorities stood by him. Similarly, without support from the Company rulers, it could not have been possible for Dwarkanath to introduce English education with the establishment of Hindu School in 1817. It can thus be argued that Hindu elites preferred the British conquest presumably because they strongly felt that the British rule was not as retrogressive as the erstwhile Mughal administration, but

---

[17] Dwarkanath's press statement in *The Times*, 4 November 1842, cited in Mittra, *Memoir of Dwarkanath Tagore*, 17–18.

an opportunity towards establishing a system of governance based on the principles of Enlightenment which shaped governance in Great Britain.

The sizable fortune that he had made from trade and commerce in competition with foreign business houses was what allowed him entry into the company of the British elites, including even the royal family. His uncritical acceptance of the principles of the British Enlightenment led directly to the popularization of Western philosophical discourses back home, which was helped along by the coming of, for instance, the Young India campaign with Henry Vivian Derozio at the helm. These forces contributed to the evolution and consolidation of a new cultural wave in India in which indigenous intellectual and cultural traditions were side-lined, if not completely undermined.

The tide turned in the late 1800s, as evinced in the writings of Rammohun Roy who was the first to articulate the relevance of the ancient Indian texts in conjunction with his championing of British Enlightenment values. This admittedly tepid reclamation of ancient Indian heritage nonetheless created conditions for a renewed focus on Vedic and Vedantic resources. The Brahmo Samaj, established in 1828 by Roy, was reinvigorated in 1840 by the second Tagore patriarch, Debendranath Tagore. This kicked off a period of intense linguistic, cultural and spiritual revolution that catapulted non-Western philosophical traditions to centre stage. Debendranath was at the forefront of this movement and took the initiative to get the Vedas translated into vernacular so as to broaden access. He, in collaboration with Akshay Kumar Datta (1820–1886), also encouraged the rendering of scientific discourse in Bengali in the regular meetings of Tattwabodhini Sabha. While Dwarkanath advocated the supremacy of British culture and philosophy, his son Debendranath called for a return to the roots by drawing attention to India's rich intellectual legacy. The clearest distillation of Debendranath's ideas, however, was yet to come. It was in the late 19th and early 20th centuries, with the arrival of the third and most illustrious Tagore patriarch, Rabindranath, that a rich and complementary balance of East and West manifested itself.

IV

As history shows, the three Tagore patriarchs,[18] Dwarkanath, Debendranath and Rabindranath, were important icons of Bengal's sociocultural heritage. Exposed to the Western sources of knowledge and cultural practices in the wake of colonial rule in Bengal, they evolved a unique blending of sociocultural voices that gradually became organic to the Indian mindset. According to the available literature, the first of the patriarchs appeared to have accepted the ideas and values that came as piggyback of colonial power which helped him to go all out against the archaic and inhuman social practices, including sati custom. Aided by Rammohun Roy, the senior-most Tagore actively participated in abolishing the brutal sati custom which had neither the sanction of the scripture nor support of the ruling authority. Challenging the orthodox forces, Dwarkanath attributed the continuity of this inhuman practice to the selfish desire of grabbing the property of the deceased male by forcing his widow to self-immolate in the pyre of her dead husband. Being disgusted with the pompous and luxurious lifestyle of his father, Debendranath resorted to a spiritual line of thinking that had its root in the ideas of Rammohun Roy and his father, Dwarkanath, who by establishing Brahma Samaj set out the platform for the former. With his initiative, the Brahmo Samaj became a major campaign for radical social transformation in Bengal in the late 19th century. Opposed to Hindu idolatry, the second of the patriarchs generated a new wave of thinking in which the Indian ancient texts, especially Vedas and Vedantic texts, received adequate attention. His son, Rabindranath, can be claimed to have universalized the ideas and values linked with Brahmo Samaj, especially those conceptual parameters that were critical to view humanity afresh. Not only did he win the Nobel Prize in literature in 1913 but also his concern for creating and popularizing a new pedagogy of learning helped build newer ways of thinking which were inconceivable

---

[18] In the well-accepted lexicon, the term 'patriarch' means the male head of the family. As history shows, the three Tagores, Dwarkanath, Debendranath and Rabindranath, played this role vis-à-vis the Tagore family.

presumably because of the hegemonic grip of the Western discourses of knowledge generation and dissemination. Being sociopolitically conscious of his historical role, the bard also devoted his energy to evolve an alternative voice which did not match with what Gandhi (1869–1948) propagated. A perusal of his essays and speeches confirms that the poet left no stone unturned to identify the limitations of the political campaign that gained momentum at the behest of the Mahatma. He also separated himself from the revolutionary nationalists, particularly as his novel *Ghare-Baire* (1916) shows, who failed to create a nationalist platform for all presumably because of their social alienation from the poor, especially the poor Muslims. Tagore can thus be said to have articulated a new and also powerful political message by mingling the idea of *karma* or endeavour with the well-being of the nation. In other words, it was a voice for togetherness and selfless work for contributing to the enrichment of communities irrespective of class, clan and ethnicity.

The three Tagores represented a voice of empowerment. Dwarkanath, for instance, stood out in the field of trade and commerce in competition with his foreign counterparts. A pioneer banker, he was one of the first generation of Indian entrepreneurs in the modern setting. His endeavour towards radical social changes entailed his organized campaign for the eradication of barbaric sati custom in 1829 following the adoption of the Bengal Sati Regulation. A true disciple of Rammohun Roy, Debendranath sustained the campaign for purging the society of evil practices and also superstitious beliefs by involving many of his like-minded compatriots in the activities of Brahmo Samaj which not just was a platform for intellectual discourses but also represented a new forum for making people aware of their social responsibilities. That Brahmo Samaj continued to remain important in Bengal's intellectual discourse was largely attributed to the hard work of Debendranath Tagore. To institutionalize the Brahmo faith, he started a Brahmo School in 1861 which was later shifted to Santiniketan in 1891. In fact, it will not be an exaggeration to suggest that Debendranath gave a fillip to his son's desire to set up first a school, Patha Bhavana in 1901, and later a university, Visva-Bharati in 1921, in Santiniketan. The last of the Tagores, Rabindranath Tagore rose to prominence due to his poetic prowess which was globally recognized when he was bestowed with the Nobel Prize in Literature in 1913. Visva-Bharati not only represented a new form of pedagogy but also evolved a new kind of all-round personality development of pupils. His idea of inclusive development was manifested in Sriniketan, an abode of wealth, which was a laboratory for experimenting with agricultural development in villages around the campus. As early as 1921, when Visva-Bharati began its journey as an alternative centre for learning in colonial India, the university adopted 50 villages to articulate its distinct approach of agrarian development. Supporting his equally enthusiastic colleagues and disciples, the poet brought villagers together in his mission for making villages economically self-sufficient. He was a believer of the idea that 'United we win and divided we fall'. Furthermore, his approach to education drew on his faith that book-based learning was futile unless it was connected with reality. The English education was tuned to the creation of a set of clerks to support the British government, while his notion of education was meant to contribute to the blossoming of human personality in all its strides. This was a type of education which was to create a mind free from prejudicial values and systems of thinking. In other words, it was a vehicle for change and not just a passport for government jobs, as was the case then. In a nutshell, by seeking to radically alter the well-entrenched prejudicial mindset, the bard articulated his zeal for socio-economic transformation at two levels: At a rather conventional level, he preferred to establish a system of education generating desires to bring about socio-economic changes which were appropriate for creating an inclusive society. At the practical level, he insisted on specific kinds of training to be imparted to accomplish the goal of all-round socio-economic development exclusively with indigenous support.

V

What brought the three Tagores together was their identical sociocultural concern to conceptualize the idea of India. It is evident that the ideas that unfolded at the behest of the early 'nationalists', including the three Tagores, are clearly reflective of the Orientalist conceptual design for homogenizing the Indians regardless of the obvious sociocultural differences among themselves. This was a deliberate constructed mode of defining the colonized by evolving a culturally specific way of conceptualizing cultural differences.[19] In its encounter with the Orient, the Western powers faced a sociocultural milieu which was manifestly different from what they experienced in the West. Being nurtured in the Western tradition, it was obvious that they would interpret the Orient in their conceptual framework which was exclusively alien to the context in which the Orient evolved. In the process, the West provided a flawed version of the Orient which failed to take into account the Orient's socio-economic and cultural complexities presumably because it was based on an equally flawed reading of Hindu tradition by reference to a set of selective sacred texts. The aim is to substantiate the contention that Hindus were united because of the eternal (*sanatani*) Hindu tradition. This argument has two interrelated components: On the one hand, by insisting that given the eternal homogenous Hindu tradition, it is logical to assume that Hindus cannot be but united as a community; from this, it follows, on the other hand, that Muslims in view of their stark sociocultural (supplemented by religious) features shall always remain different from their Hindu counterparts. As a deliberative process, Orientalism creates an environment in which certain ideas are privileged over the rest to defend those views which are supportive of the project. To build a supportive mindset for the Orientalist mission, the Orientalist selected a set of sacred texts in India which, they thought, were useful to put across the point that Hindus were homogenized as a community. This process, argued an analyst, 'included pulling Indian sacred texts into a Western cognitive grid, reinterpreting texts through translation, the application of Western classificatory methods including hierarchization, the dispersing this body of knowledge in India'.[20] Characterizing

---

[19] I am following the model that Edward Said developed in his *Orientalism* (London: Routledge and Kegan Paul, 1978).
[20] Drawing on Gyan Prakash, 'Writing Post-orientalist Histories of the Third World: Indian Historiography', in *Colonialism and Culture*, ed. N. B. Dirks (Ann Arbor, MI: Michigan University Press, 1992). Paola Bacchetta develops this point in her 'Sacred Space in Conflict in India: The Babri Masjid Affair', *Growth and Change* 31, no. 2 (Spring, 2000): 272.

the process as nothing but 'a modality of cognitive violence',[21] that it is shown to be a deliberate design to consciously construct an idea of India by suggesting that today's India is nothing but a continuity of the past in view of the prevalence of a homogenous eternal Hindu tradition. This process view of interdependence has a clear spiral effect in the sense that it creates and also embraces a system that gradually gains acceptability as axiomatic.

The Orientalist argument defends the point that the endeavour towards essentializing Indian identity was historically conditioned and supportive of a colonial design creating a mindset in its favour. Although neither Dwarkanath nor his son Debendranath ever expressed clearly that behind their sociocultural endeavour remained the endeavour to build a united India since their primary concern was to instil a sense of being proud of one's distinct intellectual prowess. Fundamental to this conceptualization is the idea that Orientalism and colonization went hand in hand. Interestingly, the process of interaction between the colonizers and the colonized was a two-way traffic which entailed that the colonized had evolved a mindset in which the Orientalist design became an integral part; as a result, it was never considered an intrusion, but one that evolved naturally. Hence, it is argued that

> Both the colonizers and colonized are morally responsible, but in two different ways. The colonizer for actively initiating the process that prevents people from accessing their own experiences. The colonized is morally responsible for propagating and perpetuating the same process [though] … in a different time frame.[22]

In the making of a colonial mindset, both the colonizers and the colonized remained critical in the sense that whatever the former germinated was zealously upheld and protected the latter. Perhaps, in its evolution, coercion must have played a decisive role at the outset and, over a period of time, the mindset did not appear to be alien at

---

[21] Bacchetta, 'Sacred Space in Conflict in India, 272.
[22] S. N. Balagangadhara, *Reconceptualizing India Studies* (New Delhi: Oxford University Press, 2012), 115.

all presumably because of its wider acceptance as 'a naturally' grown design. The contention has serious theoretical implications because it is a telos-centric argument in the sense that the goal remains well-defined and the outcome is clearly goal-driven. Nonetheless, the claim that those who were harbingers of India's sociocultural transformation were seriously engaged in creating a corpus of knowledge and wisdom by drawing attention to India's lost intellectual past. Founded in 1784, the Asiatic Society of Bengal complemented the endeavour that the indigenous intellectuals, beginning with Rammohun, had begun in the late 18th century and early 19th century. It was a subtle process that finally appears to have generated waves of thinking which gradually became predominant in the contemporary intellectual discourses. Implicit here are two arguments: On the one hand, the indigenous public intellectuals, while being involved in unearthing the indigenous intellectual resources, appear to have been shaped in a particular fashion which did not seem to be deviant from the Orientalist conceptualization of a specific sociocultural and economic reality. The so-called indigenous people can thus be said to have lost their independent voice. Based on Edward Said's monumental and also most seminal work on Orientalism,[23] it is thus argued that

> Colonialism is not merely a process of occupying lands and extracting revenues. It is not a question of encouraging the colonized to ape Western countries in trying to be like them. It is not even about colonizing the imaginations of a people by asking them to dream that they, too, will become 'modern', developed and sophisticated. It goes deeper. Colonialism denies the colonized people and cultures their own experiences; it makes them alien to themselves; it actively prevents descriptions of their own experiences except in terms defined by the colonizers. This situation makes colonialism intrinsically immortal. Colonial consciousness is not only an expression, but also an integral part, of the phenomenon that colonialism is. In that case, colonial consciousness itself becomes immortal. Colonialism is also immortal because it creates an immortal consciousness.[24]

---

[23] Edward Said, *Orientalism* (Haryana: Penguin Books, 2001; reprint).
[24] Balagangadhara, *Reconceptualizing India Studies*, 111.

The argument is persuasive to the extent that it helps us understand how a particular mindset evolved at the behest of colonizers who, instead of flatly rejecting the indigenous sources of knowledge, superimposed a mode of thinking that drew on the socioculturally liberating ideas. It is not surprising that Dwarkanath was persuaded to believe that the Western philosophical discourses, based on the Enlightenment principles, were panacea to humanity. At the same time, he, by drawing attention to the indigenous sources of knowledge, especially Vedas and Vedantic texts, also devoted his energy to show that these ideas were not, at all, alien to the Indian intellectual traditions but were integrally linked with them. The tradition continued with Debendranath who also found that a true knowledge was possible by a creative blending of both Western and indigenous discourses which was evident by his insistence on studying the core texts of Enlightenment philosophy by the members of Brahmo Samaj. Rabindranath was not clearly at variance with what he derived from his father. He also accepted the Western mode of thoughts as critical to the discovery of India's distinctive intellectual past. With this in mind, he devised the course curricula at Visva-Bharati which represented an effort on his part to develop a conceptual tool based on his comprehension of both the Western and indigenous discourses. As India's intellectual history shows, the argument also highlights, on the other hand, the point that it was a trend that was reflected in the endeavour and also written tracts of the then leading intellectuals. In his various creative texts, Bankim Chandra Chattopadhyay (1838–1894), for instance, argued strongly for imbibing the spirit of the Western discourses for he found in them a step, perhaps a strong step, in realizing the sociocultural goals that he steadfastly espoused. Similarly, Vidyasagar (1820–1891) appeared to have held the same view to save the distortion that the Hindu zealots deliberately made while interpreting the *Sastras* or the holy books. Swayed by the fact that only through hard work a nation flourished, he thus emphasized that 'the greatest duty of an individual, and his life's preeminent activity, is to be as hard-working and diligent as he can in promoting the welfare of the country in which he was born'.[25]

---

[25] Benoy Ghosh, 'Vidyasagar O Bangali Samaj', cited in Brian Hatcher, *Idioms of Improvement: Vidyasagar and Cultural Encounter in Bengal* (Delhi: Primus Book, 2020), 264.

This idea was reverberated in Dwarkanath's explanation of why the British rose to prominence. Similar to the explanation of Vidyasagar, he also admired the Britishers for being so hardworking and committed to the realization of their sociopolitical objectives.[26] Rabindranath echoed his grandfather's voice when he also attributed their success to their inchoate desire to work hard for the goals, which was evident when he stated that

> What catches [his] eyes [is] the busy air of the people! It is amusing to note the expressions of the people walking hastily down the streets, oblivious to the people around them, an expression of urgency writ upon their faces, trying with all their might and main, lest time should give them the slip.[27]

The fundamental point here is that the keenness to work hard was integral to everybody in England. It was neither forced upon them nor an outcome of any threat of punishment if they deviated. In Rabindranath's perception, it became integral to their lifestyle which evolved over generations since, as per him, 'it was a constant struggle for [their] livelihood'[28] which he further elaborated by insisting that

> The people of this country are Nature's pampered children—no one has the opportunity to sit back idly, reclining on a cushion. Not only does the soil of this country yield fruit as it does in our country by merely scratching at its surface; it has also to fight to winter's chill.... Only the fittest survive in this land, only those who have the ability may raise their heads high.... Not only does one have to fight Nature, one must also deal with much competition in the workplace.[29]

Intellectually, Rabindranath was inspired by the Enlightenment principles, like his grandfather and father, and was also appreciative of the zeal that ordinary Englishmen demonstrated while fulfilling

[26] Mittra, *Memoir of Dwarkanath Tagore*, 93–95.
[27] The second letter of Rabindranath Tagore in Rabindranath Tagore, *Letters from a Sojourners in Europe* (Kolkata: Visva-Bharati, 2008), 38.
[28] Ibid., 39.
[29] Ibid.

their assigned duties as citizens. But a sensitive poet was equally unhappy when he found that 'the working classes of this country do not seem to have any trace of humanity left in them—they seem to be placed only a step above animals,' which he condemned by saying that 'those reddened faces replete with bestiality are repulsive'.[30] It was for Rabindranath to make this argument possibly because by then he emerged as a widely accepted critical voice against colonialism not only in India but also abroad. His winning of the Nobel in 1913 in literature helped him spread his ideas across the continents, including some of the non-English-speaking countries in the east.

VI

This book is also an attempt to conceptualize the mindset that gradually became predominant in India at the behest of three Tagore patriarchs and their associates with identical sociocultural goals. An analytical dissection reveals that, at one level, the ideas that unfolded at their aegis can be conceptually formatted in the Orientalist theoretical mould, since none of the Tagores created a completely deviant mode of thinking. As a loyalist, Dwarkanath happily accepted the conceptual packages that were rooted in the Enlightenment thoughts. It was also a source of inspiration for him to probe deep into India's distinct intellectual traditions. The reason needed to be found in his determination to show to the rest of the world that the concern for humanity was not an exclusive domain of the West; there are many persuasive texts in India's intellectual repositories which, by highlighting the same concerns, pursued the same goal. Evident here is that Dwarkanath's argument was couched in the same conceptual format, though he had different sources of evidence. In other words, it was an attempt to make an identical argument that the colonizers made to prove that they were superior to the colonized. Debendranath did not seem to be different in his conceptual mould, though he focused primarily on building an indigenous repository of wisdom by insisting how Vedas and Vedantic texts were important in this regard. One hardly notices any deviation from what his father initiated in the late 19th century.

---

[30] Ibid.

What was however little different in case of Debendranath was his success in institutionalizing the search for knowledge in the ancient texts and also its sustenance by creating a committed corps of colleagues and disciples in Calcutta and also in *mufassil* towns. One of the outcomes of this effort was the foundation of Visva-Bharati in 1921 by his son, Rabindranath, which not only established an alternative form of learning but also instilled among the colonized a sense of being confident of their intellectual prowess and abilities notwithstanding the adversities which he encountered while being involved in fulfilling his mission. Given the obvious political hegemony of the British, it was not possible for Debendranath, as mentioned in Chapter 1, to completely reject English education since it was a passport to government and other jobs in British merchant houses. Nonetheless, the establishment of a school where both English and the vernacular Bangla received equal emphasis shows that Debendranath was unable to cross the hurdle. Unlike the past experiments, Visva-Bharati was a novel endeavour, for it became a platform in which the ideas of the West were as enthusiastically accepted as those from the eastern intellectual discourses, especially Vedas and Upanishads.

One is now in a position to make two arguments which will help us pursue the point that Orientalism as a thought process does not seem to be exactly appropriate to comprehend Bengal's intellectual history that started unfolding in the late 18th century at the behest of Rammohun and Dwarkanath, at the outset, and later Debendranath and finally Rabindranath. First, there is no denying that the colonizer was responsible for 'actively initiating the process that prevents from accessing their own experiences [and the colonized was] responsible for propagating and perpetuating the same process'.[31] The argument remains valid before concerted attempts were made by Rammohun who, despite having endorsed the spirit that the Western discourses were libertarian presumably because they were rooted in the Enlightenment philosophy, also generated a new genre of thinking by relooking at the indigenous intellectual resources, articulated in Sanskrit, Persian and Arabic. It was a new endeavour which evolved a

---

[31] Balagangadhara, *Reconceptualizing India Studies*, 114–115.

relatively less publicized mode of thinking presumably because of the deliberate efforts of the colonizers to completely erase the historical memory of the colonized. Once English education was made mandatory in India with the adoption of the 1835 Macaulay Minutes, the effort to popularize the 'native' languages received a severe jolt from which they hardly ever recovered. The demeaning of Sanskrit as 'a less valuable language, that what may be found in the paltriest abridgements used at preparatory schools in England' represented how the language was viewed by those who mattered in the decision-making processes in the colonial government. So the Orientalist project was based on coercion which also means, to pursue a counterfactual argument, that had India not been colonized, the thought processes would have followed a different trajectory. The most basic cognitive weakness of the Orientalist venture by the colonizers stems from the fact that there existed a chasm between the derivative ideas and their cultural roots. To this was added the acceptance by the colonized of these ideas as axiomatic which helped them perpetuate for years together. In consequences, one thus endorses the view that 'the European cultural experiences of India is [an appropriate] framework for Indians to understand their own culture [which] ... prevents them from accessing their own culture and experience' in their own terms of references.[32] The outcome is disastrous because, as a result, the Indians 'are unable to articulate or to understand their own experiences [which further led to the denial of their] experiences while they futilely and busily try to make alien experiences their own'.[33] The argument thus hinges on the point that there is one way of conceptualizing the sociocultural and economic realities regardless of the prevalent milieu. It was also manifested in Benedict Anderson's endeavour towards building 'a modular form of nationalism' which was exposed as conceptually faulty by many post-colonial writers. For instance, Partha Chatterjee in his *The Nation and Its Fragments*[34] takes issue with Anderson's conception of 'modular' forms of nationalism which hardly explains

---

[32] Ibid., 116–117.
[33] Ibid., 117.
[34] Partha Chatterjee, *The Nation and Its Fragments: Colonial and Post-colonial Histories* (New Delhi: Oxford University Press, 1994).

nationalism that had emerged in the context of anti-colonial political mobilization in India. Chatterjee accepts the basic premise about the essentially 'invented' nature of national identities and the importance of such factors as 'print capitalism' in their spread and consolidation. He however challenges Anderson's assumption concerning 'modular forms' of nationalist intervention since it ignores the point that if modular forms are made available, nothing is left to be imagined. Hence, the argument for modular forms does not seem to be tenable because the textures of the communities located in various sociocultural and economic contexts vary for obvious reasons. Second, the argument defending and also challenging the Orientalist vision provides inputs to put across the point that it is neither axiomatic nor lacks substance. As India's past intellectual history demonstrates, as soon as attempts were made to create an independent intellectual domain independent of the erstwhile Islamic discourses in the wake of the British rule, the indigenous thinkers found the Western ideas as liberating and intellectually persuasive. It was not a matter of the accident that Rammohun and his compatriot Dwarkanath were drawn to the Western philosophical discourses as they found them compatible with what they had in mind. So it worked in two ways: On the one hand, their views were consolidated out of their distaste for the prevalent ideas that the Islamic rule championed and they also derived emotional support; on the other hand, what they learnt from the ideas also justified colonialism as a means to civilize the barbarian Indians. In other words, colonialism, despite being a hierarchical and also hegemonic system of governance, emerged as a panacea presumably because of the erstwhile brutal feudal Muslim rule. Conditions were created in which the indigenous intellectuals were instinctively drawn to the libertarian views upheld by the principles of Enlightenment. This is not the end of the story which further develops also into an innate urge to unearth the indigenous intellectual resources. So Rammohun found the source of inspiration in, for instance, the Islamic Sufi philosophy, besides, of course, the Vedas and Vedantic tracts. In opposition to the Dharma Sabha, which was patronized by the orthodox Hindus, Rammohun convincingly proved that sati was neither justified religiously nor considered appropriate by any of the holy canons of Hinduism. So, here, he defended a point by showing that this brutal custom of burning widows was allowed to continue by the Hindu zealots to realize their partisan aims. Similarly, Vidyasagar, in his first well-argued text in defence of widow remarriage in January 1855, persuasively argued that the interpretation of *Parasara Samhita* which was quoted by the orthodox Hindus to justify the status quo in this regard was entirely wrong. According to him, the widely quoted *sloka* of *Parasara Samhita* on which he built his argument in favour of widow remarriage clearly suggests that 'on receiving no tidings of a husband, on his demise, on his turning an ascetic, on his being found impotent, or on his degradation—under any of these calamities it is canonical for women to take another husband.'[35]

The argument is crystal clear: Widow remarriage was not anathema in so far as the Hindu scriptures were concerned. The system continued presumably because of the hegemonic grip of the orthodox Hindus over social customs and mores which also meant that voices opposed to it were easily muzzled. So when Dwarkanath emerged on the scene, the template for sociocultural reform was already being prepared. With the foundation of a monotheistic sect of Hinduism, the Brahmo Samaj in 1828, those who opposed prejudicial sociocultural practices received a boost which gained momentum once the baton passed onto Debendranath, the son of Dwarkanath. What was common between Rammohun and Debendranath was their steadfast commitment to reinterpret religious beliefs and values by a proper analytical dissection of the well-established Hindu scriptural texts. The trend was not different because Debendranath's son, Rabindranath, also believed in the importance of Vedas and Upanishads as sources of wisdom. A careful comprehension of the endeavours of three Tagores and their associates reveals that at one level, they appeared to have been heavily influenced by the Orientalist discourses since they justified some of their sociocultural designs in terms of what they derived from the Western discourses. Memoirs of the Tagores are, for instance, illustrative here. This is part of the story which further unfolds with their equal emphasis on learning from the indigenous

---

[35] *Parasar Samhita* is cited by Benoy Ghose in his *Iswar Chandra Vidyasagar* (New Delhi: Publication Division, Ministry of Information and Broadcasting, Government of India, 1971), 64.

traditions of Hinduism. There should be a note of caution here. None of the Tagores was religious, though they were, of course, spiritualists which means that they upheld the principal religious texts not as sources of mere sermons but full of ideas to view human beings and their collective existence in a fresh light. What was unique about the ideologues of the mid-18th century was an attempt to draw out the rich intellectual resources that remained an exclusive domain of the orthodox Hindus; with the rise of the Tagores as a dominant voice of opposition which also drew sustenance from an analytical grasping of the ancient scriptures and the concomitant commentaries, the Hindu zealots lost their importance to a significant extent. The task did not seem to be an easy one presumably because the orthodox beliefs had well-entrenched social roots and also because of the fearfulness of the majority of the unknown consequences of defiance of religious instructions, given by the so-called custodians of Hinduism. Nonetheless, they hardly restrained themselves to articulate their views in opposition to the mainstream thought processes.

There is a fundamental issue that needs to be addressed at the end of this introduction. Is Orientalist mode of thinking unavoidable? The answer cannot be a categorical no because Orientalist conceptualization of the colonized was a product of a thinking that evolved over the years. The colonized nations were thus drawn to the imposed thought processes given the deliberately nurtured hierarchical relationship between the ruler and the ruled. At the dawn of colonialism, what governed the colonizers was their concern for civilizing the barbarians. Even a scholar and parliamentarian like Edmund Burke endorsed the claim that British colonialism was for India's benefit. Even after the foundation of the Indian National Congress in 1885, that the British philosophical discourses were libertarian in character was very zealously pursued. Both Dwarkanath and Debendranath appear to have been swayed by this aspect, though they stayed away from institutionalized political activities. Their priority was well-defined; along with their comprehension of the Western philosophical discourses, they also generated public interests in the indigenous literature of conceptualizing humanism. So by accepting that the Hindu traditions were equally important given their cultural connectedness with the

Hindus, Dwarkanath and Debendranath introduced a new mode of thinking which also flourished simultaneously with their appreciation of the Western philosophical tracts. In other words, given the fact that the two Tagore patriarchs developed their models by learning from both the discourses, it is difficult to suggest which of the discourses was predominant in their thoughts, though one is persuaded to argue that their ideas evolved out of a creative mixture of both the Western sociocultural ideas and their indigenous counterparts. We must also be aware of the fact that in Dwarkanath's thought, the distinction between what was Western and what was clearly indigenous was visible, while in his son's approach the indigenous ideas appear to have been privileged as a careful study of the texts that he articulated to justify his spiritual faith on the Supreme Soul. Rabindranath's ideas were far more complex; although they were visible impact of the Western discourses, his thoughts were also drawn on the Hindu religious scriptures because they provided him with refreshing inputs to reconceptualize humanity and human existence in a world when colonial power was subject to the nationalist threat which reached a different height once Gandhi emerged on India's political scene. The poet was appreciative of the Orientalist mindset, though it was, to him, an aid to critically conceptualize the indigenous sociocultural identity. Rabindranath was also politically involved in the nationalist campaign in an indirect way since he did not participate directly in the anti-British offensive, unlike Dwarkanath and Debendranath who pursued their political goal in the sense they were also involved in activities leading to the eradication of sociocultural discrimination which means that they articulated their political views by seeking to change the power relationships between the haves and have-nots. In the changed politico-ideological milieu, Rabindranath's views seem to be qualitatively different in two ways: He challenged the British rule as it was deviant from the Enlightenment principles which was manifested, for example, in his abdication of Knighthood in protest against the brutal firing of the British police in the 1919 Jallianwala Bagh incident. His condemnation was based on his appreciation of the foundational values on which the British Empire was based. Here, Orientalism was not just a mode of imitating the West but also a voice to develop a scathing critique of British colonialism. This was one side of his approach to the Empire; the other side is reflective of his careful responses vis-à-vis the colonial rule. It was evident when he declined to visit Ireland as it was likely to be a source of irritation to the rulers. His reluctance to go to Ireland in 1913 was based on his assessment that 'the English government would not be pleased with his visit to England's most disturbed country',[36] which also confirms that the bard operated strategically where necessary.

VII

Divided into three parts, *The Three Tagores, Dwarkanath, Debendranath and Rabindranath* has altogether six chapters, besides an introduction and a conclusion. Parts divide the focus of the chapters. Since it is a study of sociocultural views that developed and became prominent in colonial Bengal, and later India, during the 19th and 20th centuries at the behest of three Tagores, Dwarkanath, Debendranath and his son, Rabindranath, along with their close associates holding identical politico-ideological views. By setting the argument in the prevalent sociocultural perspective, the introduction endeavours to demonstrate that the intellectual campaign that Tagores spearheaded had its roots in Rammohun's approach to social transformation. While he wanted to build a bridge between the sociocultural differences among human beings due to their different religious identities, the tradition did not seem to have received less attention once Debendranath, the eldest son of Rammohun's colleague, Dwarkanath, emerged on the scene. No clear evidence is however available to show that Debendranath was opposed to those belonging to a different religious sect, though the fact that he upheld Upanishad as the principal source of knowledge and wisdom helps us understand his inkling.

Dwelling on the significant contribution that Dwarkanath made as a social reformer and also a successful entrepreneur, Part A, in two chapters, is an elaboration of the principal point. As is well known,

---

[36] Sirshendu Majumdar, *Yeats and Tagore: A Comparative Study of Cross-cultural poetry, Nationalist Politics, Hypernated Margins and the Ascendancy of the Mind* (Palo Alta, CA: Academia Press, 2013), 213.

being an admirer of Rammohun, Dwarkanath was associated with many of his schemes leading to radically alter the prevalent sociocultural milieu, as Chapter 1 elaborates. It was with his initiative that Bengal saw the printed weeklies in vernacular; it was also due to his effort that Calcutta saw many schools and colleagues; it was also an outcome of his endeavour that the first medical college was founded in Calcutta in 1835. Chapter 2 is about that aspect of Dwarkanath's effort which was little perplexing given the inherent reluctance of the Bengalis to get involved in trade and commerce. It was a revolutionary step since Dwarkanath who began his involvement in business as a banian (who helped the British to communicate with local suppliers given his ability to speak in English) finally emerged as one of the most successful businessmen in the Empire in the 19th century. Also striking was his collaboration with a British firm, Carr Company, which was also inconceivable, especially when colonial power was increasingly becoming politico-ideologically well-entrenched. Part B is about the specificities of the sociocultural interventions that Debendranath made to carry forward the traditions that his father built in association with his intellectual mentor, Rammohun. There are two chapters here. As mentioned above, Debendranath devised a different scheme for bringing about meaningful sociocultural transformation in Bengal. Unlike his mentor, he concentrated on the ancient Hindu religious scriptures, especially Upanishads which were, being repositories of wisdom, adequately equipped to regenerate a moribund 'nation'. By focusing on the specific projects, Chapter 3 argues that as a true disciple of Dwarkanath, Debendranath continued with the same tradition: Besides being involved in building institutions of learning, he also devoted energy and spent money in translating *Ramayana, Mahabharata* and some of the Upanishads in Bangla and English with support from the Asiatic Society of Bengal. He was also credited with the creation of another platform for religious discourses, known as Tattwabodhini Sabha; with his initiative, *Tattwabodhini Patrika* gained momentum. Chapter 4 pursues the discussion further by dwelling on his role in championing the ideas that the ancient Hindu texts, especially Vedantic tracts, espoused. For him, his efforts were directed to understand the indigenous politico-ideological vision which, he strongly felt, remained peripheral in our search of knowledge.

Debendranath was one of these rare social reformers who generated a zeal for comprehending the ancient spiritual texts. It was with his initiative that the concern for knowing India's sociocultural roots received adequate attention among his colleagues and associates. The emergence of Visva-Bharati in 1921 as an alternative centre of learning and pedagogy would not have been possible had Debendranath not laid the foundation of Brahmacharya Vidyalaya in the late 19th century in Santiniketan. Part C deals with the role that the last of the Tagore patriarchs, Rabindranath, played in pursuance of his distinctive sociocultural faith. Chapter 5 is about how the poet carved a space in Bengal's intellectual history independent of his predecessors. Inspired by Rammohun (1774–1833), his grandfather, Dwarkanath (1794–1836), and Vidyasagar (1820–91), the bard creatively blended what he derived from his intellectual mentors with what he learnt from the contextual sociopolitical impulses. Given his exposure to the Western discourses and also the ancient sources of thoughts at a very young age, he evolved a model in which one notices elements from both of them. As is well known, Rabindranath was also involved in the contemporary political struggles that drew inspirations first from the revolutionary nationalist perspective and later from the Gandhian non-violence which is dealt with in Chapter 6. The aim of the chapter is to identify the distinctive nature of his voice while challenging the British rule; he was both Gandhian and also anti-Gandhian, as the chapter demonstrates. In the process, he evolved a unique politico-ideological vision which was neither Gandhian per se nor exactly opposed to the fundamental precepts of what the Mahatma stood for. A devoted apostle of non-violence, as his plays *Visarjan*, *Muktadhara* and *Prayaschitta*, among others, show, Rabindranath opposed to the violent methods and also the discriminatory practices that the revolutionary nationalists had indulged in during the anti-Bengal partition campaign of 1905–1908, as his novel *Ghare-Baire* displays. The book ends with the conclusion that a careful scan of the roles of the three Tagore mavericks reveals that they remained one of the predominant sources of sociocultural changes in Bengal. What Dwarkanath initiated was led to fruition by his equally socioculturally sensitive son, Debendranath, which reached its zenith once Rabindranath shouldered the responsibility amid various kinds of politico-ideological challenges linked with colonial rule. Nonetheless, with his steadfast commitment to the cause, he not only raised a voice for sociocultural amity regardless of religion, caste and clan but also devised a design which unfolded with the foundation of Visva-Bharati in 1921.

VIII

Instead of being a biographical study, *The Three Tagores, Dwarkanath, Debendranath and Rabindranath* is an attempt to map out the story of a cognitive revolution complemented by a radical epistemic transformation that Bengal witnessed in the 19th and 20th centuries. There is no denying that the process had begun with the initiatives of the British Orientalists which gained momentum once the indigenous elites were persuaded to explore further in this regard. Being inspired by them, it was Rammohun who creatively devised a design by drawing upon the Western and indigenous discourses. The intellectual traditions that evolved with him received a boost once his colleague, Dwarkanath, and later his admirer, Debendranath, took it onto themselves as their responsibility to carry forward what they derived from him. Being born and nurtured in a highly cosmopolitan family, Rabindranath was naturally privy to the newly emerged cognitive vision that blossomed fully when he reigned supreme in Bengal's sociocultural universe. His personal cognitive identity can thus be said to have evolved out of his exposure to the prevalent visions and also his interactions with his family members, besides those that he received by being interactive with the literati of Calcutta. This was an era of possibilities. On the one hand, the Asiatic Society of Bengal under the care of one of the most well-informed intellectuals of the period, William Jones, insisted on unearthing the precious intellectual resources on which the Indian civilization drew its sustenance since time immemorial, while the Anglicists, led by James Mill and T. B. Macaulay, among others, on the other hand, generated an intellectual wave, supported by the colonizers, to belittle the derivative Indian intellectual traditions. Both these trends were clearly noticeable then, and the indigenous intelligentsia were hardly immune from the intellectual influences that they generated. It is thus plausibly argued that 'together, the Orientalist "positive" and the Anglicist "negative" cognitive identities constituted the seed of a new-shared cognitive identity for their indigenous followers'.[37] This was the basis on which new epistemic visions emerged. To persuasively capture the trajectory of the cognitive-cum-epistemic identity which was manifested in Bengal at the behest of Dwarkanath, Debendranath and Rabindranath, the book offers two major and one minor (or supplementary) arguments. First, the study argues on the basis of both archival and literary sources that cognitive identities hardly remained static but were in constant flux since they emerged out of a peculiar interconnection with changing socio-economic and politicocultural milieu. An analytical dissection, for instance, of the ideas of Debendranath who accepted Rammohun as his mentor and his father, Dwarkanath, who introduced him to Upanishads, substantiates the claim. The second argument hinges on the claim that while pursuing their sociocultural objectives, neither Dwarkanath nor his son, Debendranath, was hardly associated with the political struggles against the foreign rule that had already begun in Bengal. It is true that they did not participate in the struggle per se; but by being involved in changing the prevalent power relationships in the society, they coached their campaign in a clearly articulated political language. In other words, unlike Rabindranath who challenged the British Empire by abdicating the Knighthood as a mark of protest against the brutal firing of the British police in Jallianwala Bagh in 1919, their role was far more subtle since they undertook various sociocultural missions to eradicate prejudicial sociocultural beliefs. The complementary argument takes care of the concern that cognitive identity cannot be conceptualized independent of the surrounding socio-economic priorities and politico-ideological preferences. This perhaps persuasively explains why Dwarkanath was a loyalist; Debendranath appeared almost indifferent to what was happening then in the British-ruled political set-up, given his fascination and also deep-rooted interests in spiritual uplift. The scene was different when Rabindranath became a powerful voice; he not only expressed his displeasure with the British government but also supported Gandhi when he was persuaded and also opposed him when he differed. Fundamental here is the point that one's cognitive

---

[37] Subrata Dasgupta, *The Bengal Renaissance: Identity and Creativity: From Rammohun Roy to Rabindranath Tagore* (Ranikhet: Permanent Black, 2007), 238.

identity is formed in response to both internal and external stimuli. With the emergence of Gandhi as a pan-Indian leader, the contemporary political scene not only underwent a sea change but also created many constituencies of support for the nationalist struggle which were completely peripheral, if not absent. It was therefore expected that Rabindranath's approach to the collective battle against the political hegemony of the British was bound to be different since his cognitive identity evolved differently in response to different impulses.

By elaborating these arguments with reference to evidences, *The Three Tagores, Dwarkanath, Debendranath and Rabindranath* also seeks to draw out the changing intellectual perceptions that were critical to comprehend the constantly transforming texture of Bengal's sociocultural milieu. Although the chapters are individual-centric, the aim here is to view the visible sociocultural changes upon a wider canvas. Critical here is the point that one's epistemic identity is an offshoot of complex sociocultural and politico-ideological processes which may often operate at a subterranean level. With this insight, it is easier to appreciate why the three Tagores designed unique sociocultural visions and politico-ideological preferences; after all, they represented three contrasting milieu-driven perspectives.

Part A

Dwarkanath Tagore

Courtesy: Rabindra-Bhavana, Visva-Bharati, Santiniketan

It is axiomatic that specific socio-economic and politicocultural circumstances create conditions in which specific ideas unfold. The onset of British colonial rule was such an occasion which radically altered the conventional approach to governance and also humanity. By challenging the prevalent ideas concerning society, economy and politics, the British rule also contributed to the emergence of a new voice for radical social reforms in Bengal, which was colonized first following the defeat of the then Bengal ruler in the 1757 Battle of Plassey. As days passed on, the British rule developed organic roots in the province by creating hopes for better administration in contrast with the declining Mughal rule in India. By the late 18th century and early 19th century, it was possible for the colonizers to easily generate adequate support for colonial rule, presumably because it was considered to be a panacea for the subjects in view of their modernizing zeal. In a nutshell, there were two ideational aims that unfolded with the arrival of the British who seemed to have engendered enthusiasm among the indigenous elites for accepting the alien governance as perhaps the best available alternative to them. First, with many of the government initiatives, they readily welcomed the British rule given its roots in the sociopolitically progressive principles of Enlightenment; they were persuaded to believe that with the government backing, their endeavour for radical social changes was likely to succeed. One of the first Indian thinkers who stood for the colonizers was Rammohun Roy (1772–1833), for he believed that colonialism was a boon in disguise. For him, the British Raj was the destiny's prescript presumably because of the growing resentment against the existent governance. Second, as the available evidence shows, colonialism also advanced with assistance from the Christian missionaries. Hence, it is claimed that 'the urge for social reform in India is a direct outcome of Christian missions and Western influence … and all communities have felt the impact in a greater or less degree'.[1] The contemporary evidence also mentions that 'the primal impulse for social reform was communicated by the Serampore Missionaries to Ram Mohan Roy, and by him to

---

[1] J. N. Farquhar, *Modern Religious Movements in India* (New York: The Macmillan Company, 1915), 387.

the Hindu community'.² Whether it was a particular group of missionaries that inspired the Indian social reformers to undertake radical social reforms is debatable. Nonetheless, the fact remains that a large group of Bengali public figures were not only drawn to the ideas of the missionaries, the foundational values of the Enlightenment philosophy, but also became a critical source of newer thoughts which, so far, remained distant in the Bengali mindset. Second, the role of the Asiatic Society of Bengal had supplemented the urge expressed by the indigenous elites in favour of reviving the ideas that Vedas and Vedantic texts contained.³ Dwarkanath (1794–1846) was born and raised in such an environment when the Hindu archaic social values were severely challenged and serious attempts were made to bring about radical social reforms. It was an era of questioning the archaic social values that were clearly restrictive in character and prejudicial to the lower castes. A powerful voice was articulated against the social bondage, justified as integral to Hinduism by this enlightened section of the Bengali elites who, being supported by the British rulers, gained strength in pursuing their socio-economic and cultural objectives. By following the path of reform that Rammohun had set out, Dwarkanath continued the endeavour which his mentor failed to complete because of his untimely death in 1833. Being a disciple of Roy, Dwarkanath had also believed that the British rule was free from the vices of the erstwhile Muslim governance. A hardcore liberal and also a loyalist, the first of the Tagore patriarchs undertook many social activities, including the spread of education because he, like his mentor, also held the view that the campaign for social reforms was likely to lose its momentum unless one was adequately educated. A liberal Tagore also insisted on press freedom, which, being a foundational pillar of liberalism, was required to freely express views on myriad issues of governance, society and economy. The outcome was the inauguration of *Tattwabodhini Patrika* in Bangla and *The Bengal Herald* in English in 1829; while the former continued even during the 20th century, the latter was shelved with the demise of Rammohun Roy in England in

² Ibid.
³ O. P. Kejariwal dealt with this aspect in his *The Asiatic Society of Bengal and the Discovery of India's Past* (Delhi: Oxford University Press, 1988).

1833. Nonetheless, this was illustrative of how both Rammohun and his follower Dwarkanath created a space for the print media to flourish in the immediate future. Basic here is the idea that being impressed by the core Enlightenment principles, both Roy and Dwarkanath left no stone unturned to introduce these derivative ideas to the Bengalis as perhaps the only means to take them out of the superstitious values and beliefs. They were thus a harbinger of a new era which gradually unfolded as history progressed in the wake of the British rule in India.

Dwarkanath was also a pioneer in another respect. While Rammohun Roy devoted his energy to spread out and consolidate the concern for social reforms, Dwarkanath went a step further by being involved in trade and commerce in competition with his British and American counterparts. Along with establishing schools and colleges, he also had shown his capability in successfully running many business ventures in which the foreign business houses reigned supreme. He became not only one of the successful entrepreneurs in the shipping industry and banking but also a forerunner in establishing an Indian bank despite serious opposition by his British competitors. Endowed with tremendous courage, he never hesitated to get involved in any of the business ventures which, he thought, were likely to be profitable. With his reputation of being an intelligent entrepreneur, it was easier for him to collaborate with Carr Company, a British business house which was well established in shipping industry. Once Carr, Tagore & Company was formally inaugurated, Dwarkanath started the trend of collaboration as an effective business strategy. Similarly, by owning coal mines, he also established his claim that he was equipped with business acumen to manage diverse sets of business activities.

Besides contextualizing Dwarkanath's significant historical role, the above brief note underlines three immensely important points to understand Bengal's rapidly changing social, economic and politicocultural milieu in the days to come when his son, Debendranath, and grandson, Rabindranath, carried forward the tradition that he built. First, Dwarkanath can easily be said to have initiated and firmly established the idea that British colonialism, despite being unfair to the colonized on many occasions, helped develop an ambience in which many sociopolitically progressive views were allowed to thrive.

The first of the Tagore patriarchs not only agreed to spend money for founding schools and colleges as it was complementary to his ideological belief but also undertook steps to generate a voice against the faith-driven superstitions and beliefs. Second, by being one of the partners of Rammohun Roy when he started Brahmo Sabha in 1828, Dwarkanath also became one of the first crusaders against Hindu orthodoxy. Although the Sabha was dismantled in 1833, with the death of Rammohun, the Brahmo Samaj, which came into being in 1861 with his initiative, was actually a continuity of its erstwhile counterpart. As history demonstrates, both his son, Debendranath, and grandson, Rabindranath, steered the Samaj to fulfil the sociocultural and politico-ideological goals that Dwarkanath had set out as a social reformer with assistance from his mentor, Rammohun. Finally, it will not be exaggeration to suggest that Dwarkanath also helped generate a voice of protest against the government decisions, which, he felt, was constitutionally contrary. By joining hands with his colleagues in Landholders' Association and British India Association against unlawful government decrees, he created a space for the opposition to strike roots in liberal constitutional governance. The voice of opposition loomed large in the writings of Rabindranath, though his father, Debendranath, remained aloof from contemporary political activities since he preferred to focus primarily on his spiritual mission. Nonetheless, the fact that Dwarkanath was a fearless soul, of course, within the contextual constraints, was a testimony to the claim that he was a pioneer in this regard as well.

In an era when Bengal was undergoing massive socio-economic and political changes following the onset of colonialism, Dwarkanath evolved a distinctive conceptual universe which gradually became axiomatic, as history has shown. The discussion that follows in the chapters is illustrative of the claim that the first of the Tagore scions, aided by his like-minded compatriots, generated enough inputs to develop models of understanding and also reforming the prevalent socio-economic and politicocultural circumstances. It is also true that by being committed to the ideas that Rammohun developed on the basis of his own comprehension of the indigenous intellectual traditions and the derivative Western philosophical discourses, the senior of the Tagores devoted himself fully to the realization of the objectives that his mentor was unable to achieve largely due to his untimely death in England. Evident in the thoughts of Dwarkanath was a sustained endeavour to creatively blend both what he learnt from the ancient Indian texts, especially Vedas and Vedantic discourses, and what he received by being exposed to the principles and ethos of the Enlightenment philosophy. Dwarkanath was thus different from many of his contemporaries who preferred to enjoy a trouble-free life by being indifferent to those socio-economic and cultural issues which needed to be immediately addressed to finally create a country of his choice. In view of the fact that the early 'nationalists' or 'patriots' (for want of a better expression) drew on the ancient Hindu texts, they may be characterized as 'Hindu revivalists'. First, the claim is partially false because they also imbibed the progressive Enlightenment ideas; along with this effort, they also looked at the intellectual discourses that unfolded in India, especially in the Vedas and Upanishads. Second, the interpretation is entirely wrong since their endeavour was not directed to emulate thoughtlessly 'the bygone life styles ... and dead ideas, [but was] a conscious attempt to use chosen elements of the past for functions that were by and large secular and certainly futuristic'.[4] These ideas and endeavours were meant to regenerate a moribund 'nation' that appeared to have lost its vitality due to crippling sociocultural values and mores impeding the growth of a well-knit community. Being open to the Western philosophical discourses, it was easier for them to tacitly evolve a mode of challenge to the imposed alien rule which drew its sustenance from the Enlightenment concern for ensuring well-being of the mankind regardless of sociocultural hiatus. In other words, Dwarkanath and those who held identical politico-ideological concerns were instinctively persuaded to build a conceptual universe by creatively amalgamating those intellectual impulses, which, they strongly felt, were badly needed to awaken a 'nation' that was in deep slumber. Hence, it is plausible to forcefully argue that given their explicit concerns, their aim was to generate a new wave of thinking wherein 'new inter-community and intra-community linkages [were]

---

[4] Amiya P. Sen, *Hindu Revivalism in Bengal, 1872–1905: Some Essays in Interpretation* (Delhi: Oxford University Press, 1993), 12.

first established with noticeable effect'.⁵ A new era was ushered in when the urge for coming together for a common cause appeared to have been germinated amid unprecedented socio-economic and political changes once Bengal saw the ascendancy of colonial rule in the mid-18th century.

Dwarkanath stood out among the disciples of Rammohun who joined hands for fulfilling the socio-economic and cultural objectives that he espoused. By dint of his hard work, he not only created a milieu in which the argument that the urge for self-dignity was complementary to a community's sociocultural independence gained precedence but had also shown that Indians lacked neither the intelligence nor the capability to compete with the British in any field of human activities. As a pioneer in many respects, the senior-most member of the Tagore patriarchs had, metaphorically speaking, set the historical clock to precision since the sociocultural schemes and the politico-ideological voice that he articulated did not seem to have changed much, as the effort that his son, Debendranath, and grandson, Rabindranath, undertook to pursue an identical goal shows.

---

⁵ Ibid., 403.

Chapter 1

A New Ideational World

Born in 1794, Dwarkanath was adopted by Ramlochan Tagore. After the demise of Ramlochan, he had to take care of the landed property that his adoptive father left. The striking fact about Dwarkanath was that as a landlord he was not only sensitive to the difficulties of his subjects but also bitter with the archaic social traditions that he felt were responsible for India's downfall as a polity. Like some of his compatriots, he also admired the British rule for being progressive in comparison with the prevalent system of governance. He was persuaded to believe that unless the society was reformed radically, Indians continued to remain backward presumably because of the hegemonic grip of the anachronistic values and mores. With the unconditional support that he received from his colleague, Rammohun, and also a relatively pro-Indian Governor-General, William Bentinck, it was easier for him to successfully accomplish the tasks that he sought to complete. Besides being a sincere social reformer, Dwarkanath was a tough competitor with the British entrepreneurs in trade and commerce. His acquired wealth helped him undertake many campaigns that created an ambience in which many of his followers accepted the mission as their own. In other words, what emerged later in the form of organized crusades against outmoded mores and practices had their roots in the activities that evolved at the behest of Dwarkanath and his equally zealous colleagues. The aim of this chapter is to highlight those areas of the activities in which the first of the Tagore patriarchs was involved to realize his socio-economic and politico-ideological objectives at the dawn of colonialism. This was also an era of exploring various possibilities which the indigenous elites felt were of great use to establish their independent identity. This was also an era in which concerted attempts were made to draw on the ancient Hindu texts, Vedas and Vedantic texts in particular, to defend the argument that they were significant repositories of wisdom. Beginning with Rammohun and his disciples in the early 19th century, Dwarkanath pursued the goals that his mentors failed to accomplish due largely to his untimely death. What is also striking to note here is the claim that despite being committed to radical social reforms, Dwarkanath succeeded in rejuvenating his colleagues and those who held identical politico-ideological views by revamping the Brahmo Sabha which was an effort to build an organized campaign in Bengal to purge various superstitious social practices being falsely justified as integral to Hinduism. The campaign gained momentum later with the formation of Brahmo Samaj in 1843 at the behest of his son, Debendranath Tagore, and his compatriots. Nonetheless, the contribution that Dwarkanath made in regenerating interests in the need for immediate social reforms was of immense significance. It was he who set the ball rolling with a well-defined set of programmes for radical social reforms since he believed that unless his countrymen were immune from superstitious beliefs, the goals that he set out for himself remained elusive. By contextualizing the role of Dwarkanath Tagore, the chapter is also directed to demonstrate that the early liberals accepted the Enlightenment principles not because they were intellectually servile but because they felt that these values were extremely useful in radically altering the prevalent sociocultural prejudices.

Conceptualizing Dwarkanath

Dwarkanath was a liberal per se, which means that he upheld the core beliefs, namely care, concern and empathy, which are critical to the philosophy of Enlightenment. As history shows, most of the indigenous elites were swayed by these enlightening values presumably because they were libertarian and humane. Inspired by the Western discourses, Rammohun initiated processes that loomed large when Dwarkanath appeared on the scene, especially following the untimely demise of his mentor Rammohun. It will not be an exaggeration to suggest that what his predecessor failed to attain was possible for Dwarkanath. More than once, his contribution to humanity was appreciated in a language which was not common when the colonizers did not seem to be so sympathetic to the colonized. Adopted in a meeting of the Europeans in the Calcutta Town Hall on 6 January 1842, the resolution admiring Dwarkanath begins with the sentence that

> [It] is expressive of our cordial esteem for [your] public and private character and our admiration of the liberal course which [you have] uniformly pursued for the improvement and amelioration of [your] countrymen, and [your] promotion and support of all institutions which have been proposed for that object.
>
> Dwarkanath to the Governor-General, William Bentinck, 20 August 1834, cited in Ibid., 78.

The Calcutta sheriff, Mr Thomas Turton, who presided over the meeting praised Dwarkanath by saying,

> Your unwearied benevolence, your upright conduct as a man in all the relations of life, claim and have received the need of public admiration in Calcutta, of which we trust the voice will re-echoed in England.
>
> In every good work of charity, without reference to caste, to colour or to creed, you have set a very splendid example of liberality to your countrymen, and your purse has ever been as freely opened to promote objects more peculiarly affecting feelings or pursuits of Europeans, as to support the noble institutions which philanthropy suggested.
>
> We rejoice that, in you, our British fellow-subjects will one who is calculated to raise the estimate which some in England may heretofore have been disposed to entertain of the native gentlemen in India.[1]

---

[1] The 6 January 1842 address by Mr Thomas Turton, cited in Kissory Chand Mittra, ed., *Memoir of Dwarkanath Tagore* (Kolkata: Thacker, Spink & Co., 1870), 82–83.

Fundamental here is the view that Dwarkanath held those values which endeared him and even to the British residents of Calcutta. It was inconceivable, especially at a time of the ascendancy of colonial power in India, that 'a native' was held in high esteem by the members of conquering race which perhaps is indicative of (a) the heart-felt urge of the Europeans for showing that liberalism was a panacea for the mankind and also of (b) a strategy of identifying one influential person who was capable of spreading the liberal ethos to the society at large. Nonetheless, what stands out was the appreciation of the set of activities which, while being drawn on the core values of the Enlightenment discourses, also generated a voice against the well-entrenched sociocultural prejudices in the Hindu society. So despite being 'a strategy', the outcome of the changing mindset appreciative of liberalism was clearly positive so far in the superstitious Hindu minds.

There is no denying that Dwarkanath personified some of the attributes of his intellectual guide, Rammohun, which were universally known as the following address of the Committee of the Edinburgh Emigration and Aborigines Protection Society underlines. On 8 September 1842, Dwarkanath was felicitated by the Committee in the Town Hall where he was profusely appreciated for being true to the humanitarian concerns which made him 'unique' and 'truly liberal'. In the Address, it was thus unambiguously stated that

> We recognize in you a friend of that knowledge which confers dignity and power on its possessor, and also a liberal promoter of the most extended plans for the education of the youth of your country.
>
> We recognize in you a munificent patron, and practical promoter of peaceful and unrestricted commerce: of a system of trade calculated to bind nation and man to man, and to make the varied blessings of the Creator, and the useful inventions of genius, universal in their benefits to the human race.
>
> We recognize in you the fearless asserted to the rights of human industry—at this moment striving to throw the shield of protection over the humblest cultivator of the soil of your birth, and to secure for honest toil a just participation in the fruits of the field.

We recognize in you a generous supporter and in some instances the founder of the institutions of your own Metropolis, which have been established for humane purpose of mitigating the sorrows and the sufferings of your indigent and afflicted countrymen.

We recognize in you a zealous advocate of just and equal laws for all classes of the vast community to which you belong.... You have lived and laboured for the good of mankind, and it is but just you should receive our thanks in the name common humanity.[2]

Explicit here are the claims and ideas for conceptualizing Dwarkanath Tagore. That Dwarkanath epitomized all the qualities that a true liberal upheld is too evident to be denied. What is striking is also the fact that his reputation of being a benevolent guardian of the oppressed reached the shore of Scotland which clearly shows that amid difficulties, he, being sensitive to liberalism, pursued the goals seeking to ensure socio-economic well-being of all regardless of class, caste and religion. There are three important attributes that the address highlighted: First, he hardly held partisan views directed to protect the well-off sections of the society; he was equally concerned for those who were at the lower rung of the society, including 'the humblest cultivator of the soil'. Second, he was international in his perspectives because his involvement in trade and commerce was a stepping stone to bring people from various sociocultural contexts together; he was claimed to have built a bridge of communion which ultimately benefitted the humanity. Finally, as a true liberal, he promoted those ideas seeking to empower humanity to fight against odds; it was a design to confer the voice to the voiceless and also the power to combat the evil forces inflicting injustice to the disempowered. Being committed to liberal values, the endeavour by Dwarkanath to evolve 'just and equal laws for all classes of the community' was a testimony to the claim that his devotion to the cause was genuine.

What does Dwarkanath mean? He represented a new kind of human beings who, despite being colonized, proved that hard work,

---

[2] The 8 September 1842 address of the Committee of the Edinburgh Emigration and Aborigines Protection Society, cited in Mittra, *Memoir of Dwarkanath Tagore*, 100.

truthfulness and honesty helped one remain historically relevant. There are two levels of this argument: At the level of common sense, it is arguable that what he achieved was based on his own labour; at the conceptual level, the qualities that he evinced in his activities corresponded with those values that are also part and parcel of liberal ethos. Unless one is truthful and honest, one is unable to express care, concern and empathy, the fundamental pillars of the Enlightenment philosophy. So Dwarkanath was a creative blending of the values and mores derived from both the indigenous and derivative philosophical traditions. To stretch the argument little further, one may say that the widely circulated Upanishadic belief, *Vasudhaiva Kutumbakam* (the world is a collectivity of relatives) that he imbibed by being introduced to the Vedas and Vedantic texts, was manifested when he meaningfully articulated the basic conceptual ideas of liberalism. According to him, colonialism was an aberration and under no circumstances it was allowed to undermine the human values which were universal.

Dwarkanath was a wave of thoughts that were articulated on the basis of his understanding of both the Western and indigenous discourses. He was born at a particular juncture of India's colonial history when the alien rulers through the Christian missionaries and those who preferred the British administration over the erstwhile decadent feudal rule prepared a platform for the Enlightenment ideas to strike roots in Bengal. By welcoming the British, Rammohun set out those politico-ideological priorities which, he felt, were of tremendous significance in successfully pursuing his mission. As a true disciple of Rammohun, Dwarkanath steadfastly followed the path because he too shared his mentor's sociopolitical concerns. A zamindar who held completely different ideological preferences in comparison with his counterparts, the first of the Tagore patriarchs was one of the rare Bengali elites who did not seem to have been ever blinded by partisan interests. It is true that he was 'a loyalist' par excellence which was never reduced to an uncritical acceptance of the British rule. Whenever he felt strongly, he never hesitated to raise his voice in which he articulated his displeasure to the policies that the government promulgated. By being critical of the government when it was required, he also built a strong support for himself and also for the ideological priorities that he upheld. Hence, a contemporary biographer of Dwarkanath wrote that

> He strove to raise his country along with himself by dint of his hard work [because he knew that it] was the destiny of humanity, and he threw himself heartily into it, but he wanted to vary it with higher labours—even the labours of a patriot and the philanthropist.[3]

Striking here is the characterization of Dwarkanath as a patriot and a philanthropist. It was a rare combination, especially in a historical context when anti-British expression was amount to treason. Dwarkanath was not implicated presumably because he had a strong following among both indigenous and European elites presumably because he was the one who always privileged his wider concern for humanity over anything else. Hence, it was further commented that

> He possessed the first requisite of the patriot and the philanthropist, viz., a generous and broad and intense sympathy with his fellow beings ... [which] was not bounded by the restrictions of race, or creed or colour. It embraced all men requiring it. It was not a lip-deep sympathy, but was manifested in unmistakable and substantial ways.[4]

Basic here is the contention that Dwarkanath evolved a new mode of conceptualizing humanity by surpassing all artificial schisms. The sources are not difficult to contemplate: On the one hand, it was Rammohun who introduced him to the idea of universal brotherhood which remained the main creed of all religious faiths; this was one of the main pillars of his philosophical dispositions. This idea was endorsed by the core ideas of the Enlightenment discourses which, on the other hand, reinforced his belief that notwithstanding sociocultural chasms, humanity was one and the differences were artificially created to fulfil partisan politico-ideological objectives. So colonialism was a temporary phase of human history which was certain to be vanquished once humanity was upheld as prior to anything else.

---

[3] Mittra, *Memoir of Dwarkanath Tagore*, 38–39.
[4] Ibid., 39.

Dwarkanath was therefore a refreshing idea that Rammohun generated in Bengal's adverse sociocultural milieu. Although by the early 19th century, both Rammohun and Dwarkanath were supported by their colleagues in Brahmo Sabha that came into being in 1828, the orthodox Hindus deployed various means to scuttle their efforts. For instance, when the Brahmo Sabha mobilized opinion against the brutal sati custom, many of Calcutta's well-established elites petitioned to the government as it was contrary to the fundamental canon of Hinduism. Nonetheless, their effort yielded no results since the British authority, by being supportive to the campaign against widow-burning practices, created a public opinion which finally culminated in its abolition with the adoption of the 1829 Sati Regulation Act. Although this Act was enacted when Rammohun was alive, most of the tasks that he undertook were in their embryonic forms when he suddenly passed away in Bristol in England in 1833. It was Dwarkanath who carried forward the mission that his mentor failed to accomplish. By drawing on Rammohun's idea that had an effective attack on superstitious mindset, Dwarkanath devoted himself wholeheartedly to the spread of schools and colleges in Calcutta and its vicinity which helped build a new template of education in Bengal. In short, Dwarkanath was therefore a harbinger of a new world by working on the foundation that his mentor laid with support from Indian and European colleagues.

A Social Reformer

In order to discharge his responsibility as a landlord as efficiently as possible, Dwarkanath felt the need to understand the English laws for which a mastery of English language was necessary. As per his biographer, Kshitindranath Tagore,[5] what separates Dwarkanath from his contemporaries was his indomitable will and determination to achieve the objectives that he held so dear. Learning English language was one of those objectives. With support from expert teachers of English, he became not only a fluent speaker of English but also capable of clearly

---

[5] Kshitindranath Tagore, *Life Sketch of Dwarkanath Tagore* (in Bangla; Kolkata: Rabindra Bharati University, reprint, 1970). This biography of Dwarkanath Tagore was published in 1904.

articulating his thoughts in English in the public domain. According to him, the British succeeded because it drew its sustenance from (a) a mindset well-equipped to independently decide a course of action, tuned to individual and collective well-being and (b) the willingness to work hard directed to establish discipline of mind and acts.[6] To Dwarkanath, this was the touchstone for the British to be invincible in all walks of life. Having internalized the idea, he thus left no stone unturned to prepare himself intellectually which, he thought, was needed to effectively counter the British in areas that helped them to flourish as an Empire. With his sincerity and devotion to the cause, Dwarkanath became well-versed with some of the important Western conceptual texts, especially those which were critical to the foundation of the British jurisprudence. It was of great use especially because he had to face many litigations from his detractors who falsely filed many cases in the court of law. It is also well established that, in most of the litigations, he himself advised the lawyers on how to prepare the counter and also how to persuasively argue the case before the judges. This was an in-born trait in him, as Kshitindranath Tagore wrote,[7] which many of his contemporaries appreciated; many of them preferred to hire Dwarkanath to the English pleaders since he was believed to have been far more prudent in respect of the laws governing land and other household properties. As history demonstrates, two important qualities that placed Dwarkanath ahead of his British counterparts were (a) the ability to understand the complex legal procedures and paraphernalia and (b) the positive inclination to help the Indians who, because of wrong legal advice, lost their legal battle. Unlike other landlords in Bengal, he had thus qualities that eased his rise first as a successful landlord who hardly faced any serious legal entanglement and later as a triumphant businessman in competition with British and their collaborators. He had to however pay a heavy price: He was asked to resign as a Dewan (who was in-charge of Salt Board) as his detractors proved that he took bribes to illegally extend favour to a select group of people. Interestingly, the Board of which the Governor-General, Lord William Bentinck, was the chief patron accepted the charge and

[6] Ibid., 27.
[7] Ibid., 51.

relieved him of his responsibilities. Nonetheless, in the letter accepting his resignation, the following was also mentioned:

> I am directed [by the Governor-General] to convey the expression of the regret [the Board members] feel in losing the services of an officer whose talents, zeal and experience have been so long and diligently exerted in advancing the interests of the important branches of the Revenue over which the Board preside[s]. As the high sense which the Board entertain of your qualifications and integrity, and their appreciation of the advantage which the public interests have derived from your connection with this office are recorded in the proceedings of the Board, it would be superfluous to say more at present than that your past services have met with cordial approbation of the Board.[8]

As evident, Dwarkanath Tagore rose to prominence as his service to the British government was useful especially in creating a support base for the British legal system. It was he who always argued that justice was not elusive within the system of governance that flourished in the wake of colonial rule in India. It was explicit when H. M. Parker, the chairman of the Salt Board, stated that

> I have been solely actuated by what I thought due to justice and to the public service in which your assistance was so valuable, and your integrity, to any unprejudiced human being, beyond the shadow of a doubt. To say that I regret your loss in an office where your aid has been at once so valuable in itself, and so cheerfully, will but poorly express what I feel in losing your services.[9]

One must add a caveat here. That Dwarkanath was unconditionally appreciated by the British government meant that he was one of those educated Indians who uncritically accepted the alien rule, and it is obvious that their contribution deserves to be recognized. The charge is partly true and partly false: It is true because, with hindsight, it is easier to condemn those who welcomed the British rule which was nothing

---

[8] Ibid., 62.

[9] H. M. Parker to Dwarkanath Tagore, 14 October 1834, reproduced in Tagore, *Life Sketch of Dwarkanath Tagore*, 62.

but an endeavour to curry favour from the ruler; it is also false at the same time in view of the context in which the British rule was considered to be far more enlightened than the rapidly declining Muslim rule which was both archaic and backward looking. This argument holds water presumably because it is a context-driven assessment of the views that the educated Indians, in their admiration, unconditionally supported the British rule despite being foreign. For them, it was a boon in disguise because with the spreading of colonial rule, a powerful campaign was likely to unfold against superstitious values and beliefs which were justified in the name of religious texts and discourses. The argument gains ground once it is linked with the fierce challenge that Dwarkanath and Rammohun Roy confronted when they launched a boisterous attack on the most brutal and inhuman sati custom. Over these issues, two powerful groups emerged: Dharma Sabha and Brahma Sabha. Led by the orthodox Hindus, the former justified sati custom as it drew on the religious texts, they claimed; they also apprehended 'a religious war' in Bengal if this custom is abolished since it was contrary to the established social practices, supported by 'an exact reading' of the Vedas and Vedantic texts. Rammohun's mother and his younger brother challenged his effort in the court of law because, they felt, it was a debasement for the family to which he belonged; Dwarkanath was not spared either, he was abused in the contemporary press and was threatened with 'social boycott'. Nonetheless, despite being subject to abuse and bodily harm, neither Rammohun nor Dwarkanath retreated; it was with their steadfast support to the case that Brahma Sabha fought relentlessly against the torturous custom. Initially the British government was vacillating with the apprehension that following the annulment of the custom the opposition to the British rule was likely to assume massive proportions which might not have been desirable when the Empire was relatively less strong than it later became. The campaign however persuaded William Bentinck, the Governor-General, who joined hands with his Indian counterparts, led by Rammohun and Dwarkanath which finally repealed the savage sati custom. It was a victory for the Brahmo Sabha in opposition to the Dharma Sabha when the former succeeded in establishing that the burning of widows was motivated by selfish economic interests of those championing this barbarous practice. The contemporary evidence also shows that before the 1829 Bengal Regulation Act was promulgated, the Hindu Calcutta appealed to the Privy Council for its annulment. In a meeting, presided over by one of the topmost public intellectuals, Raja Radhakanta Deb, supported by Rajnarayan Roy and Ashutosh Deb, the decision to appeal was accepted along with a press report in which both Rammohun and Dwarkanath were severely condemned for their anti-religious stances.[10] What is hilarious is the fact that the expenses for this appeal were not given to the lawyer who filed the appeal in London. The lawyer was reported to have requested Dwarkanath to help him, to which the latter curtly replied that he had 'no sympathy to those who enjoyed the burning of innocent widows for their own pecuniary benefits'.[11] Hen minced no words when he further wrote that

> You cannot I am sure for one moment suppose that I, or the reformer or any son of humanity will contribute the smallest iota towards the payment of the sum which appears due to [the lawyer] on account of expenses attending the appeal against the abolition of that diabolical system of suttee.[12]

One must not forget the importance of Atmiya Sabha (organization for relatives) that Rammohun established in 1814. The purpose was to understand the critical religious texts, especially the Vedas and Upanishads. Many of his contemporaries joined at the outset with the belief that it was a forum for entertainment; they however got disillusioned soon because it was a forum for reading the text and to understand its real meaning. Those who left the Sabha had begun spreading rumours that it was a place where the forbidden meat (beef) was served to those who joined. It appeared to have affected Rammohun which was evident when he candidly remarked in his conversation with Dwarkanath that 'though my staple diet is bread and honey, the denigrators saw in them beef because that served their

---

[10] Tagore, *Life Sketch of Dwarkanath Tagore*, 89.
[11] Ibid., 90.
[12] Dwarkanath's letter of 19 August 1841, quoted in Tagore, *Life Sketch of Dwarkanath Tagore*, 91.

partisan objectives'.[13] In the mid of abuse and threat, Rammohun never gave up what he believed to be socially appropriate for India's progress as a healthy society. This is what attracted Dwarkanath to him. As evident in the contemporary description, despite being supportive of idolatry at the outset, the senior-most Tagore admired Rammohun for his grip over the Hindu texts and his concern for developing a social ambience in which logic prevailed over superstitions. On many occasions, Dwarkanath stopped his regular ritualistic prayers when he was told that Rammohun arrived to see him which enabled him to engage in a discourse with the latter. For Dwarkanath, this regular intellectual engagement was an important source of his shift from idolatry to the worship of invisible Brahma. This also helped him understand, as Dwarkanath admitted, that working hard for the benefit of the people, especially the marginalized sections, was a perfect tribute to the omnipresent God.

An Educationist

Besides being a crusader against archaic social customs, Dwarkanath was one of the leading figures in the spreading of English language because he believed that lack of knowledge of English was a deterrent to India's progress as a socioculturally compact unit. Furthermore, he also held the view that given the fact that this was the language of the ruler, one needed to be an expert in this language to interact better with the ruling authority. His keen desire to learn was manifested when he employed native English speaker to teach him English. A committed social reformer, Dwarkanath also felt that individual learning of English was not adequate. Hence, he joined hands with Rammohun when he laid the foundation of Hindu College in 1817. It was not an easy task because the British government was opposed to the opening of schools and colleges in India in a widely held view that the spread of education was responsible for the overthrow of the British in the United States. In a meeting of 1792, the directors of the East India Company endorsed the argument by reiterating that

---

[13] Dwarkanath's statement quoted in Tagore, *Life Sketch of Dwarkanath Tagore*, 65.

> One of the leading and most efficient causes of the separation of America from Great Britain, as the mother country, was the founding of colleges, and establishing seminaries for education in the different provinces.... Sound policies dictate that we should in the case of India avoid and steer clear of the rock we had split upon in the case of America.[14]

Although the argument was supported by those rabid supporters of the British rule who considered India merely to be a source of wealth; there were, however, many among the British elites, especially those parliamentarians who, being true to the values of the Enlightenment philosophy, also believed that the British rule paved the way for transforming India from 'a barbaric society to a civilized one'. Among the most vociferous proponents of this view was Edmund Burke, a member of the House of Lords. In his many speeches in the parliament, he accused those who, instead of discharging the civilizing role of the British, utilized the government machinery for personal gain. What was thus needed was to develop adequate infrastructure in India, including the system of English education to 'take the barbaric natives ... out the morass of a dingy superstitious world'. So in their mission to start English education, Rammohun and Dwarkanath found in Edmund Burke and those who held identical views enough encouragement to go ahead with their endeavour.[15] Furthermore, the British government also realized by then that it was expensive to get people from England to run administration in India. Hence, the argument veered towards creating a pool of 'English-educated native Indians' for governing India. The outcome was the creation of a College Committee in 1841 as part of the government which strongly recommended the establishment of an English-medium college. The groundwork prepared by Rammohun and Dwarkanath led to fruition with the foundation of the Hindu College in 1817. In 1853, Hindu College became Hindu School, and Presidency College was established

---

[14] The resolution adopted in the meeting of the directors of the East India Company, reproduced in Tagore, *Life Sketch of Dwarkanath Tagore*, 95.

[15] I have elaborated in my *Constitutionalizing India* (New Delhi: Oxford University Press, 2018).

at the behest of the Bengal government with support from the leading elites of Calcutta, including Rammohun and Dwarkanath.

Apart from his concern for English education, the senior-most Tagore also took personal care for the establishment of a medical college which was realized in 1835. He not only made financial contributions for the construction of buildings but also contacted those in government who, he felt, thought alike. His task was made easier since the then Governor-General, William Bentinck, offered help and the entire administration was geared up accordingly. So his initiative in this regard did not confront much of the difficulties. But when the college started functioning, Dwarkanath encountered formidable obstruction from the orthodox Hindus of Calcutta for their general repugnance to dissection of human bodies. Besides explaining why dissection was required, the contemporary media reports confirm that to show the critical importance of dissection in the study of medicine, Dwarkanath decided to be present in the dissection room along with the students 'to remove the misgivings in this regard'.[16] His insistence on the study of anatomy as integral to medical sciences 'contributed in no inconsiderable degree to render the College with such a short time a great success'.[17] Here, Dwarkanath is not only seen as a crusader of debilitating sociocultural ideas, as he left no stone unturned in attaining his mission, but was also evident in a situation that was clearly adversarial. The idea was very clear. In an era of possibilities for deep-rooted sociocultural changes, the first of the Tagore patriarchs resorted to means which, he strongly felt, were extremely useful to design a mindset largely immune from being retarded due to well-entrenched and highly socially restrictive values and practices.

A Man of Organization

Dwarkanath realized that effective reforms were possible with mass support for the cause. Having understood the importance of

---

[16] Sreenath Banerjee, *The Life of Dwarkanath Tagore* (Bhowanipore: Sreenath Banerjee, 1914), Appendix, iii.
[17] Ibid.

organization, he created a forum for the landlords because he believed that they, in view of their financial contribution to the British rule, were likely to be critical to governance. While pursuing this objective, Dwarkanath was persuaded by two principles: On the one hand, according to him, the Landholders' Society, founded in 1838, gradually became a mouthpiece of the landlords to ventilate their grievances to the government; it was also then, on the other hand, that a forum for raising the issues of the local people given their intimate contact with the latter. In other words, the landlords, in view of their being in the villages, also became a source of information for the British government. The Landholders' Society was thus useful to the rulers as it created a bridge of contact between the landlords and their subjects who paid dividends to the alien administration. It worked both ways: The landlords found a means of communication while the government had a channel of dialogue with those who mattered most in the village economy which the government welcomed by agreeing 'to receive and consider the representations of the members of Landholders' Society affecting their own interests or the good of community'.[18] The idea was appreciated by the government as the Landholders' Society emerged as a safety valve for the administration and members of the society became favourably inclined because they also found a bridge to be connected with the British rulers.

With the establishment of the Landholders' Society, it was also possible for Dwarkanath to organize campaigns against the laws affecting the interests of the landlords in areas outside the capital city of Calcutta. In other words, the landlords in *mofussil* towns were deprived of legal redressal since their complaints were adjudicated by the *mofussil* tribunals. Even if they remained dissatisfied with the verdict of the tribunal, they had nowhere to go as it was barred for them to even make an appeal to the higher court in Calcutta. Critical of this policy, which was injurious to the socio-economic interests of the landlords, the Calcutta elites, led by Dwarkanath, launched a fierce campaign for the abolition of what they characterized as 'the black law'. In a meeting convened in April 1836, he strongly argued for the repeal of the Act

[18] Ibid., vii.

XI which put an embargo for an appeal of the landlords in *mufassil* towns to the higher courts. The Englishmen living in areas away from Calcutta were also adversely affected by this restraining Act. It was therefore not surprising that many of them joined the meeting and also endorsed the view that the said Act needed to be revoked. With his persuasion, Dwarkanath built a strong group of supporters among the whites who also resolved to put before the 'Board of Directors and Board of Control of the East India Company in London ... to repeal or disallow this Act'.[19] It was a source of strength for him because by his persuasive logic, he easily put across the point before them that unless the Act is done away with, soon the Britishers would suffer just their Indian counterparts. He also insisted that for the annulment of the Act, they needed to come forward because 'little is expected from our countrymen [who] ... are timid in the extreme and very reluctant to come forward in asserting their rights'. The timidity of the indigenous people was attributed to the abuse of power by the British rulers in the *mufassil* towns, which Dwarkanath illustrated by saying that 'they have suffered for no other crime than displeasing a civil servant, or unintentionally omitting to make a *salam* [salute] when they are passing on the road'.[20] Under these circumstances, the only option left for them was to petition higher authorities for securing their rights for justice which were being denied. In order to secure their property in the *mufassil* towns, Dwarkanath therefore saw 'no reason why the "natives" ought not to support a petition to Parliament on the present occasion'.[21] His speech clinched the issue and those present in the meeting stood by him to get rid of the *mufassil* courts which were, in contemporary description, 'dens of iniquity, instead of temples of even-handed justice; ... they were marketplaces where decrees were sold to the highest bidder instead of sanctuaries for the protection of the rights of individuals'.[22] The campaign gained momentum and in December 1838, the Parliament replaced the Act by promulgating a new one which administratively approved the creation of the office of

---

[19] Ibid., xii.
[20] Ibid., xiii.
[21] Ibid., xv.
[22] Ibid., xvi.

deputy magistrate for governing the subdivisions. The first few batches of deputy magistrates selected were either 'cadets of ancient and influential families or distinguished alumni of the Hindu College'.[23] With the intervention of the newly recruited deputy magistrates,

> The subdivisions were so well-managed that not only crime was put down, and lawlessness of every kind curbed by the strong arm of law, ... and these places became the centres of civilization, schools, dispensaries, libraries and literary societies springing up in all directions; and a new and healthy tone imparted to the morale of the people.[24]

The government decree was well appreciated, especially those with landed property, because it was an opportunity for them to seek justice from the whimsical application of laws and rules by the 'lesser competent persons' in charge of executing the royal design of governance. Dwarkanath and his colleagues with similar socio-economic interests rejoiced the victory not only because their views received royal approbation but also because it ensured their rights to seek justice if it was denied at the hands of the *mufassil* tribunals, run by individuals with partisan interests. The repeal of the Act had its effect at two levels: At the level of the zamindars, it was a boon because the new system provided a design for judicial redressal of their grievances; at the level of the cultivators, it brought benefits since the whimsical imposition of rents by the tribunals was to be assessed whether it was justiciable.

One should not miss here an important aspect of Dwarkanath's character: His persuasive arguments for defending the rights of the whites in *mufassil* towns (who lost their claim to be treated at par with their counterparts in Calcutta following the 1836 so-called Black Act) brought him closer to the British elites, especially in England. His role as a loyalist was appreciated in the contemporary press because by being opposed to the Black Act, he questioned the government's decision 'to equalize the Englishmen with the Natives'[25] in *mufassil*

[23] Ibid.
[24] Ibid.
[25] Ibid., xiii.

towns, which did not augur well with some powerful critics.[26] His argument does appear to have the imprint of being an uncritical loyalist, when he stated that by seeking to equalize the Europeans with the natives, 'the Government wishes ... [to] degrade the [former] by lowering them to the state of the Natives'. However, a careful assessment of the argument in its entirety may lead one to suggest that it was primarily a contextual response with wider connotations. In order to persuasively argue his point, he thus upheld the view that if the government was allowed to proceed further in this regard, the Europeans were likely to lose their rights, just as their Native brethren 'have lost by being indifferent ... [when] their rights were taken away [which] made them slaves. Are the Englishman therefore to be made slaves also', he asked.[27] This was likely to happen because, as he adumbrated his point forcefully, 'the shackle-free Government [has] taken all which the Natives possessed: their lives, liberty, property, and all are now held at the mercy of the Government.'[28] There is no denying the fact that Dwarkanath did not unambiguously argue for the rights of the natives, though he did implicitly defend the demand for forcing the government to adopt laws which were non-discriminatory in character. It was probably expected of a 19th-century liberal such as Dwarkanath, who was out-and-out a British loyalist, to lambast the erstwhile Muslim rule. Nonetheless, it was also implicit in his argument that an uncritical acceptance of the British design was also undesirable, since history was a testimony to the fact that the natives had become slaves because they did not appear to have effectively combatted the British ascendancy in India. On the surface, therefore, the argument is that of a loyalist, though a careful reading allows one to put forth the view that Dwarkanath had also jotted down the consequences of the government being allowed to remain immune from criticism.

---

[26] His biographer Kissory Chand Mittra (1822–1873) mentioned that Dwarkanath's arguments for 'exemption of British born subjects from the jurisdiction of the ordinary courts' were attributed to his unalloyed 'loyalism to the British crown'. Mittra, *Memoir of Dwarkanath Tagore*, 68–70.

[27] Banerjee, *The Life of Dwarkanath Tagore*, xiii.

[28] Mittra, *Memoir of Dwarkanath Tagore*, 65–66.

Besides his critical role in the abolition of the so-called Black Act, Dwarkanath was also a pioneer in a campaign for press freedom. Before William Bentinck, the first Governor-General of India, unlike his predecessors who were Governor of Bengal, in 1828, the erstwhile British rulers strongly argued for press freedom, though it was not legally endorsed. The fate was not different when Bentinck endeavoured hard to legalize since the Board of Directors in London were not favourably disposed towards it, though his intervention received adequate support from the British elites in England. Bentinck's arguments appear to have persuaded his colleagues in the British parliament who defended the withdrawal of restrictions on press freedom as it was 'contrary to the fundamental principles of Enlightenment'[29] on which the British rule ought to have drawn sustenance. It was further stated that given the interests that Bentinck 'has always taken in the welfare of the natives and in that of the community at large ... he will repeal the regulation [imposing restriction on press freedom, which] will help the future Governor-General to get the law [legalizing press freedom] enacted'.[30]

Once an opinion for press freedom developed in the official circle and was reverberated in the British parliament, it was easier for Dwarkanath and his like-minded compatriots to pursue the cause. In a meeting, held on 12 May 1827, he thus declared that 'the objective of the British rule shall remain unfulfilled [so long as] natives were denied the freedom to speak freely and without being scared of government displeasure'. According to him, the withdrawal of restrictions on press freedom was absolutely essential to realize the values that the British government were keen to transmit to India. Not only did Dwarkanath speak in favour of press freedom, but his British colleagues also stressed the importance in their speeches in the 12 May congregation. The outcome was the submission of a memorandum on 20 June 1835 to the Governor-General which justified the demand for press freedom since it was complementary to the unfolding of the British rule in India in accordance with the principles and values of the philosophy of Enlightenment. A surface reading of the endeavour perhaps leads us to

[29] Banerjee, *The Life of Dwarkanath Tagore*, iv.
[30] Ibid., v–vi.

believe that the increasing support for press freedom was illustrative of how the British rulers were ideologically tuned to the grand principles of Enlightenment philosophy, though it was not exactly true. There is no doubt that the Indian elites, including Dwarkanath and his companions, had had a chance to ventilate their grievances if the freedom of the press was legalized. For the British it was accepted as another tool for strengthening the colonial rule in at least two ways: On the one hand, the airing of grievances in the public domain through the press was cathartic in its own right, which was believed to neutralize their dissent, to a significant extent; on the other hand, the freedom of press was a concession that the British readily gave, as it redeemed the British in the eyes of the natives as benevolent rulers. Therefore, this was not a no-strings-attached gift, but one that was perhaps one of the effective strategies of governance by devising a design for comprehending the public mood and also for quelling opposition by allowing the anti-British sentiments and views to come to the surface through the press. It was evident when T. Dickens, a House of Lords member, corroborated the idea in his speech in parliament that press freedom was not just a concession but also 'a fruitful tool to understand and also control public mood in India'.[31] The idea was endorsed by Charles Metcalfe, another parliamentarian who defended the point and also set out a design to control press freedom once it 'harmed the interest of the British rule'.[32] As he argued, with the promulgation of stringent laws 'the court of law provides for the safety of the State'.[33] One is thus persuaded to believe that the press freedom was both a boon and an instrument in support of the alien rule: It was a boon because it allowed the natives to aerate their grievances against the government and also those views for raising public awareness; it was also an instrument for the British since press was a bridge between the public and the ruler which was of assistance to the latter for assessing the public mood. As history shows, *The Englishman* or *The Friend of India*, the two contemporary newspapers, were appreciated by both the British elites and their Indian counterparts presumably because they

---

[31] The proceedings of the parliamentary debates are cited in ibid., vi.
[32] Ibid., vii.
[33] Ibid.

served as a link between the rulers and the ruled.[34] Similarly, *Bengal Herald* and *Bangadwut* (in Bangla) which were published at the behest of Rammohun and Dwarkanath represented the indigenous voice. So the press freedom was a watershed in India's nationalist campaign, as was evident in the upsurge of nationalist newspapers that played a significant role in spreading nationalist concerns and gradually consolidating a political–intellectual bloc. From Gandhi's *Indian Opinion*, *Young India* and *Harijan* to B. R. Ambedkar's *Mooknayak* (silenced actor) and *Bahishkrit Bharat* (ostracized India), instances abound. These ventures were key vehicles for propagating and sustaining nationalist zeal.

Dwarkanath thus represented a set of goals which, he felt, were propitious for the consolidation of a mindset questioning the age-old archaic beliefs. He was a pioneer in many areas of human existence which hardly received adequate attention from the leading public figures. Being influenced by Rammohun, he was drawn to those social issues which were hardly scrutinized thoroughly in the past. It was evident in the obituaries that the leading dailies carried. As per *The Bengal Hurkaru* of 19 September 1846, 'His country suffered a moral loss [and] … it is considered doubtful if there ever will be his like again.'[35] The sentiment was elaborated further in another editorial of *The Bengal Hurkaru* when it was claimed that

> In Dwarkanath Tagore, India has lost the man who has done most to raise her in the esteem of Europe.… It was in the liberality and comprehensiveness of his mind.… It was this free and far-looking spirit that … incited and enabled him to do good to his countrymen at home, and to exalt the name of his country abroad'.[36]

Striking here is the claim that Dwarkanath succeeded in generating interests about India in England and other parts of Europe; it

---

[34] David Kopf, *The Brahmo Samaj and the Shaping of the Modern Indian Mind* (New Delhi: Archives Publishers, 1988), 190–193.

[35] *Bengal Hurkaru*, 19 September 1846, cited in Krishna Kripalani, *Dwarkanath Tagore: A Forgotten Power* (New Delhi: National Book Trust, 1981), 285.

[36] *Bengal Hurkaru*, 21 September 1846, cited in Kripalani, *Dwarkanath Tagore*, 285.

was possible presumably because of his emergence as a successful businessman in an area that was so far dominated by the British and other European powers. Simply by dint of his hard work and strategic sense, he rose to prominence as a businessman also due to his collaboration with the Carr Company, which was also a rare endeavour in the 19th century. Besides this image of being an able businessman, he was equally famous as an effective social reformer despite being of a community to which exclusiveness was a point of religion; he not only abdicated idol worship by being associated with Brahmo Sabha, but also persuaded many of his colleagues to question the bigotry of caste and caste-driven well-entrenched social practices. While being critical to the primordial values segmenting human being around caste axes, he was one of those who also drew the contemporary attention to the ancient Hindu texts, especially Vedas and Vedantic texts. Along with his critical appreciation of these Hindu texts, he also learnt from the Western discourses, especially the Enlightenment tradition which, he strongly believed, was a stepping stone towards realizing his sociocultural and politico-ideological visions. Hence, *The Bengal Hurkaru* in another editorial of 24 September 1846 highlighted his role in bringing some of the progressive Western ideas because, instead of being xenophobic, Dwarkanath perfectly blended in him 'the best traits of European and Asiatic character' which firmly established him as an original thinker. The same kind of views were conveyed in the Bangla daily; *Prabhakar* emphasized, while underlining his philanthropic contributions to various welfare schemes, that a large group of the marginalized sections of his countrymen were benefitted by his 'liberality, and he has redeemed many a man from debt and difficulty and encouraged many an enterprise that without his aid would never have been attempted and done more, perhaps, towards developing the resources of India than any other individual'.[37]

What is reinforced here is the argument that the first Tagore patriarch became a force in colonial Bengal by being close to the people, which was manifested in his willingness to help the dispossessed; his concern for spreading education was guided by his belief that it was

---

[37] *Prabhakar* (Bangla daily) of 24 September 1846—the translated version is cited in, Kripalani, *Dwarkanath Tagore*, 288.

necessary for taking the people out of the morass of superstitions, for which he liberally spent. Being his own 'guide and guardian', Dwarkanath was also admired for his 'moral courage' which was manifested in the claim that 'he never hesitated to express his opinions freely nor to maintain them firmly, and he never servilely bowed the obsequious knee to power'.[38] One may however argue that it was easier for him to pursue his benevolent activities presumably because the top British leadership, including Governor-General William Bentinck supported him in many of the projects that he undertook. As mentioned above, he was a loyalist, and hence he always emphasized that his objective was

> To establish a community of feeling and of interest between races separated by almost every conceivable circumstances of alienation ... [and also] to efface all distinction between conquerors and conquered; and to make all in heart and mind, in hopes and aspirations, one with Englishman.[39]

Instead of nurturing ill feelings towards the colonized, the contemporary Bengali elites admired the British rule for reasons connected with the rise and consolidation of favourable mindset presumably because of the misgovernance and also communalization of the erstwhile administration. So colonial rule was a boon in disguise for the elites who never looked back given their firm belief that it was certain to release those forces which were conducive for India's progress as a civilized country. The argument was reverberated in the speech that he delivered on 4 April 1835 in The Sanskrit College and University when he unconditionally admired that

> With the foundation once solidly laid, the greatness and honour of Britain, the happiness, prosperity and independence of India can never be impaired [although he did not conceal] ... the unpleasant fact that, during his life, [he] has seem too much of conqueror's

---

[38] Ibid.
[39] Dwarkanath's address in the Hall of The Sanskrit College and University in a meeting which was presided over by Governor-General William Bentinck 4 April 1835, cited in Mittra, *Memoir of Dwarkanath Tagore*, 50–51.

spirit, of the pride of domination, of the abuse of power, and of the too general oppression of the strong over the weak [which can be mitigated by] the strong hand of authority, the establishment of a more simple code of laws, and what is of greater importance, a more efficacious administration of them.[40]

Implicit here are three important points which are critical to conceptualize Dwarkanath Tagore as a wave of thinking with reference to the contextual peculiarities. First, being born and raised in an environment which witnessed a significant change in the prevalent power relations, those who thrived under the previous political regime lost their importance with the arrival of the British. It was thus not possible for them to exercise a determining role that it had in the immediate past. Second, with the gradual decline of the earlier elites, a new set of elites, favourably disposed towards the British, emerged as a significant actor in the newly emerged sociopolitical circumstances. The trend had begun with the growing acceptance of Rammohun and his beliefs which were appreciative of the Western discourses, by, of course, not being averse to the indigenous philosophical visions. His was design of creatively blending the ideas and values from both the Western and indigenous sources of knowledge which were organizationally upheld with the formation of the Brahmo Sabha in 1828. What his mentor Rammohun left was pursued by his disciple Dwarkanath when he emerged as an important leader of Brahmo Sabha and later Brahmo Samaj that came into being in 1830. Finally, being a self-made man, Dwarkanath was tremendously confident in treading an untrodden path which was evident in his involvement in trade and commerce in collaboration with the Carr Company which was owned by a British businessman. What was also impressive was the exponential growth of the Tagore–Carr Company especially in shipping and banking. Dwarkanath was a pioneer in this respect since involvement in business was then generally socially despisable and hence Bengali elites preferred to stay away. By venturing in an area of activity which, so far, did not attract the indigenous elites, Dwarkanath, by being a serious

[40] Ibid., 51.

businessman, had demonstrated that with hard work and devotion to the cause, nothing was impossible for human beings to achieve.

Dwarkanath was an offshoot of complex interplay of historical processes following the onset of colonialism in India. Being a true liberal and a confirmed loyalist, it was easier for him to pursue the sociocultural goals conforming to the civilizational moto that the British elites put forward to colonize India. For those who were emotionally close to Rammohun, the British rule was therefore a panacea for the superstitious people. Perhaps this was a principal reason why a large section of the Bengali elites seemed to have underplayed, if not undermined, the atrocious nature of the prevalent alien governance. Basic here is the point that the loyalist elites steered a course of action which, they felt, was useful for radical social and cultural reforms; the task seemed easier presumably because of the support that the British government extended to the campaign that Dwarkanath and his colleagues, with identical sociocultural views, spearheaded.

Concluding Observations

Dwarkanath represented an endeavour which gradually flourished in colonial India. He not only brought about a radical change in the prevalent mindset but also put forward new parameters in conceptualizing humanity. Being born in an era of superstition and archaic values which were justified as inviolable given the seemingly religious sanction, the Tagore maverick, along with his colleagues, including Rammohun Roy, generated an alternative mode of thinking by creating Brahmo Samaj which gained momentum under the care of his son Debendranath and grandson Rabindranath. It will therefore not be an exaggeration to claim that Dwarkanath set in motion a uniquely conceived socio-ideological voice against well-entrenched inhuman practices, including sati customs and others forcibly ostracizing a large majority because of the accident of birth. Politically, he is liable to be condemned for his widely publicized loyalty to the British system of governance if one ignores the context in which his attitude was formed. It does not seem odd to argue that Dwarkanath was inspired by the British intellectual discourses presumably because they provided him with a powerful argument to mobilize the indigenous opinion against the brutal practices that the orthodox Hindus nurtured rather happily. As history shows, the battle between the Tagore family and the rest of Calcutta elites lost steam once Rammohun passed away in Bristol in England since it was believed, as the contemporary evidence demonstrates, that without the latter, the Brahmo Samaj was likely to fizzle out. The hope of the detractors of Brahmo Samaj was however short-lived since with the backing of Dwarkanath, Ram Chandra Vidyabagish and Bishnu Charan Chakrabarti, it rose to prominence. As a result, not only did the Samaj become a source of inspiration to those opposed to meaningful social change, but it also became a forum for creating awareness among the Bengali youths of the importance of debate and dialogues on Hindu texts rather than accepting them as axiomatic. In other words, both Dwarkanath and Rammohun and those who believed in their sociopolitical vision ushered in an era of social awakening which drew its sustenance, to a great extent, from the derivative Western ideas as well. At one level, it was an era of almost complete intellectual surrender to the Western philosophical discourses and uncritical appreciation of the British rule since it humanized humanity which was sadly missing in India. So the highly hyped loyalism was context-driven. Being loyalists, it was easier for them to push their radical social agenda, for example, the abolition of sati, repeal of the Black Act or press freedom, among others. Furthermore, with the formation of Brahmo Samaj as a counter to Hindu orthodoxy, Dwarkanath also articulated the idea that an organized campaign was likely to be most effective to combat those who continued to uphold the antiquated values and practices presumably to protect their narrow and partisan interests. There is also another aspect that deserves mention here: Unlike many of his colleagues, Dwarkanath shifted his attention from land to trade and commerce. It was an unknown terrain, and yet he excelled in the field of business in competition with the British businessmen. By dint of hard work and application of effective business tactics, the senior Tagore expanded his business empire in areas such as shipping, mines and newspapers, which, so far, remained the exclusive domain of the foreign businessmen. The allegation that in order to express his unconditional loyalty to the British he endeavoured hard to blindly imitate the British culture and life may have been true since the contemporary evidence supports. Nonetheless, it cannot also be undermined that the effort that Dwarkanath and Rammohun undertook to generate interests in the Hindu ancient texts to justify their radical social agenda also meant that they also paid adequate attention to them. The sati custom was engineered for fulfilling the narrow economic interests which would have remained elusive unless Rammohun had shown that it was neither proposed in Veda nor justified in any of the Vedantic texts. Similarly, Dwarkanath preferred typical Bengali attire (dhoti and kurta) in all Hindu social events and also illustrated that he was equally respectful to the Hindu sociocultural ethos. Nonetheless, his Western style of living, especially indiscriminate mixing up with English men and women and unhesitating drinking habit alienated his wife, Digambari, who never accepted him as his husband for his deviant behaviour. Condemning Dwarkanath as 'a fallen Hindu', she attributed this to her sin, an idea that she held till her death as she was told by the priest of the Tagore family.[41] Whether Dwarkanath tried to convince her that her understanding of the holy scripts was wrong is not known, though he mentioned that it was the result of a sustained distortion of the Hindu scripts for fulfilling 'the misdeeds of a section of selfish Hindus'.[42] Nonetheless, that he never wavered from his mission is evident from many of the social and politico-ideological activities that he undertook both in collaboration of his like-minded compatriots and also those opposed to him. With his level of popularity among the British elites, including Queen Victoria, it was easier for him to accomplish many of his feats leading to path-breaking legislations, including the banning of sati custom and 1836 Black Act, and also to compete with the British commercial magnates in business. It was also believed, his grandson Rathindranath Tagore informs, that he was almost to officially get 'an *izara* (permanent lease) of the provinces of Bengal, Bihar and Orissa in supersession of the East India Company, [which was not materialized] … on account of his sudden death under

---

[41] The idea is elaborated in Raja Bhattacharya, *Dwarkanath: Paradhin Bharater Rajputra* (Kolkata: Patrabharati, 2020), 212–214.

[42] Bhattacharya, *Dwarkanath: Paradhin Bharater Rajputra*, 214.

somewhat mysterious circumstances'.[43] The claim of Rathindranath Tagore seems to have gained acceptance among the Calcutta and London elites presumably because Dwarkanath was always warmly received by the Queen during his many visits to the royal palace. Whether it was true or false is hardly relevant; what is striking here was the belief that his contemporaries held the ability to realize objectives which remained elusive for most of them.

The life and times of Dwarkanath are testimonies of dramatic sociopolitical and cultural changes in the dawn of colonial rule in India when the Hindu Bengali elites, by being exposed to the Western derivative intellectual discourse, became well equipped to question, if not challenge, what were considered to be fundamental to the prevalent social norms. This was an ear of newer possibilities which gradually became pillars of radical socio-ideological transformation. Despite being raised in a traditional *zamindari* household, Dwarkanath was a class by himself since he created his own preferred mode of thinking and also the complementary practices which he felt were adequate to fulfil his mission in not so favourable circumstances. Implicit here are two important conceptual claims which are useful to persuasively present the contribution of the two other Tagores who owed their socio-ideological faith from the senior-most Tagore, Dwarkanath. On the one hand, being vehemently opposed to Catholicism in Hindu religion, he created a new wave of thinking which put in question some of the principle values of Hinduism which prospered due to being propagated continuously for partisan gains. So here Dwarkanath is a social reformer who defended his belief by reference to the holy texts of Hinduism. Dwarkanath also expressed, on the other hand, the desire to contribute to the social well-being by developing a collectivity with identical socio-economic and politico-ideological goals. Here too, he was a pathfinder for the Tagores who followed him. Both his son, Debendranath, and his grandson, Rabindranath, continued the same tradition: While the former strengthened Brahmo Samaj and its socio-cultural beliefs, Rabindranath, by being involved, inter alia, in rural reconstruction, fulfilled his grandfather's desire of being economically

---

[43] Rathindranath Tagore, *On the Edges of Time* (Kolkata: Visva-Bharati, reprint, 2020), 5.

self-dependent in colonized India. In other words, what we see in the activities of Debendranath and Rabindranath can be said to have been rooted in the pathbreaking thinking of Dwarkanath. By being a loyalist, it was easier for him to break many barriers; being a devout social reformer, it was hardly a hurdle for him when he joined hands with Rammohun to do away with the most cruel sati custom; being a successful entrepreneur despite being a colonial subject, Dwarkanath had put into practice the proverb that 'where there is a will, there is a way'. Notwithstanding being context-driven, the voice that Dwarkanath had articulated was thus transcendental cutting across the barrier of age and location. It is so presumably because Dwarkanath left a message which might not have been radically nationalist but was strong enough to put across the views that being a loyalist does not stand in contradiction with being an instrument for noticeable sociopolitical metamorphosis with the government support. For him, it was, in other words, easier to convince the alien rulers, given his close emotional proximity with them of the needs for government decrees for discarding policy designs that adversely affected the interests of the ruled. This is where Dwarkanath can be said to have continued with the politico-ideological traditions which had unfolded with the arrival of Rammohun on the scene.

Chapter 2

A Successful Entrepreneur

Besides being a pioneer in combatting the prevalent archaic mindset in Bengal in conjunction with his equally enthusiastic colleague Rammohun Roy, Dwarkanath was one of the first industrialists to form an enterprise in collaboration with British business partners and other entrepreneurs. He played a critical role in setting up many commercial ventures in the fields of banking, insurance and shipping companies. It was a remarkable feat since this was the domain in which the British reigned supreme. His objective was twofold: On the one hand, he firmly believed that supremacy in commerce allowed the East India Company to prevail over the Indians which instilled in him the idea of being seriously involved in commercial endeavours; his second objective was, on the other hand, to generate a strong zeal among the native Indians for industrialism because only through widespread industrialization his idea of India was sure to emerge. Inspired by his well-thought-out ideological belief, Dwarkanath therefore devoted his energy to create conditions for India's industrial growth. He thus organized the first coal-mining company and the first steam tug and river steamboat companies and was among his country's pioneer promoters in the rail network. To facilitate these enterprises, he 'launched a commercial bank, insurance companies and commercial newspapers'.[1] By 1840, the idea gained ground that eastern India was to be the centre of India's industrial revolution and Calcutta would emerge as its hub. He not only became a successful businessman but was also recognized by his British counterparts as a reliable partner which was manifested with the formation of Carr, Tagore & Company, a joint venture in 1834 in which William Carr, a successful British business magnate, joined hands with Dwarkanath. The then Governor-General, William Bentinck, was a bridge between William Carr and Tagore; it was he who sent the latter to start a joint-stock company in which the former invested an amount of ₹1,000,000 (1 million) on the advice of Bentinck. He was not only aware of the capability of William Carr but also convinced of his instinctive talents in successfully guiding business houses towards attaining the goals. Dwarkanath thus described Carr as

> A gentleman who has for some years been favourably known to the commercial circles of Calcutta as joining, in his person, talents of the highest order and most varied description, with unblemished integrity, long experience in business and a complete knowledge of mercantile affairs.[2]

A departure from the past, Dwarkanath's decision to start a new company was inconceivable then when even the rich Bengalis preferred not to get involved in commerce, which was considered a mere waste of time given the risk that it involved. Nonetheless, Dwarkanath never hesitated to embark on a venture that was completely at variance with the established sociocultural practices. The reasons are not difficult to seek. Manifested here was his uncritical faith in the mode in which the British rose to power: In other words, in view of the hegemonic presence of the British in commerce, it was easily possible for the East India Company to build its empire in India. Furthermore, he was thus persuaded to believe that the key to power and authority was success in commercial activities. It was not easy to accomplish for (a) he hardly

---

[1] Blair B. Kling, *Partner in Business: Dwarkanath Tagore and the Age of Enterprise in Eastern India* (Berkeley, CA: University of California Press, 1976), 3.

[2] Dwarkanath to the Governor-General, William Bentinck, 20 August 1834, cited in Ibid., 78.

had mentors and also (b) the obvious reluctance of the British businessmen to extend support to an Indian as a competitor in a domain in which they, so far, reigned supreme. Nonetheless, Dwarkanath's determination, complemented by his astute business strategy, helped him emerge as a successful businessman despite attempts by his foreign competitors to create hurdles of various kinds. Apart from dwelling on how he attained success as a businessman, this chapter is also devoted to a relatively underexplored, if not unexplored, aspect of Dwarkanath's activities in an area which brought him laurels from across the countries. Christened as 'Prince' by the British queen, he generated pro-Indian sentiments among the British elites in England which was inconceivable in view of the blatant racism of those who mattered in governance then. By highlighting Dwarkanath's adept handling of his British colleagues and also his British counterparts in trade, this chapter is also an elaboration of the argument that long before the rise of Gandhi in Indian political scene, there were many Indians who, despite not being 'nationalist' in the conventional sense, raised their voice against colonial domination by creating an independent space for them in which opposition to the British rule was articulated in more subtle fashion.

A Different Dwarkanath

Given the initiatives that the senior-most Tagore undertook in unsettling the orthodoxy and in championing industrialism, he can be said to have ushered in an era of questioning hegemonic social and cultural beliefs and creating new institutions based on his reading of modern Western civilization. Just as Europe experienced a wave of sociocultural evolution with the onset of massive industrialization, it was Dwarkanath's dream that India, particularly his native Bengal, would follow. The *dramatis personae* of this sociocultural campaign included Dwarkanath, Rammohun, Vidyasagar, Derozio, among others. Tragically, however, their hard work did not come to fruition because of (a) the serious opposition mounted by leading British industrialists who were threatened by the rise of Dwarkanath as an effective competitor and (b) the indifference of his Bengali compatriots regarding commerce. The steady ascendancy of Bombay, rather than Calcutta, as India's commercial hub was also responsible for the early death of the dream of making eastern India industrially solvent. Under these circumstances, Dwarkanath carved a new path for himself in trade and commerce which allowed him to break the 'myth' that Bengalis remained ill-equipped to handle transactional business. Despite being a pioneer in, for instance, shipping business along with the inauguration of the Union Bank in 1829 which was also an intervention by a Bengali of that era, Dwarkanath hardly suceeded in persuading the fellow Bengalis to undertake independent commercial ventures. There is evidence to argue that it was Vidyasagar who inspired him to venture into trade and commerce because according to Vidyasagar business was perhaps the only means whereby money generated in the country could be retained. Being persuaded by Vidyasagar, Dwarkanath plunged into an unknown territory because that was the most effective means to support his concern for India's well-being. The circumstances were not however favourably disposed towards him given the official embargo on Indians working for the government. Since Dwarkanath was still formally associated with the government as an employee, the restriction was applicable to him though there was also a rule that if an Englishman was willing to join an Indian, it was permissible. An astute individual with knife-sharp intelligence, Dwarkanath took the advantage of this legal provision which allowed him to start the shipping company and the Union Bank in collaboration with Carr Company and Mackintosh Company, respectively. He never looked back after this formal association with these two well-known British companies since his participation in running these two companies generated enough profit which helped him build his reputation as a successful business and also provided him with adequate financial support to accomplish his sociocultural goals in Bengal.

Introduction to Business

For Dwarkanath to become a successful businessman, the role of the then Governor-General, William Bentinck, was of significant importance; it was Bentinck who introduced Dwarkanath to one of the most successful British businessmen, William Carr, though it was possible only after he resigned from the government job. The story goes that once the Governor-General despite his liking for Dwarkanath declined to attend a get together since it was contrary to the protocol because given his position in the government hierarchy it was not possible for him to accept the invitation of a lower-ranking employee of the British government. Instead of upsetting him, Bentinck arranged for his wife to join the guests in the social meet. The available evidence suggests that it was Bentinck's wife's profuse appreciation for Dwarkanath as a host that brought him closer to the Governor-General; Dwarkanath also understood that since for so long he had remained a salaried employee of the colonial government, the hierarchy of position was an impediment for him to meet the top British officials at par with them. This is what provoked him to give up his job in the government which immediately helped him build a bridge with the Governor-General who was reported to have had a soft corner for Dwarkanath for his devotion to social causes.[3] As soon as the opportunity came, Dwarkanath invested ₹1,000,000 to start the Carr, Tagore & Company which was possible because he was willing to utilize his financial resources for a new venture also with the support that he received from the Governor-General. In a letter to Dwarkanath, not only did Bentinck appreciate him, he gave a commitment to support in case need arose.[4] This ushered in a new era in Bengal because now, the richest Bengalis, instead of remaining 'mere sellers of what the British companies brought to Calcutta … they were inspired to get involved in shipping products just like their British counterparts'.[5] It is also disappointing to note that Dwarkanath's dream of inspiring the Bengalis to think big did not seem to persuade his fellow countrymen to the extent that he had expected. History shows that there was hardly a businessman of the stature of Dwarkanath once he passed away in 1846. Nonetheless, he set out a new trend to establish the claim that Bengalis were not capable of competing with the British in any field, including commerce and trade.

---

[3] The description is based on Kshitindranath Thakur, *Dwarkanath's Biography* (in Bangla; Kolkata: Rabindra Bharati University, reprint, 1969), Chapter 12, 101–134.
[4] Letter is cited in Ibid., 101.
[5] Mittra, *Memoir of Dwarkanath Tagore*, 30.

The Success Story

The Carr, Tagore & Company stood out not merely because it was also led by an Indian but because it was distinct in its functioning by drawing on the ideas of the local businessmen as well presumably because they understood the nature of the market more than the outsiders. As the available studies show, it was Dwarkanath who was mainly in charge of governing the Company, while his partner, William Carr, was responsible for devising ways and means to take care of government regulations in regard to trade and commerce. The situation was a little difficult presumably because of the government's favourable tilt for the East India Company though William Carr, with his contact among some of the leading parliamentarians, helped build their business empire in course of time. Furthermore, the rising importance of Calcutta port was also a factor that supported the growth of the Carr, Tagore & Company in shipping business. By 1834, Calcutta had grown from 'an enclave port on the edge of a vast, relatively inaccessible subcontinent to become the nerve centre of an empire stretching from the Arakan in Burma to the Sutlej river in Punjab'.[6] It is also reported that Calcutta 'handled roughly half of the international trade of British India'.[7] One of the reasons why Calcutta became one of the busiest ports in the Empire is presumably because the expenses for both the raw material and labour were abysmally low. In fact, this provokes an analyst to argue that the manufacturing interests of Britain saw in Calcutta 'the spectre of a second Lancashire on the bank of the Ganges, which could beat the original with cheap Indian labour and raw material'.[8] The increasing importance of Calcutta brought about a radical transformation in the city's socio-economic life. So far, only agriculture and internal trade, in a very haphazard manner, were sources of income for the people of Calcutta. With the promulgation of the 1793 Permanent Settlement Act, the landlords left their landed estates under the care of their appointed caretakers and settled in

---

[6] Kling, *Partner in Empire*, 51.

[7] J. H. Stocqueler, *The Hand-Book of India* (Historical Print ed.; London: British Library, reprint, 2011), 11.

[8] Amales Tripathy, *Trade and Finance in Bengal Presidency, 1793–1833* (Delhi: Oxford University Press, reprint, 1980), 228.

Calcutta which became the hub of all kinds of social, economic and political activities presumably because it was the centre of the British empire. Once trade and commerce created other avenues of income, the local Bengalis had new opportunities to augment their income. Besides generating demands for labourers in the port, the business companies also needed people to help them understand the market and also the sources of supply of raw material that they wanted to export from Bengal. Known as banians, they built a bridge with the local businessmen and also helped the British businessmen to locate the places for the supply of the material that they wanted to ship out from Calcutta. The banians, being trained in communicating in English, were of great use to the British businessmen in pursuing their business goals. The striking fact to note is that it was never considered a demeaning job even by those belonging to the upper castes. There were also banians who were educated from Calcutta's Hindu College which was famous for having produced brilliant students since it was inaugurated by the effort of the Calcutta-based philanthropists. Being characterized as 'the agents of native capital', these banians, with their wealth that they earned by helping the British businessmen, helped generate a sociocultural force questioning the contemptuous disregard for working with the white men.

It was an era in which there not only were newer avenues of income but also was creation of newer types of social sensibilities, which means that what was considered to be socially unacceptable became a part and parcel of the prevalent socio-economic and cultural circumstances. In other words, the newer possibilities that radically altered the existent social, economic and cultural perception were linked with the rising importance of trade and commerce in Bengal. What was also noticeable was the increasing importance of Calcutta as a port which brought many British businessmen to the city who, along with the banians, helped build a base there. So far, the business activities were exclusively controlled by the London-based business houses; a battle erupted between the Calcutta-based businessmen with their British counterparts over the control of 'a steamship line between India and Britain'.[9] As historical evidence illustrates, in 1823, the Calcutta

---

[9] Kling, *Partner in Empire*, 58.

merchants constituted a committee to argue for a cheaper steamship line between Calcutta and London. In 1833, the committee formed 'the Bengal Steam Fund' which was headed by a leading Calcutta-based British businessman, T. E. M. Parker, and Dwarkanath Tagore was one of the members of this conglomeration. Being one of the vocal members, he persuaded his colleagues to establish the headquarter of the Bengal Steam Fund in Calcutta.[10] The tussle however continued and given the support of the British elites, located in London, the Carr, Tagore & Company and those supporting its claim lost the battle; the headquarter of the Fund was established in London. Despite his failure to fulfil the goal, Dwarkanath efforts paid off and he rose as an important exponent also of the British business houses in Calcutta. It was manifested in the willingness of the British merchants to collaborate with Dwarkanath in many of the business ventures that he undertook. One of the first instances was a joint venture in which Dwarkanath participated involved shipping and life insurance schemes. By 1834, Dwarkanath was the principal businessman in life insurance once the Mackintosh Insurance Company that was the most prominent business house became bankrupt. It was Dwarkanath who, by steering the Company out of crisis, made it a profitable venture. This was an achievement which established him as a successful businessman with perfect business acumen. One of the leading newspapers of the era, *The Bengal Hurkaru* thus admired Dwarkanath as 'a unique personality who is capable of creating wealth even in adverse circumstances'.[11] At the fag end of his life, to have an independent dock for the Carr, Tagore & Company, he formed the Calcutta Docking Company in 1836 which also justified the claim that he was one of the few businessmen who understood the importance of having independent docks for destuffing and also stuffing of the goods in the ships. It not only was a very unique logistic design but also created an exclusive space for his company which reduced pilferage to a significant extent since it was monitored by the watchmen who, being always rewarded out of the profit that Carr, Tagore & company made, discharged their duties as efficiently as possible.

[10] Ibid.
[11] *The Bengal Hurkaru*, 3 March 1834, cited in *India Gazette*, 1 June 1836.

The Distinct Role of the Carr, Tagore & Company

In conceptualizing Dwarkanath's role as a successful businessman, one should critically evaluate his role in the emergence and continuity of the Company in competition with his British counterparts. It not only ushered in a new era of Bengal's sociopolitical milieu but also evolved new thoughts which never attracted the Bengali elites in the past. A milestone by itself, the company also helped generate a new mindset in Bengal which hardly despised business; it was a significant change since, with the adoption of the 1835 Macaulay's famous minutes for the introduction of English education was made mandatory in schools and colleges, the Bengalis Carr, Tagore & Company remained contented with clerical jobs in government offices and British merchant houses. The arrival of Dwarkanath on the scene radically altered the community's perception to a noticeable extent. The scene underwent a sea change because many of his colleagues agreed to support Dwarkanath when he joined hands with the Carr Company to pursue his socio-economic mission. In other words, Dwarkanath represented a significant ideational metamorphosis in colonial Bengal because his involvement in trade and commerce created many new opportunities for earning a livelihood, besides making money. It was easier for Dwarkanath to defuse opposition presumably because the Tagore family was one of those families in the then Bengal that also contributed to many successful campaigns for radical social reforms; being as one who had clear social goals, Dwarkanath succeeded in persuading even his detractors to follow his footsteps. His established image as one who devoted wholeheartedly for common well-being is probably one of the reasons why he generated enthusiasm among his followers and colleagues. It was evident in his own declaration which he made in his communication with the Governor-General, William Bentinck. He attributed his involvement in the establishment of the Carr, Tagore & Company to his concern for 'national regeneration' and to evolve 'a model to emulate by his countrymen'. Denying that the Company was not, at all, an offshoot of his 'selfish desire and private ambition', he further elaborated his views by highlighting that 'my fortune, by inheritance and successful industry, places me above any necessity for applying myself to the labour and cares of common life'; the new partnership, as the Carr, Tagore & Company epitomized, was 'calculated to introduce the natives of India generally to more immediate participation in the objects of the European enterprises'. The Carr, Tagore & Company was a venture that would be 'upon a par with, if not in advance of, the first houses of Calcutta ... combining ... the advantages ... of European and native integrity, wealth and experience' seeking to 'the unfolding of productive energies of the country'.[12] Evident here is a twofold image of Dwarkanath: On the one hand, like most of those belonging to his generation, he was a loyalist per se. Similar to his mentor, Rammohun, he also believed that by being associated with the Empire, the liberal values would not only strike organic roots but also help build a mindset in favour of radical sociocultural transformations. Despite being condemned by a section of the Bengali elites for his uncritical acceptance of the British hegemony, he also endorsed a view, on the other hand, that without British patronage it was difficult for the indigenous business enterprises to evolve and develop. Given his unalloyed faith in the Enlightenment philosophy, he also strongly held the belief that the Empire was there to ensure India's well-being. Hence the earlier distaste for trade and commerce among the Bengali elites completely evaporated presumably because of the success of the Carr, Tagore & Company in business despite being headed by an Indian as well. The local media supported the venture since it provided the Bengali Hindus with an opportunity to compete with the British in not only literature and aesthetics but also sciences, trade and commerce. For instance, in support of this opinion, some of the leading members of the radical Young Bengal called on the natives to shake off their 'natural idleness and lethargy, and armed with the weapons of business, commerce and industry, triumph over the enemies of prosperity'.[13] Appreciative of the effort undertaken by Dwarkanath along with his like-minded colleagues who plunged into an unknown territory, the Young Bengal

---

[12] Dwarkanath Tagore to William Bentinck, 20 August 1834, Bentinck Papers, Nottingham University Library, cited in Kling, *Partner in Empire*, 73.

[13] *Jnananeshan*, 14 December 1833, cited in Brajendranath Bandyopadhyay, ed., *Sambadpatre Sekaler Kolkata, 1818–1840*, Asia, Vol. II, 331–332, available at https://archive.org/details/in.ernet.dli.2015.337369/page/n1/mode/2up

further adumbrated that 'foreigners come here and in a short time earn enough to live in comfort back home and our country is being pumped dry in the process. Perhaps things will now change. Down-trodden Hindustan will now compete with other trading countries'.[14]

A new way of making the country self-dependent appears to have been visible and Young Bengal seems to have been enamoured by this new development. It was a path which was, not so long ago, socially despised, and became a design that was worth emulating. Rather than criticizing those involved in trade and commerce, there had emerged a general opinion that income from business was useful for fulfilling socio-economic needs of the indigenous people. It was emphasized when the Young Bengal further insisted that 'may others follow the path shown by the Tagores and engage in similar ventures which are beneficial and bold and deserve praise, and thus help remove the bad name of the Hindus as idle and ignorant'.[15]

Appreciating the path-breaking contribution of Dwarkanath Tagore, the radical Young Bengal saw in him a harbinger of noticeable socio-economic and cultural changes. As history shows, as a pioneer, the senior of the Tagore patriarchs set in motion processes of significant ideational metamorphosis in Bengal. What he had initiated in the early part of the 19th century unfolded in the involvement of large number of Bengali elites in trade and commerce. They not only got involved in the production of silk and indigo but also took ample care in selling their products to the European merchants. As is well known, Dwarkanath's collaborative business in shipping encouraged many of his compatriots to proceed in this business domain. It is true that the number of Bengali businessmen was not adequate to outnumber their British competitors; nonetheless, Dwarkanath's initiative helped generate a space in which his indigenous counterparts also flourished even after he was permanently gone from his worldly existence.

One of the reasons for Dwarkanath's success was also his desire to achieve 'as much vertical integration as possible—to control the production, processing and shipping of goods exported and sold by

---

[14] Ibid., 339.
[15] Ibid.

his firm'.[16] As an astute businessman, he developed an efficient business strategy which he learnt from some of the leading companies of the period. According to the available evidence, the success of one of the top British companies, The Palmer Company, was attributed to a design of combining, for instance, the trade of indigo and sugar with the collection of raw material from those districts in Bengal which produced them in plenty. Being persuaded by this strategy, Dwarkanath imbibed it while being involved in shipping jute, indigo, sugar and silk from India to England. It was a unique mode of conducting business because no other Indian businessman tried this in the past. He was a unique landlord who connected his landed estates with commercial activities since most of the raw material that Carr, Tagore & Company carried from Calcutta was procured from there. The contemporary evidence confirms that he 'exploited his ancestral estate of Berhampur as the chief source of the indigo, sugar and silk exported by the Company that he owned along with William Carr'.[17]

The businessman Dwarkanath ushered in a new chapter in India's incipient nationalism. Being a self-made man, it was he who had shown a path of independently expressing his capacity to create space for himself at the dawn of colonialism; his rise as a partner of a British company helped defuse many prejudicial myths that the British elites nurtured by virtue of seemingly being 'a superior race'. In other words, by being an equal partner with a British-owned company, Dwarkanath raised and established a voice against racial segregation which, though muted then, gradually gained momentum, as later history demonstrates. By insisting that racial discrimination was contrary to the values of Enlightenment that informed the British civilization, he also drew attention to a serious conceptual abnegation that the colonizers deliberately nurtured in defiance of their core philosophical beliefs. Unlike the banians who rose to prominence by being dependent on the British businessmen, Dwarkanath represented a fresh wave of thinking by being involved in trade and commerce which was, as argued above, not the area in which the Bengali elites preferred to be involved. According to him, the involvement and success of the indigenous

[16] Kling, *Partner in Empire*, 83.
[17] Ibid., 84.

elites in business encouraged them to think that nothing was impossible provided it was backed by hard work and innovative thinking. The enormous success that he achieved in business made him believe that the merchants of Calcutta forced the British rulers to recognize them as integral to the Empire which, by implication, means that their contribution was enormous. It was clearly articulated in Dwarkanath's speech which he delivered on 22 May 1835 while appreciating the role of William Bentinck as India's Governor-General by underlining that 'twenty years ago, the Company treated us as slaves. Who first raised us from this state, but the merchants of Calcutta.... It was to the merchants, agents and other independent English settlers, that the natives of Calcutta are indebted for this'.[18]

The above statement is critical to conceptualize the role of Dwarkanath as 'a merchant'. There is no denying that he, by successfully nurturing a collaborative business venture with a British partner, can be said to have laid the foundation of a bourgeois initiative in which the Calcutta's *nouveau riche* acquired social legitimacy especially in circumstances when the possession of landed estates continued to be a source of social respectability in colonial Bengal. So, Dwarkanath was one of those selected few of the Bengali elites who carved a new path for socio-economic regeneration. As an initiator, Dwarkanath undertook revolutionary steps to create a new genre of thinking which, so far, remained almost anthemic to the Bengali psyche. It is also undeniable that he was bold enough to undertake the step despite the threat of being socially ostracized by the orthodox Hindus of Calcutta. Here, one must not forget the contribution of his mentor, Rammohun Roy, and his radical colleague, Vidyasagar, who always believed that the British rule was a panacea for Bengal, especially after the brutal and backward-looking administration of the erstwhile rulers. So, Dwarkanath carried forward the traditions that he imbibed by being appreciative of radical socio-ideological thoughts of Rammohun and his equally competent colleagues, as mentioned in Chapter 1. Unlike Rammohun and other Tagores, Dwarkanath stood out as a class by himself because he also had the rare distinction of pursuing a career

---

[18] Mittra, *Memoir of Dwarkanath Tagore*, 55.

of a merchant which was not exactly a run of the mill kind of activity. Nonetheless, he was constrained by the conceptual myopia of the era of merchant capital. The Carr, Tagore & Company was happy in transporting the merchandise from India to England and vice versa because he believed that the wealth generated out of this exchange was the most effective step in building a strong India. Conceptually, this idea gained credibility as the East India Company flourished by being involved in shipping profitable merchandise from the colonies to England and vice versa. The idea that struck roots in the process was that the merchant capital was a steppingstone towards creating an industrial centre which England later became, at the cost of the agricultural colonies. It is thus argued that Dwarkanath, in his enthusiasm, 'closed his eyes to the full implication of a movement grounded in the concept of industrialized England supported by the agricultural colonies [that] ... frustrated [India's] industrial development ... so long as colonial rulers ... reigned supreme in India'.[19]

Conceptually, the argument is valid though a contextual reading of historical processes may lead one to arrive at a different kind of conclusion. Dwarkanath was born and raised in an environment when the dominant views were favourably tilted in favour of the British rule presumably because it was a radical departure from the past especially in terms of sociocultural perspectives in which the contemporary views evolved and gained popular acceptance. In such a milieu, his sociocultural views were, as mentioned in Chapter 1, a break with the past. His involvement with trade and commerce was equally novel given the fact that the established criterion of social respectability was the possession of landed property: The more land one owned, the higher would be one's social status. It was Dwarkanath who changed the prevalent mindset; he broke with the past tradition by wholeheartedly accepting the challenge of participation in trade and commerce which was not, at all, considered respectable in the contemporary social parameters. So, here he was innovative in his perception and was bold enough to invest in business. There was another dimension of his career as a merchant which should not escape our notice. In circumstances, when the job of banians attracted many educated young men, his desire to

[19] Kling, *Partner in Empire*, 72.

start a business on his own deserved to be understood in the context when it was not a desirable path for the Bengali elites to follow. The far more striking was also his initiative to strike a partnership deal with William Carr, the owner of the globally reputed Carr Company which paid him off both socially and economically: Socially because, by creating for him a legitimate space as an equal partner with a British businessman, he was readily accepted by the British elites in Calcutta and in London; economically because the money that he earned by exchange of merchandise also gave him enough resources to support his social causes in Bengal. What was initiated by him was far more enthusiastically pursued by his son, Debendranath, and grandson, Rabindranath, in the days to come. There is therefore no doubt that Dwarkanath played an immensely significant role in generating (a) an awareness of being capable of competing with the British and (b) an uncompromising zeal for creating a legitimate space for the natives that flourished especially with the rise of Gandhi in the early part of the 20th century.

A surface reading of Dwarkanath's business venture may lead one to conclude that he was primarily guided by the desire to make money. The argument does not seem to be plausible because what also promoted him was to ensure benefit to the commoners. For example, it was Dwarkanath who popularized journeys by water by putting many of the steamers that he bought in this service. This endeavour made journey not only less cumbersome but also safe since those who travelled by road were, on many occasions, fatally hit by the gang of robbers. Even those who went out for pilgrimage were not sure of their return to home which also led them to formally distribute their property among the heirs. As per the contemporary media reports, it was not an uncommon feature for the pilgrim to have been violently attacked and robbed of their possessions. Even the government servants were not free from this dangerous assault when they had to take a road journey. According to an eyewitness report, a government employee was going to Patna from Calcutta, by palanquin carried by six physically well-built individuals. After a couple of nights of journey, the palanquin carriers lost the road in the middle of dense forests in the district of Rajmohol, near Patna. In view of the probable threat of attack, the government employee and the carriers left the palanquin to search for a safe place in nearby villages. In the morning, when they returned, they found that the palanquin was heavily damaged and the documents that the government employee was taking with him were also taken away. They however thanked the almighty for having saved their lives.[20] In view of the dangers, the journey by water became soon popular because it was relatively safer except perhaps the thunder and storm which sometimes resulted in the sinking of the steamer. Appreciating the endeavour that Dwarkanath undertook, Governor-General, William Bentinck, thus wrote that 'the object of allowing steamer to ply between Calcutta and other town in India is to streamline the facilities for commerce and inter-communication between the extremes of the empire'.[21] The arrangement needed to be set up to carry the stuff that the big steamers carried from England and also load the goods that they took from India. Furthermore, on occasion, these small steamers also helped their bigger counterparts navigate the waterways since the former was well-acquainted with the depth of the water from the main sea to the estuary of the Bay of Bengal. Keeping these objectives in mind, the Steam Tug Association was founded in 1837 as an auxiliary of the Carr, Tagore & Company. On his return from England in early 1939, Dwarkanath suggested that instead of being confined to these tasks, the Steam Tug Association should also get involved in shifting goods from one place to another and also, in view of the expertise of those managing the ships, the Company should also be entrusted with the responsibility of navigating the small steamers while sailing from one place to another. It was also suggested by some of the members of the governing board to have a new company for this purpose to which Dwarkanath acquiesced. The result was the formation of British India Navigation Company in 1844. What deserves mention here was the business acumen of Dwarkanath Tagore who explored a new area of generating wealth which none of his predecessors conceived. This shows that he was ahead of his age in conceptualizing newer modes of generating resources and also helped create newer types of employment which were inconceivable

---

[20] The story is narrated in Thakur, *Dwarkanath Thakurer Jibani*, 106.

[21] A note by the Governor-General, William Bentinck, 8 June 1832, cited in Ibid., 107.

then. The members of the governing body received a boost when the government announced its decision to completely withdraw from this business which, however, was not fructified presumably because none of the members had had the capacity to persuade the government which Dwarkanath had, and as a result, the application that was moved by them was rejected without getting into the merits of the argument in favour of the project. Given the fact that Dwarkanath was busy with his other preoccupation and also was not happy with the functioning of the board of governors that did not pay much attention to his suggestions which perhaps annoyed him, as his biographer, Kissory Chand Mittra, informed.[22] So, The Indian Steam Navigation Company was deprived of the judicious guidance of Dwarkanath; the situation became worse once he passed away in 1846. Furthermore, the Company lacked a proper direction presumably because the members of the Board of Governors never spoke in one voice which was an impediment for the formulation of effective policy concerning its operation. So long as Dwarkanath was on the scene, he maintained a semblance of unity which allowed the Company to function by following a roadmap; financially also, the Company was viable and earned enough to continue. Two factors appeared to have harmed the Company beyond repair: On the one hand, with the arrival of the Ganges Steam Navigation with the same business aim, the Company now faced a stiff competition which reduced the size of its business; the government assurance that it would completely withdraw from internal navigation and shipping of goods within India seemed to have put, on the other hand, the last nail in the coffin. The above brief sketch of the decline of the Indian Steam Navigation shows, as Dwarkanath's biographer, Kissory Chand Mittra, underlined, the indispensability of Dwarkanath in successfully launching and continuing a business venture. As he was busy in focusing on his mission of sociocultural transformation of Bengal, he failed to give adequate time for sustaining the venture. Still, the Company survived presumably because of the fact that he continued to remain associated with the Board despite his differences with many of his colleagues. After his death, there was none to hold the recalcitrant colleagues together. In the contemporary

---

[22] Mittra, Memoir of Dwarkanath Tagore, 111.

description, it was thus stated that 'the personal squabbles due to petty issues led to its downfall [and] … it is regrettable that the existing board members failed to stay together when the need arises'.[23] So the Company dissipated due to a lack of leadership and also the inability of the board members to rise above petty squabbles. This is also indicative of Dwarkanath having those critical qualities which made him one of the most successful businessmen in colonial India in competition with his foreign counterparts.

This is not out of the context to suggest that to run the steamship for navigation internal shipping, Dwarkanath felt that an adequate supply of good-quality coal was required. Not only there was scarcity of good coal but the supply was also erratic. To address this, Dwarkanath bought coal mines in Raniganj despite the opposition of his colleagues in the Board of Governors in The Indian Steam Navigation Company. Since he was persuaded to believe that the lack of sustained supply of coal was a serious constraint to run the shipping business, he placed his argument forcefully in the meeting which however did not elicit support from the majority. Once this plan failed, he, instead of wasting his time and energy, decided to buy a coal mine in Raniganj which was famous for good-quality coal. The purchase of a Raniganj coal mine was hailed as 'the most important single transaction of Dwarkanath's business career'.[24] Besides securing a steady supply of quality coal for Carr, Tagore & Company steamships, this possession represented an endeavour to get involved in diverse activities in trade and commerce. With this deal, the Carr, Tagore & Company 'transformed a loose partnership into an effective managerial team [because] the firm had all the requirements for success—managerial and technical skills, a distribution system and sales experience. Legal talent, influence with both the government and local magnates and capital resources'.[25]

By applying a clever business strategy, Dwarkanath carved a space in an area of business which suddenly became an important source of revenue due to the utilization of coal for running the steamships. An

---

[23] Reported in Thakur, *Dwarkanath Thakurer Jibani*, 116.
[24] Kling, *Partner in Empire*, 95.
[25] Ibid.

astute businessman, the Tagore scion realized the importance well ahead of his competitors. He was thus a pioneer in this field which, later on, attracted many of his competitors and colleagues. Besides, his business acumen, Dwarkanath was a good negotiator: By persuading the Burdwan Maharaja to lease out the coal mines in Raniganj in exchange of a very meagre sum, he proved that he not only was an effective negotiator but also devoted his energy to take it to a logical conclusion. He applied the same technique when he took 40 villages around Raniganj on permanent lease since these areas also contained good-quality coal. In other words, the demand for good-quality coal along with Dwarkanath's efficient handling of the negotiations established Carr, Tagore & Company as one of the most successful business ventures in the then British empire. Furthermore, in view of the non-availability of quality coal, the demand expanded exponentially which also helped the Company to expand its business. One of the most important buyers of this kind of coal was the government because most of the government ships needed good-quality coal to run efficiently. So the government being a regular customer sustained the demand which was also a constant source of profit for the Company.

To institutionalize the business venture in the coal industry, Dwarkanath, along with his colleagues who contributed immensely to run the business, established Bengal Coal Company in 1842.[26] One should not ignore the effective role of the Company's site manager, C. B. Taylor, in sustaining and also expanding the business by excavating huge quantities of coal from Raniganj coal mine. The local people spontaneously joined the Company despite the high risks presumably because it gave them a source of livelihood in circumstances when income of agriculture was fast dwindling. Initially, the Company had difficulty in getting adequate number of labourers to get into the mines for excavation as they were scared of the fatal consequences once they got stuck inside the mines; the fear however dissipated with the constant persuasion of local managers who, by regularly accompanying them to the mines, earned their confidence. With steadfast support

---

[26] The formation was announced on 6 April 1842 in a letter of Dwarkanath to his colleague, C. B. Taylor, the Company's manager at the mine site, cited in ibid., 115.

from those associated with the running of the Raniganj mine, and also the able leadership of C. B. Taylor, the Bengal Coal Company also rose to prominence as an important business house in Calcutta. There were many factors which explain its ascendancy and the maintenance of its hegemony in the coal business. Prominent among were, of course, the government dependence on the Bengal Coal company for sustained supply of coal; apart from running the steamships efficiently, coal was also transported to England to run some of the major industries, especially the textile industries in Manchester in England. As the contemporary evidence demonstrates, by 1860, the Bengal Coal Company procured 99 per cent Indian coal from 50 collieries in Raniganj that it owned, which was possible presumably because there was hardly a strong competitor in this field.[27]

The above description shows that Dwarkanath raised the Bengal Coal Company to a height which was also a source of jealousy for his British counterparts. But once it became viable, he appeared to have lost interest and allowed his colleagues to take critical decisions which were not always favourably disposed towards the Company. One of the factors was, as the contemporary literature underlines, was his extravagant lifestyle for which he needed money; as a result, in course of time, he did not bother to even utilize the principal funds that were kept for running the Company; it also annoyed his colleagues though they had to abide by the order of the major shareholders. Once Dwarkanath appeared to have lost interest, his British colleagues began shouldering the responsibility of running the Company which further alienated him from his own brainchild, the Bengal Coal Company. To explain why Dwarkanath began to dissociate from the Company, an analyst attributed his indifference to the fact that 'instead of devoting himself to established enterprises, he was always on the search for new directions and new opportunities [which also shows that] he was out-and-out an entrepreneur, the initiator, the promoter, but not a routine manager'.[28]

---

[27] Kling, *Partner in Empire*, 115.
[28] Ibid., 121.

There was, of course, a pattern in Dwarkanath's behaviour, as argued above. He enjoyed most the discovery of a new business path, for which he was always willing to devote his energy and time. He was a builder, and thus he hated being a maintenance engineer. As an innovator, he not only started new business ventures but also was perhaps one of those businessmen who realized the importance of joint-stock companies as early as the mid-18th century. By institutionalizing a collaboration with the William Carr Company, the senior-most of the Tagore patriarchs not only created a new mode of business activities but also had shown that collaboration with able partners was perhaps the only effective means to build a business empire.

Dwarkanath was a path finder in the sense that he knew that joining hands with like-minded colleagues was at the roots of success in business. This was the pattern that evolved in the 19th century; the most successful joint-stock company was the East India Company itself. Dwarkanath was the only Indian businessman who realized this well ahead of his colleagues and hence he initiated business collaboration with those companies which, he thought, had a bright future. The Carr, Tagore & Company was the outcome of his astute calculation. It was now established by the mid-19th century that 'the vehicle for economic development in eastern India was the joint-stock company'[29] and that it was a preferred mode of business was evident since 'it had been applied to commercial banking and insurance companies'.[30] Illustrative here is the argument that joint-stock company emerged as a form which was readily acceptable then presumably because it was also a successful mode of running a business venture. The claim that, of all the businessmen, contemporaneous to Dwarkanath, the senior-most Tagore patriarch was always interested in exploring new business ventures is also evident here. It was clear since he was devoted to not only shipping but also banking, insurance, coal, tea, steam navigation, among others. While pursuing his interests in trade and commerce, Dwarkanath and his like-minded colleagues, both Indian and British, were always innovative and not hesitant to take risks presumably

---

[29] R. S. Rungta, *The Rise of Business Corporations in India, 1851–1900*, (Cambridge: Cambridge University Press, 1970), 10.

[30] Ibid., 12.

because they understood the market better than their competitors. Given his uncritical loyalty to the Empire, Dwarkanath was never suspected and his close proximity with the British elites in England helped him scuttle many bureaucratic difficulties; his social skill in building friendship with the British elites, both in India and England, was also a source of his strength. On many occasions, his being close to the elites gave him advantages which others lacked because of their politico-ideological differences with those who mattered in the decision making. Furthermore, they designed their responses to the government directions in a very intelligent fashion which also helped them sustain their business empire. The formation of The Calcutta Group comprising the major business houses is illustrative here. Dwarkanath's colleague, William Prinsep, was instrumental in forming the group as a lobby by including, among its members, some of the important parliamentarians. By drawing on the contemporary archival resources, Blair Kling had shown that by intelligently steering the activities of The Calcutta Group representing the interests of the indigenous businessmen/capitalists, Dwarkanath along with his colleagues succeeded in securing 'many trade benefits [which were even] denied to many British companies'.[31] The system continued so long as the East India Company ruled India; the scene reversed once the 1858 Queen's proclamation shifted the authority to the monarchy. Furthermore, the fate of most of the companies that flourished under the umbrella of Carr, Tagore & Company did not remain the same also because those who were at the helm of affairs remained busy in sustaining 'old primary industries rather than to explore new industries that would compete with those in Britain'.[32] The reasons are easy to understand. With the proclamation, the colonizers had an all-pervasive control of India as an Empire. It is true that the British authorities did not close down the enterprises that Dwarkanath founded along with William Carr though their successors never attempted to explore new business ventures besides those that they established, such as steam shipping, coal mining, tea plantation and sugar refining. That they were reluctant to explore new areas was a testimony to their conscious decision

---

[31] Kling, *Partner in Empire*, 147.
[32] Ibid., 155.

to not compete with the British entrepreneurs presumably because they thought that it was likely to 'invite the government's wrath'.[33] The reluctance also reinforces a fundamental point that India continued to be 'an economic satellite of the industrially advanced nations of the West [by being] a producer of agricultural and primary products'.[34] Implicit here are two basic points in support of the argument that Dwarkanath's initiatives fizzled out due to the exclusive nature of colonialism that hardly allowed the indigenous enterprises to remain viable. On the one hand, it is evident that, at the dawn of colonialism in India, the local businessmen fulfilled their mission presumably because the spread of colonialism was dependent on the cooperation of those who mattered in Bengal's sociocultural life; the Tagore family was certainly one of those families that was socially highly respectable and economically wealthy. What was linked with this was, on the other hand, the colonizers' well-thought-out strategy of building a corps of loyalists among the indigenous elites. The idea was based on the colonizers' identical concern for developing a strong support base among those who were capable of being effective opinion-makers for colonial rule. In a nutshell, the argument that stands out is about the rise and failure of the indigenous capitalists for an obvious capitalist design which seemed to have escaped their attention. Perhaps, this is how history moves and Dwarkanath's endeavour is illustrative of a design that contains in itself the seeds of both success and failure: success, as the ventures that he undertook remained inspirational to his contemporary colleagues and also the successors; failure, as his business empire dismantled presumably because of the obvious historical processes supportive of colonialism.

In pursuance of his belief that only through involvement in trade and commerce, a country prospered, and, without economic prosperity, no nation gained respect in the comity of nations, Dwarkanath ventured in various business endeavours, as mentioned above. His last business venture was the establishment of a railway company, known as

---

[33] A. K. Sen, 'The Pattern of British Enterprises in India, 1854–1914: A Causal Analysis', in *Social and Economic Change*, eds. Baljit Singh and V. B. Singh (Bombay, Allied Publication: 1967).

[34] Kling, *Partner in Empire*, 155.

the Great Western of Bengal, in 1844. The purpose was to introduce a fast mode of transport both for the people and goods. In competition with his rival company, the East India Railway Company, owned by R. M. Stephenson, he initiated the proposal and the board of the Carr, Tagore & Company endorsed and also agreed to fund the project. It was justified since the introduction railway provided them with a mode of easy transport, especially of coal from Raniganj coal mines, and also helped the people located in those areas to come to Calcutta quickly and also with lesser hassles. The plan was to lay out railway lines till Mirzapur, near Varanasi, covering the entire coal fields from Burdwan to Raniganj. Here too, Dwarkanath had to struggle with his British counterpart, the East India Railway, which received support from the British businessmen, especially those involved in managing businesses relating to the readymade textile goods and raw cotton. In contrast, the Great Western of Bengal was supported by the indigo planters and those involved in the sugar business. As history shows, by the late 19th century, indigo no longer remained as marketable as in the past given the invention of chemicals capable of creating various kinds of colour, and sugar from India was more expensive than those exported from many sugarcane-growing African colonies. So, strategically, the East India Railway had an edge over Dwarkanath's railway company. Furthermore, the plan to extend East India Railway till the extreme north was considered to be of great use in expanding the Empire in north India till the Punjab. The outcome was the gradual dwindling of interests in Great Western Bengal and many members of the Carr, Tagore & Company did not find the investment worthwhile and the project did not take off. It was a setback for Dwarkanath and his colleagues who were keen to have railway services out of indigenous effort. But due to the discriminatory policies, the British government, instead of supporting Dwarkanath's initiative, backed the East India Railway presumably because it was a British company, and the majority of the shareholders were British. In other words, what was evident was that colonial interests were privileged at the cost of indigenous endeavours.

The storyline is similar in the case of the Union Bank that was founded by the initiative of Dwarkanath Tagore in 1829. Even during the commercial crisis that lasted almost nearly two decades (1830–1847), the Union Bank stood out presumably because of an efficient banking system which helped both the British and indigenous businessmen. Born out of the Dwarkanath zeal to develop an institution for financially supporting the business houses, especially those who needed liquid cash, the Union Bank was established as a joint-stock company with more than hundred shareholders, both British and Indian. It was one of those rare joint ventures in which racial differences did not alienate one group from another. That they worked sincerely for the cause was evident when they scuttled the effort by the London-based businessmen to establish a rival bank. The willingness of both the British and Indian shareholders to come together was 'at the root of its success [even when] the economy experienced a serious slump'.[35] Being a symbol of 'local allegiance', the Union Bank provided the businessmen with a blueprint for cooperation for 'mobilizing capital, expanding credit, engaging in exchange banking, issuing of banknotes and influencing the production and prices of agricultural commodities'.[36] Furthermore, by agreeing to have as many shareholders as possible, the Union Bank created a new model also of sharing the responsibility to many. This was also a shield in case the Bank collapsed because the loss was to be borne by many. To this was added another argument which Dwarkanath offered by saying that so long there were many shareholders, it would be difficult to bulldoze the diverse opinions so easily. As a result, the Union Bank ended up with 525 shareholders which was unprecedented for a joint stock company in the then British India.[37]

As per the account of Blair Kling, the bank saw a reversal when the shareholders disagreed to give loans to the indigo planters in view of the fast decline of its demands in the global market. Dwarkanath was alleged to have deployed subterfuge means to get the decision approved by nearly two-thirds of the shareholders. This was the beginning of the fall of the Union Bank because this incident created a chasm among the shareholders who went to the extent of calling another meeting to reverse the decision which was again defeated by Dwarkanath who, by drawing attention to the Common Agreement,

---

[35] Ibid., 199.
[36] Ibid.
[37] Ibid., 204.

mentioned that there was no provision to subject a decision to further enquiry once it was approved by two-thirds of the members.[38] Even at the cost of diverting away from the main theme, it does not seem out of the context to mention that given his legal acumen, Dwarkanath knew well how to win an argument by resorting to the legalities of the argument. With this quality he managed his zamindari far more efficiently than his counterparts in Bengal. By being trained by one of the topmost lawyers of the period, Cutler Ferguson, he acquired the knowledge of the British laws and statutes which helped him win many legal cases relating to his landed estates. His advice was solicited by not only the zamindars but also many merchants in Calcutta and England when they were deeply troubled by the legal cases. For most of them, being well-acquainted with the legal stipulations governing the Supreme Court, the district courts and the local courts, he was always a saviour. One must not forget to mention that it was one of his core characteristics, namely, whatever he wanted to learn he desired to become an expert. It was evident that he was trained in understanding the prevalent laws by an expert, just as he became an expert in English language by being taught by one of the topmost teachers in Calcutta in teaching English language. So, he not only became a reliable ally for a majority of zamindars in Bengal but also generated his image of being 'a capable individual who is both competent and reliable to the British government'.[39] This was one of the major reasons which endeared him to the British as he was intellectually capable and always desirous of exploring the new. So, unlike most of his zamindari colleagues who preferred to spend their fortune for worldly enjoyment, Dwarkanath carved a space in history by being completely socioculturally different from his counterparts. As argued above, by being steadfast in whatever he undertook impressed the then Governor-General, William Bentinck, who recommended him to one of the topmost businessmen in the Empire, William Carr, which helped him establish a joint business collaboration, Carr, Tagore & Company in colonial India. It was a rare feat especially at the dawn of colonialism when the Indians were not only despised racially but also not considered capable of

[38] Ibid., 204–205.
[39] Thakur, *Dwarkanath Thakurer Jibani*, 52–53.

pursuing any worthwhile activity. It was also perhaps due to the fact that to strike roots in India, the colonizers depended on those who supported the arrival of the British in India given their deep-rooted hatred for the erstwhile regime. Given their almost uncritical loyalty to the British Empire, Rammohun, Dwarkanath and their colleagues automatically became close allies of the rulers.

Despite the initial success, the Union Bank collapsed by 1849, three years after the death of Dwarkanath though he witnessed how the bank, due to its inefficient functioning, lost enormous liquidity which was a source of concern for him and other shareholders. He was equally responsible because the decision to sanction a huge amount of loan merely against individual guarantee, and not guarantee of property, was taken with his support as well. Known as 'the bill of exchange', the system ultimately led to the fast depletion of bank's liquidity. Furthermore, as the contemporary account shows, many of the bank workers were also involved in corrupt practices. Given Dwarkanath's presence as a major shareholder, there were not many cases of cheating which increased exponentially after his demise. Contemporary evidence shows that in many cases, there were massive discrepancies between the amount of money actually sanctioned and the amount that was mentioned in the bank ledger. To state it clearly, it happened in many cases which was one of the major reasons for the shareholders to withdraw their share. In view of the diminution of cash and also selling of bank's property, many of them did not get even what they invested. It was a source of heart burning for them which was manifested in their expression of discontent in the local media and also filing of cases in the court of law.[40] A careful analysis of how the bank collapsed reveals that it was attributed to the issuance of the bill of exchange to large number of British indigo planters, and given the fact that the day-to-day functioning of the bank was managed by white men who held most of topmost positions, it was easier for the British indigo planters and textile merchants to avail the facility of the bill of exchange. In other words, it is difficult to rule out that the racial favouritism seemed to have decisively influenced the bank's decisions in favour of the British

[40] Ibid., 146–150.

merchants. According to Kshitindranath Tagore, who wrote perhaps the most authentic biography of Dwarkanath, despite having realized that the critical bank employees sanctioned the bill of exchange rather liberally, it was not possible for him to stop since the majority of the shareholders did not stand by him. He instead extended the facility to many indigenous merchants who were unable to start businesses due to lack of money. The shareholders agreed because it was easier for the bank to recover the amount given as loans; this was not the case for most of the British indigo planters and textile merchants since they left India for England and that there would be legal remedy if a case was filed in England's courts was evident because the bank received no legal relief in most cases.[41] An upset Dwarkanath was thus reported to have lamented by saying that most of the Britishers came to India 'to plunder India's wealth by hook or crook, and if they fail they are not hesitant to indulge in cheating the colonized'.[42] Implicit in his realization are two core points that deserve careful scrutiny also to understand the nature of early colonialism in India. On the one hand, Dwarkanath's statement reveals that notwithstanding being uncritically appreciative of colonial rule, they were not expected to change their attitude to the Indians who always remained inferior in their assessment. The collapse of the Union Bank also underlines, on the other hand, the complex interrelationship that evolved between the Indian merchants and their British counterparts. The way the bank lost its credibility also suggests that Dwarkanath was neither treated at par with his British counterparts nor did he possess the authority to force the British government to accept the Indian subjects as equal to the British subjects in Great Britain presumably because of the colour bar.

The fall of the Union Bank is illustrative of both the success and failure of the nationalist endeavour which Dwarkanath spearheaded in circumstances which were not favourably disposed towards him. As he was endowed with rare qualities of bringing people together, it was possible for him to raise funds from the shareholders rather easily. Despite his success, the Union Bank was a failed venture presumably because of the adverse circumstances in which he operated. The fact

[41] Ibid., 153.
[42] Ibid.

that he was engaged in business ventures which was also an exclusive domain of the British merchants before he emerged on the scene. That he had to confront adversaries was beyond question. Furthermore, it was also evident that those who held topmost strategic positions in the bank were not reliable which was manifested when they were not hesitant in cheating the bank once opportunities arose. Many cases came to the public domain especially after Dwarkanath sailed for England in 1845 and died there in 1846. So, primarily, the internal weaknesses led to the fall of the bank in 1849. It was just the decline of a bank; the collapse had far wider ramifications, as *The Bengal Hurkaru* reported by arguing that it not only would frustrate the indigenous investors from investment in future but also helped consolidate the grip of the British merchants in trade and commerce in Bengal.

> As to the natives, who it is so desirable to see becoming members of Joint Stock Companies', the report highlights, 'the Union Bank affair has given a death blow to their confidence in such associations. We have heard several highly respectable natives declare that nothing would induce them to take shares in any of them and that such was the general feeling among their countrymen; no power of logic will ever persuade a native to take a step in this regard.[43]

The Union Bank collapsed due to a complex set of factors, including the failure of managing the administration in iron hands which allowed the cheats to flourish and gain at the cost of the shareholders. It was also the failure of the shareholder to devise effective policies to stop the validity of the bill exchange once it became a source of great loss for the bank. It was not possible for many of the shareholders to discontinue this presumably because of the inherent weaknesses of a joint stock company where decisions were adopted by the majority. One can go on finding many reasons to explain that, despite being a successful venture at the outset, the fall of the Union Bank also epitomized a clear failure of the indigenous capitalists to remain viable in competition with their British counterparts in a rather adverse politico-ideological milieu. Nonetheless, the experiment stood out

---

[43] *Bengal Hurkaru*, 28 August 1848, cited in Kling, *Partner in Empire*, 223.

as an example of coming together of both European and Indian merchants for an identical cause. There were not only European and Indian shareholders but also employees from both the racial stocks. Racism did not seem to have retarded this common venture. If it had survived, the Union Bank would have become a powerful statement of racial amity under British rule. It is thus persuasively argued that had the Union Bank continued as a successful venture, it would have 'helped to bridge the chasm that developed between Indian and European in the social, cultural and political life of Calcutta'.[44] With hindsight, the argument appears to have been drawn on a rather simplistic assessment of the nature of colonialism as a mode of exploitation in general and British colonialism in particular. As history has shown, it would not have been possible for the indigenous capitalists, despite being unalloyed loyalists, to even start an independent business venture that Dwarkanath and his colleagues succeeded at the dawn of colonialism when its tentacles were still restricted to Bengal. There are many historical accounts to demonstrate that no indigenous efforts were supported as soon as they harmed the British mercantile interests. Indian merchants were allowed to be in circulation so long as they agreed to act as an appendage to the British-guided business venture and activities in trade and commerce. What is prominent here is the point that as soon as nationalism developed as a threat to the continuity of the British Empire, the rulers took out their fangs to nip the endeavours at the bud.

Explaining the Fall of Dwarkanath's Business Empire

Dwarkanath's meteoric rise and fast decline as a merchant is both scintillating and also puzzling: Scintillating because during colonialism, the ascendancy of Dwarkanath as a successful businessman who was readily accepted as an equal partner by a British firm establishes his inherent acumen for trade and commerce; it was scintillating also because it was a rare feat when Bengalis preferred to be clerks in government and other private offices. What was little surprising for him

---

[44] Kling, *Partner in Empire*, 229.

was to rise above being a banian which some of the English educated Bengalis opted for. The banians were those who helped the British merchants to negotiate with the local producers by being interpreters given their bilingual capability. His fast disappearance also shows that it was not possible for Dwarkanath to defuse the crisis in his business ventures which were compounded also by conspiratorial designs of his competitors, besides his failure to develop a group of committed workers for the companies that he founded and ran with his financial support. As mentioned above, the fall of the Union Bank was largely attributed to his failure to contain pilferage in the bank. His trusted workers, including the British workers, who held topmost positions betrayed him, and the cracks in administration were clearly visible especially after he left for England in 1845. Nonetheless, he had shown to the colonizers that Indians were no less equipped in dealing with trade and commerce with equal capability. Inspired by the stupendous success of the Britishers as a nation by also being successful businessmen, he strongly felt that this was perhaps one of the effective ways of demonstrating the capability of the colonized in a field of activity in which the colonizers reigned supreme. Furthermore, Dwarkanath was also persuaded to believe that trade and commerce were means to generate wealth which was necessary to support his sociocultural mission; his involvement in business was also illustrative of an idea that held so dear throughout his life, namely, instead of spending money in charity, it was always most productive to create avenues for generating income by utilizing one's capability. In other words, he was not very zealous in providing monetary help to anybody, instead he was keen to develop a mechanism which needed human endeavour for which he was willing to pay. Core here is the idea that one needs to work for which one legitimately claims what one monetarily deserves. It was manifested in his decisions to engage only the local people at the lower level of the bureaucracy that run his business empire. In his perception, the involvement of the local people in his business ventures not only gave them a sustained source of livelihood but also generated confidence in them to conceive that Bengalis had the potential to flourish in trade and commerce. It was a source of developing self-confidence, as Dwarkanath perceived. In pursuance of his objective, despite supporting the proposal of the District Charitable Society for a strict vagrant law to control to wandering beggars in the city, he introduced a resolution suggesting that

> The present practice of the society, which distributes relief almost wholly in money, is inherently liable to abuse and has had injurious effect in the encouragement of pauperism. This should immediately be discontinued. In its place, a system needs to be developed to ensure that public charity should provide nothing for the poor beyond wholesome food, raiment, and necessary shelter, and it should invariably exact an adequate return of labour from all able bodied paupers who receive relief.[45]

A workaholic Dwarkanath had empathy for the poor but was not appreciative of the system which allowed able-bodied beggars to survive on others' hard work in generating wealth. By suggesting that they were also capable of contributing to the society's mission by utilizing their labour, Dwarkanath, in fact, provided Rabindranath, his grandson, with an impetus for developing a model to effectively involve the villagers in many productive works in which he was engaged following Visva-Bharati's foundation in 1921. In other words, as mentioned in Chapter 6, Rabindranath also followed the same ideational belief in the sense that he too did not support charity; instead, he employed experts to evolve various kinds of training to impart various kinds of skills to the villagers to enable them to earn their livelihood by utilizing their acquired skills for production of marketable goods.

Despite having reached the zenith in trade and commerce in the Empire in less than two decades in an atmosphere of cutthroat competition, the business ventures that Dwarkanath undertook also collapsed and none of his heirs was capable of halting the gradual downfall. As argued above, the Carr, Tagore & Company, the holding company, was virtually run by the salaried British officers who held the important positions in various companies that came under its control. Also, the shifting of interests of Dwarkanath from the established companies to ones that he ventured to create deprived the former of his capable

---

[45] The resolution of the District Charitable Society, adopted in its meeting of 28 April 1840, cited in Mittra, *Memoir of Dwarkanath Tagore*, 62–63.

handling of the existent companies; this allowed the topmost officers to be absolutely free to act in accordance with their priorities which, as mentioned above, were not always protective of the companies' financial health. Furthermore, his competitors took full advantage of the situation which not only dented the reputation of the companies but also created an opportunity for them to thrive at Dwarkanath's cost. Primary here is the argument that the Carr, Tagore & Company collapsed due to internal weaknesses which neither Dwarkanath nor his colleagues who joined hands with him were able to meaningfully address. Notwithstanding the crisis in his business empire, to the outside world, he was still 'a munificent prince ... [who] ... continued to entertain his guests [both in India and England] at parties, shower his hosts with lavish gifts and donate to charitable institutions'.[46] On a surface reading of his behaviour amid severe financial crisis, one may end up arguing that Dwarkanath was unable to comprehend the future presumably because he was swayed by emotions rather than logic. A deep reading however suggests that this was his behavioural pattern that one witnessed once he rose to prominence in Calcutta's elite circle. This was his one time-tested means to bring like-minded people both from the indigenous and British elites which helped him pursue some of the major sociocultural projects that brought about radical metamorphosis in the prevalent mindset threatening to undermine, if not delegitimize, them.

The other formidable reason was the lack of interests of Dwarkanath's legal heirs, his sons, to take care of the business houses that emerged by dint of his hard work. Although Dwarkanath legally transferred his property to his eldest son, Debendranath, his other sons also received their share as the former distributed the inherited wealth equally among his brothers, Girindranath and Nagendranath who was just 17 and had to give up his plan to be enrolled in Cambridge University for higher studies. But the fact is that none of his legal heirs had either the inclination or the capability to run the businesses at Dwarkanath's disposal. It has been thus argued that the collapse of his business empire within a year of his death is attributed to the

---

[46] Letter from Theobald Mathew to Debendranath, 17 October 1845, *Tagore Family Papers* (Santiniketan: Rabindra Bhawan, Visva-Bharati).

lack of 'intelligence, foresight and the determination to work till the goal is achieved' by his sons who were entrusted with the task of carrying forward the legacy that the senior Tagore patriarch established by years of hard work.[47] The contemporary narrative also suggests that the decision of Debendranath's brother Girindranath not to treat the shareholders with dignity alienated those who could have saved the Carr, Tagore & Company given their experience in managing the complex business affairs of the Company.[48] It will not be an exaggeration to argue that Dwarkanath foresaw the situation as his letter to Debendranath clearly stipulates. In this letter to his son, Debendranath, Dwarkanath admonished his son for his incapability in managing the salaried personnel of his landed estate and he was surprised that despite his negligence, it was a source of wonder to him that 'all [his] estates are not ruined'.[49] Dwarkanath held Ramchandra Vidyabagish who introduced Debendranath to the Upanishadic texts. In his autobiography, Debendranath mentioned that Dwarkanath lamented that though he respected Vidyabagish because of his knowledge of Upanishads, he castigated him for 'spoiling Debendranath by whispering Brahma mantra to his ears' which was taking him away from worldly affairs.[50] So disappointed was Dwarkanath that he further stated that

> Your time I am sure being more taken up in writing for the newspapers and in fighting with the missionaries than in watching over and protecting the important matters which you leave in the hands of your favourite amlas (officials)—instead of attending to them most vigilantly.[51]

Evident here is Dwarkanath's anguish over Debendranath's shifting of attention from the worldly possession to spiritual uplift which according to the former was a deterrent to the attainment of worldly

---

[47] Thakur, *Dwarkanath Thakurer Jibani*, 130–134.
[48] Ibid., 131.
[49] Dwarkanath to Debendranath, 22 May 1845, *Tagore Family Papers*.
[50] Ashis Khastagir, ed., *Debendranath Thakurer Atmajibani* (*Autobiography* of Debendranath Tagore) (Kolkata: Sopan, 2020), 47.
[51] Dwarkanath to Debendranath, 22 May 1845, *Tagore Family Papers*.

goals. It also reinforces that Dwarkanath foresaw the dismantling of his business empire once he was gone. The evidence was not difficult to seek because in the same letter, he also mentioned that

> If I was strong enough to bear the heat and climate of India, I would have immediately leave London personally to superintend—as it is—my only alternative will to write and authorize the House to get rid of the mortgaged properties and to dispose of as many as Mofussil estates as they can as soon as possible.[52]

Explicit here is the lamentation of a helpless father who failed to persuade his son to take care of the property that he amassed over the years by dint of his determined effort and hard work even in adverse circumstances of colonialism. There are two critical points that deserve careful attention: On the one hand, an astute businessman as Dwarkanath was, he realized that for protecting his business empire, his sons were neither capable nor had the inclination to continue with what he introduced amid adversaries in colonial Bengal; one should not however undermine the contribution of Dwarkanath, on the other hand, to generate interests on ancient Hindu texts, especially Vedas and Upanishads, among his son, Debendranath, who was instrumental in ushering in an era of radical sociocultural and politico-ideological transformation in Bengal. It was the beginning that blossomed fully when Rabindranath, the grandson of Dwarkanath, appeared on the scene.

Concluding Observations

By being engaged in trade and commerce as a means to generate wealth and also to demonstrate that Indians were no less capable than their British counterparts, Dwarkanath stood out as a class by himself. Rammohun inspired him to be proud of the indigenous sociocultural roots which was manifested in his involvement in many activities that the former found appropriate to radically alter the well-entrenched archaic mindset. So, as far as Dwarkanath's initiatives for social

[52] Ibid.

reform were concerned, it was Rammohun who was the chief priest. As regards his decision to partake in trade and commerce, perhaps his experience as a banian in colonial Bengal provided him with impetus to realize that business was an important source of wealth creation. Furthermore, his close proximity with the then Governor-General, William Bentinck, also allowed him to take part in many social get togethers in which the leading businessmen of the period participated. These were occasions when he impressed them by suggesting many ways to successfully run a business in Calcutta which drew him closer to them; his advice was often solicited which also enabled him to develop close contact with those individuals who managed big business houses. His sharpness of mind also brought him closer to the then Governor-General, William Bentinck, who introduced him to one of most successful businessmen, William Carr, as his biographer notes.[53] As argued, given that Dwarkanath possessed qualities which were conducive to attaining success in trade and commerce gave him opportunities to explore possibilities in area which hardly attracted the indigenous elites who appeared to be contented with their income from land as absentee landlords.

Like his mentor, Rammohun, who also championed identical politico-ideological priorities, Dwarkanath also evolved a distinct sociocultural design to disturb the status-quoist social equilibrium. It was possible for him because, similar to Rammohun, he also endorsed the same ideological path which was manifested in his strong hatred for the erstwhile Muslim rule in India since it was socioculturally backward-looking and also uncritical appreciation of the British rule in India as it was a passport to some of the enlightening modes of conceptualizing humanity. A pucca loyalist, Dwarkanath believed that the British rule was a panacea for India although he was also one of those public intellectuals who laid equal emphasis on knowing India's intellectual past, especially the Vedas and Vedantic texts. So, there were two equally important aspects of his endeavour: On the one hand, he was keen to derive ideas from sociocultural processes that made the British the ruler of the world and simultaneously he

[53] Thakur, *Dwarkanath Thakurer Jibani*, 100–102.

was equally enthusiastic, on the other hand, in unearthing the sources of knowledge from the indigenous sources. In Dwarkanath, we find a creative blending of both the Western and Eastern discourses.

That he was enamoured by the British civilization was evident in his speech that he delivered before he sailed for England on 9 January 1841. In response to a felicitation by city's big wigs on 7 January 1841, he characterized this opportunity as 'a proud moment for him and also for his country [because] it is the first time that a native of India has ever received such a testimony of regard also from the white inhabitants of our Eastern metropolis'.[54] This was indeed a proud moment for Dwarkanath because like his colleagues, he also felt that his exposure to English life was of great help in fulfilling the sociocultural and politico-ideological goals that he sought to accomplish. It was more accurately articulated when he further stated in the speech that 'the main object of my life has been to improve my native land. I viewed, as the best means of effecting this great object, the charitable institutions and social habits of Great Britain'.[55] He was also aware that he was actually carrying forward the traditions that his colleague, Rammohun, started which he admitted by underlining that 'the initiative efforts had already been made by others, and particularly by my lamented friend, the late Rammohun Roy'.[56] A person who attributed one's success in any field to meaningful collaboration, Dwarkanath also never wasted an opportunity to share his belief once he had a chance. In this speech, he thus appreciated those who gathered in the felicitation by admiring their presence as 'an approbation of his endeavour' which he articulated by saying that

> Knowing how imperfect my endeavours have been, I feel conscious that your approbation is rather applicable to the attempt than to any success which is fairly ascribable to me. The good work has commenced, to whomsoever be the praise, and my hopes are high for the result. Proud am I, indeed, that my motives and conduct should

---

[54] Dwarkanath's speech of 7 January 1841, cited in James W. Furrell, *The Tagore Family: A Memoir* (New Delhi: Rupa, 2004), 25.
[55] Ibid.
[56] Ibid.

have been so appreciated and rewarded by my fellow citizens, both of England and India.[57]

On the basis of a thorough analytical dissection, two claims can be firmly established: On the one hand, Dwarkanath was a man of action who was hardly constrained with any of hurdles presumably because he had the inherent determination to get things done by amalgamating his sharpness and the desire to work hard for achieving the objectives. To this was added, on the other hand, his willingness to build a bridge with those colleagues who held identical viewpoints. Here lies the root of his idea of evolving designs for collaboration as a means to successfully chase his dreams. In other words, Dwarkanath epitomized a rare breed of humanity that was committed to work hard for accomplishing the set-out goals. It was possible because he 'endowed with herculean energy'[58] which hardly matched with any of those who agreed to partner with him in either his social or business ventures. Out of his life experiences, he was persuaded to believe that hard work and collaboration were two effective means to do wonders which he illustrated by drawing attention to the miraculous success of the Britishers in expanding their Empire across the globe. By being appreciative of the progress that Great Britain made as a nation, Dwarkanath endeavoured to instil, among the Indians, the qualities that he saw among the British citizens during his visit to England and Scotland in 1841. He thus never hid the fact that behind his rise as a successful businessman lay, as a contemporary description confirms, in the 'great geniality of disposition and a happy capacity for adapting himself to the circumstances if that was required to save the mission'.[59] Despite being a tough competitor of the British businessmen, Dwarkanath was also admired by his critics for the courage that he had shown by challenging the British hegemony in trade and commerce. That the then Governor-General, William Bentinck, created, for him, an opportunity to not only get involved in trade and commerce but also

---

[57] Ibid.
[58] Furrell, *The Tagore Family*, 40.
[59] *Bengal Hurkuru*, 4 December 1846, cited in Mittra, *Memoir of Dwarkanath Tagore*, lv.

establish his claim as a successful businessman in stiff competition with the established business houses. As a triumphant businessman, he never undermined his battle for social causes which also put him on a pedestal of glory and fame. The point that was reemphasized in the memorial meeting held in Calcutta on 2 December 1846, was manifested when the resolution mentioned that Dwarkanath,

> Ordained by Providence to shine among his species—setting at defiance the horrors of superstition and priest craft which hold an ascendant away over the benighted land, heeding not the cries of envy and malice, rending all family considerations—braved the waters of the Atlantic for the Western hemisphere; not for self-aggrandizement, as has been wrongfully imputed by bigotry and shortsightedness, but with the laudable motive of ennobling his country, by bringing two hemispheres to a sisterly attachment and dependence.... Against those bent upon the encouragement of superstition and of deeds which call forth commiseration and pity from the heart of a true lover of India, the Prince [Dwarkanath] will be remembered for ever ... for disseminating the mind-opening blessings of education, so absolutely necessary to rise a degraded nation to the pitch of civilization.[60]

To understand the meteoric ascendancy of Dwarkanath as a businessman and also the dismantling of his business empire shortly after his demise in 1846, one is required to understand the contemporary politico-ideological dynamics linked with the consolidation of colonial power in India. That he was readily accepted by the British elites, both in India and England, was largely because he was never a threat to colonialism. A loyalist par excellence, Dwarkanath perhaps mistook the hospitality that he received in England as a manifestation of accepting him at par with his British counterparts. It was also Dwarkanath's failure to comprehend the colonizers' strategic design of creating a corps of loyalists in India to enable them to rule the colony with their support. Given the peculiar sociopolitical circumstances in which British colonialism was uncritically appreciated by the indigenous elite, it will be an exaggeration suggest that Dwarkanath's

---

[60] Ibid., lvii–lviii.

admiration for alien governance was drawn on his assessment of the displaced Muslim administration. So, from his point of view, the British Raj was a relief which perhaps persuaded him to be an uncritical loyalist of the Empire. Nonetheless, it cannot be ruled out that by demonstrating through his deeds his unalloyed loyalty to the Raj, he might have failed to unravel the ruthlessness which was to unfold soon in India. Furthermore, Dwarkanath was allowed to rise as an entrepreneur to absolutely strengthen the industrial capital in its terms and conditions; he appeared to have been accepted as a second fiddle in the mechanism that helped build the Empire by setting the priorities as per its choice. It is thus argued that 'whereas Dwarkanath conceived of India as a potentially modern, industrialized nation, the British, for the most part, saw only a vast agricultural dependency feeding raw material to British industry'.[61] In other words, senior Tagore patriarch remained a mere, but indispensable, support system to the rise and consolidation of the industrial capital that would have been considerably weakened had India not been colonized especially after the ignominious British defeat in North America.[62] Nonetheless, his accomplishment as a successful businessman in a colonized India, established Dwarkanath as a rare Indian who raised a nationalist voice by showing his capability for successfully competing with the British merchants. To be a well-established entrepreneur was not an easy task which also proved that he rose to prominence with his astute business acumen in a milieu when Indians were not treated at par with their British counterparts despite being the citizens of the Empire. Being nurtured in an environment of racial discrimination, complemented by adequately supportive administrative policies, Dwarkanath carved an independent space in the processes for generating national consciousness. While his mentor, Rammohun, can be said to have prepared the foundation for radical social reforms by holding the cudgels against archaic sociocultural values, Dwarkanath, along with pursuing the task that was left unfinished by Rammohun, also exhorted the fellow

---

[61] Kling, *Partner in Empire*, 252.
[62] Eric Hobsbawm dwells on this aspect in his *Industry and Empire: The Birth of the Industrial Revolution* (New York: The New Press, 1999).

countrymen to participate in trade and commerce to prove that Indians were capable of efficiently managing a business enterprise.

The above narrative firmly establishes the argument that Dwarkanath was an epitome of the sociocultural ideas that he derived from his predecessors, particularly Rammohun, and also represented a powerful challenge to the British hegemony in trade and commerce. As history shows, the business empire that he built collapsed almost soon after his death in 1846, presumably because of the debt that he had incurred and also the reluctance of his legal heirs, Debendranath, Girindranath and Nagendranath, to carry forward the tradition. Their lack of interest was largely due to their different priorities which were, of course, not entirely independent of what Dwarkanath publicly held. For instance, it was he who not only publicized the Vedas and Vedantic texts but also introduced a vernacular weekly, *Tattwabodhini Patrika*, to popularize Bangla. One is struck by his multitasking ability because, apart from successfully running businesses, he also devoted his energy to realize his sociocultural goals and objectives. That his sons were not equipped to match with the qualities that their father possessed was soon evident: Girindranath who tried to revive the Carr, Tagore & Company finally decided to survive on the income from the inherited landed estate; Nagendranath preferred to have a steady income which he ensured by joining a merchant as a salaried employee. Only Debendranath, by being steadfastly committed to his father's sociocultural priorities, followed the path that Dwarkanath deemed appropriate to successfully refashion the dominant mindset supporting the prejudicial and also primordial values and mores. It was Debendranath who, in other words, carried forward the battle that his father waged for creating a prejudice free society. As mentioned in Chapter 3, Debendranath was a ruthless zamindar who was happy to earn revenue even by subjecting his subjects to various kinds of tortures though with the demise of his grandmother he realized that it was futile to run after the worldly comforts.[63] Inspired by his father and mentor, Rammohun, Debendranath nurtured a new wave of thinking that turned inwards and probed deeper into the Hindu traditions.

---

[63] Khastagir, *Debendranath Thakurer Atmojibani*, 30–31.

Most of the tasks that he undertook were either expansion or rooted in the multifarious sociocultural activities in which Dwarkanath was engaged. Clearly in contradiction with his father's deep concern for internationalism, Debendranath championed a nationalistic voice that drew sustenance from the ancient Hindu texts; it was an effort that did not exactly deviate from the attempts that his father made in conjunction with Rammohun to forcefully argue that Vedas and Upanishads were also repositories of knowledge that hardly received attention presumably because of India's past history when they were considered to be sacrilegious to the rulers' religion, Islam. By effectively applying his entrepreneurial skill, Dwarkanath earned a fortune which he utilized largely to support a meaningful campaign to develop a healthy sociocultural milieu. Despite the fact that his business empire ceased to exist once he was gone, given his herculean energy and sharpness of mind, Dwarkanath became a fountainhead of a nationalistic challenge that gradually blossomed into a gigantic campaign leading to the discontinuity of the British rule in India in 1947.

Part B

Debendranath Tagore

Courtesy: Rabindra-Bhavana, Visva-Bharati, Santiniketan

Bengal in the 19th century was a laboratory for many sociocultural and political experiments presumably because of the onset and consolidation of colonial rule before it expanded to the rest of India. Rammohun generated a new wave of conceptualizing the communal identity by drawing on both the indigenous and Western thought processes which Dwarkanath upheld; after his untimely demise in 1846, the baton passed onto his son, Debendranath Tagore (1817–1905). He was however deeply troubled because his father, Dwarkanath, died with huge debt in the market which he had to repay. So Debendranath inherited nothing except the debt that his father incurred for running the business ventures that he started. As a conscientious son, it was to his credit that Debendranath settled the debt of his father and happily accepted the life of an ordinary mortal. Nonetheless, the urge that Dwarkanath ignited in him unfolded in series of activities which he undertook to translate into reality some of his father's unfinished sociocultural reforms. From being the heir of one of the wealthiest public figures of Bengal, Debendranath became overnight a pauper who had nothing but the house that Dwarkanath built for the family in Calcutta. It was not, at all, a shock to him presumably because he by then had realized the Upanishadic dictum that only through abdication one understood and enjoyed life in its fullest form. There were two sources of influences which account for this realization: On the one hand, it was his father's mentor, Rammohun, who introduced him to the Vedantic wisdom, especially Ishopanishad, that generated in him the pleasure of giving up worldly comfort. Following Rammohun's suggestion, he met a famous scholar of *Naya*, Ramchandra Vidyabagish, who helped him, on the other hand, understand the inner meaning of the *slokas* of Ishopanishad. Rammohun prepared him to raise questions on the futility of Hindu idolatry, while Vidyabagish endowed him with the logic to justify the contention.

Also striking is the fact that Debendranath was not, at all, spiritualist. He was a tough zamindar who discharged his role as ruthlessly as was required to sustain the flow of income from his landed property. A change was noticeable since the time he lost his grandmother at the age of 18 years.[1] As he himself admitted in his memoirs that so long as he was swayed by the outer charm of being wealthy, he never realized that the spiritual enrichment was at the root of all enjoyment. Being at the burning ghat for his grandmother's cremation, he further understood that worldly comfort was ephemeral; what was required was the fulfilment of the spiritual concerns, which was possible only through complete renunciation of bodily pleasure. Here too, he started questioning the idolatry because his grandmother was highly religious and a devout follower of Goddess Durga and yet she had to leave this world in a manner which was both ignominious and distasteful because she was taken to the River Ganges at least three days before her death with the apprehension that she was to die soon. He thus wanted to discontinue with the family tradition of holding idol worship at home. The worship however was not stopped because Debendranath also realized that it was an occasion when people from various places come to enjoy the festival together. So it had a social purpose which prevented him from doing away with the festival. In other words, as the festival created an occasion for bringing people together from all walks of life, it was a stepping stone for evolving a collectivity regardless of class, caste and clan. Here too, it was evident that his ideas were based on the teachings of Rammohun; in his regular meetings with Rammohun, he always discussed the underlying meaning of many of the ideas that various religious scriptures had offered. The outcome of these interactions led him to believe that the almighty had no form; it was completely formless, which was reverberated in the Upanishad-based prayers in Brahmo Samaj. What was required, he strongly felt, was selfless devotion to the almighty in order to be spiritually endowed with ideas and qualities which would not have been available otherwise.

The stark difference between Debendranath and Dwarkanath in their approach to life did not however deter the former to undertake some of the tasks that his father undertook and left unfinished. For

[1] Debendranath Tagore, *Atmajibani*, cited in Khastagir, *Debendranath Thakurer Atmajibani*, 28–29.

instance, both of them felt the need for unifying people under one platform. It was manifested because Debendranath paid adequate attention to the strengthening of the Brahmo Samaj, constituted in 1863, which was a continuity of the Brahmo Sabha, founded by Rammohun and Dwarkanath in 1830. Interested in spreading education in vernacular, he was involved in the establishment of many schools and colleges in Calcutta and its vicinity, where the medium of instruction was Bangla. Later on, English as a language was introduced since training exclusively in vernacular was not, at all, marketable in the prevalent circumstances. It revealed his concern for expanding education for both self-awakening and also generating curiosity for knowledge among the pupils. Furthermore, in collaboration with the Asiatic Society, he also arranged to translate Vedas and Upanishads in Bangla, which was most useful in transmitting the ideas contained in them to a larger section of readers.

By founding a Brahmo Vidyalaya in Santiniketan in 1861, Debendranath initiated a campaign for education in rural Bengal which culminated in the formation of Visva-Bharati in 1921 by his equally capable son, Rabindranath. While Dwarkanath contributed to the spread of education in collaboration with his colleagues who joined hands with him, Debendranath founded Brahma Vidyalaya on his own initiative which created a solid platform for Rabindranath who, by establishing a university, went ahead of his father in his mission for imparting higher learning to those in rural Bengal who hardly had an opportunity to be educated given the total absence of schools and colleges. Unlike Dwarkanath who stood out also as a successful businessman in competition with his British counterparts, Debendranath, also known as a Maharshi (great saint), generated a great impulse for education and also Bangla as a language which equipped the future generation with the capability for joining hands with one another for the 'nationalist' cause.

Debendranath's contribution needs to be gauged with reference to the context in which the 'nationalist' campaign did not appear to have gained momentum to the extent that it gained once Gandhi arrived on the scene. Nonetheless, there is no denying that by seeking to build a sentiment of togetherness, Debendranath privileged his heartfelt keenness to develop a strong education system; here, he also put forward a design of learning in which both the Western and indigenous discourses were equally critical to comprehend the complexities of human existence. It is also true that he did not exactly nurture anti-British sentiments but was aware that what brought the British rule in India was the lack of social cohesion due to multifarious reasons which never allowed the country to stand as a well-knit collectivity. According to him, one of the reasons for this failure was the prejudices against fellow human beings due to their caste and religious identities. That he was free from caste-driven segregation was evident when his son, Rabindranath, requested him to allow even the non-Brahmins to guide the weekly Brahmo Samaj prayers. His concern for Hindu–Muslim amity was manifested in his unqualified appreciation for the Sufi poet Hafeez, who always propagated that the religious division among human beings was contrary to well-established canons of humanity. As evidence shows, Debendranath was introduced to *Deevan*, a collection of Hafeez written poems, by Rammohun. It was a source of enlightenment, as Debendranath declared in his memoirs.[2]

There are three important points that deserve attention here: First, undoubtedly, Debendranath set out some of the major sociocultural goals and politico-ideological voices that gradually loomed large in Bengal and later in India as history progressed. He was also a revolutionary in his thoughts because he, despite stern opposition by his colleagues, was not hesitant in challenging schism around the caste and religious denomination. Second, by establishing Brahmo Vidyalaya in rural Bengal, he also translated into reality his concern for universalizing education which, so far, remained confined to Calcutta and its vicinity. This was a pioneering venture which fully blossomed when his son, Rabindranath, founded Visva-Bharati in 1921 in rural Bengal. Finally, unlike Dwarkanath, his father, Debendranath, by completely giving up the luxurious life of a wealthy scion, came closer to the ordinary people, which was recorded in contemporary media reports. By imbibing his father's approach to humanity, Rabindranath generated a distinct wave of thinking which his 'nationalist' colleagues, especially

---

[2] Ibid., 119–122.

Gandhi and his disciples, stuck to as a means to bring people together irrespective of the division around social axes.

Debendranath was a class by himself. A pioneer in many respects, the second of the Tagore patriarchs evolved ideas which provided newer inputs to the posterity. There is likely to be a misconception that by drawing attention to the rich ancient Hindu intellectual traditions, one may argue that he was a 'Hindu revivalist'. The claim can be dismissed in two ways: On the one hand, by insisting on the fact that Hindu ancient texts were also repositories of wisdom, he paid attention to those forgotten texts which, despite being sources of knowledge, lost their viability due largely to the colonial conspiracy. It is also true that his task of reviving those texts was rather easier because of the support that his British colleagues in the Asiatic Society of Bengal extended. Nonetheless, it was Debendranath who created a zeal for knowing these ancient tracts, especially Vedas and Vedantic texts, by persuasively arguing that, like the Western discourse, the indigenous sources of knowledge were equally critical to grasp humanity as a well-knit collectivity. On the other hand, by steadfastly working for unearthing alternative sources of knowledge which, so far, remained intellectually peripheral, he simply challenged the hegemony of the Western philosophical discourses which, by completely discarding the indigenous conceptual designs based on the ancient Hindu texts, privileged the one-size-fits-all model. In other words, as colonial discourses were complementary to colonization of India, it was obvious that the colonial rulers allowed no thought processes that harmed their sustenance in India. In this way, the argument that by supporting the study of ancient Hindu texts, Debendranath became a Hindu revivalist is highly flawed and thus conceptually misleading.

Debendranath thus not just was a social reformer but also evolved path-breaking ideas which helped the later generation create a newer genre of thinking. Rabindranath was certainly the main actor who, by drawing on his father's ideas and values, carried forward the traditions that started unfolding with the arrival of Rammohun on the scene. After the departure of Rammohun in 1833 and Dwarkanath in 1846, the baton was transferred to Debendranath who, instead of surrendering to the British completely as many of his landlord colleagues preferred, devoted his energy to champion a new world of thinking by being appreciative also of the indigenous sociocultural and politico-ideological ideas. What was almost muted in the ideas and activities of Dwarkanath who was unconditionally loyal to the British came to life, though in a limited way, in what Debendranath pursued while seeking to fulfil his mission. In short, Debendranath brought about radical ideational transformations in Bengal's sociocultural and politico-ideological milieu. By following this path, Rabindranath streamlined his ideas and activities once Visva-Bharati came into being in 1921. So Debendranath can be said to have been a harbinger of significant metamorphosis in Bengal's intellectual universe which, so far, remained clearly West-centric. Although Debendranath did not follow the path that his father, Dwarkanath, adopted, to become an important public figure in the then Bengal, one cannot completely dismiss his contribution in making what Debendranath ultimately became by instilling in him the strong determination to carry on despite failure. So the model that Dwarkanath built might not have been exactly appropriate for attaining his sociocultural and politico-ideological mission, though the idea that nothing was insurmountable if it was backed by unalloyed determination was at the root of Debendranath's constructive role at a particular juncture of Bengal's sociopolitical history. With the articulation of a new genre of thinking, Debendranath carved a distinctive mode of thinking which was further strengthened once the third of the Tagore patriarchs, Rabindranath, arrived on the scene.

Chapter 3

Continuity with the Past

Dwarkanath's eldest son, Debendranath, was expected to take care of the landed property and other business ventures that his father, Dwarkanath, had acquired. The available historical evidence shows that Dwarkanath had successfully managed his interest in social reform along with his concern for property and business. To his utter disappointment, he however felt that his son, Debendranath, was not keen to work hard for retaining what he amassed by dint of self-driven initiatives. It was evident when he accused Debendranath's tutor, Ramchandra Vidyabagish, of 'spoiling [his son, Debendranath] by whispering the Brahma mantra to his ears. He has little worldly acumen and now all his interests lie in "Brahma". He does not concentrate on worldly affairs'.[1] Being completely disenchanted with the lifestyle of his father, he also defied Dwarkanath's instruction of looking after the guests who were invited to his parties. As Debendranath himself admitted, his father wanted him to hobnob with the British and also the Calcutta elites for the sake of being 'one of them'[2] in course of time and it was necessary, Dwarkanath further felt, for

---

[1] Debendranath, *Atmajibani* (Autobiography), in Khastagir, *Debendranath Thakurer Atmajibani*, 47.
[2] Ibid., 48.

sustaining 'the family traditions which were built by dint of years of hard work'.[3] Debendranath's defiance shows that he was not cut out for the role that his father had contemplated for him. Dwarkanath did not conceal his resentment when he wrote to Debendranath on 19 May 1846 by underlining that

> Your time I am sure being taken up in writing for the newspapers and in fighting with the missionaries than in watching over and protecting these important matters which you leave in the hands of your favourite amlahs [employed office staff managing the business and landed property] instead of attending to [them] yourself most vigilantly.... These are more important things [than] fighting with the Englishmen for defending your exclusive socio-cultural faith.[4]

Debendranath did not seem to be as keen as his father in material possessions though he spent the early part of his life most luxuriously. One of the principal reasons was perhaps, as he hinted in his *Atmajibani*, that he never liked his mother being neglected by his father who being indulged in Western lifestyle never understood 'his wife's concern and love for him'.[5] There could also be his utter disgust with the pompous lifestyle that Dwarkanath followed to become closer to the British elites or one of them. At a very young age, Debendranath realized that it was impossible simply because of the carefully maintained socio-economic and cultural distance between the British elites and their Indian followers. Dwarkanath was liked by British elites in Calcutta and elsewhere simply because of his willingness to spend his wealth for their enjoyment; it was primarily 'a selfish motive of the British'[6] that drew them to him, Debendranath lamented. Nonetheless, it is fair to argue that as Dwarkanath's son, Debendranath, was exposed to his grandfather's lavish and pompous lifestyle on the one hand, and his concern for critical social issues, on the other hand, which was an

---

[3] Ibid.
[4] Dwarkanath to Debendranath, 19 May 1846, cited Mittra, *Memoir of Dwarkanath Tagore*, 15.
[5] Debendranath, *Atmajibani* (Autobiography), in Khastagir, *Debendranath Thakurer Atmajibani*, 31.
[6] Ibid., 27.

outcome of his intimate contact with Rammohun. A product of peculiar sociopolitical processes, Debendranath created a space in history that had the imprint of his father's distinct perspectives and also the indomitable influence of Rammohun. In fact, he admitted that had he not come into contact with Rammohun, he would have remained blind to the complex layers of life under colonial rule. Debendranath's close intimacy with Rammohun was, however, a source of annoyance to his father who thought that 'his son was spoiled by him', as his biographer Kissory Chand Mittra noted, 'by taking his mind away from Hinduism to Brahmo Samaj which was primarily a challenge to the strictly ritualistic Hinduism clinging to archaic customs and idolatry'.[7] Nonetheless, the bond that developed between Debendranath and Rammohun was critical to the acceptance of Brahmoism by the former who gradually became one of the chief proponents of this religio-ideological perspective, especially after the demise of the latter. Debendranath's close proximity with Rammohun's son, Ramaprasad Roy, who studied with him in the same class allowed him free access to the Roy household. As he recollected, Debendranath often met Rammohun at his residence because it was a matter of routine that he had to wait for his son to go to school together. For him, it was not, at all, a waste of time since Rammohun occupied him by sharing his thoughts on many issues, including the torturous Hindu social customs. It was also from him that he learnt the price that one had to pay if one undertook a campaign of purging Hinduism of these superstitious practices. As contemporary evidence demonstrates, Rammohun was subject to fierce criticism in the local media while he was pursuing the crusade against the burning of women once they became widows. A very interesting anecdote by Debendranath is illustrative here. Rammohun had the habit of taking breakfast with honey and home-made bread though in the then media it was reported that the food items that he was served were beef and ham.[8] Although Debendranath was too young to understand the complex ideas in which Rammohun couched his arguments while challenging

---

[7] Mittra, *Memoir of Dwarkanath Tagore*, 17.
[8] Ajit Kumar Chakrabarty, *Maharshi Debendranath Tagore* (Kolkata: Paschim Bangla Akademy, 2013; reprint of the original publication of 1916 of the text), 94.

the forces championing Hindu orthodoxy, he was enamoured by his ability to elaborate the points so lucidly in support of the contention that he strongly believed. As he himself noted in his autobiographical text, 'I was never intimate with the Raja [Rammohun] and he never rendered any advice though his strong determination to realize the social and economic objectives that he held so dearly endeared him to me'.[9] Inspired by his thoughts, Debendranath naturally became a true apostle of the ideas that he internalized by being privy to listen to the discussion that Rammohun had with his father, Dwarkanath. In view of the fact that Debendranath was instrumental in bringing back the ancient Hindu texts (Vedas and Upanishads) as critical to contemporary intellectual discourse, one is inclined to argue that had he not endeavoured to revive interests in these texts in conjunction with his like-minded colleagues in Bengal they would have lost salience given the uncritical acceptance by the educated Bengalis of the Derozians who, while seeking to popularize the Western philosophical perspective on humanity, created a social ambience in which Christianity seemed to have been preferred. Had Debendranath not undertaken the task after Rammohun, 'Hinduism would have disappeared which would have, it was apprehended, led to the consolidation of Christianity in Bengal'.[10] The idea gained ground since Derozians generated a fierce campaign 'to uproot Hinduism in its entirety [since, according to them,] it was backward, superstitious and an impediment towards human progress'.[11] Although, as per some of the contemporary descriptions, Derozians were 'adept at destroying the fundamental cultural ethos of Bengal', there was hardly a strong voice against them until Debendranath arrived on the scene.[12] The aim here is to highlight the argument that being heavily influenced by Rammohun Debendranath evolved a genre of thinking which, like his intellectual mentor, creatively blended the Western discourses with their indigenous counterparts to evolve a unique approach to human existence. He was, in other words, neither a rabid follower of the Western mode

[9] Ibid., 98.
[10] Ibid.
[11] Ibid.
[12] Ibid.

of conceptualizations like the Derozians, nor had blindly endorsed the principles that had emerged out of the ancient discourses of Hinduism.

A Landlord Per Se

After the untimely demise of Dwarkanath at the age of 51 in 1846 in England, the responsibility of managing the large landed estate and other properties that he left was vested in his eldest son, Debendranath Tagore. Although the available literature on Debendranath focuses primarily on his spiritual life and his significant contribution to the strengthening of Brahmo Samaj, there is another part which projects him as a very worldly person who acted as a tough zamindar while protecting his landed property. As is well known, Debendranath, to repay the loan that his father incurred, sold most of the family's landed estate which left only three zamindari estates at his disposal. Here his letters to his son-in-law, Sharadaprasad, are illustrative. There are two features of these letters that immediately draw our attention: On the one hand, they demonstrate Debendranath's unflinching attempt to guard the landed property in remote areas of Bengal which, because of his absence, remained little neglected after Dwarkanath's sudden death. Distinct is also the feature, on the other hand, underlining a change in his stance vis-à-vis the cultivating peasants and the officers who were engaged in collecting rent. So long as Dwarkanath was alive, Debendranath did not bother with the income that the zamindari estate had generated; he was enjoying the rural beauty, as his letters and other texts reveal. Once his father died, one notices a significant transformation of Debendranath being an ardent admirer of nature to a strict administrator who devoted wholeheartedly not only for raising the rental income from his zamindari but also to evolve mechanism for augmenting production with high-quality manure and implements.

A care analytical scan of these letters shows that a prudent Debendranath left no stone unturned while fulfilling his role as an effective landlord. In other words, these letters draw our attention to a relatively unknown aspect of Maharshi's life where the zamindar Debendranath seems to have prevailed over his other persona of being indifferent to worldly possessions. One should not jump the gun however because Debendranath's devotion to spirituality and concerns for radical social reform in opposition to Hindu obscurantism also remained critical to his life which did not match with these letters. This confirms the argument that like many of the important social reformers in Bengal or elsewhere, Debendranath had also undergone noticeable transformation in life which cannot be captured, at all, if one concentrates on one particular phase of his life.

Illustrative of Debendranath's deep concern for shielding his landed property are these letters with many of his specific instructions for executing his decision in this regard. In his letter of 29 December 1875 to Sharadaprasad, Debendranath ordered to 'suspend the rent collector since he failed to perform his duties in collecting the amount of rent'[13] that Debendranath had fixed. While asking his son-in-law to get a replacement, he further set out stringent qualification, including 'efficiency' and 'truthfulness'. If nobody was found suitable, Debendranath left the instruction for

> 'not appointing anyone [and to carry the work] with the help of the caretaker [who, according to him], despite not having the exact qualities, is, by being honest to the core, fit enough to be of help in collecting rent for the time being'.[14]

Here Debendranath was just like any other zamindar in Bengal: Protective of his income, he would not excuse any losses due to negligence on the part of rent collectors. As a landowner, he was neither lenient nor accommodative of his subordinates' mistakes. On one occasion, he did not hide his disappointment when the rent collector failed to deposit the rent within time 'by being too soft to the cultivators, they failed to fulfil their obligations to the zamindars that cannot be tolerated'.[15] Appreciating the caretaker, Debendranath also rejoiced

---

[13] Debendranath to Sharadaprasad, 29 December 1875, cited in Nilanjan Bandyopadhyay, *Collection of Debendranath's Letters* (Santiniketan: Rabindra Biksha, No. 51, Rabindra Bhawan, 2011), 15.

[14] Ibid.

[15] Debendranath to Sharadaprasad, 2 July 1877, cited in Nilanjan Bandyopadhyay, *Collection of Debendranath's Letters* (Santiniketan: Rabindra

when he had won a litigation over land with an English landlord, though he ended the letter by reminding the second time that as far rent was considered no mercy was possible.[16] In another letter, he also directed to lodge a police complaint if the cultivators of Noorpur in east Bengal 'declined to pay the rent'.[17] Unable to accept the loss of rent from his landed estate, he also insisted on retrenching one of his erstwhile trustworthy staff responsible for managing his property since he was alleged not 'to have given enough effort to arrange to collect the amount of rent that was expected to be collected'.[18] He was also aware that to sustain a smooth flow of rent to his exchequer, he needed to take care of the order given by the British magistrate. One of the letters is illustrative here where he unhesitatingly sanctioned ₹5,000 to the flood victims in Sahajadpur just 'to please the British magistrate [who] passed an order directing the local landlords to financially assist the hapless victims in areas severely affected by flood'.[19] The same argument was reiterated when Debendranath ordered Sharadaprasad to release adequate funds to the English school inspector, F. W. Taylor, who requested him to donate for constructing a school building in Krishnanagar.[20] He was not willing to give up his landed estate was evident by his annoyance when he lost a litigation which led to abdicating his right over certain portion of his estate to a rival zamindar. While attributing this loss to an inefficient lawyer, he asked the caretaker to replace him as quickly as possible to avoid

Biksha, No. 51, Rabindra Bhawan, 2011), 16.

[16] Ibid.

[17] Debendranath to Sharadaprasad, 11 May 1878, cited in Nilanjan Bandyopadhyay, *Collection of Debendranath's Letters* (Santiniketan: Rabindra Biksha, No. 51, Rabindra Bhawan, 2011), 20.

[18] Debendranath to Sharadaprasad, 21 October 1878, cited in Nilanjan Bandyopadhyay, *Collection of Debendranath's Letters* (Santiniketan: Rabindra Biksha, No. 51, Rabindra Bhawan, 2011), 22.

[19] Debendranath to Sharadaprasad, 30 June 1879, cited in Nilanjan Bandyopadhyay, *Collection of Debendranath's Letters* (Santiniketan: Rabindra Biksha, No. 51, Rabindra Bhawan, 2011), 25.

[20] Debendranath to Sharadaprasad, 1 May 1883, cited in Nilanjan Bandyopadhyay, *Collection of Debendranath's Letters* (Santiniketan: Rabindra Biksha, No. 51, Rabindra Bhawan, 2011), 38.

further loss.[21] Moreover, he also asked Sharadaprasad to punish 'the officer responsible for handling litigation as regards his landed property … to send a message to others so that it does not recur in future'.[22] He was assiduous when it came to collecting rent from his landed property is evident from his devising a plan of leasing his land for five years. Debendranath took this step to not lose rental income under any circumstances.[23] His consciously articulated devices for ensuring his rental income from the estate that his father bequeathed run through these letters. Here the landlord, Debendranath, is mistakenly one of the other landlords that Bengal witnessed following the adoption of the 1793 Permanent Settlement Act. As mentioned above, with the departure of the zamindars from the areas in which they had their landed estate, a new group of people emerged in agrarian Bengal who, without owning land but by being ruthless executioner of collection of rent for the landlord, were reported to have created a reign of terror in rural Bengal, as the contemporary print media reports.[24] While endorsing that the local cultivators suffered severe torture in the hand of the rent collectors, R. C. Dutt also condemned the effort by 'their brethren to undertake various plots to ascertain rent collection on time'. The brutality in this regard helped the British to financially support the British expansionist policy. According to him,

> It is not an exaggeration to state that Bengal, with its Permanent Settlement, yielding a steady and unvarying income from the soil, enabled the British nation to build up their Empire. [Reinforcing the argument, he further stated that] it may therefore be said with

---

[21] Debendranath to Sharadaprasad, 26 July 1880, cited in Nilanjan Bandyopadhyay, *Collection of Debendranath's Letters* (Santiniketan: Rabindra Biksha, No. 51, Rabindra Bhawan, 2011), 27.

[22] Debendranath to Sharadaprasad, 11 December 1880, cited in Nilanjan Bandyopadhyay, *Collection of Debendranath's Letters* (Santiniketan: Rabindra Biksha, No. 51, Rabindra Bhawan, 2011), 29.

[23] Debendranath to Sharadaprasad, 6 May 1881, cited in Nilanjan Bandyopadhyay, *Collection of Debendranath's Letters* (Santiniketan: Rabindra Biksha, No. 51, Rabindra Bhawan, 2011), 31.

[24] Bengal Horkara, 18 September 1883, cited in Kalyan Kumar Sengupta, *Pabna Riot and the Politics of Rent, 1873–1885* (New Delhi: Peoples' Publishing House, 1974), 131.

strict truth that the conquest of Lod Hastings, like the conquest of Lord Wellesley, were made out of the resources furnished by Permanently Settled Bengal.[25]

There is no denying that for the zamindars, the only consideration was to generate income from the landed estates; and more so once the Sunset Law was implemented. Debendranath was, as the above letters show, not an exception in this regard. On one occasion, he was very upset because the amount of rent that he received from 'Shahjadpur and Birahimpur was far less than what he expected'[26] which resulted in the removal of the caretaker of these two estates. Stern in his message to Sharadaprasad who was in charge of looking after Debendranath's landed estate, he further stated that 'lapses of this kind cannot be tolerated in future'[27]; he also threatened Sharadaprasad with dire consequences if he was found to be 'negligent'[28] in discharging his responsibilities. By giving him authority to take over the leased land in case the landowner was a defaulter,[29] Debendranath emerged as a hard task master insofar as the collection rent was concerned. It was clearly revealed in the letter of 4 June 1883 when the zamindar, Debendranath, insisted that under no circumstances the cultivators were to be allowed to harm his economic interests; to pre-empt them, he also allowed the caretaker to deploy coercive methods, if it was necessary. Reiterating that the caretaker needed to be extra careful and always alert so that 'the enemies cannot raise their heads ever'.[30] It is most likely that these letters allow Debendranath to be characterized as one who, similar to his counterparts in Bengal, seems to have been highly protective of his rental income. The argument has

[25] Ramesh Chandra Dutt, *The Economic History of India*, Vol. 1 (New Delhi: Oxford University Press, 1976; reprint), 282–283.

[26] Debendranath to Sharadaprasad, 31 May 1881, cited in Nilanjan Bandyopadhyay, *Collection of Debendranath's Letters* (Santiniketan: Rabindra Biksha, No. 51, Rabindra Bhawan, 2011), 33.

[27] Ibid.
[28] Ibid.
[29] Ibid.

[30] Debendranath to Sharadaprasad, 4 June 1883, cited in Nilanjan Bandyopadhyay, *Collection of Debendranath's Letters* (Santiniketan: Rabindra Biksha, No. 51, Rabindra Bhawan, 2011), 38.

substance as the above letters amply demonstrate that he, unlike his father, Dwarkanath, was far more attentive to his responsibility as the patriarch of the Tagore family by ensuring a steady rental income to take care of the family expenses, including those which helped them sustain their societal reputation as one of the leading families of Calcutta elites. His ruthlessness, on occasion, was thus guided by certain practical considerations which one would have missed had the letters been read out of the context. Tagore family was one of the British loyalists continued even when Debendranath took over the mantle of the family which came out very clearly when he instructed Sharadaprasad to provide financial assistance to the British magistrate for their endeavour towards supporting the construction of a school building or helping the hapless flood victims. In light of these evidences, one is also inclined to suggest that it did not seem odd for Debendranath to extend financial support because he was nurtured in an environment where his father, Dwarkanath, regularly spent money for various kinds of social services. Furthermore, by being involved in activities contributing to the welfare of the poor and underprivileged, as his later life shows, Debendranath agreed to be associated with the efforts that the British rulers undertook to take care of the interests of the poor and also to advance education in Bengal.

These letters are a testimony to the claim that Debendranath, like other zamindars in Bengal, was governed by his class interests which led him to be firm in his dealing with the rent defaulters. As well as in protecting his rights as a landlord, he also, like his counterparts in rural Bengal, endeavoured to evolve a mechanism to execute his authority vis-à-vis tillers of the soil. Being a zamindar, he hardly wavered in this regard, as the letters amply demonstrate. The striking fact is that despite zamindars being ruthless on many occasions, there were hardly many serious peasant rebellions to disturb the balance of power. One needs to locate the reason in the symbiotic relationship between the zamindars and their *prajas* (subjects) that had ceased to exist, especially after the adoption of the 1793 Permanent Settlement Act,[31] which radically altered the socio-economic circumstances in

---

[31] Sugata Bose clarified this point in his 'The Roots of Communal Violence in Rural Bengal: A Study of Kishoreganj Riots, 1930', *Modern Asian Studies* 16, no. 13 (1982).

rural Bengal. In view of the stringent application of the Sunset Law by the British rulers which fixed a scheduled date in a year when the rent was to be deposited to the government; if the zamindars failed, their rights over their landed property became illegal, and the government was authorized to sell the property. With the growing commercialization of zamindari estate and the shifting of the landlords to Calcutta, the rural Bengal had undergone radical socio-economic transformation. In the absence of the landlords, those who acted on their behalf hardly had any sympathy for the tillers which caused an alienation between the zamindars and the *prajas*. That the new Act was a source of oppression by the *zamindars* was emphasized by Warren Hastings, the Governor-General of Bengal, who, in a minute of 1819, wrote that 'The Permanent Settlement subjected almost the whole of lower classes throughout these provinces [where the Act was executed] to most grievous oppression; an oppression too so guaranteed by our pledge that we are unable to relieve the sufferers'.[32]

To not lose their property, the landlords gave a free hand to the caretakers who, in their turn, became ruthless to please their employers; the landlords too remained captive of the situation in which their primary concern was to retain their property regardless of the consequences.[33] While interpreting these letters which are reflective of Debendranath's concern for the landed property that he inherited, one should be sensitive to the socio-economic milieu in Bengal that underwent significant metamorphosis following the acceptance of the 1793 Sunset Law. In the changed circumstances, Debendranath's expressions and decisions did not seem odd since it was natural for the *zamindars* to be protective of their landed property which gave them economic power and social status in Bengal by being rich. So, while defending his right over as a landlord, Debendranath was true to his class position which he was naturally not willing to undermine by being benevolent to the defaulters of rent. Perhaps, at the back of his

---

[32] Cited in A. F. Salahuddin Ahmed, *Social Ideas and Social Change in Bengal* (Kolkata: Minerva, 1976), 118.

[33] One of the reasons that accounts for the Pabna Riot of 1873 was the oppression that they underwent by the landlords' (and especially their rent collectors) insistence on collecting rent by resorting to many coercive steps which Kalyan Kumar Sengupta captures in his *Pabna Riot and the Politics of Rent, 1873–1885*.

mind remained the fact that Dwarkanath rose to prominence among the British and indigenous elites of Calcutta largely because of the wealth that he amassed from his income out of business and landed estates in Bengal. Despite belonging to a relatively lower category of Brahmins (*pirali* Brahmins), the Tagore family with Dwarkanath at its helm, acquired a high social status presumably because of the wealth that it had. Furthermore, the fact that the colonial rulers accepted Dwarkanath as a reliable ally also made his position invincible. Although Debendranath later developed a sense of being indifferent to material possessions, so long as his father, Dwarkanath, remained as the patriarch of the family he remained captive to the socio-economic goals that the latter so assiduously pursued to expand his influence and acceptability among those who wielded power and authority, both social and political. Revealed here is his distinctive personality trait demonstrating that despite being born and raised in one of the richest families of the then Calcutta, he derived his ideological predilections from the Upanishadic messages that he had from Rammohun in course of his regular interactions with him. Dwarkanath, his father, did not appear to have opposed Debendranath meeting with Rammohun though he later expressed his anger when he found that it was at the initiation of his friend, Rammohun, that his son was deviating from Hinduism and was engaging in spreading the message.

An Organizational Endeavour

One notices striking changes in Debendranath's personality: An erstwhile landlord gave up the worldly comfort rather instantaneously once he realized that it was not going to help him achieve salvation (*moksh*) in life. Being ideologically baptized by Rammohun, he developed his powerful critique of Hindu idolatry and his admiration for Brahmoism which was manifested in many of his activities, including the foundation of a Brahmo school in Santiniketan in 1863, construction of a prayer hall (Upasana Griha) in 1888, starting of a weekly paper, *Tattwabodhini Patrika*, in 1843, among others. In view of the organized activities that Debendranath undertook during his lifetime one is persuaded to argue that he always endeavoured hard to creatively blend the theory with practice. It was rather easier for him to get involved in these activities because he was aided by equally competent colleagues with similar ideological faith. A new era ushered in when concerted attempts were made to create an Indian identity on the basis of indigenous social and intellectual resources as the reformers believed that by being oblivious of the ancient Hindu texts the Indians had done a great disservice to their identity as independent thinking beings. To translate his ideas into practice, Debendranath contributed to the formation and sustenance of the National Association, British Indian Association and Bharatbarshiyo Sabha in 1858–1859. Two points merit attention here: On the one hand, these organizations were undoubtedly attempts at redefining Indian identity in circumstances when Indians were ridiculed for being a nation of followers. By holding regular meetings of these organizations, it was also sought to be established that only by asserting their identity as independent of colonial values and ethos, Indians no longer remained servile to the colonial power but were potentially strong enough to fulfil their sociopolitical objectives within, of course, colonial rule. The viewpoint needed to be publicized also meant, on the other hand, that, by being appreciative of values of Enlightenment and political liberalism, Indians upheld the ideological priorities that flourished in Britain. In other words, concern for the country was, under no circumstances, a threat to the British authority; their devotion to the cause of the nation was articulated, not as an opponent, but as ones who expressed their 'nationalist' sentiments within the government-set parameters to sustain colonialism.

A scan of the associations reveals that Debendranath and his colleagues with similar ideological preferences were guided by two major considerations. First, given lack of interest in Bangla as a language among the youths, they found it incumbent on them to undertake steps for renewal of interests which was possible, they thought, only by holding regular intellectual discourse in the mother tongue in the public domain. It was a difficult task since with the acceptance of the 1835 Macaulay Minutes the English education became mandatory which automatically led to the dwindling of the importance of Bangla as a language. Second, as English was a passport to white-collar jobs it was obviously certain to become most popular. The zealous appreciation of the Bengali educated middle class for English also ruined the possibility of the revival of Bangla as a medium of intellectual discourses.

Under these circumstances, the initiatives that Debendranath and his compatriots took was a boon in disguise; it was an organized effort, on the one hand, to instil interests in the language among the youth and was also, on the other hand, an effective design to generate and defend the argument that pride in one's mother tongue was a source of strength.

Keeping the above objective in mind, Debendranath and his like-minded colleagues were instrumental in the establishment of the following organizations, which, they felt, also needed to be strengthened to spread the message for popularizing one's mother tongue: First, Sarvatattvadipika Sabha (an organization for discussion of multiple intellectual discourses) was founded in 1832 with inspiration from Rammohun Roy, though his son, Ramaprasad Roy, and his uncritical admirer, Debendranath Tagore, shouldered the responsibility of running the organization by mobilizing supporters and raising funds for the expenses they required to carry on its regular activities. The main purpose of this Sabha was to resort to Bangla as a mode of addressing the participants; the organizers also proposed to start a Bangla weekly, which, by publishing essays and poems in Bangla, was tuned to the Sabha's sociocultural goal. Second, in 1838, Debendranath was associated with the formation of an organization, known as Sadharon Jnanoparjika Sabha (organization for seeking wisdom). Compared to the Sarvatattvadipika Sabha, this organization generated interests among some of the then top intellectuals who appeared to have dismissed the effort as nothing but a bubble which would burst soon. Nonetheless, their enthusiastic participation in the Sabha had shown otherwise; many of the Calcutta's individuals, known for their academic grits, joined the Sabha and also contributed to the publication of three volumes in 1840, 1842 and 1843. Altogether, there were 14 well-researched essays with the argument that Bangla could easily be a medium of expressing serious ideas and thoughts for universal consumption. Third, a collectivity, christened as Bangobhasanubadak Samaj (an organization for translating in Bangla) or Vernacular Literature Society, was founded in 1850 with the purpose of translating some widely read and globally famous books in Bangla. Although the purpose was to make books written in English available to Bangla readers, the majority of the members of the Sabha were Englishmen, including D. Bethune, H. Prat and M. Townshend. Besides Debendranath Tagore, the other two local representatives were Rashomoy Dutta and Jaya Krishna Mukhopadhyay. In view of the fact that many other organizations, including The Asiatic Society, School Book Society, Knowledge Society, Christian Trust Society, had also embarked on translation, the Vernacular Literature Society picked up only those books which remained to be translated. Besides making available important books which needed to be brought to public attention, the Society also felt that not only it contributed to the available Bangla literature but also the endeavour towards translating a text was certain to enrich one's ability to understand and express the sense in which a foreign author wrote while articulating specific thoughts. Later in 1851, the Sabha started a monthly magazine, *Vividarthasangraha* (collection of many), which soon became popular presumably because of the lucidity of the language and also the diverse themes on which essays were written. Its publication was proscribed because one of the members, Rajendralal Mitra, wrote a review of Dinabandhu Mitra's *Neel Darpan*[34] in which the British rulers were severely criticized for forcing the cultivators to produce indigo in place of paddy and wheat. The Sabha undertook a project of publishing a *Panjika* (almanac) or an annual calendar containing important dates and statistical information such as astronomical data and the tide tables. This was a grand project involving very renowned Sanskrit scholars, including, inter alia, Vidyasagar, Pyarichand Mitra, Rajendralal Mitra, James Long. Once it was published it was sold out immediately though the sale started dwindling presumably because the readers expected it to be a text with astrological predictions which was, however, not the purpose for which it was planned. Within two years of its publication in 1855, the Sabha decided not to publish the almanac for, instead of contributing to its profit, it became a burden which led to its closure. Despite the fact that the Sabha lasted for only 15 years (1850–1865), there is no denying that it created a zeal among the youth to write on relevant

---

[34] Ranajit Guha wrote a persuasive text on Neel Darpan in his 'Neel-darpan: The Image of Peasant Revolt in a Liberal Mirror', *The Journal of Peasant Studies* 2, no. 1 (1974).

social issues in Bangla. Besides funding and helping to raise funds for the Sabha, Debendranath Tagore devoted much of his attention to not only encourage young writers but also create enthusiasm for learning and writing in Bangla. It was a gigantic task indeed especially because of the hegemonic grip of the English education which obviously attracted many because it was a passport to clerical jobs. On the whole, the effort was appreciated as it endeavoured to explore means to spread Bangla in contrast with the increasing importance of English though it was unfortunate that it did not last long. One of the reasons was perhaps the opposition of the *Sambad Prabhakar*, one of the most contemporary dailies, which was critical from the very beginning because it was an initiative based on the ideas of the 'secluded few of Calcutta's elites'.[35] Furthermore, it failed to generate adequate interest among the readers due to the Sabha's inability to comprehend what was attractive to the readers. By choosing serious theoretical treatises for translation, the readers of the Sabha's publications were confined to a minority which explains why they never became financially viable. It was, on the one hand, a failure on the part of the members of the Sabha to understand the mindset of the Bengali readers and also their indifference and, on the other hand, to the new prose style that the Sabha sought to popularize.

To translate their concern for Bengali language, Debendranath and his colleagues in Brahmo Samaj established David Hare Memorial Society in 1843 and instituted an award in Hare's name for the best writer in the Bengali language. A famed social activist and pedagogue, David Hare, is known for his contributions to the preservation and enrichment of Bangla. Two of the first recipients of the Hare award were Tarasankar Tarkaratna for his essay, '*Bharatbarshiyo Striganer Vidyasiksha*' (the education of Indian women) and Rangalal Bandyopadhyay for his essay, '*Sareersadhanee Vidya*' (healthcare knowledge). Further to this endeavour, they also founded Bethune Society in 1851 immediately after the demise of J. E. D. Bethune that year. The purpose was to recognize the significant contribution that Bethune made towards developing and also spreading Bengali language. Hence,

---

[35] *Sambad Prabhakar*, Kolkata, 17 January 1866, cited in Kashtagir, *Debendranath Tagore: Atmajibani*, 265.

unlike the David Memorial Society, the Bethune Society also focused on sociopolitical issues, besides, of course, on English, Bengali and Sanskrit literature. During its existence for 40 years (1851–1891), the Society published essays on various topics in science, history, travel, women's education and also healthcare. Although the chairman of the Society was always an Englishman, it was also an attempt to bring the Indian elites under one platform was evident when many Indian elites joined the Bethune Society. As part of his effort to consolidate like-minded individuals, in 1854, Debendranath also established *Samajunniti-Bidhayanee Suhrid Samiti* (organization of friends for social reform) that complemented Vidyasagar's endeavour towards legally stopping polygamy and widow remarriage. The contemporary evidence shows that the Samiti had held many meetings with Vidyasagar when he plunged into campaigns for rescinding these cruel social practices.[36] Debendranath also felt that these evil practices survived due to lack of education, especially among women who hardly ever raised their voice despite being social victims, which led him to establish a school for girls in Kashipur in north Calcutta.

The sustained efforts by Debendranath and his compatriots particularly in Brahmo Samaj provoked those unconditionally supporting British colonialism which was manifested in the establishment of Bengal British India Society in 1843 by George Tomson, a British trader settled in Calcutta. Even Dwarkanath Tagore and his colleagues, Raja Radhakanta Deb and Ramkamal Sen, did not join the Society notwithstanding their appreciation for British rule in India simply because it was racist in its tone and spirit. As a counter, the British Indian Society was formed in 1851 which was an amalgamation of the Landholders' Society and British India Society. With the initiative of Debendranath Tagore and Raja Radhakanta Deb, the Society was created to bring Indians together. Besides frequently addressing the public in many meetings, the members of the Society decided to start a weekly, christened as *Hindu Patriot*, which was probably the first nationalist mouthpiece in India. Interestingly, there was no debate on the title of the weekly which perhaps suggests that Muslims

[36] Khastagir, *Debendranath Tagore: Atmajibani*, 268.

did not seem to have been considered integral to the Calcutta elites. The reason lies in the hatred that they nurtured against the erstwhile Muslim rule that unfolded with the sharp critique of Muslim ruler by Bankim Chandra Chattopadhyay and Rammohun Roy. Nonetheless, *Hindu Patriot* raised the nationalist voice in an unprecedented fashion is undeniable. Illustrative of the claim is an editorial in the weekly on 14 January 1858 which says that

> Can a revolution in the Indian government be authorized by Parliament without consulting the wishes of vast millions of men for whose benefit it is proposed to make. The reply must be in the negative. The time has nearly come when all Indian questions must be solved by Indians.[37]

Critiquing the 1853 Charter Act in view of its clearly racist bias, the Association organized many protest meetings which were mostly presided over by Debendranath Tagore and Radhakanta Deb. This was a watershed in the mindset of the Calcutta elites who, so far, had hardly criticized the British rule in such categorical terms. The loyalist citizens of the Empire also became critics of their rulers for undermining, if not ignoring, the indigenous views while devising rules and regulations meant for them. The idea was still in its formative stage though it was clear that the Calcutta intelligentsia became politically baptized to raise a critical voice which, so far, remained muted, if not absent. It is true that Bengali elites seemed to have been contended with the British rule though they, by being opposed to the British prejudicial attitude, clearly evinced an endeavour towards firmly claiming their independent identity which needed to be respected just like any other white British. As an example, one can cite the strong critique by *Hindu Patriot* of the 'infamous shoe question' which was about the embargo that the Council of Asiatic Society and the Trustees of the Museum imposed on Vidyasagar, on entering the Society with his 'native shoes' or *chappal*, in local parlance. The Indians were, in other words, restrained to go inside the museum or the office of the Society

---

[37] Cited in Brian A. Hatcher, *Vidyasagar: The Life and After-life of an Eminent India* (Oxford and London: Routledge, 2014), 211.

with their shoes. Opposed to this decision, Vidyasagar wrote scathing critique of the Trustees of the Asiatic Society in various periodicals including *Hindu Patriot*. While supporting the criticism of Vidyasagar, the editor or *Hindu Patriot*, Harish Chandra Mukherjee wrote that

> In the remotest degree of countenancing, [the logic of the] regulation is nothing but a source of amusement [because] ... if there is a mark of respect attached to the leather, it is immaterial as to what form the leather may take. We hope [that] the Council of the Asiatic Society and the Trustees of the Museum will have the good sense not to make the native gentlemen feel that to enter their rooms is to court insult.[38]

This can be said to have been a part of many protests against the colonial design of degrading the 'native' Indians, which stood contrary to the fundamental ethos of Enlightenment philosophy seeking to establish fraternity regardless of class, creed and colour. The protest not only was justified by reference to the contradiction of the regulation with the core values of Enlightenment but also had projected what Rabindranath Tagore had characterized as 'a symbol of [Vidyasagar's] indomitable individuality'.[39] The shoe controversy of 1874 seems to have built a bridge that connected many of the Bengali elites who, so far, remained non-committal, if not scared, to colonial racist designs in governance. As history demonstrates, despite having held contrary views on many social issues, such as sati customs, polygamy, widow remarriage, among others, the Bengali elites came closer in their opposition to the racist British rule. It was an era of the germination of nationalism that grew in importance as decades passed on. With the increasing number of *Samitis* (organizations) and inauguration of many printed periodicals, the era is also a testimony to the realization by the 'native' Indians of what colonialism meant to the colonized and also their urge for combatting the colonizers in case their self-dignity is brutally violated. Newer possibilities had emerged which blossomed

---

[38] *Hindu Patriot*, 26 July 1874, cited in Benoy Ghose, *Iswar Chandra Vidyasagar* (New Delhi: Publication Division, Ministry of Information and Broadcasting, Government of India, 1971), 118.

[39] Ghose, *Iswar Chandra Vidyasagar*, 118.

in full form in the days to come. The claim that merits attention while assessing these collective endeavours is that besides creating a zeal for respectful self-identity which informed the latter nationalists, the era is also a testimony to the fact that without adequate social reform or radical metamorphosis of the indigenous mindset, the battle for liberty, equality and fraternity was likely to be easily defeated.

An Educationist

Debendranath, like his father, Dwarkanath, paid adequate attention to the spread of education as it was, he strongly felt, an antidote to superstition and other prejudicial beliefs. It is also a matter of surprise that he was not as vocal for education among women as he was for men which is perhaps a reflection of how he failed to surpass the contextual prejudices against female education. Nonetheless, his endeavour towards making education easily available was evident when he, along with his compatriots, took ample care in fulfilling his mission in this regard. His contribution was significant in the spreading of education, and, as a part of his initiatives, several schools came up in Calcutta and also in Santiniketan. One should not however forget that behind the effort what governed them was also to contain the increasing importance of Christianity which was an integral part of the course curricula in schools, founded by the British government. It was highlighted in the first meeting which led the foundation of Tattwabodhini Sabha in 1839. Appreciating the venture, many Calcutta elites joined hands with Debendranath and his colleagues when the idea was put in the public domain which also received adequate attention in the contemporary print media. While referring to this initiative, the *Calcutta Courier* wrote that

> [A] NEW SCHOOL—We have been given to understand that a new school, having for its object the education of the rising youths in the vernacular languages of the country is about to be established in Calcutta under the auspices of some enlightened native Baboos. It is to be conducted on the same principles as the new College Patshala. The boys will further receive religious education which is a new feature in the system of native instruction. It is said that

new books suited to the capacities of youth are now in course of preparation in the vernacular languages by Baboo Debendranath Tagore, the son of Baboo Dwarkanath Tagore.[40]

The initial zeal for the school however soon disappeared; perhaps this type of education was not, at all, appropriate for getting jobs in the public offices. Despite their enthusiasm matched with hard work, the Bengali elites had to finally agree to abandon the project three years after it was inaugurated in 1840 as the *Pathshala* failed to attract students. Two factors were responsible for the decline of this school: On the one hand, the insistence that the medium of instruction was Bangla was a deterrent since it did not help those who passed out of this school to get jobs in the government offices and other fields, for which the knowledge of English was mandatory. The government's opposition from the outset because of the introduction of lessons in Hindu texts, especially Vedas and Upanishads, also prevented many guardians from sending their kids to the school to avoid being identified with those who apparently were opposed to government designs of education. Notwithstanding with its ephemeral existence, the school generated 'a nationalist sense' among the pupils was beyond question, as *Tattwabodhini Patrika* hailed the effort by stating that 'Debendranath's initiative to ideologically baptise the Bengali youths in nationalism failed presumably because it was little premature'.[41] The failure of the school to attract students was attributed to 'the excessive emphasis of indigenous learning as a means to generate nationalist sentiments and feelings'.[42] Appreciative of the effort since it was potentially a good endeavour, the *Tattwabodhini Patrika* also underlined that had the school lasted it would have been 'an important source of generating a sense of togetherness which was sadly wanting in Bengal'.[43] The dismantling of the school however hardly dampened the spirit of Debendranath Tagore and his colleagues; they restarted the

---

[40] *The Calcutta Courier*, Calcutta, 4 June 1840, cited in Khastagir, *Debendranath Tagore: Atmajibani*, 273–274.
[41] *Tattwabodhini Patrika*, Chaitra, 1837 (Shakabda), cited in Kashtogir, *Debendranath Tagore: Atmajibani*, 274.
[42] Ibid.
[43] Ibid.

school in Bansberia, a small locality in the vicinity of Calcutta in 1843. As the school became less important because Bangla was the medium of instruction, the school-governing body decided to provide education in English as well which attracted as many students as possible to make it a viable project. With his persuasion, many of Debendranath's colleagues introduced basic texts in English which however did not prevent them from explaining difficult concepts, especially in Science subjects in Bangla. Akshay Kumar Dutta, one of Debendranath's close confidants, wrote a book on the basic ideas of Science in Bangla which was a very popular supplementary reading for the students even among those pursuing their courses in English medium schools. Despite being a hardcore rationalist, Dutta also believed that

> Merciful God has created us and continues to protect us throughout our lives by the many beneficial laws that he has ordained.... [H]e has mercifully instilled in us intellect and a religious faculty so that we may live our lives freely and happily by ascertaining and observing all his beneficial laws.[44]

A pioneer in articulating difficult ideas in vernacular, Akshay Kumar Dutta can be said to have dismissed a well-entrenched view that Science subjects remained incomprehensible unless they were taught in English. Besides his reputation as a good teacher who handled the difficult concepts in sciences, he also strongly held the view that without being united no progress was possible. It is thus stated that 'Akshay Kumar maintains that as God has implanted in man faculties, such as affection, pity and devotion, many must live in association with others in rural and urban communities to attain a nobler life through the fulfilment of these facilities'.[45] With capable teachers, the school received accolades even from those who at the outset dismissed the effort as nothing but an abortive attempt. However, due to serious financial

---

[44] In a school textbook, Dutta introduced his analysis of the idea of science with this statement. *Charupath* (in Bangla, new edition, Part 2 Calcutta: Harishchandra Majumdar, 1921), 1–2.

[45] Bimanbihari Majumdar, *History of Political Thought: From Rammohun to Dayananda, 1821–1884*, Vol. 1 (Calcutta: Calcutta University Press, 1934), 130–131.

crises, the school had to be shut down. Here too, Debendranath suffered due to his ill luck. With the unmanageable financial crises as a result of the downfall of the major pillars of Tagore's business world, the Union Bank and Carr, Tagore & Company (shipping), it was not possible for Debendranath to continue funding the school. The British educationist, Alexander Duff, did not lose this opportunity. Given the fact that Tattwabodhini Pathshala gained popularity because students were also instructed in Bangla, he decided to open a school with facilities for teaching in both Bangla and English. While inaugurating a Free Church Mission School in Calcutta, Duff thus announced that 'the Free Church Mission School provides instruction in English and Bengali [which] has already been commenced elsewhere'.[46] What is evident is the sustained effort that Bengali elites undertook in which Debendranath continued to remain an important source of inspiration. Despite having failed to achieve the goals that they aspired to attain, these efforts were regularly cited by the latter nationalist activists as attempts to combat the colonial hegemony in education. As mentioned later, Rabindranath Tagore, the last of the Tagore mavericks, referred to these well-meaning emotional designs that his father along with his colleague with compatible ideological preferences undertook in adverse circumstances.

It is true that neither Dwarkanath nor his son, Debendranath, took part in the nationalist struggle since their priority was different and the prevalent socio-economic and political context did not seem to have been prepared then. Nonetheless, their contribution in creating a milieu for independent thinking which finally led to the nationalist outbursts in the late 19th century and early 20th century cannot be ignored. They, in other words, helped build an intellectual atmosphere to begin appreciating indigenous texts and ideas; it was thus not a matter of coincidence that both father and son paid adequate attention to learn and spread the ideas that the ancient Hindu texts, especially Vedas and Vedantic texts, evolved. Their argument that these ideas and viewpoints were far more relevant to comprehend India's civilizational importance since they had emerged out of the

---

[46] Alexander Duff's statement was printed in the *Friend of India*, 6 April 1848, cited in Khashtagir, *Debendranath Tagore: Atmajibani*, 274.

contextual experiences of the authors of these invaluable texts. To fulfil the objective, Debendranath first acquired a printing machine in 1840 which also printed books in Bangla and English for the students studying in Tattwabodhini Pathshala; donated by Ramaprasad Roy, the youngest son of Rammohun, this printing machine was utilized for publishing *Tattwabodhini Patrika*. The idea was supported and adequate funds were handed over to Debendranath by his father, Dwarkanath, though the latter did not pay much attention since he was busy in managing his business empire. In other words, Debendranath's decision to publish a knowledge-based periodical was appreciated by his father who donated adequate funds for sustaining the *Patrika*. While announcing the decision to start the *Patrika*, Debendranath justified the venture as most appropriate because (a) it would not only be an effective instrument for spreading the ideas and viewpoints of the Brahmo Samaj but also connect the members of the Samaj scattered all over Bengal with one another, and (b) it would also acquaint the readers with those ideas and messages which contributed to the unfolding and also consolidation of humane values and concomitant ethos in circumstances when their importance was fast dwindling. Inaugurated in 1843, *Tattwabodhini Patrika* had a very powerful editorial committee comprising the then leading intellectuals of Calcutta who, besides Debendranath, included, inter alia, Vidyasagar, Debendranath, Rajendralal Mitra, Anandakrishna Bose, Radhaprasad Roy, Shyamacharan Mukhopadhyay. As opposed to *Sambad Prabhakar* which was famous for highlighting the cheap and vulgar stories, *Tattwabodhini Patrika* gained instantaneous popularity primarily because of the seriousness of the authors who wrote while dealing with complex social, economic and political themes. Although Debendranath wanted the *Patrika* to be a mouthpiece of the Samaj by focusing exclusively on ideas and themes of Upanishads, it never became so primarily because his colleagues in the editorial board did not concede and also the fact that one of the reasons for its wider circulation was the publication of essays focusing on multiple themes highlighting relevant issues, such as education, women's education, agriculture, science, religion and various modes of prayer among the Indians, among others. Until 1877, the *Patrika* was published regularly and its popularity remained unabated. With the disintegration of

Brahmo Samaj in three contrasting groups in 1878, the *Patrika* became a mouthpiece of the Adi Brahmo Samaj which lost its popularity by being opposed to radical social reforms which was its forte in its past incarnation and also supportive of the caste system, religious prejudices against non-Hindus and also the unconditional appreciation of the British government. Here too, the ideas that Debendranath held so dear to him lost their salience presumably because they did not appear to have developed organic roots in the prevalent socio-economic and political contexts. During its life span of 34 years (1843–1877), *Tattwabodhini Patrika* played a critical role in spreading awareness regarding not only the evilness of certain prevalent social practices but also the pernicious influence of colonial rule. Hence, despite having lost its radical character due to internal feud among those who started, it can safely be argued that the *Patrika* ushered in an important era in India's intellectual history that set in motion urges for radical socio-economic and political transformation even in adverse politico-ideological milieu.

As well as publishing *Patrika*, Debendranath and his colleagues also undertook steps to start a school exclusively for Hindus in opposition to those schools where only Christian students were preferred presumably because of their specific religious identity. What triggered their effort was the 'forcible' conversion of some of those who were working for the Tagore family. For Debendranath, it was an ominous development for the Hindu society, and this needed to be countered by preparing a mindset in support of Hinduism. The idea was translated in the formation of a Hindu Hitarthi Vidyalaya (a school for salvation of Hindus) in 1846. Appreciating the endeavour, the contemporary newspaper, *Sambad Bhaskar*, wrote that 'it was a timely intervention by the Bengali Baboos with Debendranath Tagore at the helm of affairs'.[47] They worked hard for its popularity and success was evident with the success of the Board to raise adequate funds out of voluntary contributions made by Bengali Hindu elites. Besides being involved in collecting money, Debendranath and his compatriots travelled extensively to locate capable teachers for the school, as it is reported

---

[47] *Sambad Bhaskar*, 7 April 1846, cited in Khastagir, *Debendranath Tagore: Atmajibani*, 282.

in the contemporary media.[48] Notwithstanding a good beginning, the school soon faced many difficulties, especially regarding the rigidity in pursuing ideas, tilted in favour of Hindus in opposition to those who had emanated from other religious texts. When some of the teachers reacted strongly to the religious strictures, the battle came into the open which led to their resignation; by readily accepting their resignation, the school Board also endorsed that the definite sociocultural identity of the school was established beyond doubt. Being associated with the school, Bhudev Mukherjee highlighted this aspect in his autobiography, *Bhudev Charit*, by underlining that 'the insistence on teaching only the Hindu texts alienated some of those teachers who held eclectic views since in India emphasis on an exclusive religious identity shall not always be accepted to all'.[49] By being adamant in supporting the argument which allowed no space to other religious faith, the members of the board of the school failed to appreciate, Bhudev further argued 'the sentiments of those teachers who believed that other religious texts were also sources of knowledge and social well-being'.[50] This was an example when the teachers were asked to resign; in 1848, a teacher, Kailashchandra Bose, was removed since he accepted Christianity which was contrary to the charter of the school. This had a snowballing effect since three teachers left the school as a mark of protest. As soon as this controversy subsided, the school was again troubled when son of a prostitute was admitted. The Bengali Hindu elites joined hands with Debendranath Tagore to condemn the decision because it was an attempt to 'malign the Hindu society and also defame those associated with the school, [which] nobody was willing to swallow'.[51] As a consequence, two of the principal architects of the school, Radhakanta Deb and Debendranath Tagore, resigned from the board and many of his colleagues followed him. With their initiative, they founded Hindu Metropolitan College in 1853. Endowed with good teachers, the school attracted many students, including some who left the Hindu college. Soon, it became an

[48] Ibid.
[49] Bhudev Mukherjee, *Bhudev Charit*, 121, cited in Khastagir, *Debendranath Tagore: Atmajibani*, 283.
[50] Ibid.
[51] Ibid.

important centre of learning which was innovative in terms of both pedagogy and the nature of disciplines that the students were offered. The contemporary evidence, while admiring the endeavour, suggests that Metropolitan College, by appointing 'highly educated and learned teachers ... with established reputation in their respective fields of studies.'[52] Many students of the Hindu College left for joining the Metropolitan College which forced the Hindu College authority to restrict the entry of outsiders since it was apprehended that the latter were sent to persuade the Hindu College students to desert for the Metropolitan College. It was also reported in contemporary media that students willingly came to the Metropolitan College simply because the course curricula and the teachers were modern and competent, respectively. Hence it was not an outcome of 'a crafty strategy ... but an expression of interests for academic and pedagogic excellence'.[53] With the decline of students in the Hindu College, it was not possible for the board to continue the College; furthermore, many of those who financially supported the College to run its activities had withdrawn by then. A new phase in college education had begun with the intervention of the government of Bengal directly in education which resulted in the formation of Presidency College in 1855. In course of time, this college gained momentum for two reasons: On the one hand, it had no dearth of funds given the sustained financial support by the government; on the other hand, there was no shortage of students presumably because it was government-supported college which helped the graduates get public jobs rather easily, besides, of course, the level of teaching was excellent.

The establishment of Presidency College in 1855 was a watershed in higher education in Bengal in three ways: First, exemplifying a new trend in providing education, Presidency College represented an endeavour which was fully funded by the government; in other words, now, the government participated in an activity which, so far, remained an exclusive private domain. Second, the arrival of Presidency College

---

[52] Binoy Ghose, *Samayaik Patre Bangla Samaj*, 67, cited in Khastagir, *Debendranath Tagore: Atmajibani*, 285.
[53] Binoy Ghose, *Samayaik Patre Bangla Samaj*, 68–69, cited in Khastagir, *Debendranath Tagore: Atmajibani*, 285.

also signalled the gradual withdrawal of the philanthropists who, for furtherance of education in Bengal, were not hesitant to offer financial support to this effort. Examples abound. Besides Tagore patriarchs, Dwarkanath and Debendranath, there were many Bengali Hindu elites who readily extended financial effort whenever initiatives for starting schools and colleges were undertaken. This confirms that as much as Rammohun, Dwarkanath and Debendranath 'recognized the degree to which spiritual and moral life depended upon careful and diligent effort'.[54] Finally, Presidency College was the culmination of a process that started with the acceptance of the famous 1835 Macaulay Minutes for making English education mandatory. The colonial design of creating a class of men who were Indian by birth but English in taste and culture was fully articulated with the foundation of Presidency College which, gradually not only became an excellent academic centre in India, but also created an ambience in which debates and dialogues were appreciated, of course, within the boundary that the colonial government had set out for these. This is not the place to highlight the role of Presidency College in Bengal renaissance and also the rise and consolidation of nationalistic views but, suffice it to say here that, Presidency College, despite its origin in colonial initiatives, gradually became as well a place for nationalism to grow and spread among the educated Bengali youths in adverse circumstances due to hegemonic colonial control.

Despite Debendranath's critical role as an educationist who also took part in many initiatives for establishing educational institutions along with his like-minded colleagues, there are two aspects which merit attention here. First, his contribution to education was marred by his reservation for women's education though he allowed his daughter Saudamini to be formally admitted in Bethune School; except Saudamini, he did not allow his other daughters to go to school for education. In fact, he did not seem to have appreciated the idea of women's education since it was, according to him, 'an intervention of unknown cultural forces into the inner private domain'. It was reinforced when his son, Satyendranath Tagore, sought his permission to

[54] Brian A. Hatcher, *Idioms of Movement: Vidyasagar and Cultural Encounter in Bengal* (Delhi: Primus, 2020), 225.

take his wife, Jnanadanandini, to England, he vehemently opposed and the plan was shelved because, according to Debendranath, it amounted to 'a total disregard to the well-established social customs and mores [that developed] over ages as appropriate for sustaining a social order'.[55] The second point that projected a different Debendranath was his decision to completely withdraw English education from schools in his *zamindari* estate in Shelaidaha. It stood in contradiction with this belief that English education was necessary for opening up one's intellectual horizon. The reason was difficult to seek, except perhaps, was his view that given the general lack of interests in education, the introduction of English was likely to be a deterrent since it was not so easy to learn and also the fact that it was a language of the Englishmen who eat 'forbidden meat, for example, beef and pork, [which was likely to] create and also substantiate the image of Debendranath of being a deviant Hindu'.[56] In rural Bengal, it was perhaps a judicious decision for him who, being a landlord interested in collecting rent from his subjects, appeared to have privileged his partisan interests over his social concern. Nonetheless, the above scan of the endeavours that he undertook in collaboration with his colleagues with compatible social, economic and cultural concerns reveals that Debendranath stands out as for his decisive contribution to the spread of education in Bengal just like his father, Dwarkanath, who, being persuaded to believe that education kindled curiosity and quest for knowledge, initiated a campaign that assumed massive proportions once the baton passed onto his son, Debendranath.

Concluding Observations

The above discussion shows that Debendranath represented an era of significant social, economic and politicocultural transformation in Bengal which led to processes of change elsewhere in India. A careful study of his life reveals how the colonized Bengal metamorphosed

---

[55] Debendranath to Satyendranath, cited in Khastagir, *Debendranath Tagore: Atmajibani*, 288.
[56] Debendranath on education, *Sambad Bhaskar*, 8 August 1859, cited in Khastagir, *Debendranath Tagore: Atmajibani*, 287.

from being a space that allowed colonialism to flourish to a hotbed of nationalism (though in a muted form) which gradually blossomed into a gigantic campaign for political freedom during the period when his son, Rabindranath (1861–1941), played a similar role. In conventional terms, Debendranath was not a nationalist, but was, undoubtedly, a patriot who privileged social reforms over other socio-economic priorities. Like his father, Dwarkanath, he strongly felt the importance of mobilizing opinion by organizing like-minded colleagues and compatriots for a cause that, he felt, needed to be pursued with elan and commitment. For instance, he channelized his desire to counter Hindu orthodoxy by constituting Brahmo Samaj in 1833 along with his colleague, Rammohun Roy. Seeking to instil the values of 'righteousness, sinlessness and devotion to the effort that [members of Samaj] agreed to undertake', the Samaj brought fresh air in Bengal's sociocultural environment.[57] By reviving the Samaj in 1842, Debendranath continued a tradition that, he thought, was an important instrument for radical social changes that he had in mind. What was most striking in Debendranath was his steadfast endeavour in creatively blending ideas that he derived from the Western sources with what he received from the indigenous Hindu and Islamic traditions. It was therefore not surprising that he was equally excited while reciting Upanishadic hymns simultaneously with the innovative writings of Hafez, the Sufi poet. His firm belief that human beings attained salvation by not complete abdication of worldly life but their success in discovering the supreme being in worldly existence. This was possible by not competition or coercion but unconditional lover. He became emotionally close to Hafez since he always championed the claim for devotion to the supreme being without expecting anything in return. While accepting Hafez's dictum he actually reverberated the vision that Upanishadic faith in the idea of complete surrender to the almighty.[58] The idea was embryonic in the past, but had blossomed in its full form when Samaj reappeared with much zeal and spirit at the behest of Debendranath and his associates. Two important points deserve to be highlighted: First, by disparaging competition and coercion in persuading human

---

[57] Hatcher, *Idioms of Movement*, 225.
[58] For details, see Chakrabarty, *Maharshi Debendranath Tagore*, 660–671.

being to a faith, Debendranath, in a very subtle manner, provided a powerful critique of the design that the Christian priests forcibly pushed in Bengal, of course, with support of the colonial masters. It is true that the Brahmo Samaj and its activists failed to halt the march of Christianity since conversion to Christianity allowed access to many material benefits which would not have been available. Second, the endeavour by Debendranath and his supporters raised an alternative voice in colonial Bengal which, despite not being exactly political, helped build an ambience in which the clamour for freedom rested. So, by seeking to create an independent sociocultural space, the Samaj generated a momentum which gained massive proportions in the decades to come. In other words, the initiative that Dwarkanath had undertaken gradually gained momentum in the late 19th century and its aftermath presumably because it developed organic roots in Bengal.

On the surface, Debendranath can be said to have been an ascetic barring a few years of youth when he discharged his role as a landlord just like any of his counterparts in Bengal. As soon as he gave up his worldly possessions to repay the loan that his father had incurred, he became a different person though he continued his social activities amid great financial difficulties. A careful scan of his sociocultural activities even after he lost all his properties shows his firm commitment to the causes that he held so dear. It was a cause for refashioning human minds which needed to be purged of all the prejudices dividing one group of humanity from another on the basis of socially constructed yardsticks of chasm. Hence, Debendranath never dissociated his aspirational hankering for divinity from his worldly concern for socio-economic well-being for all. This was a foundational concept which the later nationalist articulated by challenging the artificially justified schism around many social axes. Mahatma Gandhi's cudgels against caste segregation or religious segmentation were rooted in the campaign that Debendranath spearheaded. In clear terms, Debendranath established that the concern for humanity was neither contrary nor an impediment towards pursuing the Upanishadic goal of complete salvation or *moksha* in Sanskrit. One should add a caveat here: It was not possible for him to be completely irreligious presumably because religion continued to remain an effective instrument for bringing socioculturally disparate people together; by completely discarding the well-entrenched archaic social practices which were justified as religion-driven, Debendranath drew on the Upanishadic wisdom to reconceptualize humanity in a perspective which was both novel and threatening to the Brahminical hegemony. The impact of the revival on interests in the original Vedantic texts was far reaching than what was felt then, as mentioned below.

Debendranath was a harbinger of radical sociocultural metamorphosis. Because he was persuaded to believe that the source of wisdom was the classical Hindu texts, he drew his attention to them to spread the idea. The far more striking was his endeavour to translate them into practice which was evident when he took personal care in developing organizations for this cause. As argued above, he not only established Tattwabodhini School in 1840 but was also instrumental in persuading many of his colleagues to write books in vernacular which were published in the printing press the Samaj owned. One of his most significant achievements is surely the establishment of a Brahmo Vidyalaya in 1888 in Santiniketan which laid the foundation of Visva-Bharati as a university that came into being in 1922 at the behest of his capable and illustrious son, Rabindranath. In so doing he not only articulated an alternative voice but also helped build an independent intellectual domain of thinking which drew on ideas other than those derived from the Western philosophical texts. In the context of the 19th century, it was a revolutionary effort for two complementary reasons: On the one hand, it firmly established the claim that India had a long intellectual history, longer than what became the mainstream texts in the wake of colonial rule. By regularly publishing Bangla commentaries on the Vedantic texts which Rammohun had initiated, *Tattwabodhini Patrika* that came into being in 1843, was a perfect vehicle for spreading the message. Its social impact was, on the other hand, far more significant in a context when there were mass conversions of Bengali Hindus to Christianity and also increasing attraction to English education. For Debendranath, it was not, at all, an aberration because, by being reduced to an instrument of Brahminical hegemony, Hinduism not only became divisive but also strengthened the belief that it was primarily a practice-based religious faith. As a result, the valuable inputs for humanity that the Vedantic texts provided remained hidden presumably because it was necessary to sustain the prejudicial practices protecting the interests of a social segment. So, Debendranath's effort was a powerful step in igniting interests in indigenous wisdom on the one hand, and also a challenge on the other hand to the Western discourses that reigned nearly supreme given the colonial patronage. In light of this, it can persuasively be argued that he set in motion processes which generated not only an urge for intellectual independence from the mindset sustaining colonialism but also a set of ideas seeking to weaken, if not completely delegitimize, the authoritarian Brahmanical voice in the religious domain. A social reformer par excellence, Debendranath can thus be said to have prepared the ground for his son, Rabindranath, who carried forward the mission that Debendranath upheld while being engaged in multiple sociocultural activities with the aim of creating and also consolidating a mindset in support of libertarian ideas and views based on his comprehension of indigenous and non-Western sources of wisdom. Furthermore, by unfolding newer conceptualizing modes of thinking, Debendranath not only built a bridge between Dwarkanath and his grandson, Rabindranath, but also generated a momentum among the Hindu educated youth to stand independently despite challenges.

Chapter 4

Breaking with the Past

As a Tagore scion, Debendranath was both a conformist and a rebel at the same time: He was initially a conformist as mentioned in Chapter 3, for he took ample care in protecting and also augmenting income from the Tagore's landed estate. The evidence shows that he left no stone unturned to discipline the recalcitrant cultivators in his estate. He was not, at all, different from any of his zamindar colleagues, and the local media published many stories of how he exercised his authority even by deploying coercive methods. This was a different Debendranath who did not match with his rebel persona. He later became a rebel by pursuing a path which was contrary to what was expected of a son of a successful zamindar because he was reluctant to take care of his father's business empire since it was not his priority. Dwarkanath realized this when he was alive and admonished Ramchandra Vidyabagish who introduced Debendranath to the world of Vedas and Upanishads; he also felt that it was Rammohun who spoiled his son because only with his persuasion Debendranath was drawn to the Brahmo Samaj. A unique personality, Debendranath, the eldest son of Dwarkanath also owed a great deal to his father. As mentioned in chapters 1 and 2, the senior-most Tagore patriarch also participated in significant sociocultural campaigns in Bengal to purge the society of evil practices that were justified as having been drawn on the religious texts. For him, it was an attempt by a section of uneducated priests along with their supporters to carry on with these practices to realize their partisan aims. The task was not an easy one in view of the well-entrenched supportive mindset. Nonetheless, Debendranath, being a social rebel, was also persuaded to believe that unless they were effectively challenged, they would become part and parcel of Bengal's social life. Once the goal was set, many of his colleagues holding identical sociocultural views joined hands with the campaign that Debendranath spearheaded in the late 19th and early part of the 20th centuries.

In view of his upbringing in a highly cosmopolitan family, Debendranath was exposed to the philosophy of Enlightenment of the Western variety. Moreover, Dwarkanath's regular interactions with the enlightened British colleagues in Calcutta also allowed him to be privy to many discussions on radical sociocultural and politico-ideological discourses. Alongside, he was privileged to have been exposed to the ancient Hindu texts, especially the Vedas and Upanishads. So, on the one hand, by being drawn to the Western philosophical discourses, he understood the serious limitations of most of the prevalent sociocultural customs that were considered too axiomatic. With an opportunity to read the ancient Hindu texts, he also came to realize that Indian thinkers had also put those liberal ideas in the public domain long before they were articulated by their Western counterparts. Like Bankim Chandra Chatterjee (1838–1894), he appeared to have held the view that these valuable and innovative ancient Hindu texts were deliberately put aside by the Muslim rulers for obvious politico-ideological reasons though he was not a Muslim baiter like some of his hardcore Hindu colleagues. One should not forget here that it was Rammohun who intellectually prepared Debendranath to effectively challenge the Hindu orthodoxy which was possible because of his realization that none of the Hindu religious texts ever justified torturous sociocultural practices. Here, there is a parallel between Debendranath and his father, Dwarkanath, since both of them strongly held these views. Hence, it is plausible to argue that while battling against Hindu orthodoxy, Debendranath pursued the same politico-ideological vision that flourished in Bengal initially at the behest of Brahmo Sabha which later became Brahmo Samaj. Basic here are two points that merit attention: The Hindu orthodoxy was challenged by some of the leading public intellectuals, including Rammohun, Dwarkanath, among others, on the one hand; to strengthen their voice, they also organized themselves institutionally as they felt, on the other hand, that it was necessary to combat the forces supportive of the archaic system for torturing fellow human beings in the name of religion.

By seeking to develop a voice against ritualistic Hinduism, Debendranath was a true follower of the viewpoint that Dwarkanath evolved in collaboration with his like-minded colleagues. Hence, his task was little easier because (a) the literature in support of the campaign against orthodox views and beliefs was available which was gradually enriched by Debendranath and his compatriots and (b) the campaign also gained momentum by involving those who thought alike and once there was a platform, the Brahmo Samaj, they had the courage to come together for a cause. In other words, it is argued here that the campaign in which Debendranath was involved brought many of his like-minded colleagues together as they were also convinced that it was the only effective option. Those who came in touch with Debendranath and other Brahmo Samaj members held the cudgels against the ritualistically justified orthodox sociocultural practices. It was thus not surprising that the campaign that began in the late 18th century developed its tentacles in various parts of Bengal and also outside.

There is a misconception that the sociocultural challenges that unfolded with Rammohun were nothing but attempts at Hindu revivalism.[1] Perhaps a surface reading of the concomitant historical processes may lead one to draw such a conclusion. The aim of this chapter is to argue that it is a simplistic reading of what finally persuaded the leading intellectuals of Bengal to endorse the sociocultural issues that were potentially a serious threat to Hindu orthodoxy. Fundamental point here that the chapter elaborates is linked with a massive social churning that led to the rise and consolidation of an equally powerful sociocultural campaign involving those who thought

---

[1] Amiya P. Sen, *Hindu Revivalism in Bengal, 1872–1905: Some Essays in Interpretation* (Delhi: Oxford University Press, 1993).

alike. Underlining the argument that the campaign was not broad-based though that it affected the Bengali sensibilities to a significant extent was evident when Debendranath's son, Rabindranath, emerged as its chief priest. The chapter thus makes a wider argument that the voice that Rammohun and his compatriots raised in the mid-18th century against religious orthodoxy continues to provide impetus to the campaigns against bigotry drawing sustenance from specific interpretation of one's religious beliefs.

Sociocultural Milieu

Debendranath was a product of a specific sociocultural milieu. On the one hand, he was exposed to the Western philosophical discourses because he was privileged to have access to a well-stocked library at home which Dwarkanath built by getting books also from England. It was possible for him to read books in English and Sanskrit primarily because Debendranath learnt these languages by competent tutors. So, intellectually, he was at an advantage given his access to the available literature in English and Sanskrit. Despite being a pampered child since he was raised in an extremely wealthy family, Debendranath was also a witness to the culture of supporting the poor, both in cash and kinds, by his father. He was also privileged to have regularly met Rammohun during his visit to the Tagore household although he did not seem inclined so passionately when he saw him first. One important incident appeared to have acted decisively in bringing Debendranath closer to Rammohun. As he mentioned in his memoir, the fact that Dwarkanath always stood near the main gate to receive Rammohun even if the latter visited him during his regular prayer. In other words, for his father, welcoming Rammohun was prior to his prayer though, under normal circumstances, nobody was allowed to disturb him in the family temple. This was a watershed incident in Debendranath's life as he elaborated that given his father's willingness to meet Rammohun even when he did not want to be distracted otherwise meant that Rammohun possessed those distinctive qualities which his father appreciated most. That he had many interactions with Rammohun gave him an opportunity to clearly set out a definite sociocultural vision for fulfilling his politico-ideological objectives.

Debendranath also noted that, on many occasions, he hardly had a chance to open a dialogue with him because he was always mesmerized by his views and accepted them as axiomatic. There were also occasions when to be a part of the same horse buggy in which he was travelling was also a source of inspiration to Debendranath. Rammohun was, to him, not just a teacher but also one who shaped his vision that helped him devise a meaningful sociocultural design in support of the mission that he sought to accomplish.

There are two core points that need attention here: On the one hand, Debendranath represented a new era when priority was not to augment income from landed property but to engage in sociocultural campaigns for making people socially aware. Because he believed that only by being socially aware, Bengal, and, for that matter, India, was certain to shake off the age-old shackles which are serious impediments for radical sociocultural transformation. Unless that was achieved, the country continued to remain servile to the alien powers. Further, the campaign that was initiated by his father in collaboration with Rammohun needed to be strengthened by involving the youth. The steps were to be taken accordingly. Here we must add a caveat. It was easier for Debendranath to organize sociocultural movements, tuned to eradicate socioculturally backward practices, since he hardly received any opposition from the British rulers. In other words, since his social reform campaign was, under no circumstances, a threat to the government, he was never restrained; instead, many of his British colleagues, both in Bengal and England, admired his zeal for such an act despite opposition of well-established Bengali elites who characterized him as 'a fallen Hindu' and thus deserved to be socially boycotted. There was another aspect, on the other hand, which is equally critical to understand the zeal with which Debendranath carried his campaign in otherwise adverse circumstances. It will not be an exaggeration to suggest that being a son of Dwarkanath who was also socioculturally baptised by Rammohun, Debendranath had an advantage here. By the time he became prominent in Calcutta's elite circle, there were many who were persuaded to hold the view that radical social change was a stepping stone for political rejuvenation of the countrymen. The argument that India too had something to contribute to humanity was persuasively articulated by emphasizing that the ancient Hindu texts, Vedas and Upanishads, in particular, were repositories of knowledge and wisdom and not, at all, xenophobic in texture and spirit. The argument was a serious endeavour to draw interests in and also popularize these texts as equally important in conceptualizing human history. Here too, one should not belittle the role played by Debendranath's predecessors, including his father and Rammohun, who undertook many steps to unearth these indigenous sources of knowledge and wisdom which remained peripheral since the erstwhile Muslim regimes desired so.

The purpose here is to put across the point that (a) the prevalent sociocultural context supplemented the endeavour that Debendranath and his compatriots undertook and (b) by drawing on the intellectual resources that his predecessors generated, it was easier for the eldest son of Dwarkanath to steer the campaign in accordance with the plan that they prepared jointly with those who held identical sociocultural views. This is one aspect of the argument that justifies some of the radical sociocultural steps that Brahmo Samaj adopted at the behest of Debendranath and his like-minded colleagues. The other equally important aspect is linked with the point that Debendranath also set in motion processes that loomed large even after he disappeared from the scene which means that he also surpassed the contextual constraints. As mentioned in Chapters 5 and 6, it was Rabindranath who owed a great deal to the sociocultural traditions that unfolded with the initiatives of his father with his friends by his side but did not blossom fully which justifies the claim that for the bard since the task was relatively easier, he focused on many other areas of human life which hardly received attention from the earlier sets of social reformers. So, Debendranath's emergence as a committed social reformer was not, at all, an accident of history but an outcome of complex sociopolitical processes, also rooted in endeavours of his predecessors who felt alike.

Triggering Factor

It is axiomatic that ideas and values are context-driven which are transmitted from one generation to another. In the case of Debendranath, the role of Rammohun was most critical in shaping his socio-ideological preferences. Having personally met Rammohun since he visited his residence often to meet his father, Dwarkanath, given the social concerns that former shared with the latter. As mentioned above, the young Debendranath was awestruck when he first saw him face-to-face. One of the reasons that brought him close to Rammohun was Debendranath's emotional proximity with Ramaprasad Roy who was Rammohun's son; being his classmate in school that Rammohun founded, Debendranath had free access to Rammohun's house which was not very far from where Tagores lived. In his memoir, the second Tagore patriarch mentioned that the huge fruit garden bearing juicy fruits, such as mango and lichi, attracted Debendranath to Roy's residence. As he reminisced, one day when they were struggling to get lichi from the tree, Rammohun noticed and asked them to not sweat out under the scorching sun, and, later, he asked the gardener to collect lichi for them which both Debendranath and Ramaprasad consumed to their heart's content. There were occasions when Rammohun allowed him to sit next to him in the swing in the garden. In the absence of any verbal communication even when they were in the same swing, the emotional proximity of Debendranath with the individual who spearheaded a campaign for the abolition of sati despite severe opposition of most of the elite Hindus of Calcutta which also included his mother and brother was a source of inspiration to him. He inspired the young Debendranath given his steadfast commitment to radical social reforms is acknowledged by the latter though he was still not persuaded to believe the ideological deficiency of Hindu idolatry. Debendranath had an opportunity to broach the matter when he invited him to attend the religious festival of the worship of goddess Durga. Having declined to participate in the festival, Rammohun had also an occasion to explain why Hindu idolatry is a clever way of taking people away from spiritualism since the almighty is formless. While defending his argument against the idol worship, Rammohun forcefully argued that none of the Hindu religious texts, including Vedas and Upanishads, referred to idolatry though it was justified as having been drawn on them which also meant that it was a ploy of a section of Hindus to mislead others by distorting the texts. Persuaded by Rammohun's logically justified arguments, Debendranath convinced his brothers to not take part in the festival though they were present in the evening near the sanctum sanctorum largely due to the presence of their father, Dwarkanath, who they were all scared of.[2]

The claim here is justified that Rammohun was a critical influence insofar as Debendranath's ideological preferences were concerned. There was no denying that Rammohun who, by his erudite explanation of some of the difficult ideas of Vedas and Upanishads, convinced Debendranath of the futility of Hindu idolatry. It did not escape Dwarkanath's notice who also realized that his son, Debendranath, was gradually drifting away from the worldly enjoyment. He expressed his annoyance by saying that 'your involvement in many activities linked with social and educational reforms hardly left time to deal with some of the burning issues of zamindari estates, especially the dwindling of income from land'.[3] Although he never castigated Rammohun, he expressed his resentment against Ramchandra Vidyabagish who was introduced by the former to Debendranath as his guru for understanding the difficult ideas particularly of Upanishads. As Debendranath recollected, his father was so annoyed with Vidyabagish that he mentioned in public that the latter was 'spoiling Debendranath by whispering Brahma mantra to his ears; given his very little knowledge about worldly issues, he got easily swayed by these ideas ... which resulted in his complete withdrawal from worldly affairs'.[4] That Debendranath evolved distaste for worldly enjoyment was again evident soon. In response to requests from his friends, he agreed to invite Bengalis in the grand get-togethers in his farmhouse which were earlier organized exclusively for the whites. Debendranath was in charge of welcoming the guests and also looking after them so long as they remained. Debendranath decided to stay away from one of these regular get-togethers since it clashed with one of the important meetings of Tattwabodhini Sabha. His absence was noted by Dwarkanath who, instead of admonishing him, just conveyed his displeasure by warning that 'the attraction to religious discourses was futile unless you are

---

[2] The entire narrative is drawn on the fifth chapter, cited in Khastagir, *Debendranather Atmajibani*, 36–37.

[3] Dwarkanath to Debendranath, 19 May 1846, cited in Mittra, *Memoir of Dwarkanath Tagore*, 15.

[4] Khastagir, *Debendranather Atmajibani*, 47.

assured of a comfortable life, for which one is required to be engaged in productive works'.[5] With this warning, Debendranath realized that his father was not favourably disposed towards his involvement in Tattwabodhini Sabha or activities for spiritual uplift at the cost of neglecting the property that he was to look after once he was gone.[6] Dwarkanath's concern was natural for he pursued his sociocultural mission rather easily while being devoted to the maintenance and also expansion of his worldly possessions. As mentioned in Chapter 2, Dwarkanath is credited with the pursuance of his sociocultural mission along with income augmentation out of his business ventures and landed estate. He was truly a multitasker who efficiently amalgamated his concerns for social causes and fulfilment of worldly goals.

Rammohun's spiritual persuasion worked well in Debendranath perhaps because he was disgusted with the pompous and also secluded life of a son of a wealthy zamindar who supplemented his income from commerce. In view of his exposure to the reality by being often interactive with Rammohun and his colleagues in Tattwabodhini Sabha, he was also persuaded to believe that the hierarchical social division among human beings was engineered by those with partisan motives. In a most eloquent way, Rabindranath, who considered his father as a pathfinder for him, argued that Debendranath uncritically accepted Rammohun's thesis presumably because he also realized that division was an impediment to human progress. While elaborating the point, the bard further mentioned that artificially generated customary practices stood in the way of 'bringing people together'; 'human civilization', he added, 'cannot advance so long as human beings are separated from one another, which helped, as history shows, the evil forces to develop and assume devastating proportions'.[7] The containment of these evil forces was not an easy task, the poet warned. Steadfast commitment to the cause and willingness to work hard towards its accomplishment were required. In his words, 'a wealthy nation easily attracts our attention, but we tend to forget the amount of sacrifice of

---

[5] Ibid., 48.
[6] Ibid.
[7] Rabindranath Tagore, *Charitrapuja* (in Bangla; Kolkata: Visva-Bharati, 1997), 54.

those who made it happen'.⁸ By reminding Indians of the importance of sacrifice for a cause and togetherness amid sociocultural diversity, Rammohun reiterated those ideas which were transcendental in nature. Hence it is argued that

> The roots from which [he] drew [his] sustenance are, as [he] himself set forth, a reassertion of the highest cultural heritage of India as the cement of binding the diverse people of India into a united nation and, secondly assimilation and adaptation of the culture of the West [which also reaffirms that] ... he was the initiator of the awakening of India to the modern world—the world of scientific progress and national thought.⁹

Argued here is the point that, for Rammohun, spiritual elevation did not merely mean the comprehension of the complex religious ideas but was also conceptualized as a means to unite people together irrespective of social, economic and cultural chasms. His primary concern was to build India as a nation on the basis of her internal spiritual resources combined with what the Western discourses provided to complement the effort. The philosophical discourse that he unfolded was based on his belief that nations were bound by loyalty to a common cause, that of abiding welfare of all its citizens, and every citizen should feel responsible for the welfare of all regardless of differences on any count. It was evident when he forcefully argued that

> Everything that stood in the way of the pursuit of this aim should be abjured. Customs, traditions and usages that caused and maintained divisions among sections of the people had to be scrapped and new social morality based on social equality and recognition that the welfare of man is the objective of religion as well as politics had to be established.¹⁰

Rammohun's conceptualization of new social morality is based on his understanding of the kernel of Islam, Christianity and Hinduism.

⁸ Ibid., 55.
⁹ Sachindra Lal Ghosh, *Raja Rammohun Roy: Pathmaker of Modern India* (New Delhi: National Council of Educational Research and Training, 1970), 88–89.
¹⁰ Rammohun's statement is cited in ibid.

Being trained in Persian in Patna since it was then a passport to government job, he was well-equipped to read the original scripture of Islam. It has been recorded that he was drawn to Sufism which corresponded with the Vedantic School of Hinduism and was more appreciated as a novel approach to human welfare than 'heretics by the narrow and orthodox school of Mohammedans'.[11] His thorough study of the Christian scriptures, including, Old and New Testaments, also enabled him to realize that no religion was anti-humanity; or, the core message that each religion conveyed was to ensure common well-being regardless of social, economic and cultural division. Thus, he argued that

> The consequence of my long and uninterrupted research into religious truth has been that I have found the doctrines of Christ more conducive to moral principle and better adapted for the use of rational beings than any other which have come to my knowledge.[12]

The above argument was directed to defend the point that the segregation of one set of human beings from another in terms of one's religious faith is clearly artificial and deliberately constructed. The purpose was, as Rammohun strongly felt, to create a barrier of segmentation among human beings which needed to be discarded to develop humanity as one and indivisible. It was stated categorically in his 1820 text, entitled The Principles of Jesus: The guide of Peace and Happiness, that

> The simple code of religion and morality is admirably calculated to elevate men's ideas to high and liberal notions of one God ... and is also so well fitted to regulate the conduct of the human race in the discharge of their various duties to God, to themselves and to society, that I cannot but hope the best effects from its promulgation in the present form.[13]

---

[11] J. N. Farquhar, *Modern Religious Movements in India* (Norwood, MA: Norwood Press, 1915), 30.

[12] The statement of Rammohun is quoted in ibid., 32.

[13] The statement from Rammohun's book, *The Principles of Jesus: The Guide to Peace and Happiness* is quoted in ibid.

A careful analysis of the ideas that Rammohun articulated in the above statements suggests that what prompted him to engage in radical social reform, including the ban of cruel sati custom, was also to establish that customary practices seemingly drawn on religion had neither religious sanction nor happened to be true to the religious scriptures. It was done deliberately to fulfil the partisan motives of a section of the community at the cost of the majority. On the basis of his threadbare discussion of the issues that contributed to the distortion of the religious discourses, Rammohun raised the cudgels against the dominant voice which always, for justifiable reasons, stood by the archaic mindset in support of these prejudicial practices. A strong believer of Deistic theology, Rammohun never accepted any religious instruction as axiomatic. It was evident when he prepared the trust deed for Brahmo Samaj which was published on 23 January 1830. To restore Hindu worship to its pristine purity, it was mentioned in the deed that the space bought by the Samaj for prayer

> [It] shall be used as a place of public meeting of all sorts and descriptions of people without distinction as shall behave and conduct themselves in an orderly sober religious and devout manner for the worship and adoration of the Eternal, Unsearchable and Immutable Being who is the Author and preserver of the Universe but not under or by any other name, designation or title.... [there will be] no sermon preaching discourse prayer or hymn be delivered or used in such worship but such as have a tendency to the promotion of the contemplation of the Author and Preserver of the Universe to the promotion of charity morality [sic], piety benevolence virtue and the strengthening the bonds union between men of all religious persuasions and creeds.[14]

Rammohun's spiritual discourses represent, as the above inputs confirm, a specific voice which he endeavoured to spread through an organization, the Brahmo Samaj. By setting out rules and regulations, he also evolved a specific pattern of congregational worship which was not so common among the practitioners of Hinduism. Nonetheless, the design that he devised was readily accepted by his

---

[14] Farquhar, *Modern Religious Movements in India*, 35.

followers and colleagues which helped the Brahmo Samaj to flourish as a powerful alternative to what appeared to have made the Hindu society sterile and clearly deviant from the core principles and practices of Hinduism. With the consolidation of the Samaj, a battle line was drawn between the conservative Dharma Sabha, led by Radhakanta Deb and Rammohun's brainchild, Brahmo Samaj.

What brought Debendranath close to Rammohun was his heartfelt desire supplemented by his selfless endeavour to radically alter the predominant mindset in favour of artificial social, economic and cultural segmentation among the Indians. In so doing, he also evolved a unique conceptual paradigm by creatively blending the Western discourses with the Eastern counterparts. It was evident in his appreciation for the Upanishadic idea that 'seeing oneself in others and vice versa helps dissipate hatred for others'.[15] This was articulated more or less in the same fashion in the Western discourses, especially when the principles of the Enlightenment philosophy were espoused by the utilitarian thinkers, including John Locke, Jeremy Bentham, J. S. Mill, among others. Based on care, concern and compassion, the Western thinkers did not seem to have held views which were contrary to what Upanishads championed.[16] Rammohun was thus one of those social reformers who was neither obsessed with Hindu scriptures nor xenophobic in his attitude towards the seminal texts in Western discourses. It was easier for Debendranath to appreciate the mindset that gradually became decisive among his colleagues in *Tattwabodhini Sabha* given his intellectual proximity with Rammohun and also the exposure to the seminal Western texts which Dwarkanath collected for his personal library.

Debendranath accepting Rammohun as his pathfinder was also evident when he protected Brahmo Samaj which was founded at the behest of the latter after his demise in Bristol in England in 1833. Given the deliberate attempts of the orthodox Hindus under the stewardship of Radhakanta Deb, the task was not an easy one since he had a large following among the Hindus of Calcutta. As argued

[15] Tagore, *Charitrapuja*, 60.
[16] Amiya P. Sen pursued this argument in Chapter 5 of his *Rammohun Roy: A Critical Biography* (London: Penguin, 2012).

above, the Samaj lost its appeal to a significant extent with the sudden demise of Rammohun in 1833; the Samaj had a temporary relief with the munificence of his colleague, Dwarkanath, though the situation did not seem to be favourable when Debendranath emerged on the scene presumably because of the intellectual challenge confronting the Samaj from three sources: (a) From English-educated youth, especially the Young Bengal, (b) from Christian Missionaries and (c) orthodox Hindus, organized by Radhakanta Deb. For most of the elite Bengalis, the Samaj became, at the behest of Debendranath Tagore, another form of religious sectarianism. The charge did not seem to be unfounded, as the contemporary evidence shows, because Debendranath, despite having rescinded idolatry, introduced worship of the formless God by showing his love and devotion by doing what was required to be done. Further to this, he also designed a specific form of prayer and adoration, which he characterized as *Brahmopasana*, or the worship of Brahmo. It acted favourably for him since most of the members supported him when he introduced regular prayer in a specific format. Here we must note a caveat: Unlike his intellectual mentor, Rammohun, Debendranath was far from being a deist because he believed in prayer and worship of God which allowed human beings to be in communion with the spiritual force. Since the Vedas and Upanishads were sources of his belief, he wanted his colleagues to read them in original Sanskrit. Hence, he sent four students to Banaras (Varanasi) to copy from the original Vedas which were later translated into Bengali and English by the scholars of Asiatic Society of Bengal with financial support from Debendranath'.[17] It was a planned effort on his part to defend that his spiritualism was based on Hindu *shastras* which was manifested when Debendranath compiled the code of conduct for the Brahmos, in the form of *Brahmo Dharma*. Based on theological and ethical concerns, the Dharma is said to have creatively amalgamated Debendranath's religiosity with his colleague's, Akshay Kumar Dutta, rationalism.[18] A careful delineation of the precepts of the Dharma reveals that Samaj insisted on the imbibing of those qualities

---

[17] O. P. Kejariwal dealt with this point in detail in his *The Asiatic Society of Bengal and the Discovery of the Past* (Delhi: Oxford University Press, 1988), 71–72.

[18] David Kopf, *The Brahmo Samaj and the Shaping of Modern Indian Mind* (New Delhi: Archives Publishers, 1988), 106.

which were tuned to the common well-being. By justifying that these were values with transcendental importance, Debendranath generated an argument to draw on the ancient texts, especially Upanishads. In other words, given the claim that Upanishads upheld all those devices to bring about human welfare regardless of differences, it was easier for him to persuade his colleagues. Dutt's rationalism was reflected in the precepts for the code of conduct. Based on his belief that family was the nursery of basic social virtues, he delineated those steps which, he thought, were useful to build a well-knit family. According to him, the consolidation of a social bond was based on 'sincerity, devotion, purity, forgiveness and gentleness [while] social evils strike roots if these values are undermined'.[19] Once the family bond was solid, social togetherness flourished, believed Debendranath who, to consolidate the unity, thus stressed the importance of 'self-reliance, perseverance of effort and the utility of hard work'.[20] Undoubtedly, one sees how strongly Debendranath was influenced by his father, Dwarkanath, who also believed that the success in any venture was dependent on these qualities. As mentioned in Chapter 3, by dint of his hard work, he rose to prominence in trade and commerce which was neither the forte of the then Bengali elites nor appreciated as a means for generating wealth. Similar to his father, Debendranath always held the view that the qualities that human beings acquire instinctively needed to be nurtured by 'self-improvement by hard work' which helped one to successfully cross hurdles. As a pious individual, he never undermined the importance of being 'righteous' while pursuing one's socio-economic goals which was manifested when he stated that 'labouring in the path of righteousness will help to overcome the miseries of poverty and to know yourself as competent to acquire riches throughout life'.[21] Emphasized here are the ideas that contributed to Dwarkanath's rise as a successful businessman in British India who also pursued many sociocultural missions.

One is also struck with another similarity between the father and son: Both of them believed that mere charity was not an effective

[19] Akshay Dutt's statement is quoted in ibid., 107.
[20] Kopf, *The Brahmo Samaj*, 107.
[21] Ibid.

device to counter poverty. By referring to an essay in the *Sulabh Samachar*, the Brahmo Samaj's mouthpiece, David Kopf, has shown that neither Debendranath nor his colleagues ever endorsed the idea of giving alms to the poor because 'giving alms to beggars is not an act of kindness [since] it is wrong to live on another's charity'.[22] Instead, what was suggested was to provide them useful means to get involved in productive works for the society. As demonstrated in Chapter 3, Dwarkanath held the same view when he insisted that 'one should exact an adequate return of labour from all able-bodied persons who survive on other's charity'.[23] Interestingly, the idea was carried forward even later when the last of the Tagore patriarch, Rabindranath, was at the helm of affairs for he too was persuaded by the argument that regular financial support made a person lazy and get accustomed to this if it was not discontinued soon; instead, he was in favour of training them to acquire marketable skills to earn livelihood. Fundamental here is also the claim that for eradicating poverty, willingness to work hard for the cause was needed: Dwarkanath built a business empire along with many educational institutions with support from his colleagues who thought alike; Debendranath also followed his father's footsteps by being involved in establishing schools and colleges in Calcutta and its vicinity while his son, Rabindranath, not only laid the foundation of a centre for learning at Santiniketan, away from the metropolitan city of Calcutta, which gradually flourished as one of the best academic institutions, known as Visva-Bharati that started its journey in 1921. Illustrative here is the point that three Tagores held identical views by highlighting the well-established belief that without perseverance and hard work, nothing substantial was achievable.

Debendranath: Reiteration and Recasting of Socio-ideological Preferences

As mentioned above, Debendranath confronted Christian Missionaries, Young Bengal and also orthodox Hindus, led by Radhakanta Deb, while pursuing his socio-ideological preferences. Inspired by

---

[22] The essay in *Sulabh Samachar* is cited in ibid.
[23] Mittra, *Memoir of Dwarkanath Tagore*, 62–63.

Rammohun and also his father, Dwarkanath, he was determined to take them in their stride. Hence, he decided to create an alternative platform, other than Brahmo Samaj, Tattwabodhini Sabha in 1839, to champion his views with reference to the Vedas and Upanishads; the Sabha continued independent of the Brahmo Samaj till 1859 when it was merged with the latter. A careful study of the activities that he undertook reveals that he was a true follower of Rammohun and, at the same time, he did not also carry forward the ideas that the former held so dearly. At one level, Debendranath was persuaded, like his intellectual mentor, Rammohun, to oppose Hindu idolatry; at another level, unlike Rammohun, he accepted Vedas and Upanishads as the true sources of knowledge which he reiterated in regular prayer and also in his commentaries on these texts. To champion his ideas, the Tattwabodhini Sabha adopted *Tattwabodhini Patrika* in 1843 as its mouthpiece. There is a parallel here between Dwarkanath and his son because similar to the former, who started *The Bengal Herald* in 1829 in collaboration with Rammohun, Debendranath too agreed to publish a newspaper since it was an easy means to reach many. In the first edition of the *Patrika*, 3 September 1843, the members of Brahmo Samaj accepted a code of conduct for them which was, despite being drawn on Rammohun's concern for Vedantic texts, also a departure from his ideas in substantial ways. Like Rammohun, they also identified Upanishads as sources of knowledge and idol worship was also rejected. What differentiated Debendranath from his mentor was his insistence on accepting the Upanishadic hymns and rituals as axiomatic which Rammohun never endorsed presumably because he was a true believer of religious pluralism. In other words, despite having appreciated Rammohun's idea of one God, Debendranath preferred the Upanishadic means to reach the almighty. Opposed to caste segregation as it was an impediment for individual fraternity, Debendranath always privileged the zeal to contribute to common well-being over sectarian desires. Nonetheless, by insisting that Brahmos needed to stand by other Brahmos, he seems to have also championed the schismatic human existence. Whether it was reflective of the well-entrenched rivalry between two elite families of Calcutta, led by Radhakanta Deb and Dwarkanath, respectively, it cannot be entirely ruled out that both the families held identical views vis-à-vis the Christian Missionaries who were, according to both, first to be pushed out of Calcutta. It was a common ground that brought Radhakanta-led Dharma Sabha and the Brahmo Samaj together. Characterizing this as 'a miracle', the *Tattwabodhini Patrika* admired Debendranath for having accomplished what his father, Dwarkanath, failed. Despite attempts by many, the feud between two Sabhas was reported to have been fomented by the Calcutta elites as it 'gave them enough time to spend on evolving tricks to humiliate those belonging to groups, opposed to each other'.[24] Perhaps, the common enemy, Christian Missionaries, and also common socio-ideological goals, organizing the Hindus, led the recalcitrant groups to come together. It was categorically mentioned in his memoir by Debendranath when he stated that 'the disagreement between the Dharma Sabha and the Brahmos disappeared in an effort to establish a free school for children against the missionaries'.[25] The joint effort helped gather more than 1,000 people on the day of inaugurating the school. The separation ceased to exist was manifested when Debendranath announced name of Radhakanta, the erstwhile arch opponent of Dwarkanath as the president of the school board while Debendranath was its secretary.[26] It was a remarkable feat on part of Debendranath to accept his senior, Radhakanta, as the president and also the credit for persuading him to work together belonged to him since some of the hardcore Brahmos did not endorse the proposal. Whatever might have been the processes, the outcome was appreciated by Bengali elites since it enabled them to put in place an alternative school in defiance of the Macaulay-inspired system of learning that flourished at the aegis of Christian Missionaries.

Debendranath in a New Garb

The transformation of Debendranath from one who always privileged worldly comforts to an ascetic is well elaborated in his memoirs.[27] As

[24] '*Dwarkanath and Brahmo Samaj*', published in *Tattwabodhini Patrika*, 3 October 1837.
[25] Khastagir, *Debendranather Atmajibani*, 102.
[26] Inputs are available in ibid., 105.
[27] Ibid., 36–40.

mentioned in Chapter 3, Debendranath was an effective zamindar in the sense that he augmented income from his landed estates by being, on occasion, very ruthless in realizing rent from his subjects. The same Debendranath had undergone a significant metamorphosis following the death of his grandmother when he was just 18. Once he saw the death of his near one, because, as he admitted, his grandmother was one he loved most, he realized the vacuousness of worldly comfort and worldly desires. In front of death, the ultimate moment of merging with the Superior Soul, human beings were so helpless despite being the richest. He experienced 'a profound sense of bliss'[28] that led him to understand that there was nothing permanent in life. In his own words, he expressed his feelings by saying that

> A day before his grandmother's death, while sitting on the bank of the Ganges where, by following the contemporary rituals, she was taken given the advice of the *kabiraj* (the house physician) that her days were numbered, he was drawn to the idea that what was permanent was death which allowed the soul to merge with the almighty. And, he developed distaste for everything worldly; the sandbank appeared to be more comfortable to sit than the comfortable cushioned chair which gave him uninterrupted joy and blissful existence.[29]

This was an incident that seems to have triggered in Debendranath the extent to which the worldly enjoyment was futile. He was castigating himself for having been deprived of this indifference to worldly comforts; he further reminisced that the idea was always there, but it was his inability to internalize it since he was swayed by the pomp and luxury that he was accustomed to by being part of a wealthy family. He further argued that such a blissful enjoyment was not achievable by 'human deeds; it was possible if the Superior Soul was kind enough to bestow on you'.[30] Being grateful to the almighty, he elaborated his feelings by reiterating that without 'providential blessings, it was not

---

[28] Brian Hatcher, 'Remembering Rammohan: An Essay on the (Re)emergence of Modern Hinduism', *History of Religion* 46, no. 1 (August 2006): 65.
[29] Khastagir, *Debendranather Atmajibani*, 28.
[30] Ibid., 29.

possible for him to experience the heavenly bliss amid luxurious life that he had'.[31] It was 'God's command' that he was privy to listen to.[32] Fundamental here are two points that deserve careful scrutiny to comprehend Debendranath's radical transformation from a pampered zamindari scion to an individual who instinctively became apathetic to worldly pleasure. On the one hand, his grandmother's death was an eyeopener in the sense that he now realized that the final outcome of human beings was death which, instead of being a source of pain and agony, was actually *moksha* or salvation from one's worldly existence. Human beings thus become free from all worldly agonies and pains. The death also instilled in him, on the other hand, an earnest quest for heavenly peace by deciding to become a spartan. It was a deliberately chosen mode to recluse from a life of material comforts to which Debendranath was accustomed to.

The transformation can be said to have been expedited by Debendranath's regular meeting with Rammohun who persuaded him of the futility of idol worship which later was articulated in his strong opposition to Hindu idolatry. With his persuasion, his brothers also agreed with him though were unable to express presumably because they knew that Dwarkanath would be terribly angry and upset with their decision. Nonetheless, the idea gained ground among them presumably because of the discussion that Dwarkanath had on this especially with Rammohun when he visited the Tagores. Unable to decipher the difficult texts of Upanishads, the young Debendranath searched for a teacher which remained unrealized till he was introduced to Ramchandra Vidyabagish, a Vedic scholar, by one of the accountants, but well-versed with some of the ancient Hindu texts, Shyamacharan Bhattacharya, when he failed to explain the meaning of an Upanishadic hymn.[33] The story of how he was drawn to this hymn is interesting. As he himself recounted, when he was in quest of a teacher who was well-equipped to teach him the complex ideas of Upanishads, he chanced upon a stray page of Isa-Upanishad. Although he knew Sanskrit, he failed to decipher the meaning of the

---

[31] Ibid., 31.
[32] Ibid.
[33] Ibid., 37.

hymn. He went to Shyamacharan Bhattacharya who was unable to help him, but, on his suggestion, he contacted Rammohun's friend, Ramchandra Vidyabagish, given his profound knowledge about the Vedas and Vedantic texts. When Vidyabagish was shown the page, he immediately identified that it was the first hymn of Isa-Upanishad.[34] The *sloka* reads as follows:

> *Eesha Basyamidong Sarbbaang Jat Kincho Jagatyang Jagat;*
> *Teno Tyakteno Bhunjeeta, Ma, Gridha Kashyoswdhyanong.*

Ramchandra Vidyabagish read the hymn and explained its meaning to Debendranath which was a revelation to him. As he explained, it was about transitional nature of pleasure that one derived from worldly possessions; besides highlighting this, the hymn was also about the omnipresence of the Supreme Soul or *Ishwar* (God) and whatever we enjoyed in life was decided by the Supreme Soul; furthermore, only by abdicating the sense of possession, one would be equipped to realize the God's desire. By implication, it meant that whatever steps human beings undertook to gratify their worldly needs had to be endorsed by the Supreme Soul; otherwise, it would remain unrealized forever. Fundamental here was the idea that human beings were unable to accomplish whatever they desired and it was possible only with God's blessings. Hence, one was required not to be passionately attached to the material goods since they did not belong to them; in other words, the wealth that the rich individuals possess does not belong to them; they are mere custodians of this since it is believed that the human beings cannot claim ownership of the wealth that is generated by the Almighty for humanity as a whole.

Once the hymn was explained in intelligible words by Vidyabagish, he realised that it was 'nectar from paradise [that] streamed down on him'.[35] He found a way to reach his spiritual destiny which was constrained presumably because he was not sure whether ascetic life was a stepping stone towards attaining the goal. By being convinced that this Isa-Upanishadic *sloka* helped him identify the real spiritual

[34] Ibid., 38.
[35] Ibid., 39.

path for salvation or *moksha*, he now internalized the futility of worldly enjoyment. It was now easier for him to deprive himself of the material comforts because that was the only way to reach the final goal of his life. Hence, it is argued that, as soon as he understood the crux of the hymn, he now saw 'a divine presence (and purpose) behind creation ... and he also saw a new purpose for his own life'.[36] To translate what he realized he held onto himself 'a strong desire to spread [the messages] of a true religion'[37] which remained vitiated by the self-claimed pandits in Bengal who were patronised by a section of orthodox Hindus to achieve their partisan goals. The idea dawned on him because he was persuaded to believe that lack of understanding of Upanishad's complex conceptualizations of the spiritual path led to the rise of distorted explanations; in this regard, he was fortunate to have met Rammohun who introduced him to a competent Vedic scholar, Ramchandra Vidyabagish. Vidyabagish not only guided him to understand the Isa-Upanishad but also created a zeal to read other Upanishads. A pragmatic Debendranath also realized that unless his endeavour was supported organizationally, his principal goal remained elusive. Hence, he gathered his relatives and like-minded friends and colleagues to discuss with them the future roadmap for disseminating the wisdom that Upanishads had for humanity. The idea was unanimously endorsed and the Tattvaranjini Sabha was formed for this purpose. The aim was to grasp and spread the inherent wisdom of the Hindu ancient texts to a wider section of people. By fixing the date of meeting on every Sunday, Debendranath made this as a regularly held weekly affair. In the second meeting, Ramchandra Vidyabagish was invited as the main speaker or Acharya in the parlance of the Tattvaranjini Sabha. On his suggestion, it was renamed as Tattwabodhini Sabha which formally appeared on the scene on 6 October 1839. Since the Sabha was a congregation of those seeking to comprehend the meaning of Upanishads, the members set out its object as 'the diffusion of the deep truth of all our *shastras* and knowledge of Brahma as inculcated in the Vedanta'.[38] Here too, one finds an imprint of Rammohun's idea of monotheism.

---

[36] Hatcher, 'Remembering Rammohan, 68.
[37] Khastagir, *Debendranather Atmajibani*, 39.
[38] Ibid., 41.

Debendranath was guided by his concern to establish Upanishads as one of major sources of wisdom which was logical given the deliberate distortion of these spiritual texts by those for their narrow gains. So, on the one hand, it had a very strong social message and, on the other hand, it was also a warning to the self-proclaimed experts who thrived presumably due to mass ignorance and indifference to get to the bottom of Hindu ancient scriptures.

On a surface reading, Debendranath's support for idol worship at the Tagore household stands in contradiction with his devotion to the formless one Supreme Soul. However, a deeper probing convinces one why he was not in favour of completely doing away with this practice. As is well known, the two annual religious events in the Tagore family were the worship of Durga and Jagadhattri in the spring which attracted visitors from all walks of life, including the top government officials. It was a tradition that Dwarkanath continued by spending a huge amount to treat his guests. Despite having been convinced by Rammohun of the futility of idol worship, Debendranath and his brothers did not have the courage to stay away from the place of worship so long as Dwarkanath was alive. Once the baton was transferred, Debendranath did not support the discontinuity though he was one of the most powerful voices against Hindu idolatry. That he agreed to hold the festivals was evident when he mentioned that these were the occasions when people from various parts of the city congregated besides the family members who stayed in different places. Hence, the stopping of the festivals caused sudden disruption of social communion which was likely to be a source of mental agony and pain for many. Furthermore, being a person with serious concerns for others, he also felt that it was not desirable to hurt someone's belief in idol worship. Also, as a person appreciative of democratic deliberations before a decision was adopted, he awaited the views of his brother, Nagendranath, who was then in England. On his return he placed the proposal before him and Nagendranath did not concede by reiterating the views that 'since the spring festivals (worship of Durga and Jagadhattri) are an occasion for a get together among relatives, friends and other acquaintances, it will not be judicious for us to just halt them as they were more of a social communion and less of religious festivals'.[39] In view of the financial stress, the Tagore family stopped the worship of Jagadhattri in 1849 although the worship of Durga continued. True to his spiritual belief, Debendranath never stayed in Calcutta during the spring festival since it was celebrated with idol worship. He never hid his commitment. An illustration of how he admonished the priests in Assam's Kamakhya temple will prove the point. As soon as he reached the temple premise, on 22 October 1850, he was surrounded by many priests who were insisting on taking one of them as his priest. He not only expressed his displeasure but also declared that because he did not believe in idol worship, he decided not to go inside the temple.[40]

There are therefore reasons to believe that Debendranath was a powerful voice against idolatry which was evident in his decision to oppose idol worship. He however qualified his approach to the issue: At one level, Debendranath was clearly a staunch opponent of idol worship; at another subtle level of human conceptualization, he did not appear to be so, as he himself admitted. According to him, Vedas and Upanishads supported prayers to fire (*agni*), air (*vayu*), Indra (power) and Surya (power) which meant the ancient priests imagined various forms which they attributed while offering prayers; they were conceptualized in their senses which further meant that different forms had emerged in their imagination. Furthermore, given the belief that these natural forces contributed to the well-being of human existence, they needed to be propitiated which also gave them a status of superpowers and hence were required to be mollified by regular prayers. Fundamental here are points that Debendranath offered: On the one hand, he argued that human minds could never be fully immune from imagining specific forms to the natural powers that were believed to have been protecting the universe; it further meant, on the other hand, that the Vedantic texts did not entirely reject idol worship because they provided conceptual justification for imagination of forms of those natural forces that we experienced in our senses.[41] Despite having appreciated Debendranath for his nuanced understanding of

---

[39] Ibid., 105.
[40] The event is described in detail by Debendranath in memoir; ibid., 107.
[41] This discussion is drawn on Khastagir, *Debendranather Atmajibani*, 79–82.

Vedantic texts, the discussion did neither initiate a debate nor persuade the members of Tattwabodhini Sabha for a second thought on the emptiness of idol worship.

The Tattwabodhini Sabha Covenant

Distinctive about Debendranath was his consistent attempt to spread the Upanishadic messages to his colleagues, friends and acquaintances in opposition to Christian Missionaries, Young Bengal and also orthodox Hindus, led by Radhakanta Deb's Dharma Sabha. Opposed to Hindu orthodoxy, Rammohun evolved a mode of thinking in which Islamic Sufism, Christianity and also Vedantic texts coalesced. Debendranath was different from his mentor in the sense that his primary concern was to awaken Hindu sensibilities by focusing exclusively on Upanishads. Neither Islam nor Christianity seemed to have had any impact on his thoughts though he was intellectually very close to Rammohun who helped him understand the vacuousness of idol worship since it had no backup from any of the basic texts of Hinduism, Islam or Christianity. Debendranath clearly deviated from Rammohun in the sense that he appeared to have provided 'a Hinduized version of *Brahmo Dharma*' which was different, both in texture and spirit, from either what his father, Dwarkanath, believed or his intellectual mentor, Rammohun, upheld. It was evident when he brought out the covenant for the Tattwabodhini Sabha which was written by Debendranath's colleague, Akshay Kumar Dutt, who wrote what he was asked to. In other words, it was a text that was conceptualized by Debendranath and was put into words by Akshay Kumar Dutt in accordance with what the former dictated. Characterized as *Brahmo Dharma*, the text was actually a checklist of Upanishadic hymns which were further classified according to what was required to be followed to be a true Brahmo. Also, a philosophical treatise, the *Brahmo Dharma* is a compilation of the Upanishadic ideas which help humanity prosper as a well-knit multitude regardless of class, caste and ethnicity. We must note a caveat here: As a social reformer, Debendranath adopted a specific course of action that drew sustenance from Upanishads which means that it was based on his belief in the Hindu scriptural texts. His ideas corresponded with his father and mentor at one level, namely, like them, he did not accept the primordial social divisions, justified as axiomatic by the Hindu zealots; at another level, he held starkly opposite views from both of them because given his exclusive faith in the Upanishads, he evolved a model which was derivative entirely of the ancient Hindu texts.

The *Brahmo Dharma* is, at the outset, a running text based on Debendranath's own comprehension of Upanishadic *slokas*; later the text was divided by the author himself into 16 chapters dealing with specific modes of acquiring knowledge, enriching one's spiritual strength and enhancing one's capability for ensuring common well-being. In other words, this text was also a design to accomplish spiritual goals. A careful study of the texts shows that the first chapter deals with the steps that allowed human beings to enjoy the work in which they were engaged. Since these steps were meant to contribute to the collective pleasure, they were bound to be inspirational to those seeking to create conditions for humanity to flourish as a close-knit unit. The second chapter was an appreciation of the Supreme Soul because of the creation in which human beings prospered as they were largely an offshoot of its selfless effort. While the second chapter dealt with who created the world, the third chapter was an elaboration of how humanity was guided by the almighty in accordance with rules and regulations that remained elusive to human beings presumably because they evolved naturally. By arguing that Brahma was inconceivable in human senses, the text, in the fourth chapter, underlines that given its vastness and also apparently magical style of functioning of nature, no endeavour towards conceptualizing Brahma would succeed. So, it was suggested, in the fifth chapter, to accept as one that was omnipresent and also designed the creation in accordance with what contributed to humanity as a whole. The sixth and seventh chapters dwell on various modes of prayer which were essential to understand and reach the Supreme Soul. Since only by uninterrupted prayer, one was capable of spiritually improving oneself, the text, *Brahmo Dharma*, emphasized that there was no other alternative; only by being patient and steadfastly devotional, one was able to realize the goal that every human being desired to achieve. That Brahma was immanent is the main concern of the eight chapter. Argued there was the point that Brahma, being omnipresent, continued to be part and parcel of humanity; it further means that even if the Brahma was invisible, no one could deny the existence since the creation moved in a pattern since time immemorial presumably because there was the spirit that steered it in consonance with what the Supreme Soul deemed fit for humanity. The ninth chapter is an attempt to bring the almighty to the mortal human beings by providing an analogy of two birds inhabiting the same tree: While the former is the creator who maintained the tree and the latter were human beings, being looked after by the former. Core here is the point that God and human beings coexist which we tended to undermine, if not forget. In the tenth chapter, the text emphasizes the importance of communion with God which remained a distant goal so long as human beings naturally formed a unit disregarding artificial barriers around caste, class or ethnicity axes. As mentioned above, prayer with steadfast commitment and devotion was the only mode of reaching the Supreme Soul; it was emphasized in eleventh and twelfth chapters. It is evident in the twelfth chapter that Debendranath stressed the importance of prayer because only during prayer human beings were capable of being immune from the worldly attachment provided, of course, they attained a level of concentration when they remained absolutely focused on what they were supposed to under the circumstances. The principal point that the text highlights in thirteenth, fourteenth, fifteenth and sixteenth chapters is about the purity of heart because that was the primary requirement for successful prayers. Three conditions were identified which helped the individual attain the purity of heart: (a) One needed to generate a belief that without securing the collectivity of which one was integral, one had no future which means that only in interdependent existence human beings existed as what they were; (b) amid various temptation for individual gains at someone's cost, one was required to develop sense that this practice was despisable because it was an impediment towards ensuring common well-being; and (c) unless one understood the value of being associated with the collectivity, one's prayers were futile. Fundamental here is the reiteration of the ideas that his predecessors, Rammohun and Dwarkanath, practised to bring about radical sociocultural metamorphosis in Bengal. As mentioned in Chapter 3, the Brahmo Samaj lost its vitality to a significant extent with the untimely demise of Rammohun in 1833 and later Dwarkanath in

1846. Their task remained incomplete which gained momentum when Debendranath shouldered the responsibility by institutionalizing an alternative voice of the Tattwabodhini Sabha which ran as an organization in conjunction with the erstwhile Brahmo Samaj, formed in 1828 at the behest of Rammohun, Dwarkanath and their colleagues with identical sociocultural concerns.

The *Brahmo Dharma* is basically a checklist of activities that members of Tattwabodhini Sabha were expected to cling to for the fulfilment of the ultimate spiritual goal. These activities are divided into three interrelated components: (a) Activities helping the members to learn the core ideas of Upanishad; (b) the activities that help build a conducive mind to proceed towards spiritualism; and (c) the activities which are required to be undertaken to attain salvation or *moksha*. As the available evidence suggests, the text was based on Debendranath's own comprehension and internalization of Upanishads' fundamental principles which he himself corroborated in the introduction to the *Brahmo Dharma* by saying that

> These ideas are neither manifestation of my blind faith in Upanishads, nor an articulation of my illogical fascination, nor a reflection of my alleged madness for imbibing those values; but it is based on my own realization of the truth that I have understood by meaningfully grasping the principles that are articulated in Upanishads; it is also a blessing of the almighty in disguise because without the blessings, it could not have been possible.[42]

Unique here is the confirmation of Debendranath's unconditional faith in Hindu texts, especially Upanishads. By defending that these ideas were neither whimsically constructed nor generated out of narrow concerns, the second of the Tagore patriarchs carved a space in the campaign for sociocultural reforms in Bengal. One must undermine the claim that by being a vociferous champion of Upanishads, he deviated from the spiritual path that Rammohun preferred by creatively blending the humanitarian aspects, drawn from Islam, Christianity

---

[42] Debendranath's statement is quoted in Chakrabarti, *Maharshi Debendranath Thakur*, 237.

and, of course, Hinduism. He was also starkly different from his father in his conceptual preferences. Unlike Dwarkanath, Debendranath was vehemently opposed to idolatry which was manifested by the fact that during annual religious festival around the worship of Goddess Durga, he usually stayed away from Calcutta. Despite being remarkably different from his intellectual mentor, Rammohun, and his day-to-day guide, Dwarkanath, he imbibed the spirit in which both of them treated humanity. It is true that Tattwabodhini Sabha was an exclusive organization of the caste Hindus which means that neither Muslims nor Christians were allowed to be accepted as members. There is also the point that needs to be emphasized that Debendranath did not seem to be clouded by artificially created caste division segregating one section of Hindus from another. At the beginning, the Sabha was dominated by the upper caste though as time passed, many belonging to the so-called lower castes joined the Sabha. As per the evidence, no attempts were made to address this so long as Tattwabodhini Sabha existed. In the Brahmo Samaj phase, when Debendranath's son, Rabindranath, who was the secretary, requested his father to allow non-Brahmins to be the main priest of the regular prayers, to which he, Debendranath, immediately conceded though it was contrary to the established practices.[43] This was undoubtedly a revolutionary idea since, as per the contemporary evidence, many hardcore members of Brahmo Samaj expressed annoyance with Debendranath for his approval of the suggestion by his son. Nonetheless, given his firm belief that the Supreme Soul never segregated humanity, he stuck to his view and declared that Hindus regardless of their caste identity were allowed to conduct the regular prayers. As history progressed, notwithstanding occasional opposition from the orthodox Brahmos, the idea gained acceptance and there were many non-Brahmin priests who conducted prayers even during the lifetime of Debendranath. The examples however multiplied once Rabindranath took over the mantle of the family at the beginning of the 20th century after the demise of his father in 1905.

[43] Rabindranath Tagore, 'My Father', reproduced in Khastagir, *Debendranather Atmajibani*, 311.

Designing a New Conceptual Mould

A careful scanning of the historical processes reveals that the campaign that Rammohun started amid severe adverse sociocultural milieu was carried forward by his disciple, Debendranath, in an organized way. In other words, it was a voice, persuasive enough, that Rammohun articulated against Hindu catholicism which gradually blossomed into a massive movement in the late 19th century largely with support from the educated sections of the middle class. Since the purpose here is to highlight the contribution of Debendranath, the discussion of how his like-minded colleagues contributed to the cause is outside its purview. Nonetheless, the role of the other important social reformers of the late 19th century and early 20th century is referred to while pursuing an argument defending the point that it was a collective venture that flourished despite opposition by Christian Missionaries, excessively radical Young Bengal and also the well-entrenched Hindu orthodoxy. One has to add a caveat here because instead of completely ignoring the points of differences with the above-mentioned forces, the Debendranath-led Brahmo Samaj also drew on them to develop a persuasive intellectual defence and also to devise a correct strategy to combat them. One notices here a continuity of a trend of learning from the British philosophical discourses which trained the early social reformers, including Rammohun, Dwarkanath, among others. Instead of being xenophobic, by devoting time and energy to understand the Enlightenment principles, they also had demonstrated their willingness to internalize some of them since they inspired some of the leading sociocultural campaigns against the prejudicial sociocultural practices. So, it is fair to argue that the template of sociocultural metamorphosis was transmitted from one generation to another and one of the sources that instilled in those early social reformers a voice to challenge the orthodox practices was their critical understanding of the religious texts which were then distorted for partisan aims. Brian Hatcher succinctly makes this point in his study of Rammohun's sociopolitical views. According to him, 'Debendranath would not have undergone his spiritual awakening without Rammohun, since that awakening was precipitated by a reading of ... Isa-Upanishad as mediated by Ramchandra Vidyabagish'.[44] The argument is absolutely justified along with the point that had Debendranath not carried forward the ideas that Rammohun propounded, they would have hardly become a source of inspiration to the next generation. In other words, with his capacity to gather the like-minded individuals around him, it was Debendranath who helped Brahmo Samaj flourish as a powerful instrument for a sociocultural campaign against archaic values, principles and practices, initially at the behest of Tattwabodhini Sabha and later the revamped Brahmo Samaj.

The Samaj faced severe crises too. While explaining how Debendranath defused crises, he admitted that the financial support from his father took care of the day-to-day expenses for running the Samaj and the intellectual prowess of Ramchandra Vidyabagish helped the Samaj convincingly tackle the criticisms. In the midst of stiff opposition by the conservative Hindus with adequate financial support from Deb, some of the followers of the Samaj were completely demoralized. In these circumstances, Vidyabagish emerged as a saviour, admitted Debendranath who also stood by him because the Samaj was the only platform to discuss, understand and also spread the indigenous discourses beyond Calcutta which was being carried out by distributing *Tattwabodhini Patrika* also in *mofussil* towns. According to Debendranath, much of his endeavour succeeded largely because of the care that Vidyabagish extended to the Samaj in a context when it was vilified as an attempt to take India backward intellectually by seeking to popularize ancient Hindu texts. As he stated, 'when our hope almost disappeared, it was Ramchandra Vidyabagish who chose an appropriate course of action that took the Samaj out of the crisis'.[45] It was he, argued Debendranath, who sustained the Samaj, which no longer attracted many of its erstwhile members after Rammohun's death, by religiously performing the ritual even if there was nobody to listen to the Upanishadic discourses that he regularly delivered.[46]

---

[44] Hatcher, 'Remembering Rammohun', 76.
[45] Debendranath Thakur 'Brahmo Samajer Britanta' (Activities of Brahmo Samaj), cited in Chakrabarti, *Maharshi Debendranath Thakur*, 124.
[46] Ibid.

Debendranath did not adopt Rammohun's universalism, instead he preferred to focus on the Vedantic texts to defend his radical sociocultural aims. Two reasons appear to be plausible here: On the one hand, he sincerely believed that Rammohun's ideological predispositions drawing on Islam and Christianity likely alienated the radical Hindus who were associated with him given their strong opposition to these two religious discourses especially in the changed political context in the later 19th and early 20th centuries. With growing Hindu extremist forces against British government, it was suicidal, felt Debendranath, to champion any of the ideas of the Old or New Testament. Similarly, the views that Islam also caused severe damage to Hindu civilization by the erstwhile jingoistic Muslim rules also created an ambience in which Hindus were subject to severe torture because of their different religious identity. Given the predicament that Debendranath had by being born in a particular sociocultural milieu, it was difficult to discard the well-established ethos of the period. Unlike his radical colleague, Keshab Chandra Sen (1838–1884) who openly condemned the orthodox sociocultural practices even by antagonising some of the senior members of the Brahmo Samaj for being obstinate conservative, Debendranath, who can never be labelled as 'orthodox' or 'conservative', did not categorically support the clamour for abolition of caste hierarchy. This was reflective of an attempt on his part to strike a balance between the old and new members of the Samaj. For instance, in a letter to his Samaj colleague, Rajnarayan Basu (1826–1899), he unambiguously mentioned that 'according to him the Brahmos should not undergo the sacred thread ceremony as it represents an endeavour to divide the society vertically. Furthermore, if sacred thread is given up by the Brahmos, how can one refer to one caste identity in later life'.[47]

Aware that the caste system was certain to disappear given the growing momentum of the campaign questioning it 'as an aberration in Hinduism'[48], he was still uncertain whether it was judicious on his part to wholeheartedly support the movement seeking to demolish the

---

[47] Debendranath to Rajnarayan Basu, 8 February 1854, quoted in Chakrabarti, *Maharshi Debendranath Thakur*, 317.
[48] Ibid.

caste system in its entirety. Perhaps being persuaded by his mentor, Rajnarayan also expressed his uncertainty when he wrote in an essay justifying the opinion of Debendranath as appropriate in that sociocultural context. He thus argued that

> 'it is difficult, if not impossible, to do away with the caste system so instantaneously; in its place there will emerge another system of segregation among human beings because not everybody is the same in terms of physical strength and intellectual capability'.[49]

A logically argued stance, the point simply underlines that a system with deep organic roots cannot be so easily thrown out; what was thus required was a continuous campaign by highlighting that it is vacuous and also an instrument of exploitation of human beings by their socioculturally and also economically well-endowed counterparts. Supportive of a sustained campaign against the system, Debendranath also believed that the society did not change so fast; it changed incrementally out of the incessant struggle of those who understood that it was an impediment of social communion. It was persuasively argued in his essay entitled 'social reform' in which he adumbrated the idea that the consequences of sudden disruptions in sociocultural relations among human beings occupying the same social space were likely to be disastrous; hence, he suggested adoption of a mechanism which helped build 'strong viewpoints against archaic values and ideas because they were harmful to the humanity'.[50] However, the striking, for him, is as follows:

> the campaign for the complete abolition of the caste system did not seem prior to the prayer for attaining salvation though he believed that so long as the well-entrenched mindset appreciative of idolatry survived, no voice was adequate enough to root-out the caste system.[51]

---

[49] Rajnarayan Basu argued this point in an essay which is reported by Chakrabarti, *Maharshi Debendranath Thakur*, 316.

[50] Ibid.

[51] Debendranath to Rajnarayan Basu, 8 February 1854, Chakrabarti, *Maharshi Debendranath Thakur*, 317.

Nonetheless, that he was well-aware of the forthcoming changes was evident in another letter that he wrote to Rajnarayan Basu on 23 August 1870 in which he identified the reasons for the steady decline of knowledgeable Brahmins. In a rather castigating tone, Debendranath noted that

> Brahmins of today lack the knowledge that their earlier counterparts had though. Given their hardcore nature and also reluctance to accept the newer socio-cultural views, they will never be acceptable to the new generation. Furthermore, the well-founded charge that today's Brahmins have become excessively greedy is another factor that also alienates them from society.[52]

Does the above persuasive argument indicate that Debendranath was being tilted in favour of the campaign against caste segregation? There is hardly any conclusive answer though there is enough evidence to substantiate the claim that he was equally annoyed with various types of machinations that the Brahmins devised for their narrow gains at the cost of those who blindly believed them. Moreover, they were neither trained in the scripture nor were interested in learning from those well acquainted with the religious scriptures which persuaded Debendranath to join hands with his colleagues who gave a clarion call to boycott these misleading brahmins. He was thus persuaded to accept that even non-Brahmins who were religiously drawn to the ancient Hindu scriptures were 'allowed to chant the sacred Vedic hymns within the Samaj'.[53] This was a revolutionary step which was further manifested when he allowed a discussion on whether or not the non-Brahmins were eligible to occupy the pulpit in the regular prayer, held on Wednesdays. The decision that emerged out of the long discussion was to agree 'to accept a non-Brahmin conductor (or *acharya*) of the regular prayers only on the first Wednesday of the month'.[54] Many of

---

[52] Debendranath to Rajnarayan Basu, 23 August 1870, quoted in Chakrabarti, *Maharshi Debendranath Thakur*, 319.

[53] Debendranath to Rajnarayan Basu, 8 February 1854, quoted in Chakrabarti, *Maharshi Debendranath Thakur*.

[54] Debendranath Tagore to Keshab Sen, 7 July 1865, cited in Sen, *Hindu Revivalism in Bengal, 1872–1905*, 42.

his colleagues were unhappy with this decision which confirms that the Samaj failed to surpass the prevalent sociocultural constraints; the outcome was that the decision was kept on hold till 1909 when Rabindranath, despite opposition from some of the hardcore Brahmos, allowed his non-Brahmin colleague of Patha Bhavana, Kunjalal Ghosh, to conduct the weekly prayer on Wednesday.

Ideationally, Debendranath was far ahead of the historical phase in which he rose to prominence. He not only vehemently opposed caste segregation in pursuance of the ideas that he imbibed from his mentor, Rammohun, but also was one of the most powerful proponents for gender equality which was then almost inconceivable. Being aware that history represented a cycle of change, he was always welcome to the new ideas which he characterized as epitome of transformation. It was therefore not difficult for him to read the writings on the wall. The claim for gender parity was one of them which Debendranath readily accepted despite being opposed by many of the orthodox Brahmos. As contemporary evidence shows, his son, Satyendranath, the first Indian Civil Service Officer, after his return from England argued persuasively for equal sociocultural status for women which convinced Debendranath. He not only articulated his views in a booklet entitled *Freedom for Women* in 1891 but also took his wife out in his car which was then socially blasphemous since women were expected to travel from one place to another in a covered palanquin. The system developed as no women were seen in public. Furthermore, Debendranath never objected to his daughters and daughters-in-law when they started wearing long skirts, instead of the traditional saris, along with shoes and socks. As soon as the women of Tagore displayed their changed attire, the orthodox Hindus left no stone unturned to publicly humiliate him as a deviant Hindu. This hardly affected him since he was convinced that the change of dress was of no consequence so long as they remained tuned to the fundamentals of humanity. It is striking to note that had Debendranath put an embargo on what Satyendranath embarked upon he would not have had the courage to defy his father. The fact that Debendranath did not intervene was a testimony to his approval.[55] There is another account which further

---

[55] The elaboration of the idea is drawn on Chakrabarti, *Maharshi Debendranath Thakur*, 330–331.

illustrates Debendranath's openness in accepting different dress codes. His eldest daughter reminisced that in response to his cousin's complaint that Tagore's daughters' presence in the open roof was a source of humiliation for the entire family, Debendranath smilingly retorted that 'since society had changed, the earlier rules remained vacuous and hence, he did not find it objectionable'.[56] So firm was his belief that he never wavered in pursuing the steps that he deemed appropriate for eradicating gender discrimination. What illustrates better than his determination to admit his two daughters for education in the school that J. E. D. Bethune founded in north Calcutta despite being threatened by orthodox Hindus of socially ostracizing him and his family. When people gave an ultimatum that they would never accept food in his house, he equally forcefully responded by sarcastically saying that they were many of his friends who would love to dine with him.'[57] The situation became worse when he searched for a bride for his third son, Hemendranath, since nobody was willing to establish matrimonial link with him; once his bosom friend, Horodeb Chatterjee, agreed, he tried to dissuade him given the possibility of harsh social consequences against him and his family which failed to restrain him. The wedding took place 'with police protection apprehending that the house was likely to be ransacked by the orthodox forces who were reported to have deployed local goons for this.'[58]

Debendranath was a rebel in the sense that he was never hesitant to undertake steps that he deemed appropriate to translate into reality his ideas of sociocultural transformation. A renaissance man, in the real sense, the second of the Tagore patriarch, carved a definite space in history by consolidating the conceptual ideas that he learnt from his mentor, Rammohun, and his spiritual guru, his father, Dwarkanath. While Rammohun campaigned for universalism by drawing upon Sufism in Islam, New Testament of Christianity and Vedas and Upanishads from the Indian scriptural traditions. A strict believer of idolatry, Dwarkanath also held Upanishads as the most significant of the religious texts. Debendranath devised a new socioreligious path. Staying away from Rammohun's religious

[56] Ibid., 331–332.
[57] Ibid., 333–334.
[58] Ibid., 334.

universalism, he concentrated on Upanishads; questioning idolatry which he derived from Rammohun, he came closer to his father when he uncritically accepted Upanishads while his sociocultural discourses. With his conceptual novelty, it was not difficult to gather around him those committed individuals who stood by him despite opposition by the Young Bengal, Christian Missionaries and also the Hindu orthodox forces, organized by Radhakanta Deb who, however, later became his close associate when he started a school as an alternative to the prevalent English schools that flourished in Calcutta at the behest of the government. So, Debendranath was not just a social reformer but also a persuasive thinker who creatively blended a set of complementary practices with an equally convincing set of theoretical insights that he internalized after having understood the crux of Upanishads.

Concluding Observations

Conceptually, Debendranath was a watershed in Bengal's intellectual universe for three fundamental reasons: First, as argued above, the second of the Tagore patriarch did not exactly carry forward the tradition in which he was nurtured because he neither endorsed Rammohun's religious universalism nor accepted the idolatry of his father, Dwarkanath; he created new conceptual parameters for social reform. In this sense, he was clearly a break with the past. Second, although he devised a new set of parameters, he cannot be said to have designed a new format of persuasion as he drew on ancient Hindu texts, including Mahabharat and Upanishads. The texts that he left for posterity reveal that his only source of inspiration was Upanishads. However, most appreciable was his endeavour to get them translated into Bangla and English for spreading those ideas on which Upanishadic hymns were based. Finally, despite being enamoured by Upanishads, he always raised his voice along with his compatriots holding identical views against the prejudicial sociocultural practices segregating one section of people from another as they were contrary to the core religious scriptures. He not only created circumstances in which non-Brahmins were allowed to chant Upanishadic mantra in the Brahmo Samaj congregation but also built a strong campaign against caste discrimination which annoyed orthodox Hindus for obvious reasons.

Although Debendranath carved an independent space in India's intellectual history, he also continued a tradition that unfolded with the arrival of Rammohun on the scene. Both Rammohun and his colleague, Dwarkanath, devoted their energies to creating a sense of togetherness as perhaps the only means to contribute to well-being for all. Debendranath too had the same aim because he believed that 'one's prayer for common good is futile unless that helps others to realize the aim of the prayer'.[59] In other words, emphasized here was the concern bringing people together for a common cause. A careful study of the steps that he undertook to realize his sociocultural mission also reveals that he was protective of the Hinduized rituals as far as possible since he felt that sudden break with the past was likely to cause severe social commotion which needed to be avoided under all circumstances. The logic was simple: He did not want to disturb the applecart of orthodox Hindu forces drawing sustenance from the rituals which, they felt, were key to Hinduism. By not discarding them completely, Debendranath seemed to have devised a strategy to not provoke them as challengers which would likely have brought them to a head on collision with Brahmo Samaj. Furthermore, there are reasons to believe that being nurtured in an environment in which many of the Hindu rituals were passionately practised throughout the year, it was not so easy for him to rescind them completely. He was also persuaded to appreciate the view that social progress was a slow process and could thus not be achieved instantaneously. By simply throwing away the rituals at one go, one would have attained temporary mental satisfaction at the cost of, Debendranath warned, alienating many. So, it is understandable that his aim was to generate an opinion for Brahmo Samaj's sociocultural mission not by following the radical Young Bengal but by seeking to persuade the dissenters slowly but steadily to appreciate what he espoused. As he himself admitted, 'his goal is to transform Hinduism to Brahmoism by purging the former of prejudicial sociocultural practices and values'.[60] His objective was,

[59] Ibid., 336.
[60] Ibid.

therefore, to reform Hinduism by not being a complete deviant but generating and also consolidating views against those values and practices which were, he considered, highly debilitating.

The set of activities that Debendranath undertook also reveals that he endeavoured to establish the importance of individuals in social decision-making which was a clear deviation from the established ideational preferences. The root of this idea that privileged individuals can be traced back to his extensive study of the Western literature drawing on the Enlightenment philosophy and support of individuals as the centre of social discourses. As mentioned above, he was privy to the texts upholding liberalism since the library at home had those books which Dwarkanath brought with him from England. By arguing for the importance of individual identity, he however did not entirely abdicate the significance of social collectivity for the former flourished well only by being integrally connected with the latter. This is a unique conceptual approach in which the opposition to the so-called traditional values and mores was considerably tempered by his uncritical appreciation for individual preferences. Unlike the radical Young Bengal or the orthodox Dharma Sabha of Radhakanta Deb, Debendranath was neither in favour of complete overhauling of Hindu society like the former nor persuaded to accept the latter by uncritically appreciating the prevalent sociocultural views and practices. He was truly a social reformer who agreed to maintain the available rituals and practices not as they were transmitted from one generation to another but by making them useful for individual identity to flourish in human collectivity. It was evident in a statement that he made in context of a ritual that sisters observed for ensuring brothers' well-being. The wish of the sisters was articulated by a prayer to harm the death God, Yama. When his elder daughter mentioned this, he, as she reminisced, immediately retorted that 'instead of seeking to cause harm to Yama, she should have prayed for his well-being and his brother's well-being as well'.[61] Evident here was Debendranath's conviction in the Upanishadic concern for *Vasudhaiva Kutumbakam* (the world is one family). Fundamental here is the point that what prevailed over

[61] Ibid., 337.

Debendranath was his devotion to the cause of humanity. Despite the fact that he did not endorse Rammohun's idea of religious universalism, he, by not underplaying his concerns for human welfare regardless of caste, clan and religion, actually pursued the goal that the latter pursued during his lifetime.

That he was not exactly a follower of Rammohun nor his father, Dwarkanath, was evident since he endeavoured to creatively blending their ideas in an equally creative conceptual format which was neither deviant from nor exactly imitative of the past ritualistic practices. While defending his stances, he thus persuasively argued that

> We have accepted some of the Hindu rituals not because we are scared of the orthodox Hindus but because we deem them appropriate for the cause that we have been fighting. We do not accept the view that all the past rituals are to be rejected since they belong to the past; likewise, we also do not endorse the argument that whatever we receive as past rituals need to be accepted. True to our protestant ethic, we have agreed to retain those rituals from the Hindu corpus that we find to be untainted by vice. It is not logical to characterize these rituals that we have salvaged from the said corpus as idolatrous. For instance, funerary rituals are merely an expression of the grief that one experiences at the passing of one's parents, and they are innocent of the villainy that plagues the rest of the iniquitous religion that we call the Hindu Dharma. Hence, the observance of these traditions is not, in my view, contrary to the ideals of the Brahmo Samaj.[62]

Let me reiterate the point with which the chapter begins: Debendranath is one of those rare social reformers who led a campaign which drew nourishment from the past discourses for defending his new philosophical discourses by forcefully discarding simultaneously what he deemed inappropriate for humanity. Metaphorically speaking, the ideas that he evolved were both a clear departure from the past and also a reinforcement of the traditions compatible with the Brahmo politico-ideological vision. He was truly a renaissance man who not only represented the concerns of an age when concerted attempts were

---

[62] Debendranath to Rajnarayan Basu, 11 September 1862, quoted in ibid., 340.

made to recognize individuals as important for the multitude, but also firmly established the criticality of some of the collective sociocultural practices as integral to universal well-being. What made him a class by himself was perhaps almost the complete absence of views on contemporary political situations, unlike his mentor and his father who were loyalists per se. The reasons need to be located in his well-defined priority; Debendranath privileged sociocultural reforms as his primary goal because, he strongly felt, unless Hindus were persuaded to question the prejudicial sociocultural practices and the concomitant values, actual freedom could never be realized. For Rammohun, the support of the British government was necessary as he was involved in a campaign for the abolition of sati which required political intervention; Dwarkanath too needed government help because he, to sustain his business empire, also owed a great deal to British rulers. Debendranath was left alone because he was engaged in an endeavour for reforming Hinduism which lost its vitality by being crippled with age-old debilitating sociocultural practices. He was readily accepted by British rulers as their companion since Christian Missionaries, who worked at their behest, had the same aim. So Debendranath, by complementing their efforts, was said to have acted in sync with the missionaries. It establishes the claim that, by being steadfast to his commitment, the second of the Tagore patriarchs foresaw some of the ideas that his son, Rabindranath, put into practice by evolving compatible sociocultural devices to carry forward the traditions that his grandfather and his father bequeathed.

Part C

Rabindranath Tagore

Courtesy: Rabindra-Bhavana, Visva-Bharati, Santiniketan

By 1861, when the last of the Tagore patriarchs was born, British colonialism had undergone a sea change. With the adoption of the 1858 Queen's Proclamation, Indian administration was brought under the British parliament which ended almost 100 years of the Company Raj. The year of his birth was not historically distinct, as the bard himself characterized, though it was believed that the parliamentary governance was a stepping stone towards realizing the best of values of the principles of Enlightenment since it drew its ideological sustenance from them. Given his father's astute handling of the situation which adversely affected the family following his grandfather's untimely death in England, Rabindranath was relatively immune from some of the serious worldly shocks. Despite serious difficulties, Debendranath never allowed his children to suffer and worked hard for their physical and emotional well-being. It was not thus surprising that Rabindranath received the best possible academic training from the home tutors amid serious financial stress confronting the Tagore family; his reluctance to go to school was never an impediment towards his instinctive quest for knowledge presumably because he had good tutors and also had an easy access to the library at home that his grandfather built by purchasing books which, he thought, were useful for justifying his sociocultural reforms that he undertook along with his colleague-cum-mentor, Rammohun Roy. Furthermore, by accompanying his father to various places, including the Himalayas, Rabindranath had had an opportunity to interact with disparate people and was also drawn to the pristine beauty of nature in the remote Himalayas. Fundamental here is the point that the poet derived his intellectual nourishment from not only the books but also the nature which influenced his thinking in myriad ways.

Like his father, Rabindranath recorded his memoirs at different phases of his life. For instance, *Jibansmriti* (autobiography) was published in 1912, *Chhelebela* (boyhood) in 1940 and *Atmaparichay* (knowing oneself) which, a posthumous collection of six of his essays, was brought out in 1943. Given these written tracts, it is easier to articulate his ideas which he evolved by being sensitive to the prevalent socio-economic and politico-ideological milieus. Nonetheless, he had his own doubts which he expressed when he categorically stated that

It is not easy to know oneself. It is difficult to organize life's various experiences into a unified whole. Had God not given a long life, he would note have permitted me to reach seventy years of age, I could hardly have got a clear picture of myself. I have tried to make sense of my life at different time through its various activities and experiences. The only thing I have been able to conclude about myself that I am a poet, nothing else, no matter all the other things I may have done with my life.[1]

Evident here is Rabindranath's own assessment of his own life, although it is clear that he wanted to be identified as a poet. Nonetheless, his creative texts, including the poetic creations, have developed a serious politico-ideological discourse based on his personal experiences of life and the values that he imbibed as a result. There was another source of influence, namely the ideas that the Upanishads transmitted. As the bard himself mentioned, 'There was something remarkable about our family. It was as if we lived close to the age of pre-Puranic India through our commitment to the Upanishads. As a boy', he further added, 'I grew up reciting slokas [hymns] from the Upanishads with a clear enunciation. We had no experiences of the emotional excesses prevalent in Bengal's religious life. My father's spiritual life was quiet and controlled'.[2]

Core here are three significant points which will be of aid to understand the poet's inkling and also the reason for being less vocal about his commitment to the Upanishads. First, that he was introduced to the ancient Vedantic texts, particularly Upanishads, is evident here. It was possible for him presumably because he was born in a family that began nurturing the ancient Hindu texts since the mid-18th century with the foundation of Brahmo Sabha in 1830 at the behest of his grandfather Dwarkanath and his like-minded colleagues. Second, the appreciation for Upanishads came naturally to him since his father,

---

[1] Rabindranath Tagore, *Atmaparichay* (Bengali; Kolkata: Visva-Bharati, 1993; reprint), translated by Uma Dasgupta; Rabindranath Tagore, *My Life in My Words* (New Delhi: Penguin, 2006), xiii
[2] Ibid., 4.

Debendranath, always espoused these ideas that he derived from these relatively forgotten texts in his interactions with his children. For the bard, the discourses that he heard from his father were persuasive since they, being indigenous, were organically connected with the Indian mindset. Finally, by being strongly influenced by his father, Rabindranath preferred not to publicly announce his spiritual commitment to these valuable tracts. To him, religion was a private domain and needed to be kept to oneself.

While being drawn to the Upanishads, Rabindranath also endeavoured to explore other literature, especially the English literature, which, being a repository of knowledge, provided him with a different lens to view humanity and human civilization. Important here is the claim that the poet was open to many intellectual values and ideas which made him see the nationalist search for an independent identity in a completely different perspective. As he himself admitted, 'along with [the study of Upanishads], there was a genuinely deep love of English literature among my elders [who were] clearly swayed by Shakespeare and Sir Walter Scott'.[3] Also striking here is to note that the Tagore family was hardly enamoured by the political campaign that the Moderates and Revolutionary Nationalists had launched in the late 19th and early 20th centuries, as evinced particularly in his 1916 novel, *Ghare-Baire* (home and the world) and his *Atmaparichay*, though the Tagore family 'was at the centre of plans for establishing the patriotic Hindu *Mela*, a National Fair, whose principal organizer was Nabagopal Mitra'.[4]

The above discussion of the probable sources of the bard's intellectual nourishment helps us to know why he viewed the world as he did through his myriad writings. First of all, there is no denying that by being born in a family, the poet had had access to both the indigenous and derivative discourses. It was possible because he belonged to that family in Calcutta which had deep connection with Britain and the British society that evolved in the city. Despite being socially boycotted and sternly criticized by a majority of Hindus, Rabindranath's

[3] Ibid.
[4] Ibid.

grandfather, Dwarkanath, was hardly dissuaded from crossing the *kala pani* (sea voyage) to go to England and happily endorsed those ideas and practices, which, he thought, were useful to bring about radical sociocultural changes in Bengal. His appreciation of the Western discourses did not however deter him from exploring the indigenous sources of wisdom which was manifested in his deep-rooted concern for unearthing the ideas and values the ancient Hindu texts preserved. The trend continued once Debendranath emerged as an acceptable cultural ambassador for Bengal. So by being part and parcel of a family, it was easier for Rabindranath to develop a mode of thinking and conceptualization which had imprints of both indigenous and Western sources of wisdom. Being raised in an era that favoured exploration of newer ideas, including from the derivative sources of knowledge, the bard evolved a unique style of articulation by creatively amalgamating what he imbibed from the family with what he learnt out of his own experiences of the world and nature. The second important aspect of Rabindranath's upbringing was that he, due to the sudden loss of wealth which Debendranath's father Dwarkanath amassed by dint of his hard work, had hardly had pompous lifestyle that his father had which the poet captured by saying that 'the wealth of lamps that his grandfather had lighted … went out with him'.[5] Furthermore, that wealth could be a source of high social status was not known then which was evident when Rabindranath wrote that 'the pride arising from the difference of wealth has come to our country from the West [and] … when money began to flow into the houses of office goers and businessmen, articles of foreign luxury became the measure of respectability'.[6] Rabindranath was immune from this largely because he had a saintly father who abdicated the worldly comforts that he had access to by being the son of a wealthy father. The third critical factor in shaping Rabindranath's mental universe was the nationalist zeal that his father epitomized. Debendranath 'genuine regard for … his country' was visible in many of the activities that he undertook to popularize those ideas which helped generate patriotic concerns for the country at a time when, as Rabindranath underlined, 'our

[5] Ibid., 7–8.
[6] Ibid., 11.

educated men then at arms' length both the language and thought of their native land [which] ... his father never appreciated'.[7] In order to illustrate his point, he referred to an example when Debendranath expressed his annoyance by returning a letter with a marriage proposal for Rabindranath to the sender because it was written in English.[8] This was a powerful statement on two counts: On the one hand, it revealed that unless one was proud of one's cultural resources, none of the efforts that they undertook was likely to create a self-conscious multitude. By setting an example, Debendranath conveyed a significant message, on the other hand, to seek to instil the sense of pride in one's own history.

As the chapters show, Rabindranath was a repository of ideas which had had imprints of what he derived by being raised in a family that creatively blended both modes of thinking from both Indian and non-Indian sources. There are two conceptually innovative ideas that the chapters contain. First, instead of highlighting the poetic persona of the bard, the aim here is to show that his literary creations were based on his uniquely textured sociopolitical ideas. For instance, his novel *Ghare-Baire* cannot be conceptualized unless one is acquainted with his 1904 seminal text, *Swadeshi Samaj*. Two of his immediate concerns were (a) self-reliance and (b) pride in one's sociocultural roots. Here too, one is reminded of his father's heartfelt urge to develop an independent mindset, the lack of which, he believed, was responsible for India being intellectually servile to the West. Second, along with his concern for self-reliance, he also raised serious questions on the mainstream nationalist campaign when, he felt, it was reduced to fanaticism. The 1910 novel *Gora* and 1934 *Char Adhyay* (four chapters) are illustrative here. Once Gora, the protagonist in the novel, during his trip to the remote villages in Bengal, confronted the well-entrenched religious and caste prejudices permanently segregating one set of people from another; he understood why it was difficult for the struggle against the British to succeed. Similarly, *Char Adhyay* is also a scathing critique of blind nationalism and blind adherence to a leader which was an impediment towards generating a sense of

[7] Ibid.
[8] Ibid.

belongingness to a collectivity. Second, by dwelling on the specific kinds of activities that Rabindranath suggested in his writings and also deeds, the chapters also highlight that he was an organic intellectual who pursued seriously what he believed for contributing to the rise and consolidation of a collectivity with self-esteem and righteousness. His persuasive critique of nationalism (1916) articulates how the Western notion of nationalism was vacuous in India which he beautifully narrated in *Gora* by underlining that essentialization of sociocultural identity of the countrymen was suicidal for the effort of those seeking to politically mobilize people against colonialism. The Sriniketan experiment that he inaugurated in 1928 also epitomizes his unstinting endeavour to generate among his associates the zeal and also the willingness to work for common well-being, especially those at the lower rung of the society in Bengal villages.

Rabindranath was not just a thinker with novel politico-ideological views, but he also represented a new wave of thinking to awaken the moribund nation. He was political without being political, which means that while challenging the existent power equations that emerged in the wake of colonialism, he expressed categorically his preferred mode of protest in numerous texts and speeches. Unlike Gandhi, he hardly directly participated in any of the nationalist campaigns that the Mahatma spearheaded, although his written tracts are left with revolutionary messages for those who pledged to fight for India's political liberation from the British rule. So he was also a mobilizer, though not in the conventional sense, since many of the freedom fighters, including the mainstream leaders, drew ideological inspiration from his novels, songs, verses and, of course, the critical essays on important socio-economic issues.

Chapter 5

Intermingling of Ideas

Also known as Gurudev, Rabindranath Tagore (1861–1941) was truly a renaissance man since he evolved his thoughts by creatively blending ideas from various Western and non-Western intellectual sources. Born in 1861, the last maverick of the Tagore family witnessed radical socio-economic and political changes in Bengal and India. While Dwarkanath and Debendranath were busy in eradicating evil customary practices which were claimed to have been drawn from ancient Hindu texts, Rabindranath had also intervened in the prevalent political processes that underwent radical changes during the period he remained as one of the foremost public figures. We should not however forget that he was involved in many sociocultural activities that his father and grandfather had initiated, namely the spread of education and also the importance of organizing like-minded colleagues for the causes that he privileged. It is therefore not surprising that the last of the Tagores devoted a great deal of attention to wage a sustained battle against superstitions dividing people on the basis of birth in specific caste groups or due to different religious faith, besides, of course, gender prejudices against women.

Representing a confluence of thoughts, Rabindranath evolved a unique conceptual framework to understand the prevalent sociocultural circumstances. In his ideas, we find a very subtle mixing of views that he derived from his grandfather, his father and also contextual inputs.

Hence, it is naturally implausible to comprehend the complex set of ideas that the last of the Tagores generated to realize his sociocultural mission. Like his father, he was drawn to the Vedantic texts and upheld the Upanishads as the epitome of knowledge and wisdom. He was also appreciative of the conceptual mould that his grandfather, Dwarkanath, developed in collaboration with Rammohun, by drawing on the Western discourses which is evident in his many creative writings. It was articulated particularly in his many travelogues. That he was also critical of the ideas, derivative of the Western discourses, which was visible in his powerful critique of nationalism since the very conceptual format of essentializing India's diverse sociocultural identity was neither valid nor theoretically supportive of explaining the complex Indian identity. Emphasized here is the argument that Rabindranath did never blindly imitate what he derived from the available intellectual discourses; he subjected them to a very careful scrutiny before it was accepted as intellectually exciting. Politically too, he maintained an independent existence unlike his grandfather who was a loyalist per se and his father who remained indifferent to contemporary politics since he had other priorities. As is well known, he was not hesitant to abdicate Knighthood in protest against the brutal killing of innocent people in Jallianwala Bagh in 1919.

The chapter makes two major arguments, complemented by a secondary argument. First, given the evidence that Rabindranath drew on both the Western and indigenous discourses while expressing his views, this chapter elaborates the point by providing a textual analysis of his creative writings. The second argument hinges on the claim that by being impressed by the nature of socio-economic development of the West, especially Russia and the United States, he, in his critical essays, insisted on imitating some of the plans and programmes that made it possible. His Sriniketan experiment is illustrative here. Supportive of these major arguments, the chapter also makes a secondary argument by emphasizing that the main purpose of Rabindranath was to bring people from different walks of life together for a common cause. By pursuing the same aim that his father and grandfather sought to fulfil, Rabindranath institutionalized the desire by establishing Visva-Bharati in 1921 which was not merely a centre of learning, but also devised a system to evolve a sense of compassion for the underprivileged and backward sections of the society.

Unfolding of the Ideas and Schemes

Politically, he was a priest of nonviolence; his novel, *Rajarshi*, 1887 (which was transformed into a play *Visarjan*, 1890) is illustrative here. In another 1890 play, *Prayaschitta* (atonement), Rabindranath sharply reiterated the message through Dhananjoy Bairagi who also appeared in a later play, *Muktodhara* (the waterfall), which is discussed below. Willing to hold the bull by its horns, Dhananjoy was ready to face the physical assault by the zamindar's forces who were duty-bound to comply with his directions. He thus exhorted that he 'was going to the zamindar's *kachhari bari* (the administrative office) to oppose his decision to impose rent despite severe drought in his *zamindari* estate'.[1] In his defence, he argued that 'the taking away of food from the starving children is as good as keeping the God starved, [which is] nothing but deception to the almighty'.[2] Instead of physically countering the zamindar and his coercive forces, he also appealed to the villagers 'to have faith in the almighty who will take care of these hapless *prajas* for being strong in absorbing even organized physical attack on them'.[3] There is another interesting dimension of his humanism which he amply displayed while discharging his role as a zamindar. At the beginning of the play, *Prayaschitta*, Tagore showed that the prince, Udayaditta, was devastated by the decision that the zamindar (who happened to be his father as well) took in opposition to the earnest appeal that his subject made for waiving of rent in view of the severe drought there.[4] This led to the banishment of the prince who was punished for being, as the zamindar defended, 'obstinate and his unconditional support to a rebel, Dhananjoy'.[5] There are two

---

[1] Rabindranath Tagore, *Prayaschitta* (Atonement), 1890, reproduced in Rabindranath Tagore, *Rabindra Rachanabali*, Vol. 5 (Santiniketan: Visva-Bharati, 1940; reprint), 224.
[2] Ibid., 228.
[3] Ibid., 240.
[4] Ibid., 219.
[5] Ibid., 220.

important politico-ideological features that *Prayaschitta* epitomizes: On the one hand, *Prayaschitta* is a testimony to Tagore's emotional chords with the subjects in his zamindari estate. Unlike his father, Debendranath, who did not seem to have been so kind so long as he managed Dwarkanath's zamindari estate, Rabindranath was far more accommodative while addressing the genuine grievances of those who belonged to his estate. On the other hand, it can persuasively be argued that it was perhaps one of the first categorical statement supporting nonviolence; in other words, by insisting on absorption of the pain, Dhananjoy can be said to have laid out a conceptual foundation of nonviolence that Gandhi had already experimented in South Africa (1893–1914) and it was to become an effective mobilization strategy in India once he led the anti-British campaign. It was also evident when he wrote a scathing critique of violence in his novel, *Ghare-Baire* (1916), which was based on his experience of the 1905–1908 Swadeshi Movement that was organized to annul the first partition of Bengal in 1905. The dialogues between Sandip who supported violence and Nikhilesh who focused more on deficiencies of violence epitomizes Tagore's own ideological priority in favour of nonviolence; the idea was reverberated in his novel, *Gora* (1916). One of the most clearly written texts in favour of nonviolence is available in the dialogues of Dhananjoy Bairagi in the play *Muktadhara* (1922). Here, while clearly articulating his views questioning violence, Dhananjoy Bairagi insisted on abjuring violence since its impact was ephemeral; furthermore, it was likely to cause serious human devastation which, instead of contributing to humanity, was certain to cause irreparable damage. His statement that 'the true man within us is a flame of fire. He consumes all hurts in light. Only the brute beast is hurt. The brute beast is flesh, and it goes whining when it is struck'.[6] Condemning the desire to hit back the perpetrators of violence, Dhananjoy defended his point of view by suggesting that in view of your brute passion for revenge, 'your eyes are still red with passion and your voice lacks music'.... That's only because in your secret hearts, you want to hurt which creates a

---

[6] Rabindranath Tagore, *Muktadhara* (The Waterfall), cited in Sisir Kumar Das, ed., *The English Writings of Rabindranath Tagore*, Vol. 2 (New Delhi: Sahitya Akademi, 1996), 183.

sense of fear'.[7] The argument in favour of nonviolence is developed further than those who 'don't want to hurt ... have no fear [because if] nothing hurts you ... then the hurt will receive its death blow'.[8] Hence he declared that 'I must not in this voyage burden my boat with those who fear and those who frighten others'.[9] In other words, according to Tagore, so long as violence remained integral to the human mind, it was impossible to attain human emancipation in its true connotation. So what was required to be done was to kill the evil desire to set things right by violence, and once that was done away with, the feeling of being scared completely disappeared. Fundamental here is the idea that unlike his illustrious ancestors, Rabindranath devised a politico-ideological design in support of nonviolence long before Gandhi appeared on the scene. One of the reasons was certainly the influence of Upanishadic texts that Tagore was introduced to at a very young age by being raised in a family in which they were considered to be an important source of knowledge for humanity.

The Context

In his memoirs, Rabindranath mentioned that he was born in 1861 which 'is not an important date of history, but it belongs to a great period of our history of Bengal'.[10] While explaining why 'it was a great period', Tagore wrote that it was so because 'the currents of three movements had met in the life of our country'.[11] What were those three movements? First, it was a religious movement which Rammohun spearheaded by reopening 'the channel of spiritual life which had been obstructed for many years by the sands and debris of creeds that were formal and materialistic, fixed in external practices lacking spiritual significance'.[12] Basic here is the argument that due to superstitious beliefs which were shown to have derived their

[7] Ibid., 184.
[8] Ibid., 183–184.
[9] Ibid., 184.
[10] *Rabindranath Tagore: My Life in My Words*, selected and edited with an introduction by Uma Dasgupta (New Delhi: Penguin, 2006), 4.
[11] Ibid.
[12] Ibid., 5.

sustenance from the main religious texts of Hinduism they governed human minds to a significant extent. It was Rammohun Roy (1772–1833) who, by demonstrating the deliberately created superstitious beliefs as deviant from the classical texts, was said to have introduced a new mode of thinking that unfurled new debates and thoughts in the domain of religion. The second movement was about a literary revolution, the main priest of which was Bankim Chandra Chatterjee (1838–1894), who, in his creative texts, inaugurated a new genre of Bengali prose that was free from the Sanskritized mode of articulating one's written texts. While appreciating the role of Bankim in this regard, Rabindranath thus wrote that

> This man was brave enough to go against the orthodoxy which believed in the security of tombstones and in that perfection which only belonged to the lifeless. He lifted the deadweight of ponderous forms from our language and with a touch of his magic wand aroused our literature from her age-long sleep.[13]

Rabindranath owed a great deal to Bankim, as he mentioned in many of his speeches. For him, the Bangla language stood on its own as an independent mode of articulation and expression. A visionary who created, in other words, a space for Bangla which was simply inconceivable in the immediate past, presumably given the reluctance to go beyond the mode of expression that was largely derivative of Sanskrit. As a result, Bangla literature remained confined to a very limited group of readers which also prevented publishers from printing many copies as it was not profitable then. Furthermore, since most of the authors preferred not to deal with the social issues, but focused on historical and religious themes in a very conventional manner that hardly provoked new readers. For Bankim, it was a revolutionary step because (a) it was a courageous decision to tread a new path and (b) it was equally a bold step to challenge those authors who flourished by following the traditional mode. As mentioned below, in view of the changes that unfolded with Bankim as a pioneer, Rabindranath admitted that he was indebted to him; otherwise, his task would have been

---

[13] Ibid.

difficult given the well-entrenched bias for Sanskritized texts which the then leading authors upheld. So, it will not be unfair to argue that as a litterateur, Rabindranath's debt to Bankim was enormous simply because he absorbed and also effectively addressed much of the difficulties confronting the latter when he rose to prominence in the world of literature. The third movement was one of condemning those who, by being blind to the Western discourses, were never hesitant to denigrate the Indian past. Articulating 'a voice of indignation', the movement, argued Tagore, 'heaped humiliation by those who were not oriental' by directly supporting 'the contemptuous spirit of separateness [to hurt] us and [caused] great damage to our own world culture'.[14] The outcome was disastrous because 'it generated in young men of our country distrust of all things that had come to them as an inheritance from the past. Our students, imitating the laughter of their European school masters, laughed at the old Indian pictures and other works of art'.[15] Condemning the spirit of rejection, Tagore sharply argued that it was 'the result of hypnotism exercised upon the minds of the younger generation by people who were loud of voice and strong of arm'. It was a well-nurtured design which gained acceptance because of the following:

> A long period of encouragement in developing an appetite for third-rate copies of French pictures, for gaudy oleographs abjectly cheap, for the pictures that are products of mechanical accuracy of stereotyped standard, and they still consider it to be a symptom of superior culture to be able disdainfully to refuse oriental works of creation.[16]

Implicit here is the bard's powerful critique of appreciation of blind borrowing of ideas and discourses from the Western world regardless of their qualities. It was a crusade against imitation without assessment on the part of those who enjoyed imitating what they received from the Western world. It was clearly a servility of mind which was allowed to thrive largely due to the failure of those to create a critical mindset that

---

[14] Ibid., 6.
[15] Ibid.
[16] Ibid.

was well equipped to distinguish between what was good and what was despicable irrespective of their origin. It was not a reactionary movement, but, as the poet characterized, 'a revolutionary one, because it set out with great courage to deny and to oppose all pride in mere borrowings'.[17] Tagore's strong arguments against derivative ideas and discourses should be mistaken as a blind support to the past ideas and values because not all of them were 'necessarily humanistic',[18] which also meant that he applied the same yardstick while selecting what he felt was conducive to human well-being.

A careful scan of the movements reveals that Tagore, by being nurtured in an environment in which these three movements prospered, epitomized the newer concerns and ideas which came out of these revolutionary campaigns. The new literary genre that Bankim articulated was a source of inspiration to the bard, as his literary creations unambiguously demonstrate. Similarly, the support that Dwarkanath accorded to Rammohun when he started Brahmo Samaj in 1833 and the role that Debendranath played in revamping the organization since 1843 also acted critically in shaping the voice of protest against Hindu orthodox that Rabindranath most powerfully articulated in his creative texts and various activities that he undertook to pursue his cause. At the mundane level, it was most humiliating for both Dwarkanath and his son, Debendranath, since they took an active part in spreading the protestant messages. The family members were 'ostracized because of [their] heterodox opinions about religion, [which allowed them] the freedom of the outcaste'.[19] This was, instead of becoming a source of weakness, an inspiration, argued Rabindranath, 'to build our own world with our own thoughts and energy of mind. We had to build it from the foundation, and therefore had to seek the foundation that was firm'.[20]

It was an advantage for the youngest Tagore maverick because the family had broken from the mainstream which

---

[17] Ibid., 7.
[18] Ibid.
[19] Ibid.
[20] Ibid.

[It] led [him] from [his] young days to seek guidance for [his] self-expression in [his] own inner standard of judgment. The medium of expression doubtless was my mother tongue. But the language which belonged to the people had to be modulated according to the urging which I as an individual had.[21]

Implicit here is the point that it was easier for Rabindranath to tread an unknown path since there was hardly a blueprint to follow; he was allowed to create a world of his own on the basis of his own comprehension of the milieu in which he was born and nurtured. Given the low caste identity of being a family of *pirali* brahmin and also the radical sociocultural views, the Tagores were ostracized, which, instead of being an impediment, 'liberated [them] from the responsibility of conforming to all those conventions that had not the value of truth, that were mere irrational habits bred in it the inertia of the racial mind'.[22] This was an emotional freedom on which the third Tagore maverick built his conceptual world, on the one hand; on the other hand, Rabindranath was born in the aftermath of the adoption of the 1858 Queen's Proclamation which brought India directly under the control of the British crown that radically altered the nature of governance in India in comparison with what existed at the aegis of the East India Company. The Tagore family was hardly immune from the changes that unfolded with the new Proclamation. As Rabindranath narrated, 'the conventional code of life for our family thereupon became a confluence of three cultures: The Hindu, the Mohammedan and the British'.[23] Dwarkanath was known for being true to 'the Victorian manners, economical in time, in ceremonies and in the dignity of personal appearance'.[24] A new era had ushered in which 'the modern city-bred spirit of progress had just triumphed

---

[21] Rabindranath Tagore, *Talks in China* (Kolkata: Visva-Bharati, 1925), 24–25.
[22] Rabindranath Tagore, 'Ideals of education', cited in Sisir Kumar Das, ed., *The English Writings of Rabindranath Tagore*, Vol. 2 (New Delhi: Sahitya Akademi, 2002), 611.
[23] Rabindranath Tagore, 'A Poet's School', in Rabindranath Tagore, *Towards Universal Man* (Mumbai: Asia Publishing House, 1962; reprint), 289–290.
[24] Ibid., 290.

over the lush green life of [India's] ancient village community'.[25] By underlining the radical change in the texture of governance, the bard also highlighted the idea of the inevitability of the British influence since it was obvious that with access to the Western discourses the socio-economic character of the colony was bound to change which was to be accepted. For the poet, it was a source of knowledge which however did not involve a complete rejection of the indigenous sources of knowledge, as some of his predecessors evinced in the past.

As is evident now, Rabindranath represented a confluence of three sociocultural forces emanating from the Hindu, Muslim and British cultural ethos. The politico-ideological scene was less complicated during his grandfather's time since the Bengali elites appreciated the British rule as a saviour in contrast with what existed before. There were of course sporadic challenges to colonialism which hardly received attention from among them. Despite being socially ostracized, the wealth that Dwarkanath earned gave him a respectable place in the society, both in India and also in England. What however disturbed him were the archaic social practices which led him to organize campaigns against them in collaboration with his colleagues holding identical views. The 19th century was an era of significant social changes in Bengal in many respects: While Rammohun raised voice against brutal sati custom, Dwarkanath assisted him to create Brahmo Samaj in 1833 as a protestant organization seeking to purge Hindu society of all prejudicial mores and practices. The Samaj initiated education, even for girls, and also took meaningful steps to develop Bangla as a language. Most of the tasks that Dwarkanath undertook were easily carried forward presumably because of the financial support that he provided out of his own income from zamindari and other business ventures. His capable son, Debendranath, continued with what his father started though was restrained largely because of the lack of adequate financial support which was attributed to the fact that he had to repay the debt that the former had incurred during his lifetime. Nonetheless, by dint of capacity to mobilize colleagues with similar views, Debendranath continued with some of the projects that

[25] Ibid.

Dwarkanath had initiated. The Brahmo Samaj was revamped in 1882; the school education received adequate attention since many of the Calcutta elites came forward to support him. Politico-ideologically, he, unlike his father, largely remained neutral which means that he was neither very close nor opposed to the authority. Presumably because he strongly felt that political freedom could never be a panacea unless evil social practices were completely eradicated and human beings were treated at par with one another by jettisoning the habit of looking down upon one section of humanity by another due to caste and gender identities. Debendranath was also known for his endeavour for reviving interests in Upanishadic texts which was evident when he persuaded the Asiatic Society of Bengal to translate Vedas and Isa-Upanishad in Bangla. Like Dwarkanath, he also participated in building schools and also Metropolitan College which continued in competition with Presidency College that received government grants while the former was funded completely by donations. What was most striking was his success in spreading his distinct religious views which Brahmo Samaj articulated beyond Calcutta. The establishment of a Brahmo School in Santiniketan in 1888 was the outcome of this effort. As is well known, the Brahmo School was an initiative that laid the foundation of Visva-Bharati which came into being in 1921 as an alternative centre for learning and pedagogy.

There are three complementary points that emerge out of an analytical scanning of the politico-ideological activities of the first two Tagore mavericks, Dwarkanath and Debendranath, which will help us contextualize the massive contribution that the last Tagore, Rabindranath, made to translate into reality some of their ideational endeavours. First, it is true that Dwarkanath did not confront the British rule presumably because he felt that it was a relief from the earlier Muslim rule. Nonetheless, his heartfelt desire which he accomplished by his intelligence and hard work shows that he sincerely desired to be independent in adverse circumstances. Debendranath followed his father's footsteps since he also nurtured the idea that freedom did not necessarily mean the attainment of political power but also deliverance from the socially crippling human urges and practices. Besides publicizing his views in written tract, *Tattwabodhini*

Patrika, he also collaborated with his colleagues who founded schools and other centres of learning to spread education; it was he who took personal care to evolve interests in the ancient Hindu texts, especially Vedas and Upanishads, because he strongly felt that without comprehending and internalizing our deep-rooted sociocultural traditions, the argument for independence remained vacuous. Second, being open to the Western discourses and the concomitant sociocultural traditions, Rabindranath's grandfather, Dwarkanath, created an ambience in which these derivative ideas flourished. It was a seriously pursued attempt on his part to spread those ideas which ran contrary to many of the evil social practices which were claimed to have been drawn on the ancient Hindu texts. It led to a mental liberation which helped build a new discourse in Bengal challenging the orthodox and prejudiced mindset. Along with his exposure to the Western philosophical discourses, Debendranath worked hard to popularize the paradigmatic indigenous discourses which Vedas and Vedantic texts generated, but, due to our negligence, they remained narrowly confined, if not hidden. Rather than accepting the discourses derivative of the Western world as axiomatic, Debendranath evolved a milieu in which the indigenous discourses gained a respectable place in Bengal's intellectual horizon. Finally, it was evident that the two Tagores, instead of exclusively concentrating on augmenting their wealth, devoted a great deal of energy and money in fulfilling their philanthropic goals. Their role was complementary to the efforts that some of the contemporary leading public figures had already undertaken. In two significant ways, they were different. Unlike some of their colleagues, neither Dwarkanath nor Debendranath nurtured communal animosity towards the Muslim subjects in their landed estates. Instead, there were instances to demonstrate that they, to create a milieu in which Hindus and Muslims interacted freely with one another, invited the villagers regardless of religious identity for the festivals that were organized in their estates; furthermore, as well as holding the Hindu festival, the Durga Puja, the Tagores also were equally enthusiastic in celebrating the Muslim festival Eid. Their purpose was to build symbiotic relations with the subjects which allowed them to be attentive to other sociocultural objectives that they wanted to accomplish.

The above discussion is tuned to the argument that Rabindranath was an epitome of the ideas that he received from the earlier Tagores, Dwarkanath and Debendranath, besides, of course, the contextual inputs that he derived himself by being integrally connected with the prevalent socio-economic and politico-ideological circumstances. At one level, he was a social reformer par excellence, at another, he was a powerful political voice which, on many occasions, refashioned the mainstream nationalist outlook. The texts that he left for posterity are a testimony to the fact that his 'receptive and imaginative mind would never accept anything as final'.[26] In clear terms, his son, Rathindranath, thus wrote that 'no sooner was anything decided then his mind began to revolt against it, and he would not be content until he had found an excuse to alter the decision'.[27] It was a mindset reinforcing the idea that Rathindranath further argued,

> [S]tatus quo had no meaning for him. This applied not only to his daily life, his wanting to change his habitation, his food, his dress and such like things, but to his creative activities as well. Whenever his mind revolted against current conventions, whether in literature, in religious beliefs, in social customs, in education or in politics, he would fearlessly criticize and expose what he considered wrong or unjust. At the same time, he had constructive ideas to offer as an acceptable alternative and was ready to carry them out himself if no one else dared to do so. This spirit of revolt against accepted principles and practice coupled with the desire to experiment with new ideas, persisted till the last day of his life.[28]

What was critical in his thinking was his firm commitment to the cause of humanity despite having known that this was likely to not persuade his colleagues in a situation when rabid nationalism appears to have been privileged. Nonetheless, he stood by his concern for universal humanism despite being vehemently criticized by his nationalist colleagues, including the Mahatma, who fought for national

---

[26] Rathindranath Tagore, *On the Edges of Time* (Kolkata: Visva-Bharati, 2020), 159.
[27] Ibid.
[28] Ibid., 159–160.

independence as prior to anything else. Here Rabindranath stood out since what he defended as critical to human existence was contrary to what others felt. In fact, it is argued that the Mahatma and his nationalist compatriots pursued a mode of coming together as a unit, or nation, in the prevalent sense of the term which was not exactly new since it was, as evidence shows, a transmission of a constructed idea that gradually transformed into a nation.[29] It is true that the bard was convinced that the idea of nation could never be anything but humanist since the countries seeking to fulfil their nationalist agenda were bound to be brutally selfish, as history illustrates. That he remained committed to this conceptualization is amplified in his corpus of writings. There is a clear indication of this in his preference for the word of Bharatvarsha and not India while elaborating his distinctive ideational inklings. In a creative literary piece, *Nababarsha* (new year), published in 1902, he expressed unambiguously what he meant by Bharatvarsha by saying that to him,

> Bharatvarsha that will ultimately remain is not only ancient, but also concealed, vast and generous. We—who speak in English, who disbelieve, who tell lies, who boast—year by year, we shall dissipate, disappear, like the waves in the ocean. Silent, *sanatan Bharat* will not suffer any loss as a consequence.[30]

Here, persuaded by the Upanishadic dictum, Rabindranath made a departure from the dominant Europeanized thoughts. In his perception, the Bharatvarsha did not seem to be a geographical unit but a sociocultural concept which was neither static nor fluid, but drew on certain fundamental ethos supportive of a vibrant society. Presumably because of being an epitome of universal humanism, Tagore championed Bharatvarsha as a model of inclusive human existence despite being aware that it was contrary to the mainstream conceptualization of the nation. His insistence on the Vedantic texts was not, at all, an

---

[29] Rosinka Chaudhuri made this point in her essay, 'Hemchandra's Bharat Sangeet (1870) and the Politics of Poetry: A Pre-history of Hindu Nationalism in Bengal?' *Indian Economic and Social History Review* 42, no. 2 (2005). https://doi.org/10.1177/001946460504200203

[30] Tagore, *Rabindra Rachanabali*, Vol. 9, 609, cited in Ibid.

endeavour to go back to the past but one to derive inspiration for the present. It was therefore not surprising that Gora in his novel *Gora* (1916), despite being a *sanatani* Hindu who religiously followed all the rituals to prove himself a genuine Brahmin, had no qualms when he vehemently criticized the divisive caste system and also the prejudicial attitudes that caste Hindus nurtured to maintain social distance with their Muslim brethren. The Bharatvarsha that he was looking for was not the one that existed in reality. As a result, the deeper he penetrated into the rural life,

> The more a certain thought began to trouble his mind. He observed that in these rural areas, social restrictions were far more powerful than in educated and cultured society. In every household in the villages, food, sleep, rest, work, everything was conducted, day and night, under the unblinking gaze of society. Each individual had a very simple faith in popular traditions, never questioning such things. Yet social restrictions and adherence to customs did not empower them at all in the fields of activity.... Beyond adherence to tradition, there was no other good that they wholeheartedly acknowledged, or were willing to understand. It was prohibition, enforced through punishment or partisanship, that they regarded as supreme. The awareness of what must not be done entrapped their nature in a net from head to toe at every step, through various forms of discipline.... There was no broad unity among them that could draw them all together in good times or bad.[31]

That the poet never compromised with his commitment to universal humanism is established beyond doubt, as his creative writings unequivocally demonstrate. While dwelling on the foundational ideas that informed the poet in his endeavour in the development of his distinct sociopolitical discourses, it has been argued that a large chunk of his ideas is also derivative of what he learnt from Vidyasagar, Rammohun and his father, Debendranath Tagore. The outcome of his intellectual interaction was Tagore's appreciation for healthy exchange of ideas between the present and past and also between the East and

---

[31] Rabindranath Tagore, *Gora*, in *Classic Rabindranath Tagore* (New Delhi: Penguin, 2011), 575.

West. Unlike the Hindu zealots who seem to be blinded in their perception of India by defining her exclusively in the Hindu cultural ethos, Rabindranath argued that 'India's history is not the story of the Hindu alone. We are part material in that history; and if we cannot fit ourselves into the scheme ... we will be condemned to death in the court of humanity'.[32] Conforming to this conceptualization, he further mentioned that

> The objective of Indian history is not to set up Hindu or some dominance, but to secure a special kind of fulfilment for humanity, a level of perfection that must be gained for all. In the course of this fulfilment, if Hindu, Muslim and the British have to submerge the aggressive parts of their individuality, it may be hurtful to their national pride but it will not be reckoned as a loss in the scales of truth and human rights.[33]

This is an important aspect of his sociopolitical discourse which is an unambiguous statement on any kind of socio-economic and religious discrimination. Here, Tagore, being influenced by the trio, Vidyasagar, Rammohun and his father, Debendranath, imbibed the spirit of human beings as one unit regardless of differences in terms of class, caste or ethnic-driven distinctive sociocultural features. He was for a society in which the exclusive identity based on one's religious affiliation with a denomination of faith was clearly rejected as it stood in contradiction with the aim of building the world as one.

An Innovative and Compassionate Social Designer

Rabindranath represented a new philosophy which was a creative amalgamation of the ideas that he received from his predecessors, including his grandfather, Dwarkanath (1794–1846), and his father, Debendranath (1817–1905). His claim in the *Jeevan-Smriti* (memoirs)

---

[32] Rabindranath Tagore, 'East and West', in Tagore, *Towards Universal Man*, 131–132.
[33] Ibid., 131.

that he internalized 'three movements in him' explicitly states that he owed a great deal from these derivative inputs. The written tract, entitled *Charitrapuja*,[34] is an explicit statement on the influences that he imbibed from Rammohun, Vidyasagar and his father, Debendranath. Later, he wrote extensively about Gandhi's contribution to social reform and political awakening in India. Unlike his grandfather, Dwarkanath, who focused primarily on social transformation and hardly had inclination for political freedom, Rabindranath felt otherwise presumably because he was nurtured in a politico-ideological milieu in which independence from the British rule was a clarion call for the Indians at the behest of the Indian National Congress and its widely accepted leader, Mahatma Gandhi. Like his father, Debendranath also devoted his zeal for social reform and spiritual uplift. In this respect, there is no doubt that the father and son were heavily influenced by Rammohun as their activities demonstrate. Along with their concern for radical social reform, both Dwarkanath and Debendranath paid adequate attention to spreading education as it was, they strongly felt, necessary to effectively counter superstitious mindset. Although the Indian National Congress was founded in 1885 at the behest of a retired British civil servant, A. O. Hume, there is hardly any evidence to show that Debendranath was also involved in any of the activities that unfolded in India with its foundation though at the fag-end of his life the revolutionary terrorists spread out, especially in Calcutta and other major *mofussil* towns in east Bengal, to champion the nationalist cause. It was Rabindranath Tagore who consistently pursued his politico-ideological views based on his concern for humanity which, he always exhorted, was prior to freedom from political bondage. For instance, in his essay on plague in *Bharati* in 1898, he not only condemned the government decision to incarcerate Bal Gangadhar Tilak for criticizing the administration for failing to provide adequate relief to the plague victims in Bombay but also underlined the importance of hygiene as an antidote to the epidemic. That it was just a mere statement was evident when in 1898 the plague epidemic engulfed the city of Calcutta killing many of those who lived in the shanties in the outskirt of Calcutta, he campaigned vigorously

---

[34] Rabindranath Tagore, *Charitrapuja* (Kolkata: Visva-Bharati, 1805; reprint).

for financial support to the victims and also for vaccination which was not readily accepted by the people given the widespread apprehension that it was also as lethal as the disease itself. That Tagore's initiative was effective was manifested soon when the infection was contained and no longer remained as virulent as before. With the establishment of a school in Santiniketan, Patha Bhawan in 1901, Rabindranath translated his desire to evolve an alternative centre of learning and pedagogy amid the available systems of English education that flourished due to the patronage of the ruler. This was also an opportunity to experience Bengal's rural life which was qualitatively different from his past interaction in rural Bengal as a zamindar. Vehemently opposed to the political strategy of the Congress activists of both the Moderate and Extremist variety,[35] Tagore was in favour of getting involved in rural reconstruction which did not receive attention from among the Indians presumably because of their deliberately maintained sociocultural differences with the rural folks. Besides being critical of the well-entrenched habit of being indifferent to those in rural India, Tagore also attributed the consolidation of the British Empire to the laziness of the Indians in even doing things for their own well-being. While elaborating his argument he thus stated, in his 1904 tract, *Swadeshi Samaj*, that it was most disheartening to note that so long as

> Indians are content to receive forever all welfare grants for the nation for a tremendously powerful machine, then whatever its advantages, it cannot lead to a worse situation for us. That we do not have any means for removing our want other than the inhuman influence known as the government—to let such a notion find roots in our mind would be to lose our country in the truest sense. Actually, the primary cause behind the fact that our motherland is not our own is not that the country is under foreign rule. The real reason is that we have not been able to make the country where we have fortuitously taken birth, our own and closest to our hearts

---

[35] For details of the nature of moderate and extremist nationalist intervention, see Daniel Argov, *Moderates and Extremists in the Indian Nationalist Movement, 1883–1920, with Special Reference to Surendranath Banerjee and Lajpat Rai* (New York, NY: Asia Publishing House, 1968).

through service, sacrifice, penance, knowledge and understanding. We possess only what we build with our intelligence, life and love.[36]

Explicit here are the ideas that one needed to be organically linked with one's country. Given the long foreign rule, Indians tended to unconditionally depend on foreign help in everything which made them mentally servile to the administration. Rabindranath's argument evolved around his concern for making India self-dependent which, he thought, was at the root of social, economic progress and politico-ideological prowess. It was thus further stated that

> What was worse was that there was hardly a positive response when the country needed help from her people. For everything, including providing food, water, education, we are habitually dependent on the government. It is here that the country has considerably lost its elan and capability; by delinking herself from the people, the country has completely alienated from the core of her heart; this is most tragic and also deplorable. The argument that India will attain her past glory once Swaraj [political freedom] is attained is just like acknowledging the mother after inheriting her money. [Hence,] I insist that, instead of wasting time on demanding help from the ruler for our well-being, we should first own our country through selfless service and unconditional sacrifice; we need to organize ourselves for the cause that is intimately connected with the solemn aim of bringing people together irrespective of caste, religion and the arrogance of being a town-bred.[37]

These are foundational ideas on which Rabindranath Tagore built his conceptual universe. His creative texts, novels, short stories, plays, dance drama, among others, are a testimony to this claim, as mentioned below. His aim was to inspire the Indians to undertake social activities which were certain to contribute to common well-being. Ideologically, it was an attempt, on the one hand, to create an awareness for building a communal identity which was meant to generate

---

[36] Rabindranath Tagore, *Swadeshi Samaj* (Kolkata: Visva-Bharati, 1939; reprint), 3.
[37] Ibid., 2–3.

enthusiasm for involvement in projects for welfare to all; it was also an endeavour, on the other hand, to question of the habit being heavily dependent on the government which was an easy way to abdicate one's own responsibility. It was clearly a political statement seeking to galvanize the moribund nation. Tagore was not hesitant to declare that it was at the root of our mental decadence that we never felt that the country belonged to us. As a result, we preferred to remain indifferent to the socio-economic ills that crippled India beyond rejuvenation. The argument was most sharply put in his address to the 1907 Pabna session of the Bengal Provincial Congress Committee. According to him, one of the major sources of our weakness was as follows:

> Our indifference to the genuine socio-economic problems of our own ilk. We don't bother if the villagers suffer due to multifarious problems, including the lack of supply of potable water; we have no concern if the cows have nowhere to graze since there are barren lands all over; we don't have a place where we can sit together to discuss common problems. With the lack of interest in education, the uneducated youths have been used to provide false witness in many false legal suits because it is a source of income for them. In view of the absence of an adequate sewage system, malaria reappears every year. We have no stock of food in case of famine. This is most appalling because we have no food, we lack good health, we experience no joy, we have no confidence in ourselves; we hardly cooperate with one another; we readily accept attack on us since we don't have the ability to counterattack; when death is imminent, we accept it as fated; instead of going for medication, we happily depend on providential assistance when our relatives are dying.[38]

Critical here was his concern for inclusive development in the country which he put into practice with the establishment of Sriniketan where he focused on how to augment agricultural production to take care of the basic needs of the people associated with it. Based on his experience as a zamindar, he realized that what was lacking most was the initiative of the villagers seeking to accomplish what they felt

---

[38] Amitavo Chaudhuri, *Zamindar Rabindranath* (Rabindranath as a Zamindar; Kolkata: Visva-Bharati, 1976), 17.

was necessary for their own well-being. The idea was not novel for Upanishads and, in so many verses, stipulated that mankind is strong enough to pursue its own agenda without providential help which would come automatically in case there was desire. This was absent presumably because of the lackadaisical attitude of the countrymen that flourished in the wake of the British rule. As a perceptive soul, Tagore also understood that putting the entire blame on the alien rule was not most logical because the indigenous mindset that was rooted in the ruthless Brahminical grip on our social life, which instead of being challenged, was readily accepted by the people at large. The 1907 Pabna address is critical to comprehend the thoughts that Tagore had articulated by emphasizing that (a) one needed to be self-sufficient and to accomplish the goal (b) one was required to generate zeal to work together for common causes.

The Politico-ideological Context

As argued above, Rabindranath derived some of the landmark ideas from his ancestors and also from his own comprehension of the ancient Hindu texts, especially Vedas and Vedantic texts. Unlike his grandfather and father, he also participated in the contemporary politico-ideological battle that the nationalists had waged against colonial subjugation. While Dwarkanath and Debendranath accepted the colonial rule largely as a boon in disguise, Rabindranath, instead of following their footsteps, challenged the government since it was an impediment to India's natural growth as a nation. One must be careful because he did not understand India in the conventional conceptual format of a nation, as discussed below; his idea of nation was an appreciation for the socioculturally diverse and disparate India as a geographical compact. For him, India was, in other words, not just an expression of diversity but one that allowed people with stunningly contrasting sociocultural preferences to remain together and thrive. In his poem, *Bharat Tirtha* (the Indian pilgrim), he envisioned an India imbued with the noblest of her national ideals of 'tolerance, acceptance, exchange, striving for human perfection through a loving and reverential appreciation of nature and identification of the infinite within the finite, the form within the formless'.[39] True to his belief, Tagore thus unambiguously articulated,

> All shall give and take, mingle and be mingled in, none shall depart dejected
>
> From the shore of the sea of Bharata's Great Humanity!
>
> Come, O Aryans, come, non-Aryans, Hindus and Mussulmans-
>
> Come today, O Englishmen, come, oh come, Christians!
>
> Come, O Brahmin, cleansing your mind
>
> Join hands with all-
>
> Come, O Downtrodden, let the burden
>
> Of every insult be forever dispelled.
>
> Make haste and come to Mother's coronation, the vessel auspicious
>
> Is yet to be filled
>
> With the sacred water sanctified by the touch of all
>
> By the shore of the sea of Bharata's Great Humanity![40]

Here is clamour for togetherness, the concern for being together regardless of sociocultural and politico-ideological differences. *Bharat Tirtha* is a testimony to Tagore's heartfelt desire for uniting a nation that was disparate around many axes. There are perhaps two important sources of this idea: On the one hand, Tagore was heavily influenced by the Upanishadic vision of India as a compact sociocultural reality which degenerated over time by the rulers for fulfilling their partisan aims. It was also possible that he was equally disenchanted with the nationalist campaign that failed to create a common platform against a common foe. Besides Hindu–Muslim division which was an impediment for a united opposition against the British hegemony, Hindus

---

[39] Manish R. Chatterjee, '*Rabindranath Tagore: Sadha of Universal Man, Baul of Infinite Songs*', https://academic.udayton.edu/monishchatterjee/tagore/sadhaka.html.

[40] Translated from the original Bengali poem written by Rabindranath Tagore.

were also disparate politico-ideologically for socioculturally justified practices and mores. So, the poem was not merely a poetic creation but a powerful statement on social, cultural and economic divisions that pulled India down as a political compact, and also a scathing critique of the nationalists' failure to devise a design for togetherness. The politico-ideological was qualitatively different since neither Dwarkanath nor his son, Debendranath, confronted such a situation since the political opposition to the British rule did not appear to have acquired such massive proportions that Tagore witnessed. Seeking to fulfil their sociocultural objectives, the earlier Tagores were thus politico-ideologically conditioned differently. Their language of opposition had completely different nuances; they expressed their resentment mostly in a muted form when the colonial rule deviated from the well-established Enlightenment principles. By the time Rabindranath Tagore appeared on the public scene, the situation had undergone a sea change. His public opinion for political freedom from the alien rule ran counter to the mainstream nationalist voice. The most striking is that he held the same views when he espoused earlier while challenging those championing the goal for establishing India as an independent polity. Like his grandfather and father, he felt strongly that unless socially nurtured evil forces were completely eradicated, political freedom was futile. So, to realize freedom in its true spirit and connotation, it was required to develop a social compact which could hardly be crippled by partisan beliefs and preferences. The argument was most unambiguously made in his 1916 novel, *Ghare-Baire* (home and the world), where Nikhilesh, one of the main characters, stated that he believed that

> When you can't summon up the enthusiasm to serve the country by thinking of her merely as the country and its people as mere human beings, when you need to scream and shout out mantras and call her a goddess and go into a trance, then you love the craze more than you love your motherland. The need to place an obsession above Truth is an indication of our innate servility. When we set our minds free, we are no longer as strong. Unless we place an illusion, or an image or some framework of the establishment upon our listless consciousness as a rider, we cannot function. As long as we don't acquire a taste for the plain Truth, as long as we need such

an obsession, it is obvious that we haven't acquired the strength to receive our country in all the glory of freedom. Until then, whatever state we are in, either an imaginary spectre or a genuine presence, will continue to trouble us.[41]

The argument is loud and crystal clear. A mere statement makes no sense unless it is complemented by steadfast commitment and endeavour. The novel, *Ghare-Baire*, is a scathing critique of the Swadeshi Movement in Bengal (1905–1908) which the then Congress, especially its revolutionary nationalist wing, launched. Tagore was opposed to the campaign because it drew on violence and coercion: It resorted to violence to terrorize those who were reluctant to join and they also coerced the hapless poor Muslims to appreciate the bonfire of foreign clothes against their wishes since they were naturally reluctant as they were too poor to buy khadi which was comparatively expensive than foreign clothes. While unabashedly condemning the endeavour of the Swadeshi nationalists, Nikhilesh brought out very ambivalently his politico-ideological priorities in favour of nonviolence long before it was tested nationally at the behest of Gandhi in the second decade of the 20th century. As he elaborated, he had

> Always considered coercion to be a form of weakness. The weak man doesn't dare to judge fairly. He will avoid the responsibility of justice and arrive at his goal through unfair means. [Hence, he] will not use an excitement like Dutch-courage to do [his] duty for [his] country. [He'd] rather tolerate inefficiency than raise [his] hand against a servant. [his] very being balks at the thought of doing or saying something to someone in anger. [Since he was not] yelling 'Vande Mataram' and going around kicking up a ruckus ... [his restraint was castigated] as a form of feebleness and thus disrespectful.[42]

It is not just a statement but contains some of the foundational ideas that Tagore sincerely nurtured so long as he was an important

---

[41] Rabindranath Tagore, *Ghare-Baire* (Home and the World), translated in *The Classic Rabindranath Tagore* (New Delhi: Penguin, 2011), 689–690.
[42] Ibid., 689.

public figure in the nationalist era. Aware that his ideas did not have many takers in the context of the Swadeshi Movement in Bengal, he remained steadfastly committed to his belief which was manifested when Nikhilesh in the same novel melancholically expressed that

> Today [he] earned everyone's displeasure since [he has] not sat down with a glass of liquor in my country's honour. People think [that he was] either scared of police or [he was] angling for a title. The police think [that he was] masquerading as a good soul because [he has] other hidden agendas. Even so [he continued] on this road strewn with skepticism and humiliation.[43]

The novel *Ghare-Baire* is Tagore's own assessment of the inner debates that figured prominently among those participating in the Swadeshi Movement which was articulated in the mutual criticism between Nikhilesh who stood for constructive, rural work and also 'who [did] not see the country as an icon but as a land of very poor, exploited people' and Sandip, whose 'extremist rhetoric exalts the country as a Goddess and [who was] indifferent to the fate of the poor Muslims'.[44] Seeking to capture the complexities of the Swadeshi campaign, Rabindranath laid out foundational ideas which became part and parcel of his ideological predilections. Instead of being confined to Calcutta and main *mofussil* towns, he evolved a new genre of politics which was a sharp critique of the old-style politics 'trying in vain to placate the foreign ruler and talking big in a foreign tongue'.[45] Contrarily, he urged, as the novel underlined, that the volunteers should 'go to the villages instead, spreading social and political enlightenment in the melas and through magic lantern lectures; and, above all, [they should] try to revive our traditional Samaj, channelling all constructive work through it once again'.[46] As is evident, being terribly upset when he saw the hapless subjects in his zamindari estate, it was possible that he said what he wanted to say through Nikhilesh. His constructive work and

---

[43] Ibid.
[44] Sumit Sarkar, *The Swadeshi Movement in Bengal, 1903–1908* (new edition, New Delhi: Permanent Black, 2010), xxiii.
[45] Ibid., 45
[46] Ibid.

benevolent attitude towards his subjects were based on his humanitarian concern for those who were required to be helped; in that context, it was admirable though, like any of the zamindars who survived and also flourished on rentier income, his model did not however address the problems that emanated from the exploitative agrarian relations that alienated the tiller of the soil from the landlords.

The novel is therefore a clearly written statement of the ideas that evolved and also the texture of the Swadeshi campaign which finally forced the British government to revoke the first partition of Bengal. Being emotionally involved with the demand for rescinding partition, Rabindranath wrote extensively to openly support the campaign. The dialogical interaction between Nikhilesh and Sandip, despite having completely contrasting views on the movement, helps us understand the nature of the campaign which also manifested a constant ideological battle among the nationalists on the basis of their varied political viewpoints. As historians have shown, there were three trends in the Swadeshi Movement in Bengal: First, the Moderate tradition, of which Surendranath Banerjee was the chief priest. The aim of the Moderates was to attain swaraj but only through constitutional means. In his *A Nation in Making,* Banerjee thus wrote

> We religiously avoided unconstitutional methods and the wild hysterics that breed and stimulate them. Even when attacked by the police, we did not retaliate and then appealed to the court of law for redress.... Soul-force we believed in, but ... it could be employed to any useful or national purpose ... by men trained in the practice of self-restraint and the discipline of public life.[47]

With confidence in the three Ps (petition, prayer and protest), the Moderates believed in peaceful methods of protest as they believed that it was the best means to win concession from British rule. It should not be forgotten that their aim was to persuade the rulers to grant concession and under no circumstances they accepted any political campaign which deviated from what they strongly believed. Aghast

---

[47] Surendranath Banerjee, *A Nation in Making: Being the Reminiscences of Fifty Years of Public Life* (London: Humphrey Milford, 1925), 286.

on the rapidly changing nature of the Swadeshi campaign, Banerjee resented by saying that

> What a deterioration in the public life of the province, when mendicancy and malice are the weapons, offensive and defensive, employed by those who call themselves the apostles of self-government and promise *Swaraj* to their countrymen! Swaraj means self-restraint which is now a distant goal … it means, as now employed by a certain class of people, license to use the meanest of mean tricks for the furtherance of their ends. If this is what we are to have in the green, what may we not expect in the dry?[48]

Despite being severely critical, the Swadeshi Movement was a source of inspiration that did not escape Banerjee's notice. It ushered in an era of significant 'transformation of public feeling and of the wild excitement which must precede a revolutionary movement'.[49] According to him, it was manifested in 'the new ideals and the new methods [that] moved the people, and imparted to them an impulse that bore fruit in the manifold activities of an awakened national life'.[50] Ideologically, the Swadeshi Movement was not just a campaign for reversal of the partition of Bengal, it was synchronous with, argued Banerjee, 'the national awakening which the [Swadeshi Movement] in Bengal had created'.[51] Based on Banerjee's assessment, it can safely be argued that the Swadeshi Movement was the culmination of a series of campaigns against the misrule of the British government. While Surendranath was a constitutionalist, his detractors, the revolutionary nationalists, or the Extremists in the conventional historiographical parlance, endorsed militant means to fulfil their ideological goals. In contrast with constitutionalism of the Moderates, the revolutionary nationalists exhorted, as their mouthpiece, the *Hitabrata*, underlined, that 'the blood of the innocent will be washed by the blood of white oppressors. How long will the people of this country have more patience? The English have lost the confidence of

---

[48] Ibid., 125–126.
[49] Ibid., 197.
[50] Ibid., 198.
[51] Ibid., 197.

the people, soon they will also lose their Empire'.[52] Besides politico-ideological attacks on the British Empire, the nationalists, both the Moderates and revolutionary nationalists, insisted on being self-reliant especially in fulfilling the basic economic needs to develop *atmashakti* or inner strength. While being appreciative of this aspect of the Movement, Tagore characterized the endeavour as 'a more definite call to turn away from conventional old-style politics to build up our own strength through constructive economic and education work—*swadeshi* and national education'.[53] The Swadeshi Movement can thus be acclaimed to have set in motion politico-ideological processes that became integral to the nationalist campaign in the days to come, especially during the phase when Gandhi became the most widely acceptable leader. By changing the nationalist vocabulary, the Moderates and their detractors, revolutionary nationalists, were also most innovative while articulating their oppositional voices: On the one hand, the Moderates, by unconditionally supporting the constitutional form of governance, created an ambience for its growth in India which helped build a constitutional government even after decolonization in 1947; by drawing inspiration from India's ancient texts, the revolutionary nationalists, on the other hand, inspired their followers to understand them as well to devise a more effective mode for mobilizing people for the nationalist cause.

Unlike the earlier Tagores, Rabindranath was nurtured in a politico-ideological environment when the British Raj was vehemently challenged. The Swadeshi Movement was perhaps one of the first effective counterattacks that the nationalists had organized, which was succeeded by many as history progressed. A perusal of his creative texts, including novels, plays and other written tracts, suggests that Rabindranath's unique approach to humanity was also heavily influenced by the prevalent socio-economic and political contexts. As a zamindar, he was, unlike his father, far more sensitive to the causes of the tillers of the soil. In an essay, published in *Bharati* in 1898, entitled

---

[52] *The Hitabrata*, 29 April 1906, cited in Argov, *Moderates and Extremists*, 116.
[53] Rabindranath Tagore, '*Bangabhibhag*', 1904, cited in Tagore, *Rabindra Rachanabali*, Vol. 3 (Calcutta: West Bengal Government, 1983).

'Mukhojje-Barrujje' (Mukherjee versus Banerjee),[54] he attributed the alienation of the subjects from the zamindars to their indifferent attitude to those who contributed to their wealth. The exploitative zamindars remained a cynosure of the subjects because the former were hardly forthcoming when the latter suffered. To bridge the gulf between the zamindars and his lower-caste subjects, he undertook many steps since he believed that the social distance was at the roots of this schism. When he was to be formally declared a zamindar in Silaidaha in 1891, he decided to not attend the ceremony because those who belonged to lower castes were not allowed to sit along with the upper castes. The officials of the estate were reluctant to accept the order since they justified their stance by saying that the priests could not be persuaded to which Tagore agreed to go ahead without them. It was unprecedented because he invited his Muslims and Hindu subjects regardless of their caste to sit together on this occasion. While defending his stance in this regard, he argues that it was a festival of 'togetherness and so long as the division on the basis of religion and caste persisted the aim shall remain elusive'.[55] Furthermore, he took ample care of these hapless villagers who, being poverty-stricken, had hardly had two proper meals a day. In his letter to Indira Devi, his niece, he thus wrote that 'he felt miserable because he was appalled by the terrible suffering and hardships that his *prajas* were subject to largely due to the exploitative officials who privileged their partisan gain over what they were expected to do while discharging their duties on his behalf'.[56] Although he initiated many welfare measures, it was not an easy task at the outset because his officials always tried to befool him by insisting that for running the administration in the estate one needed to be respectful to the precedents; being opposed to the conventional mode of governance, Tagore was not persuaded by the argument which again led to skirmishes with those associated with the administration though, in a short period of time, Tagore,

---

[54] Rabindranath Tagore, 'Mukhojje bonam Barujje (Mukherjee versus Banerjee), cited in Amitava Chaudhuri, ed., *Zamindar Rabindranath* (Kolkata: Visva-Bharati Granthan Bhibhag, 1976), 18–19.

[55] The address by Rabindranath is quoted in ibid., 41.

[56] Rabindranath to Indira Devi, cited in Chaudhuri, *Zamindar Rabindranath*, 83.

by learning the new techniques of managing the estate, did not allow them to prevail over him. It was a battle between him and his officials, which however he won rather comfortably. Needless to say, he now became far more confident as a zamindar.[57] Along with his heartfelt desire to support the hapless and exploited section of the subjects, he also devoted his energy to develop a sense of concern, care and empathy for others. Disgusted with the complaint that the maintenance of a road in the zamindari estate would help people in the neighbouring estates, Tagore realized that it was linked with the selfish mindset that was neither humane nor sensitive to the basic concerns of humanity.[58] These instances show that Tagore endeavoured hard to create a milieu in which a sense of community and also belongingness emerged. Appreciating his initiatives, the district magistrate of Rajshahi, L. S. S. O'Malley, wrote that

> It must not be imagined that a powerful landlord is always oppressive and uncharitable. A striking instance to the contrary is given in the Settlement's Officer's account of the estate of Rabindranath Tagore, the Bengali poet whose fame is world-wide. It is clear that to poetical genius he adds practical and beneficial ideas of estate management, which should be an example to the local zamindars.... Employees are expected to deal fairly with the raiyats and unpopularity earns dismissal.... Remissions of rent are granted when inability to pay is proved.[59]

The above description suggests that as a zamindar, Rabindranath was neither as brutal as his father, Debendranath, nor as lenient as his grandfather. His primary concern was to ensure the well-being of his *prajas* along with the desire to build a sense of belonging to a community regardless of caste, religion and wealth. A careful scan of the character, Nikhilesh in *Ghare-Baire*, reveals that Tagore provided a model to creatively blend these two objectives. He differed from his colleagues who, by following specific politico-ideological designs, alienated the Muslims, to a significant extent. Opposed to

---

[57] Chaudhuri, *Zamindar Rabindranath*, 76–77.
[58] Example cited in ibid., 79.
[59] The report is cited in ibid., 44–45.

Sandip's argument justifying the force that his colleagues applied to the poor Muslim *prajas* for accepting the bonfire of foreign clothes, Rabindranath stood his ground by saying that it was not possible for them to afford the expensive khadi clothes. What was thus required was to provide them with cheaper clothes to meaningfully execute the Swadeshi agenda. Application of force, instead of contributing to the cause, was sure to damage the objective that Sandip and compatriots sought to realize.

Basic to Rabindranath's concern was to undertake those social welfare activities that were humanly possible to accomplish. The situation was not however favourably disposed in view of the foreign rule and also lackadaisical attitude of those who while claiming for national freedom remained totally indifferent to the socially marginalized and economically dispossessed countrymen. Because he believed that 'the country is not just this land and soil but also the people who always remain neglected ... [and] why should they tolerate that'.[60] As an illustration, he narrated an anecdote on the basis of his experience of being part of the 1907 Pabna Conference of the Bengal Provincial Congress. He was disheartened because 'none of those who dominated the political arena in those days felt that the villagers belonged to this country'.[61] Rabindranath referred to a dialogue that he had with one of the leading Bengali politicians who dismissed his argument that for our political progress, 'the underdogs of our society must be helped to realize that they are also part of this country'.[62] For his utter contempt of the hapless villagers, Tagore realized that

> Our patriots had picked up their lesson from an imperfect study of ... history. One of the advantages of such a mentality is that it finds it easy to wail over foreign rule, to get heated about it, to write poems about and to run newspapers. But the moment one recognizes the vast multitude of his countrymen as his own people, in spite of their apparent insignificance, he cannot abdicate his

---

[60] Tagore, *Ghare-Baire*, translated in *Classic Rabindranath Tagore*, 734.
[61] Rabindranath Tagore, *Letters from Russia*, 28 April 1930 (Kolkata: Visva-Bharati, 1984), 19.
[62] Ibid.

responsibility towards them which is the one that he is habitually accustomed to ignore.[63]

This was perhaps the most clearly stated assessment of the political voice of the nationalists during the Swadeshi Movement. It was a voice of deceiving the countrymen though to remain politically correct, these nationalist watch dogs expressed their emotional attachment in their public statements, both verbally and in written forms. For Tagore, it was hypocrisy of the highest order which he detested from the core of his heart. Hence, instead of grand plans, Rabindranath always preferred to initiate projects which were easy to complete. As he said,

> I am unable to take care of the country as a whole; but it is within my capability to meaningfully address the socio-economic ills of two or three villages. With our hard work in which the villagers will also be involved, the villages will get what they don't have, so far, like schools, good sewage system and adequate medical care; once they work together, the villagers will also realize what they can accomplish if they remain together.[64]

The purpose was also clearly stated. As Tagore felt, the striking socio-economic developments in these adopted villages proved how togetherness with a will to work for all contributed to the rise of socio-economically self-sufficient villages. These examples were a source of inspiration for the rest of the country. Furthermore, he also underlined that mere financial aid was futile since once that amount was exhausted the poor became the same. Hence, he argued that 'Charity spoils the people since it cannot end their misery. [Since] the plight of the majority of the people is the same ... [one] ... cannot pour in money from the outside and make for the milk which isn't there'.[65]

How to banish misery from the country? Rabindranath had innovative plans: He was opposed to charity since it was hardly an effective

---

[63] Ibid., 19–20.
[64] Rabindranath's statement is cited in Amitava Chaudhuri, *Zamindar Rabindranath*, 20.
[65] Tagore, *Ghare-Baire*, translated in *Classic Rabindranath Tagore*, 724.

solution. He devised a plan for imparting skills to the villagers in pottery, carpentry, weaving and other handicrafts for which he prepared a group of those who acquiesced with his ideas and were entrusted with this task. Furthermore, he also chalked out a design of cultivation to avoid subinfeudation due to fragmentation of land. Based on his first-hand experiences, he thus suggested that 'let the peasants join their lands together and till them by machine plough'[66] which was readily accepted as a plan but soon lost its appeal since the peasants declined to come together presumably in view of well-entrenched sociocultural differences among themselves; the bard understood the situation, but was appalled because his effort failed to generate a sense of belongingness for a good cause. Nonetheless, the poet was hardly dissuaded and he devised other plans to translate his beliefs into reality. As mentioned below, his idea of bringing people together was articulated later through his conceptualization of cooperatives in the villages around Visva-Bharati which came into being in 1921. His primary objective was to unify the nation by approaching them in the language and also the festivals with which they were emotionally affiliated. What was thus required was to champion those ideas, values and customs which would help us build a community. It was possible with the organization of mela or country fair at regular intervals which provided a platform for various kinds of cultural performances and entertainments that

> [They] would have made people converse from great distances. There indigenous goods and agricultural implements would have been exhibited. There awards would have been given to the best minstrels, *Kirtan* [songs appreciating gods and goddesses] singers and *Jatra* [country drama] groups. There the common people could have been given instruction about basic hygiene with the help of magic lanterns etc., and all strata of people could have discussed in simple Bangla all that they have to say and all that they have to discuss about their weal and woe.[67]

[66] Tagore, *Letters from Russia*, 21–22.
[67] Rabindranath Tagore, *Swadeshi Samaj (in Bangla), 1904* (Kolkata: Visva-Bharati, 1908), 12.

This was an easy option to revive the idea of togetherness among the villagers because, as the bard justified,

> If you invite people to attend a political meeting they will come with misgivings, it will take time to open their hearts—but those who assemble for a Mela come with open minds, so this is an occasion when you can feel the heart of the nation. The day the villagers take a holiday putting away their ploughshare that is the day to come close to them.[68]

These melas were an occasion when the people from various parts of the region flock together without any rhymes or reasons. They enjoyed it since they were able to interact with people in an atmosphere of festivity. Thus, the bard stated that

> During the Mela, the villagers forget their narrowness [which] was a step to building a compact of humanity in which neither religion nor any other divisive indices work. Just like the monsoons that come and fill up the water bodies by bringing water from the sky, the Melas connect the villagers with the universe that remains so distant to them by being confined to the narrow social boundary of the village.[69]

As *Ghare-Baire* and other written tracts which were written at the backdrop of the Swadeshi Movement that witnessed the estrangement of the Muslims from their Hindu counterparts, Tagore also found melas to be a platform for erasing the communal animosity. Since people visited melas without prejudicial baggage, Rabindranath insisted that the educated youth should take this opportunity to persuade both the Hindus and Muslims the need for coming together to combat the separatist forces which, rather than contributing to the welfare of all, were likely to gain by dividing the communities by attributing the social ills and economic backwardness of one community vis-à-vis another due to different religious identity. Tagore thus suggested that to combat these divisive plans, what was needed

---

[68] Ibid., 13.
[69] Ibid., 12–13.

to be done was to 'remove the deficiencies leading to the suffering of the villagers due to the absence of schools, roads and potable water, and lack of adequate grazing ground for the domestic animals, such as cows, goats, etc.'[70] Only by being involved in social work, the villagers, regardless of their religion, joined hands together to create an ambience in which they understood the importance of being together in adverse circumstances. Besides mela's utility in bringing people together, it was also an effective mode for generating funds for the development of villages. Thus Tagore suggested that for organizing the melas where many sellers congregated to sell their products, the villagers, along with the zamindars, were required to create a fund with their contribution; those who sold products needed to donate a portion of their profit to the landlord which would be utilized for welfare activities of the villages within the specific zamindari estate.[71] In two ways, the melas therefore were avenues for disseminating indigenous cultural resources, on the one hand and in so doing, they also, on the other hand, kept people away from those cultural shows and events which were purposefully organized to undermine the local cultural traditions. Basic to his concern was a seriously pursued endeavour to bring people regardless of socio-economic and political distinctions together. Mela was one of those effective modes which was instinctive to the villagers' psyche that was likely to create oneness in the context of divisive social and political tendencies.

Concluding Observations

Rabindranath represented a uniquely textured mode of thinking which evolved out of his dialogical interaction with multiple sociocultural ideas, rooted in different civilizational traditions. It is thus not unfair to argue that the bard imbued what he felt appropriate to attain the goal that he set out for himself and for the country. In a nutshell, Rabindranath, by being open to ideas from multiple sources, carried forward the traditions that he inherited from his predecessors, Rammohun, Vidyasagar and his father, Debendranath, which he

[70] Ibid., 13.
[71] Ibid., 14.

clearly stated in his *Charitrapuja* published in 1908. As argued above, what was distinctive about the poet was his willingness to learn from the many good practices that he witnessed during his visits to various parts of the world. It is difficult to dwell on each and every aspect of his conceptualization in this section; what is thus attempted here is to highlight the principal point that Rabindranath wanted to put across in his manifold writings. There are three broad trends one sees in this thought process: First, he always believed that oppression by the ruling authority was likely to lead to violent eruption unless its sources were addressed meaningfully. This is an argument that he categorically stated in his letters from Russia. Part of his third letter of 25 September 1930 is worth citing. In a very eloquent manner, he thus made his point by saying that

> Once upon a time, the French Revolution was caused by the pressure of widespread inequality. The oppressed realized that the humiliation and misery of inequality were universal. Thus, it was during that revolution that the message of liberty, equality and fraternity was carried across the frontiers of France. But it did not endure. [After having visited Russia, he realized that] ... the revolutionary appeal is universal. In the world of today, the people of [Russia] at any rate are thinking of the interests of the whole of humanity, transcending all national interests.[72]

By referring to the French Revolution and also Russia's radical socio-economic transformation following the 1917 October Revolution, Rabindranath reinforced his own assessment of how people rebelled and under what circumstances. It was, for him, derivative of his study of both the revolutions. This argument does not seem to be novel; what was novel was his emphasis on the assumption that unless the oppressive system was done away with, revolution was inevitable because, he argued further,

> The important thing is that today suffering humanity has nobler vision of itself on the world stage than before, for in the past they saw themselves in isolation, they were unaware of their real power

---

[72] Tagore, *Letters from Russia*, 11–12.

and relying on Fate they endured everything. Today, even in their utter helplessness people conjure up the Kingdom of Heaven where oppression disappears and humiliation is no more. For this very reason, oppressed humanity is in revolt everywhere.[73]

Here, he pitched the argument at a different level: Critical of those who believed that being poor or oppressed was divinely ordained, he forcefully argued that it was created deliberately to protect partisan interests of the strong and also those who cunningly continued to befool a section of the demography for their narrow personal gain. This was also an articulation of Rabindranath's revolutionary self because he, by justifying that sustained oppression by the ruling class always led to revolution, perhaps warned the colonizers in India. The argument was further elaborated by him when he mentioned that oppression destroyed social harmony which was manifested in the increasing distance between the strong and weak. 'The flow of life in the social body', he adumbrated further, 'has been obstructed by division of society into masters and slaves, into those who enjoy and those who are deprived, leading to disease and anemic emaciation on the other. In all civilized societies today, the messenger of death finds entrée through this opening'.[74]

Also striking was the style in which the poet presented his ideas which were also applicable to colonized India. At his heart always remained the concern for the underprivileged who lacked the voice to pursue their socio-economic aims in opposition to the privileged. It is evident that there is a common pattern in how Rabindranath makes an argument based on his creative amalgamation of many philosophical discourses that he was privy to. The argument that historically oppression fuelled violent overthrow of the prevalent system of governance was repeated when he explained that 'in our country, the gate of [the messenger of death's] entrance seems opened wider than elsewhere which is an indication of how volatile the situation is'.[75] While an optimistic Rabindranath charted out a course of action for

[73] Ibid., 12–13.
[74] Ibid., 147.
[75] Ibid., 147–148.

the Indians, he was however equally uncertain when he realized that the Bengalis, being totally blindly imitative of the British culture, did not appear to be able to understand what he endeavoured to convey. He was astonished and aghast when he interacted with Bengalis in England who 'complain about their countrymen and culture to the English, which even an Anglo-Indian, who is fond of India, will not. The Bengali himself introduces the subject and then proceeds', argued the poet, 'to laugh at and also ridicule India's cultural ethos, among other things'.[76] Characterizing them as Indo-Bongos, Rabindranath made further caustic remarks by drawing upon a published essay in *Bharati* which his brother Satyendranath wrote. Reiterating the point that the poet mentioned, Satyendranath further clarified that once we reach the English shore, 'we lose our love for our own country and find our countrymen repulsive, calling them barbarians. All that is British is acceptable; whatever is Indian is worth discarding. Alas!'.[77] It is evident that Rabindranath was terribly disgusted. Nonetheless, he did not give up his effort to persuade them to imbibe those qualities which the Britishers nurtured over the years to rise as one of the most powerful nations in the world. Impressed by their willingness to work hard, the bard also mentioned that this desire was also visible in their 'mental universe', by which he meant the willingness and also the capability of being innovative in thinking; this was, as he further went on, at the roots of their success. To clarify his point, he drew an analogy with the speed in which electricity moved to explain how the human mind came up with new ideas as fast as the speed of electricity. In comparison, since we use the archaic lamps, made by mud, we tended to take so much time to light the lamp and there was hardly the hurry that we noticed among the Englishmen. By drawing upon this analogy, Rabindranath highlighted how our lackadaisical attitude was at the root of our decline and also at our failure to rejuvenate the moribund nation.[78]

---

[76] Rabindranath Tagore, *Letter from a Sojourner in Europe* (Kolkata: Visva-Bharati, 2008), 70.

[77] This essay by Satyendranath Tagore entitled 'Bharatvarshiya Ingraj' appeared in *Bharati* (in the year 1284 BS), reproduced in ibid., 76.

[78] This section is a summary of the arguments that Rabindranath offered in his *Pather Sanchay* (in Bangla; Kolkata: Visva-Bharati, 2008; reprint), 120–121.

What was unique was the poet's equal concern to understand Asian civilization. He visited China, Japan, Vietnam, Java, among others. He was persuaded to believe that there were many commonalities between India and these countries simply because they belonged to the same civilizational space. In one of his trips to China, by appreciating the Chinese 'as the most long-lived race, [derivative of] the wisdom nourished by the faith in goodness, not in mere brutal strength',[79] he thus declared that 'I speak of Asia because I am proud of our continent'.[80] This emphatic faith in being an Asian did not however make Rabindranath a xenophobic; he was always ready for a creative blending of ideas which were of help to human progress. It was very categorically stated in a speech that he delivered during his trip to Beijing in 1924, he emphatically declared that

> In Asia, we must unite, not through some mechanical method of organization, but through a spirit of true sympathy ... [and] there lies our strength. But it would be degradation on our part, and an insult to our ancestors, if we forget our own moral wealth of wisdom, which is of far greater value than a system that produces endless materials and a physical power that is always on the warpath.[81]

In this 1924 speech, the poet highlighted the importance of spiritual commitment to humanity which Chinese civilization had always upheld. Striking here is that he reiterated the same concern during his visit to Java in 1927. In a letter to his secretary, Amiya Chakravarty on 17 September 1927, besides appreciating the spiritual wealth of the Javanese, he was also impressed by the creative interpretation of Indian epics, *Ramayana* and *Mahabharata*, with reference to their own sociocultural ethos. He thus referred to

---

[79] Rabindranath Tagore, *Talks in China*, compiled by Sisir Kumar Das, ed., *The English Writings of Rabindranath Tagore* (Kolkata: Rabindra Bhavana, Visva-Bharati, 1999; reprint), 55.
[80] Ibid.
[81] Ibid., 51–52.

The living way in which [these epics] have entered into their lives [which clearly shows that], instead of being mere replica, [these texts] ... have taken new forms in their progress through these people's own age-long ideas and imaginings, by the constant use that has been made of them for the purposes of their daily life. Their ethical conceptions have not been received as a ready-made whole from some scripture, but have become incarnate, as it were, in the epic characters who have come to represent for them the standard of excellence or of degradation.[82]

Implicit here are two important ideas that figured prominently in Rabindranath's approach to humanity: On the one hand, he never wavered while arguing for Hindu civilizational ethos being eternal which was manifested in the characterization of Hinduism as a *Sanatani Dharma*. As his visit to Java confirms, 'the Hindu traditions are still a reality and even the Moslem invasion and the adoption of that agate-like religion could not obliterate their inherited cultural tradition'.[83] This further affirms, on the other hand, the adaptability of Hinduism as a civilizational ethos which also flourished in different forms in various parts of Asia where Hindus travelled. One is also persuaded to argue that for Rabindranath, Hinduism was a not an institutionalized religion as Islam or Christianity but a way of life that flourished in accordance with the prevalent sociocultural and economic milieu. Fundamental here is the point that unlike religious zealots, the ideas of the last of the Tagore patriarchs can never be conceptualized in a neat format given the nuanced ways they unfolded. It was reinforced quite unambiguously when, to him, Hinduism represented a mode of living which was organically linked with the surrounding sociocultural and economic realities.

Being spiritually strongly grounded in his own sociocultural roots, Rabindranath truly remained an apostle of renaissance which means that he was never blind to the importance of values and traditions that built civilizations of various kinds. We must add a caveat here because

---

[82] Rabindranath Tagore, *Letter from Java* (Kolkata: Visva-Bharati, 2010), 116.
[83] Rabindranath to (most probably) J. K. Birla, 16 September 1928, reproduced in ibid., 228.

the bard was never hesitant in raising voice against a civilizational faith that appeared to have harmed humanity. For instance, at one level, he appreciated Wester science because it 'gives us power of reason, enabling us to be actively conscious of the worth of our own ideals'.[84] At another level, he hardly restrained himself when he condemned the devilish power of machine which 'is ready to smite and devour us, for which we must be rescued by that living power of spirit which grows into strength, not through mere addition, but through organic assimilation'.[85] It was based on his belief that

> No one nation today can progress if others are left outside its boundaries. Let us try to win the heart of the West with all that is best, and not base in us, and think of her and deal with her, not in revenge or contempt, but with goodwill and understanding in a spirit of mutual respect.[86]

Instead of appreciating the claim, live and let live, Rabindranath's sociocultural approach to humanity was based on accommodation of diverse civilizational essences and values based on mutual respect. It was possible for him because he not only was respectful to the non-indigenous intellectual traditions but also had devoted his energy to champion what he so sincerely believed. An organic intellectual par excellence, the poet thus evolved a model that, by drawing sustenance from both the derivative traditions of the West and also Asia, created a new genre of thinking on the basis of his own creative assessment. There is no denying that in espousing the Vedantic texts as sources of knowledge and wisdom, Rabindranath carried forward the tradition that developed first with Dwarkanath's concern for unearthing the indigenous intellectual resources, especially from Upanishads, and later with his father, Debendranath, who completely immersed in his drive for popularizing the Vedantic texts. This is one side of the story. The other side is manifested in the poet's own search for

---

[84] Rabindranath Tagore, *Talks in China*, compiled by Sisir Kumar Das, ed., *The English Writings of Rabindranath Tagore* (Kolkata: Rabindra Bhavana, Visva-Bharati, 1999; reprint), 52.

[85] Ibid., 51.

[86] Ibid., 52.

knowledge in the Western philosophical discourses that was accompanied simultaneously by his steadfast commitment to explore the Asian discourses. As a result, it was possible for Rabindranath to generate a mode of thinking which, despite being based on familiar derivative philosophical premises, was hardly imitative, but an innovative design of conceptualizing humanity and human needs in a new perspective.

Chapter 6

Deriding 'Nationalism'

Unlike his father, Rabindranath Tagore was raised in an environment when India's freedom struggle was no longer confined to the metropolitan cities of Calcutta and Bombay but had its tentacles spread across the country. Especially by the end of the 19th century, the Indian National Congress, founded in 1885, can be said to have prepared the ground for the nationalist struggle to strike roots in areas beyond the cities and towns. A witness to the rapidly changing texture of the nationalist counter to the British rule, Rabindranath also responded to the anti-British struggle in his own fashion. One of the most clearly articulated responses was his novel *Ghare-Baire*, published in 1916, which was based on the poet's own assessment of the Congress-led nationalist campaign. Rabindranath was not swayed by the Congress workers who opted for violence and also specific designs for political mobilization that alienated the Muslims who were demographically preponderant in Bengal. As mentioned in Chapter 5, the verbal dwell between Nikhilesh and Sandip, who ideologically differed from each other, clearly demonstrated that Rabindranath was neither for coercion nor for pursuing those policies harming the poor Muslims. For instance, Rabindranath was opposed to bonfire of foreign clothes since they were cheaper than the homespun Khadi; asking the poor Muslims to support the Congress in this regard was based on the lack of concern for them which later became an important reason for them to leave Congress and join the Muslim League, founded in 1906. Rabindranath wrote many critical essays in favour of his views which did not augur well with those who dominated the Congress leadership. That his assessment was correct became true as the nationalist campaign progressed. The visible bias against the Muslims by the Congress was responsible for their growing estrangement from the mainstream nationalist campaign. The most revealing was his sustained attack against the religious schism between Hindus and Muslims. Published in 1910, the novel *Gora* is another example where the bard graphically illustrated the development of a hardcore Hindu mindset as detrimental to the nation comprising diverse religious communities. Basic here is the point that Rabindranath felt the need of combatting religious-cum-social prejudices against Muslims, especially in Bengal where they constituted a majority.

With the arrival of Gandhi on India's political scene, Rabindranath's views on the nationalist campaign had undergone a sea change. Despite being critical of Gandhi's clinging of *Sanatani* Hinduism, he also admired the Mahatma for his capability of bringing people together cutting across sociocultural boundaries from all over the country. It was possible for him because his campaign besides an endeavour for political freedom was also an attack against those who amassed wealth at the cost of the poor. His effort was also directed against the artificial caste segregation, which subjected those belonging to the lower castes, especially Dalits.

One thus notices two compatible visions in Rabindranath's approach to nationalism. One must note a caveat here because he was opposed to the Western conceptualization of nation, nationalism and national identity that tended to view humanity by totalizing one's identity in exclusive terms around the religious, linguistic and cultural axes. *Ghare-Baire* represents his clearly articulated views on why he was unable to appreciate the nationalist mobilization by the revolutionary nationalists just because it was out-and-out sectarian. Part of the *Gora* was devoted to demonstrating how Hindu–Muslim amity was essential for human liberation in India which also means that for Rabindranath mere political freedom was not adequate to achieve his humanistic mission. Nonetheless, his support for Gandhi as one who succeeded in mobilizing people irrespective of sociocultural chasms was based on his belief that the goal was likely to be achieved under the Mahatma's stewardship of the freedom struggle.

In view of Rabindranath's concern for the nature of nationalist political mobilization, this chapter pursues two major and one minor arguments. The major arguments hinge on the poet's clear assessment of the nationalist struggle that evolved first at the aegis of the revolutionary nationalists in the late 19th and early 20th centuries and later under Gandhi's care. The minor argument is made with reference to Rabindranath's appreciation for the ideas that were not exactly anti-Gandhi but had elements of sociocultural thrusts against the Mahatma. More specifically, this is an argument that evolves out the bard's personal concern for Subhas Chandra Bose who was thrown out of the Congress because of his disagreement with Gandhi and his hardcore disciples. We must also underline the contention that Rabindranath, despite being an important player in the nationalist mobilization, was not, at all, a nationalist in its European sense; he was a patriot par excellence. His writings are illustrative here. By highlighting critical sociocultural issues, Rabindranath brought into the nationalist thinking those concerns that did not appear to have received adequate attention as Gandhi believed that since Swaraj or political freedom was a prelude to radical sociocultural transformations, there was no need to deal with them then. Except B. R. Ambedkar, none of those associated with the campaign for removing the British realized the importance of effectively dealing with sociocultural concerns. That what Rabindranath felt became true was evident in India's post-colonial history. Instead of being socioculturally deviant, division around caste and religious identity continues to remain as critical to democratic India as it was in the nationalist phase.

A Gandhian Rabindranath

At one level, Rabindranath was truly a Gandhian since he endorsed many of the politico-ideological methods that he deployed to develop a strong anti-British campaign. At another level, he was a reluctant Gandhian because he, with different views, did not openly support though he never ventilated them in public presumably to not weaken the political battle that he had waged for freedom from colonial rule. And, yet, at another level, he was just opposed to Gandhi since he was not persuaded to accept the Gandhian mode of thinking as it was contrary to logic and bordered on superstitious beliefs. There were three Rabindranath as far as his assessment of Gandhi was concerned.

Basic here is the argument that Tagore endorsed and criticized the Gandhian ideals on the basis of his conceptual universe. His support for Gandhi drew on the latter's concern for creating a self-reliant nation which did not appear to be an easy task given the age-old habit of the Indians of abdicating responsibility by resorting to many excuses. While elaborating his viewpoint, he thus mentioned that

> The habit of dependence has come down to us from time immemorial. In the olden days, one rich man used to be the mainstay of the village and its guide. Health, education and all else were his responsibility. [As a result], the common man's capacity for self-reliance was enfeebled.[1]

This was one of the crippling features that weakened communities and created conditions in which the zeal for being self-reliant was always missing. In his *Swadeshi Samaj* (1904), the bard devised many designs to generate the concerns for self-dependence for fulfilling the basic economic needs. What complemented such a lack of interest in becoming self-reliant was also the selfishness of the villagers in withdrawing from activities for others' well-being or comfort. To illustrate his point, Rabindranath referred to an exchange that he had with the villagers of Silaidaha who declined to take the responsibility of maintaining a road since it also benefited the villagers from the adjoining villages. In response to the poet's request to them for shouldering the maintenance of the road, the villagers replied that because it was going to help the gentlefolk of Kushtia, 'they would rather put up with the inconveniences [as] … they could not bear the thought

---

[1] Rabindranath Tagore, 'City and Village', reproduced in Rabindranath Tagore, *Towards Universal Man* (Bombay: Asia Publishing House, 1962; reprint), 319–320.

that other should also enjoy the fruits of their labour'.[2] Furthermore, like Gandhi, he also held that India's 'real problem is not political, but social'.[3] Persuaded by Gandhi's campaign for eradication of social inequalities and mutual distrust and hatred, Tagore evolved a specific mode of action and behaviour which he articulated in his appeal to the countrymen by saying that

> They must not delay a moment effectively to prove that they are in earnest to eradicate from their neighbourhood untouchability in all its ramifications. The movement should be universal and immediate, its expressions clear and indubitable. All manner of humiliation and disabilities from which any class in India suffers should be removed by heroic efforts and self-sacrifice.[4]

What brought Rabindranath closer to Gandhi was his emotional bond on the basis of the latter's willingness to undergo suffering for humanity. What caught even his arch enemies by surprise was his determination to win them over by happily being subject to physical torture and unbearable pain which means, wrote Rabindranath, that 'he realized his mission not by the application of coercive force but by selfless sacrifice for a cause'.[5] Despite being a great political leader capable of organizing millions of Indians for the cause of freedom from the British rule, the poet also strongly believed that 'as a moral reformer [Gandhi stands out] because none of his other activities limits his humanity; rather, they are inspired and sustained by it'.[6] It is striking to note that the poet too confidently argued that none of the reforms that Gandhi initiated was new; they all were 'proposed and preached by his predecessors and contemporaries'. By being curt in his remarks, he further underlined that

[2] Ibid., 320.
[3] Rabindranath Tagore, 'Nationalism in India', reproduced in Rabindranath Tagore, *Nationalism* (Madras: Macmillan, 1985; reprint), 58.
[4] Rabindranath Tagore's appeal to the countrymen, 22 September 1932, reproduced in Das, *The English Writings of Rabindranath Tagore*, Vol. 3, 328.
[5] Rabindranath Tagore, *Mahatma Gandhi* (in Bangla; Kolkata: Visva-Bharati, 1998), 45.
[6] Rabindranath Tagore, 'Gandhi the Man', in Ghosh, ed., *The English Writings of Rabindranath Tagore*, Vol. 4, 458.

> Long before the Congress adopted them, I had myself preached and written about the necessity of a constructive programme of rural; reconstruction in India; of handicrafts as an essential element in the education of our children ... which will be of help in giving them a skill and also a source of livelihood; of the absolute necessity of ridding Hinduism of the nightmare of untouchability.[7]

Nonetheless, he also admitted that his ideas never became as powerful as they were when Gandhi adopted them which he articulated by stating that

> They have never had the same energizing power in them as when [Gandhi] took them up; for now, they are quickened by the great life-force of the complete man who is absolutely one with his ideas, whose visions perfectly blend with his whole being.... His emphasis on the truth and purity of the means from which he has evolved his creed of nonviolence, is but another aspect of his deep and insistent humanity; for he insists that men in their fight for their claims must only so assert their rights, whether as individuals or as groups, as never to violate their fundamental obligations to humanity, which is to respect life.[8]

Implicit here are three core points of Gandhi's sociopolitical ideas: First, the Mahatma was concerned with absolute equality which means that he was not agreeable to the artificial segmentation among human beings. It is not thus surprising that he raised his voice against caste discrimination and also schism around religious axis. The second point that Tagore highlighted was Gandhi's concern for nonviolence which the former emphasized again and again in his speeches and creative writings. His novel, *Rajarshi*, which he also transformed into a play with the title, *Visarjan* (sacrifice), and also *Prayaschitta* (atonement) are illustrative here. Finally, according to Tagore, it was the Mahatma who taught us that we should fight for our rights; or, in other words, he conveyed the need for being self-reliant which Tagore also strongly felt and was explicit in his 1904 tract *Swadeshi Samaj*.

[7] Ibid., 458–459.
[8] Ibid., 459.

The views that both Gandhi and Rabindranath held are almost identical. The reasons are not difficult to find out since both of them were inspired by the core values of the Enlightenment philosophy. Baptized in the Enlightenment philosophy of the British variety, Gandhi was unable to appreciate the brutal colonial rule in India which neither upheld the Enlightenment values nor drew sustenance from the ideational university that it espoused to create. A study of Gandhi's texts also reveals the racist regime in South Africa was hardly different in this regard which confirmed his view that colonizers behaved alike vis-à-vis the colonized. In South Africa, despite being the citizens of the Empire, the Indians were subject to discrimination, presumably because they came from colonial India. Fundamental here is the point that colonialism is bound to be exploitative, otherwise the primary objective of colonialism of enriching one section of humanity at the cost of the other remained unfulfilled. Many studies substantiate this observation. Long before Gandhi confronted the British rule, it was Dadabhai Naoroji who, in his *Poverty and Un-British rule in India* (1901), argued similarly that the deviation from the core values of the Enlightenment resulted in the creation of a system of governance which violated them at the slightest pretext. Following this line of thinking, Gandhi too provided a scathing critique of the British rule in India because of its failure to govern India by being true to these core principles which insisted on creating 'sameness' in humanity. Rabindranath was akin to the Mahatma in so far as his ideological faith was concerned. By being born and raised in a 'cosmopolitan' family, he was exposed to the British philosophical traditions, including the Enlightenment values. It does not therefore seem odd to argue that Tagore, by being influenced by the derivative Western traditions as well, articulated his thoughts accordingly. He was thus not hesitant to suggest that following the onset of the British rule in India,

> The increased facilities of communication and exchange of thought, the teachings of history, the unity of government, the rise of literature and the efforts of the Congress over a period of time have together begun to make us realize that we belong to one country and are one people; that whether in joy or in sorrow, our destiny is

one; and that we cannot prosper unless we discover the ties which make us one, and seek to strengthen them.[9]

This was a great thing to have happened, Tagore admitted. Core to his belief was the idea that 'oneness' was required to accomplish the socio-economic and political objectives that we strove to attain. By being convinced that the British rule was one of the critical factors in bringing socioculturally disparate people together by means, of course, of coercion and also the free flow of Enlightenment ideas in support of conceptualizing humanity as one. He thus hardly wavered when he declared that

> The consciousness of Indians being one has been growing in us, but it has till now been intermittent and an object of intellectual awareness alone. Because we did not realize this truth with our whole being, we were not able to put our heart into our endeavours or to serve the country with the dedication she demands.[10]

There are two levels at which this argument can be pitched: At the conceptual level, Tagore unhesitatingly admitted that the idea that only through unity, the concern for the collectivity was formed and consolidated which, however, remained elusive given the well-entrenched division around caste, class and religious axes. At a mundane level, there was an implicit hope that only through a sustained endeavour it was possible to accomplish. The earlier it was realized the better for the Indians because

> The habit of submitting to conditions into which one is born as predestined and inevitable is the strongest link in the chain of our political servitude. However, our contact with Europe has awakened us to the universal laws of cause and effect; and it has given us a set of values against which scriptural dispensation and age-old convention disclaim in vain.[11]

---

[9] Rabindranath Tagore, 'Presidential Address, Bengal Provincial Congress, 1908', reproduced in Rabindranath Tagore, *Towards Universal Man*, 110–111.
[10] Ibid., 111.
[11] Ibid., 346.

Given his faith in the philosophical priorities on which the British society rested, Tagore reinforced the argument of early nationalists, including Dadabhai Naoroji, Gopal Krishna Gokhale, Surendranath Banerjee, among others, which also reverberated in Gandhi at the outset of his political career. It was therefore not surprising that Tagore, while being critical of 'the British conqueror', was not hesitant to admit that 'there was also a vast faith in the British character. How else could we have', the poet further underlined, 'come to the conviction that on grounds of human decency we could demand equal partnership in India's administration'?[12] These statements confirm that Tagore and Gandhi thought alike in some of the major social issues and also the contribution of the British rule in evolving those sets of ideas that helped Indians challenge the archaic and customary values and ideas. One of the reasons was certainly the fact that they were products of the same socio-economic and cultural milieu that unfolded with the beginning of the British rule in India. Furthermore, their regular intellectual exposure to the progressive British ideals emanating from the Enlightenment philosophy consolidated their belief in liberal sociocultural values. In a nutshell, the Tagore–Gandhi bonhomie was based on their identical ideological priorities which were both context-driven and also inspired by the indigenous intellectual traditions. It therefore does not seem odd to argue that they joined hands in combatting those age-old divisive sociocultural values which, by creating and sustaining artificial segregation in the society, did not allow the Indians to come together regardless of their primordial loyalties to caste, religion and ethnicity. Being unanimous in condemning the nationalist design of homogenizing the socioculturally diverse people, both Tagore and Gandhi developed a sharp critique of nationalism which, by creating conditions for the growth of homogenized universalism, generated forces for social uprootedness and deculturation. Contrary to the derivative idea of nationalism that tends to homogenize human identity, both the bard and Mahatma reconceptualized the phenomenon with reference to India's contextual peculiarity. The emotional affinity was, according to him, an outcome of being integrally with those

[12] Ibid., 347.

civilizational values in which sociocultural diversities were hardly undermined; instead, they were upheld to sustain the underlying unity among the Indians located in various parts of the country. It confirms the argument that given their temperamental attachment with universal humanism, it was perhaps easier for them to articulate their approach to 'national unity' accordingly. For them, nation did not mean essentialization of one's identity but a form of togetherness by being appreciative of inherent diversity among those inhabiting a specific location which further means that their viewpoints were context-driven.

The Un-Gandhian Tagore

Despite being persuaded by Gandhi's approach to nationalism, Tagore did not, on many occasions, toe his line of thinking since it was contrary to many politico-ideological preferences that the former upheld while leading the mainstream nationalist campaign against the British. As he argued in his *Ghare-Baire* (home and the world), published in 1916, he never supported the Swadeshi campaign (1905–1908) since it, instead of cementing a bond among the Hindus and Muslims in Bengal, created a fissure among them which gradually became unbridgeable and thus politically weakened the future nationalist campaign. A careful study of the Gandhian onslaught on the British reveals that it had two complementary aspects: The acts of omission and those of commission. Tagore was persuaded by neither. As is well known, the Gandhian Non-cooperation Movement had both elements of omission (withdrawal) and commission (actively disobeying). By giving a call to withdraw from the schools, colleges and other places of learning imparting English education, Gandhi's strategy can be defined as an act of omission while insisting on burning foreign clothes was an act of commission. Being in disagreement with these twofold strategies, Tagore completely dissociated him from the Non-cooperation Movement. Unable to appreciate the strategies since it was neither an aid towards consolidating unity among the Indians nor was conducive to its growth, he condemned the campaign, especially the decision to undertake 'bonfire of foreign clothes' when the homespun was beyond the reach of the poor. While defending his argument in opposition to the Mahatma's endorsement of this strategy, the bard thus said,

> The clothes to be burnt are not mine, but belong to those who most sorely need them. If those who are going naked should have given us the mandate to burn, it would, at least, have been a case of self-immolation and the crime of incendiarism would not lie at our door. But how can we expiate the sin of the forcible destruction of clothes which might have gone to women whose nakedness is actually keeping them prisoners unable to stir out of the privacy of their homes?[13]

In a similar vein, he critically evaluated the clamour for withdrawal from schools and colleges as suicidal to the Indian youths. It was a wrong strategy since the alternative that the nationalists were involved in developing by evolving an indigenous system of education was still in its embryonic stage. Under these circumstances, the call for boycotting English education was not, at all, a judicious step, argued Tagore. A believer in praxis, Rabindranath criticized the Mahatma as sternly as possible to not humiliate him but to place before him the arguments that he evolved to defend his unique perspective. He addressed the issue at two levels: At the conceptual level, he argued that in the absence of an alternative pedagogical mode of articulation, English education advanced without being opposed in a meaningful way. In other words, had the nationalists paid attention to the development of a system of education in which indigenous knowledge had also had a pace, the situation would have been different. Hence, he argued that

> What has caused the mischief is the fact that for a long time we have been out of touch with our own culture and therefore the Western culture has not found its perspective in our life very often and found a wrong perspective giving our mental eye a squint.[14]

---

[13] Rabindranath Tagore, 'The Call of Truth', reproduced in Sabyasachi Bhattacharya (compiled and edited), *The Mahatma and the Poet: Letters and Debates between Gandhi and Tagore, 1915–1941* (New Delhi: National Book Trust, 1997), 83–84.

[14] Rabindranath Tagore, 'Reflections on Noncooperation and Cooperation, Modern Review, May 1921', reproduced in reproduced in Bhattacharya, *The Mahatma and the Poet*, 58, 62.

The points of differences between Tagore and Gandhi developed two contrasting approaches to the Non-cooperation campaign; according to Tagore, it was politically ill-considered to expect that the non-cooperation as a strategy was likely to strengthen the nationalist bond while Gandhi always believed that it was Tagore's misconception about the nationalist mood that evolved in the wake of the campaign. There was thus hardly a common ground in this regard between them. Although the poet stuck to this point since it was an outcome of his firm belief; he also expressed his agony when he mentioned that

> It is extremely distasteful to me to have to differ from Mahatma Gandhi in regard to any matter of principle of method. Not that, from a higher standpoint, there is anything wrong in so doing but my heart shrinks from it. For what could be a greater joy than to join hands in the field of work with one for whom one has such love and reverence?[15]

As mentioned above, it was painful for the poet to divaricate from what Gandhi stood for though he hardly wavered since it was based on his well-thought-out views. He thus justified that his 'conscience cannot accept the Mahatma's field of work as own. That is a regret which will abide with me always. It is, however, God's will that man's path of endeavour shall be various, else why these differences of mentality?[16]

His stern opposition to Gandhi's cult of *charkha* was drawn on his belief that it was not adequate to achieve that the latter had especially in the context of colonial rule which was a deterrent for the Indians to become self-dependent, and also the inability to compete with the machine-produced clothes by the khadi. In other words, since the *charkha* was not a viable substitute, Gandhi, as Tagore strongly felt, was following a wrong strategy. He thus unambiguously stated that

> How often have my personal feelings of regard strongly urged me to accept at Mahatma Gandhi's hands my enlistment as a

---

[15] Rabindranath Tagore, 'The Cult of Charkha', reproduced by Das, *The English Writings of Rabindranath Tagore*, Vol. 3, 547.
[16] Ibid.

follower of the *charkha* cult, but as often have my reason and conscience restrained me, lest I should be a party to the raising of the charkha to a higher place that is its due, thereby distracting attention from other more important factor in our task of all-round reconstruction.[17]

Noticeable here are the respectable ways in which the poet articulated his differences with the Mahatma. He hardly fumbled when he critically evaluated the impact of *charkha* on India's socio-economic regeneration though he firmly stated that it was not possible for him to endorse Gandhi's path of *charkha* as it was simply inadequate in fulfilling his goal. Gandhi also responded to the poet's critique by arguing that he was misunderstood by the latter for his inability to comprehend the nature and also texture of Non-cooperation. According to him,

> Non-cooperation is the nation's notice that it is no longer satisfied to be in tutelage.... An India awakened and free has a message of peace and goodwill to a groaning world. Non-cooperation is designed to supply her with a platform from which she will preach the message.[18]

Similarly, Tagore's insistence on retaining English education so long as there was not a perfect alternative did not augur well with the Mahatma. Here too, the point of criticism was based on the poet's complete failure, believed Gandhi, to comprehend the strategy. As he held, English education was a device to enslave the Indians emotionally since 'it is being studied because of its commercial and political values'.[19] With the hegemonic grip of English education, the vernacular education lost its importance as mode of learning which was also disheartening to the Mahatma for it resulted in the emergence of a rootless race.

The differences between the poet and the Mahatma were primarily ideational in the sense that they drew on contrasting approaches

---

[17] Ibid., 547–548.
[18] M. K. Gandhi, 'Poet's Anxiety', *Young India*, 1 June 1921, reproduced in Bhattacharya, *The Mahatma and the Poet*, 67–68.
[19] Ibid., 65.

to the mode of nationalist protest. They diverged from each other significantly when the devastating 1934 Bihar earthquake resulted in massive human loss. For the Mahatma, it was God's caprice to the Hindus for sustaining untouchability. In other words, it was clearly 'a divine chastisement'[20] according to Gandhi who attributed a physical phenomenon to the providential intervention. A rationalist to the core, it caused severe pain to the bard since he was terribly disappointed by the Mahatma's insistence on linking the earthquake with a specific kind of human behaviour. It was not only misleading but also debilitating given the inherent flaw in the argument. According to him, the most painful was Gandhi's assertion of a completely irrational mode of explanation of the earthquake as the providential vengeance on certain parts of Bihar in 1934. He was appalled too because once this was declared by him, it was most likely to be accepted as axiomatic by most of his followers who gathered around him for magnetic capacity to draw the masses. It was evident when he expressed his anguish over the Mahatma's characterization of earthquake as divinely ordained by saying that

> If we associate ethical principles with cosmic phenomena, we shall have to admit that human nature is morally superior to Providence that preaches its lessons in good behaviour in orgies of the worst behaviour possible.... What is truly tragic about it is the fact that the kind of argument that Mahatmaji uses by exploiting an event of cosmic disturbance far better suits the psychology of his opponents.... [He thus felt] profoundly hurt when any words from [Gandhi's] mouth may emphasize the elements of unreason ... which is a fundamental source of all the blind powers that drive us against freedom and self-respect.[21]

The argument is crystal clear: Rabindranath condemned Gandhi in strong words since it was an endorsement of superstitious beliefs which the former was determined to weed out from among the Indians. As

---

[20] Tagore to Gandhi, 28 January 1934, reproduced in ibid., 156.
[21] Tagore's statement of protest against Gandhi's characterization of Bihar earthquake being an expression of 'divine chastisement', *Young India*, 16 February 1934, reproduced in Bhattacharya, *The Mahatma and the Poet*, 158.

is well known, the poet privileged emancipation from sociocultural prejudices as prior to swaraj or political freedom. He not only articulated this message in many of his critical essays but also developed the same theme in his creative writings as well. One may like to refer to the dance drama, *Chandalika* (1938), where the poet depicted the atrocities that were meted out to the *chandals* (untouchables) by the caste Hindus simply because of the accident of birth. Prakriti in *Chandalika* was a victim of being born to lower-caste parents; she was socially ostracized for no fault of hers. Due to her birth in *chandal* family, she hardly grew up like any of her counterparts among the caste Hindus as the well-entrenched sociocultural chains never allowed her to forget her identity as a low-caste girl. One should link Rabindranath's battle with Gandhi over the portrayal of the earthquake as a manifestation of God's displeasure with his fundamental ideological preferences. Under no circumstances, he was ready to accept the arguments in support of superstitious thinking which was sought to be established by the Mahatma in this regard. While Gandhi might have been persuaded by the strong logic in which the counter argument was couched, he however did not accept so when he retorted to the poet's accusation of being one who, by reinforcing sociocultural prejudices, helped consolidate an archaic mindset. In an intelligent way, the Mahatma articulated his response at two levels: At one level, he admitted that 'the earthquake was no caprice of God nor a result of a meeting of mere blind forces'; at another level, by associating the occurrences of droughts, floods, earthquakes and other physical events causing devastations to human existence, he also argued that he thus 'instinctively felt that the earthquake was a visitation for the sin of untouchability [because] ... our sins have more force to ruin the human beings than mere physical phenomenon'.[22] A surface reading of the debate may lead one to draw a simplistic conclusion that the poet was scientific while the Mahatma was not. It is simplistic because their aim was different. The poet was involved in generating ideas for eradicating sociocultural deficiencies which were, according to him, a deterrent to India's ascendancy as a well-knit community. The aim is laudable if it is conceptualized in a long-term perspective. For Gandhi, the

[22] M. K. Gandhi, 'Superstition vs Faith', *Harijan*, 28 February 1934.

aim was diametrically opposite; he was certainly concerned about the debilitating impact of sociocultural chasm on the collective political platform that unfolded with his innovative leadership and care during the nationalist phase. Given his perfect understanding of the human psyche, he launched a scathing attack on those who practised untouchability by resorting to an analogy which was, he also believed, misleading. Nonetheless, he forcefully argued his point in opposition to that of the poet simply to put across his view that unless untouchability was completely rescinded, the campaign for swaraj was likely to be defeated in view of the possible withdrawal of providential support for the cause. It was a persuasive logic especially in then India given the uncritical acceptance of many of the superstitious beliefs by the people at large. As an astute political campaigner against perhaps the mightiest Empire of the 20th century, Gandhi's comprehension of the Bihar earthquake as God's caprice has substance though not exactly rational, as the bard emphatically argued in his critique of how the Mahatma viewed the phenomenon.

The aim of this subsection is to highlight the ideational 'rivalry' between the great minds of India, the poet and the Mahatma. A deeper probe reveals that the latter was keen to wrest political power and he devised his conceptual mode of thinking accordingly, while the former was firm believer of human emancipation in its true sense since political freedom was futile if human beings were chained in the prevalent sociocultural prejudices. As shown above, these two principal protagonists for India's liberation differed on many issues which were fundamental to the existence of human beings as they were. There are reasons to believe that the differences had their conceptual root in the Mahatma's reluctance to appreciate the contribution of Rammohun Roy in bringing the ideas of the East with those of the West. Critical of Gandhi's characterization of Roy as 'a pygmy while [he reveres] him as a giant',[23] he openly came out with statements admiring his greatness in setting in motion the process for radical sociocultural transformation in India. According to him, 'Rammohun Roy was the first great man in our age who

[23] Tagore, 'The Cult of Charkha', reproduced by Das, *The English Writings of Rabindranath Tagore*, 547–548.

had the profound faith and large vision in his heart for the unity of soul between the East and West [he followed him] though he is practically rejected by my countrymen'.[24] In his booklet, *Charitrapuja* (1895), he further elaborated his firm belief that had Roy not raised his voice against the prejudicial customs detrimental to the progress of humanity, it would not have been possible to forcefully argue for 'human salvation only by sternly attacking the archaic mindset drawing sustenance by a distorted reading of the ancient texts, especially those governing humanity'.[25] Furthermore, what impressed the poet was Roy's endeavour at building a bridge between the noble ideas of the East with their counterparts in the West which confirmed, felt the bard, that he was 'open to political ideological predilections provided they contribute to humanity'.[26] There were hardly persuasive evidences to show that Gandhi ignored Roy's contribution to humanity at the onset of the Company rule in India; he however played down his role presumably as a political strategy since Roy was also condemned by a large contingent of Indians as 'an uncritical loyalist to the British'.[27] which was largely governed by the contextual compulsion.

The differences came out in the open when the Mahatma gave a call for Non-cooperation Movement in 1921. As demonstrated above, they differed radically from each other by being true to their politico-ideological predilections. In conformity with his ideational priority, the poet had no qualms in registering his protest as soon as the Movement was launched for, he believed that

> The word non-cooperation chokes [him because he] cannot get over the shame that it carries. It will always proclaim that the fact that our non-cooperation came to us by a road of ignominy; that it

[24] Rabindranath Tagore, *Letters to a Friend* (London: George Allen & Unwin, 1928), 109.
[25] Rabindranath Tagore, *Charitrapuja* (in Bangla; Kolkata: Visva-Bharati, 1895), 60.
[26] Ibid., 65.
[27] *The Collected Works of Mahatma Gandhi*, Vol. 20, 540. Evidently, it was, as the Mahatma felt, 'an appropriate political strategy', ibid.

missed its true route, and did not enter into the heart of our country through the great triumphal arch of love.[28]

Gandhi perhaps launched a scathing attack on the poet when he dismissed his argument as not only 'being stretched beyond comprehension' but also derivative of his understanding of the nature of the campaign. It was a decisive blow to the poet when he characterized Tagore's perception as being flawed for his appreciation of birds while they were flying was possible only when they had enough food to generate the strength of flying. Non-cooperation was an organized attack on the British to force the government to address the basic human needs of food, clothes and shelter. Hence, he argued that

> I have the pain of watching birds who for want of strength could not be coaxed even into flutter of their wings.... I have found it impossible to soothe suffering patients with a song of Kabir. The hungry millions ask for one poem, food. They cannot be given it. They must earn only by the sweat of their brow.[29]

Implicit here are two points: On the one hand, while criticizing the poet for being extremely 'romantic' about human life, he also implied that no radical change was possible so long as India reeled under the foreign yoke; hidden here was also the message, on the other hand, that the sociocultural transformation needed to be brought about by the Indians themselves.

We must add a caveat here because the difference between these two great minds did not seem to have an abiding effect on their personal respect for each other. Both of them drew on the ideas that they evolved for defending mankind against atrocities of any kind; they held, of course, different approaches: For the poet, the eradication of sociocultural prejudices was prior to political freedom which Gandhi

---

[28] Rabindranath Tagore to C. F. Andrews, 7 January 1921, reproduced in Uma Dasgupta (edited and introduced), *Friendship of Largeness and Freedom: Andrew, Tagore and Gandhi—An Epistolary Account, 1912–1940* (New Delhi: Oxford University Press, 2018), 269.

[29] M. K. Gandhi, 'The Great Sentinel', *Young India*, 13 October 1921, reproduced in Bhattacharya, *The Mahatma and the Poet*, 91.

did not endorse for he believed that with the attainment of political freedom the poet's espoused cause could easily be attained. At different levels, their bonhomie endured as history has shown. Even at the height of differences of opinion, the poet longed for Mahatma's friendship which he stated in his letter to C. F. Andrews by admitting that 'I wish it were possible for me to join hands with Mahatma Gandhi and thus at once surrender myself to the current of popular approbation'.[30] Despite his strong disagreement, he further mentioned that 'today to disagree with Mahatma and yet to find rest in one's surroundings in India is not possible and therefore I am waiting for my escape next March (when the poet was slated to go abroad) with an impatient feeling of longing for him'.[31] At the emotional level, they appeared to have been closer, while, at the political level, they never wavered in disclosing that they held different politico-ideological preferences. The idea was made clear when the poet opposed vehemently the decision of the British government to introduce self-government in India with the tacit support of the Gandhi-led Congress party. Critical of the view that 'self-government is simple, like the eyesight to the eyes—it is already there, only the lids have to be opened'.[32] It was made clear that this was completely myopic when he further elaborated his point by underlining that

> The most vitally valuable part of Self-Government is the "self". When it comes from to us as a gift, packed in a tin from outside, then the very "self" is smothered to death, and its tortured ghost become for us an eternal incubus.... Borrowed Self-Government is that fettered self-government, – it has the open road, but not the free legs. And yet what was it that hindered us to take upon ourselves the full responsibility of our own education, sanitation, prevention of crimes, and such other duties that God himself ... had given us to perform entirely according to our own way?[33]

---

[30] Rabindranath Tagore to C. F. Andrews, 7 January 1921, reproduced in Dasgupta, *Friendship of Largeness and Freedom*, 279.
[31] Ibid.
[32] Ibid., 271.
[33] Ibid., 269–271.

It was, according to him, tantamount to

> The mutilation of Man's personality for petty material gain [and] he is thus reduced into a machine.... Such deliberate impoverishment of our nature seems to be a crime—it is a cultivation of callousness which is a form sacrilege [because] ... deadness life in all forms gives rise to impurities—by enfeebling our reason, narrowing our vision, creating fanaticism through forcing our willpower into abnormal channels.[34]

Their differences had also surfaced in the context of the 1934 Bihar earthquake which was elaborated above; they differed from each other again on the sordid rivalry in the Indian National Congress which led to the forcible resignation of Subhas Chandra Bose as the Congress president in 1939 following his victory in opposition to Gandhi-nominated candidate Pattabhi Sitaramayya (1880–1959). In an address, while admiring Bose's valour, the bard thus noted that

> Today you are revealed in the clear light of the midday sun—there is no room for doubt to darken the sky.... you have made allies out of your troubles and obstacles have proved to be so steps in the ladder of your success. That you could do so, was owing to your refusal to accept defeat. We, in Bengal, need to emulate this strength of character than anything else.[35]

Impressed by his sacrifice for the cause, the poet was not, at all, hesitant in his admiration of Bose because he did not cling to the position as it meant to him a submission to an authority against his will. It did not escape the bard's attention which he emphatically declared by saying that 'I only invoke the will of the country and may pray that that will might actuate and strengthen your will'.[36] The poet however did not miss the woods for the trees which was reinforced when he clarified that his appreciation for Bose was not, at all, directed towards

---

[34] Ibid., 293.
[35] Rabindranath Tagore to Subhas Chandra Bose, 2 August 1939, reproduced in Das, *The English Writings of Rabindranath Tagore*, 716.
[36] Ibid., 719.

undermining the great effort that the Mahatma had undertaken to liberate mankind from servility. In an unambiguous way, he thus elaborated his point when he adumbrated that

> Let no one misapprehend that in my provincial pride I want to separate Bengal from the rest of India or that I want to place anybody on a seat of rivalry with the Mahatma who has brought in a new age in the realm of politics and has thus made India's name famous in the comity of nations. My appeal is being made today because I want Bengal fully and substantially to cooperate with India and because I want this valuable cooperation to bear real fruit. I do not wish that a powerless and weak Bengal should lag behind empty-handed while the other provinces bring their own offerings to the Motherland.[37]

Fundamental to Rabindranath's philosophical moorings remains a concern for the country as a whole; he also emphatically believed that it was Gandhi who infused new spirit and zeal to the Indians while leading a fierce campaign against the British rule. Perhaps he was not sure whether his admiration for Subhas Chandra Bose who had to succumb to the pressure of the Congress High Command in 1939 was interpreted by his countrymen as an attempt to hail the Bengali pride at the cost of the 'nation'. So, in an endeavour to address perhaps his unfounded concern, he reiterated his belief in India's political unity. While laying down the foundation of Mahajati Sadan, a hall for mass meeting where Bose was felicitated after his resignation as the Congress president, Rabindranath reinforced his views by saying though this Hall of India

> [It] will lay the foundation of Bengal's prowess, but our strength will not lie in arrogant nationalism suspicious of friend and foe. We shall invoke Bengal's magnanimous heart of hospitality to which our humanity has found liberation we shall seek freedom in many-sided cooperation. Valour and beauty, resolute work and creative imagination, devotion to truth as well self-dedication in public service—may these unite in benediction to our land.... May

[37] Ibid., 718–719.

Bengal's arm give strength to the arm of India, Bengal's voice give truth to India's message; may Bengal, in service of freedom for India, never make itself ineffective by betraying the cause of unity.[38]

The two great men came together when Rabindranath's brainchild, Visva-Bharati, was on the brink of crisis due to lack of adequate funds at its disposal. Denied help from his near and dear ones for the maintenance of this seat of learning, the poet expressed his helplessness to the Mahatma; it was most distressing when the bard himself admitted that

> When I am 75, I feel the burden of my responsibility growing too heavy for me, that owing to some deficiency in me that my appeal fails to find adequate response in the heart of my people though the cause that I have done my utmost to serve is certainly valuable. Constant begging excursions with absurdly meagre results added to the strain of my daily anxieties and have brought my physical constitution nearly to extreme verge of exhaustion.[39]

Rabindranath's appeal for raising funds for Visva-Bharati immediately elicited Gandhi's positive response. He was appalled that the poet at this age had to undertake another begging mission for Visva-Bharati. By assuring that it was a burden too, he reaffirmed his support to the great cause by saying that 'you may depend upon my straining every nerve to find the required money'.[40] He not only promised help but also, by agreeing to become one of the trustees of Visva-Bharati Trust, permanently associated himself with the mission that the poet had embarked upon. In his acceptance letter, he vowed to discharge his role for he believed that 'acceptance of the burden by me of Visva-Bharati could mean nothing to me unless it at least meant that I would be able to discharge the financial burden'.[41] It was a blessing in disguise for the bard who, as he admitted himself, was denied any kind of help in

---

[38] Rabindranath Tagore, 'At Mahajati Sadan', 18 August 1939, cited in Ghosh, ed., *The English Writings of Rabindranath Tagore*, Vol. 4, 606–607.
[39] 'Tagore's Appeal for Funds to Gandhi about Visva-Bharati', 12 September 1935, reproduced in Bhattacharya, *The Mahatma and the Poet*, 161.
[40] Gandhi to Tagore, 13 October 1935, reproduced in ibid., 182.
[41] Gandhi to Tagore, 2 March 1937, reproduced in ibid., 166.

building this great institution. While expressing his agony, he thus mentioned to the Mahatma that

> I have struggled almost single-handed for about forty years for a cause which has failed to fund a helping hand in a neighbourhood jealously antagonistic and therefore when I am nearing the end of my journey suddenly to be blessed with an unquestioning sympathy lavish in generosity overwhelms my famished heart with joy.[42]

Their views coalesced in so far as the future of Visva-Bharati was concerned. For Gandhi, Visva-Bharati was both 'a national and international institution'[43] which needed to be protected by all means; for the poet, this seat of learning was 'like a vessel which is carrying the cargo of my life's best treasure and [he hoped that] it may claim special care from my countrymen for its preservation'.[44] It is now plausible to argue that the differences that were visible at the outset did not seem to be so fundamental since both had the same mission which was articulated by the Mahatma in his obituary of Rabindranath when he captured the versality of the poet by saying that he was 'an ardent nationalist who was also a humanitarian [and] ... there was hardly any public activity on which he has not left the impress of his powerful personality'[45] This was perhaps the most-glaring tribute to the bard who represented rare qualities that humanity seemed to have been deviated from. Gandhi's ultimate aim was to bring about qualitative transformation of mankind which also the poet upheld in his multifarious activities. One however finds a lot of politico-ideological compatibility of ideas between what B. R. Ambedkar espoused and Rabindranath held before him: Both of them were vehemently opposed to the sociocultural prejudices; and also believed that unless they were effectively addressed, political freedom was just equal to the change of rulers.

---

[42] Tagore to Gandhi, 7 November 1937, reproduced in ibid., 207.
[43] Gandhi to Tagore, 19 February 1940, reproduced in ibid., 178.
[44] Tagore to Gandhi, 2 February 1940, reproduced in ibid.
[45] Obituary of Rabindranath by Gandhi, 7 August 1941, reproduced in ibid., 216.

As the above detailed discussion shows, the debate between Gandhi and the poet represented a well-argued endeavour towards highlighting different methods to reach an identical goal; it was not a battle between the Mahatma who justified earthquake as God's caprice and Rabindranath who insisted on earthquake being a geological phenomenon. Referring to this aspect of the debate, many commentators sought to capture the differences in binary terms when it was far more nuanced and context-driven. In other words, it was not a debate between the so-called archaic Gandhi and a rational Rabindranath; instead, it was a debate that drew sustenance from how they conceived the contextual issues in accordance with their respective politico-ideological preferences. The bard's opposition to the Non-cooperation Movement was based on his firm belief that it was likely to fail without developing an alternative. In other words, a mere act of 'omission' was suicidal in the absence of a system to carry forward the task that the nationalists took onto themselves. Similarly, the poet's condemnation of the idea of nationalism was based on his acceptance of the Upanishadic ideal that India was not territorial (*mrinmaya*) but ideational (*chinmaya*) which he defended by saying that 'I love India, but my India is an idea and not a geographical expression'. Hence, he always insisted on human emancipation, a concept that had global ramification. Drawn on his conceptual affinity with the dictum of Ishoponishad, *Teno Taktyano Bhunjita* (by giving up for others benefit, one enjoys most), the poet thus devoted his energy for the liberation of mankind which remained a difficult goal to achieve largely due to the consolidation of greed and partisanship among human beings. A surface reading of the debate may lead to conclude that they had different politico-ideological paths which hardly met, though a deeper analysis shows that despite having pursued different modes of attaining their respective mission, their differences were not as substantial as they seemed to be presumably because both of them drew their intellectual sustenance from identical ideational sources. The argument can persuasively be made if one draws attention to the fact that both of them strongly argued for human emancipation which was not possible to attain, as per Gandhi, so long as colonialism survived in India while the poet, despite having sternly objected to the continuity of alien rule, also highlighted the contribution that it had made by opening up a new vista of knowledge associated with the Enlightenment philosophy. Behind his endeavour at bringing the East and West together remained the belief that the prosperity of humanity could be ensured only by intellectually uniting these two geographically segregated areas of the globe. Gandhi implicitly made this plea when he also mentioned that the British citizens per se were not his enemies but only those who sustained the systemic oppression of human beings in the wake of colonialism. There was hardly a difference except perhaps the fact that the poet remained steadfastly committed to the ultimate goal of human emancipation while the Mahatma did not seem to be so obsessed with the aim since he believed that with the departure of the British, the task could easily be accomplished.

Two Contrasting Perspectives

Tagore and Gandhi differed radically from each other since they saw Indian nationalism in two contrasting perspectives. Like Gandhi, Tagore viewed that nationalism, insisting on 'homogenized universalism', was incapable of bringing disparate people together; he was thus persuaded to believe that nationalism was ideologically vacuous, if not completely inappropriate in the Indian context. At the conceptual level, despite having conceded what the poet held, the Mahatma did not seem to be hesitant to resort to nationalism as a mode for political mobilization. For him, it was a sense of belongingness on the basis of a common sentiment opposed to the British rule and its immediate revocation. Here, instead of being constrained by the conceptual limitations of the idea of nationalism, Gandhi evolved a national identity by being sensitive to the politico-ideological priority. In other words, as a mode of essentializing identity, the concept of nation was perceived to be an ideological template for cementing a bond among the socioculturally disparate communities. As far as Gandhi was concerned, to attain political freedom, homogenization of the communities was the first and foremost step which was rather easily accomplished by generating a sense of 'sameness' or a nationalistic devotion to the cause of the community. Gandhi's preferences can be understood at two levels: At the conceptual level, the Mahatma was perhaps close to Tagore in the sense that nationalism was simply an inappropriate category to understand a country comprising many socioculturally distinct communities. At the level of perception, it was not so since the sense of being integral to a united self, or nation, for want of better words, contributed and also consolidated the idea of 'oneness' which was essential for political victory against the well-entrenched British rule.

The argument that Gandhi offered to justify that for him, nationalism was just a cementing factor in the context of the campaign against the alien administration. Tagore remained steadfast in his conceptual understanding of the idea of nation, nationalism and national identity. According to him, what Gandhi suggested had justified expediently an argument which did not seem to have substance because political freedom did not ensure human emancipation in its true spirit and content. Being true to his conceptual inclinations, the poet made a scathing critique of Gandhi's defence of nationalism by saying that

> Those of us in India who have come under the delusion that mere political freedom will make us free have accepted their lessons from the West as the gospel truth and lost their faith in humanity. We must remember whatever weakness we cherish in our society will become the source of danger in politics. The same inertia which leads us to our idolatry of dead forms in social institutions will create in our politics prison-houses and immovable walls. The narrowness of sympathy which makes it possible for us to impose upon a considerable portion of humanity the galling yoke of inferiority will assert itself in our politics in creating the tyranny of injustice.[46]

Tagore's assessment of Gandhi's politico-ideological views did not seem to be odd because of his firm belief in human emancipation which was not possible with mere political freedom so long as we were governed by our archaic social values and mores. Gandhi had his priority which led him to privilege political freedom over anything else since he was persuaded to believe that freedom from socially restrictive practices and prejudices could be addressed effectively once the British colonialism came to an end. Here Gandhi felt like his

[46] Tagore, *Nationalism*, 74.

nationalist compatriot, B. R. Ambedkar, who also held the view that without political power at the disposal of the Indians it was difficult, if not impossible, to completely eradicate the well-entrenched and socially justified backward customary practices. A careful scan of the arguments made by Gandhi and Tagore reveals that while Gandhi was interested in realizing a short-term goal, Tagore was in favour of fulfilling his wider concern for humanity which was linked with radical metamorphosis of the predominant mindset supporting the divisive social practices around the axes of caste, religion and ethnicity. Hence, for him, nationalism itself became gradually illegitimate, while for Gandhi it was a means to galvanize the masses for the nationalist struggle against colonialism and he also believed that the nationalist campaign in India was a symbol of the universal struggle for political justice and cultural dignity. At one level, Tagore's conceptual approach to nationalism stood in contradiction with what Gandhi had propagated since the latter believed that the nationalist aspiration was not adequate to accomplish what he sought to attain. At another level, they seem to have come closer. A thorough examination of how Gandhi evolved into a nationalist voice whén he accepted nationalism as a politico-ideological tool for mobilizing masses suggests that he built his idea of nationalism 'upon the contradiction between nationalism which entered India as an imperial category and the nationalism which sprang up out of democratic aspirations, hoping that the latter would someday supersede the former'.[47] While Tagore developed his model presumably on the basis of what he derived from the Upanishads that always espoused the cause of humanity regardless of division, Gandhi articulated his ideas in a non-canonical form in which the local appears to be equally critical in his conceptualization. Nonetheless, despite not having conceded Tagore's views on nationalism in its entirety, 'the Mahatma shared the poet's moral concerns'.[48] Basic here is the fundamental point that neither Tagore nor Gandhi had ever discarded the importance of morality in pursuing the nationalist cause which never appeared to be insignificant to them. Gandhi's intervention laid the

---

[47] Ashis Nandy, *The Illegitimacy of Nationalism* (Delhi: Oxford University Press, 1994), 77.
[48] Ibid.

foundation of a uniquely conceptualized idea of nationalism which, instead of being restricted given the European genealogy, was potentially a decisive mode of collectivizing people for a politico-ideological goal that brought them together even in adverse circumstances.

Unfolding of Political Difference between the Mahatma and Rabindranath

This is an interesting chapter in the relationship between Gandhi and the bard which unfolded after Subhas Chandra Bose had an ignominious exit from the Congress despite having won the 1939 Congress presidential election largely because of the machinations in which Gandhi had a critical role from behind the scenes. A moralist to the core, the poet was never persuaded by the argument of Gandhi that he put forward in his defence. For the first time, the bard came out openly in support of Bose who was, as Tagore felt, wrongly thrown out of the Congress to fulfil the partisan political agenda of the mainstream political leadership. According to Tagore, by being a part of the conspiracy to dislodge Bose, Gandhi displayed a political trait which was everything but moral. By dedicating his play, *Tasher Desh* (the land of cards, which was originally written in 1933) to Subhas Chandra Bose in 1939, Tagore did not hide his sympathy for the former which did not augur well with Gandhi and his hardcore disciples. Nonetheless, he hardly revised his opinion and participated in the inauguration of a nationalist auditorium in Calcutta, Mahajati Sadan (a platform for congregation for all), where Subhas Chandra Bose was felicitated. It was a matter of shame for Tagore that Bose, who was elected unanimously as the Congress president in the 1938 Haripura Congress session, was forced to resign and unceremoniously shunted out after his victory against the Gandhi-nominated Pattabhi Sitaramayya (1880–1959) in the 1939 Tripuri Congress session. In his opinion, the decision of Gandhi and his colleagues, instead of helping them, was likely to weaken the nationalist campaign. He articulated his anguish in an open message to the press in which he unambiguously asserted that

> Whether the cause of the present unhappy situation be political or personal, whether the resulting bitterness was avoidable or inevitable, I have no doubt that no exercise of political power or

wit on either side will cure it. Only an appeal to our moral self can remind us that though much has happened that can justify this fatal unmindfulness of our permanent need of national unity at a time when we are still marching, handicapped by the lack of almost every material means, nothing is more dangerous than mutual suspicion and fault finding which may betray it. I, therefore, appeal to my countrymen, not only of Bengal but of all India, to forgive little things for the sake of great ends.[49]

Fundamental here was Tagore's explicit condemnation of divisive politics that led to the overthrow of Subhas Chandra Bose. The poet pitched his argument at two levels: At the political level, he was persuaded to believe that the forcible resignation of Bose was the outcome of internecine feud in the Congress which was likely to cause irreparable damage to the nationalist struggle. At the conceptual level, it can be argued that the bard's support for Bose and opposition to Gandhi and his colleagues who were main priests of this deplorable Congress design reflected his concern for togetherness notwithstanding the well-entrenched, but inherent differences. It indicates that so long as nationalism was a political tool for bringing disparate people together, it remained a cementing factor. In other words, one is likely to commit an error in assessing the conceptual model of nationalism unless one is aware of the nuances in which it was articulated by the poet.

After his ignominious exit from the Congress, Bose was admired in Bengal for his stand against the Congress bigwigs. In a felicitation congregation, Tagore was present and he appreciated Bose for such a courageous act in a context when 'we tend to escape our responsibility to our countrymen'.[50] The argument was elaborated when he further stated that it was unfortunate that we failed to realize that

> Divided against ourselves we are weak at home while adverse forces mobilize outside Bengal's frontiers. Our economy, method of work,

---

[49] Rabindranath Tagore, 'An Appeal to the Countrymen' after the resignation of Subhas Chandra Bose following the refusal of the Gandhi disciples to join the Working Committee that he, as the Congress President, was supposed to constitute, reproduced in Ghosh, *The English Writings of Rabindranath Tagore*, 762.

[50] Rabindranath Tagore, 'To Subhas Chandra Bose', 19 August 1939, cited in Das, *The English Writings of Rabindranath Tagore*, Vol. 3, 716.

our moral tone are woefully inadequate. Our politics is like a boat in which the oars do not keep time with the helm. When the mind is ridden by an evil fate it acts like a virus in a worn-out body. That is how we become divided against ourselves, we throw out our well-wishers, make strangers of friends, insult those who are worthy of respect, and, in this way weaken our ranks from the rear.[51]

The contemporary situation confronting Bengal did not seem to be propitious presumably because of the failure of the Bengalis to rise above petty gains and partisan aims. Under these circumstances, Tagore hailed Bose as an appropriate leader to galvanize a moribund nation because

You have made allies out of your troubles and obstacles have proved to be so many steps in the ladder of your success. That you could do so, was owing to your refusal to accept defeat. We, in Bengal, need to emulate this strength of character more than anything else.[52]

It was a herculean task, the poet was aware in the circumstances when the sense of being diffident and also the rising tide of factionalism appeared to have gripped the Bengalis which he articulated by saying that 'for various reasons Bengal has been denied many opportunities by her own people'.[53] A perennially optimist, Tagore, however believed that it was absolutely temporary which was evident when he stated that 'by her own courage and initiative Bengal should forge blessings out of this fate [and] let her determination not to accept apparent defeat, [but] lead Bengal to her triumph'.[54] Tagore's emphatic call for generating zeal for oneness was perhaps based on his own assessment of the organizational decay of the nationalist campaign in Bengal due largely to the internecine feud among the top leadership of the Bengal Congress which was apparently plagued severely by internal weaknesses. Apart from some districts in Bengal, it was not possible for the province to remain united in opposition to the British government

[51] Ibid.
[52] Ibid.
[53] Ibid., 717.
[54] Ibid.

which helped the ruler continue without much difficulties.⁵⁵ As the available evidence shows, the provincial Congress was unable to adequately organize people in both the pan-Indian movements that Gandhi led in the context, Non-cooperation Campaign (1920–1922) and Civil Disobedience Movement (1930–1932), except perhaps particularly in Midnapur and some parts in east Bengal.⁵⁶ This was a matter of pain for the bard which, he rightly pointed out, was an impediment of a successful nationalist mobilization against the mighty British administration. The scene was further complicated with the rise of the Muslims as a strong political block which also succeeded in organizing people on the basis of their separate religious identity and also the age-old mistreatment by the Hindus of their Muslims brethren especially in east Bengal. Once the principle of 'head counts' was accepted in the partially guaranteed democratic governance, the Muslim, by being demographically preponderant in Bengal, became a force to reckon with.⁵⁷ Under these circumstances, he thus caustically asked the Bengalis not to derive pleasure

> In sitting in opposition and refuting other man's viewpoints in the pride of [their] sterile intellect [because] ... the need of the day is not arguments by a spontaneous will to do things [as their earlier generation did] ... in the context of the 1905–8 Bengal partition movement ... when Bengal rose like one man against the mighty power of the Crown. [The people of Bengal] did not then sit idle and deliberate in the fashion of wiseacres as to whether it was possible to oppose and defeat (circumvent) the design of the foreign power. What she did then was to will with all her heart.⁵⁸

---

⁵⁵ I have elaborated this aspect of Bengal politics in my *Subhas Chandra Bose and Middle Class Radicalism in Bengal, 1928–1940* (London: I. B. Tauris & Co., 1990).

⁵⁶ This is the theme that I have dealt with in my *Local Politics and Indian Nationalism, Midnapur, 1919–1942* (Delhi: Manohar, 1997).

⁵⁷ Abul Mansur Ahmad provided a detailed account of how the Muslims became alienated from their Hindu counterparts in his *Aamar Dekha Rajnitir Panchhas Bachhar* (Fifty Years of Politics as I Saw; Dhaka: Kitabistan, 1983).

⁵⁸ Tagore, 'To Subhas Chandra Bose', 19 August 1939, reproduced in Das, *The English Writings of Rabindranath Tagore*, Vol. 3, 717–718.

Here Tagore made a wider point regarding the sterile character of the Bengalis which was also an outcome of the British conspiratorial design of weakening them as a race by resorting to many steps. An analytical scan of Bengal's politics once the province ceased to be a centre of the nationalist campaign for a variety of complex factors shows that one of the reasons for the decline of Bengal as a political centre was factional politics at the top level of the mainstream provincial leadership.[59] Furthermore, the failure of the Bengal Congress to bridge the socio-economic gap between the Hindus and Muslims because of their class and religious prejudices against the latter, as the 1916 novel *Ghare-Baire* demonstrates, was also an important factor for the weakening of the organizational grip of the Congress leadership in the province. Given his admiration for Bose, Tagore thus exhorted him to take the leadership to awaken the Bengalis by reminding them of their moral responsibility in strengthening the nationalist campaign by being united as one. Urging those who thought alike, he thus forcefully argued that

> Let Bengal's millions speak in one voice, in firm and clear accents that the seat of leadership is ready for you. May you resolve the spirit of mutual mistrust in the Bengalee, may his diffidence be over. May your example put meanness and niggardly conduct to ignominy and shame. Let Bengal, through upholding and maintaining her self-respect in victory and again defeat, uphold and maintain the prestige of her accredited leader.[60]

It is clear that the poet preferred Bose to take the leadership as perhaps the only way to galvanize the masses and address successfully the weaknesses that impaired the rise of Bengal as a community. At one level, this was the thrust of the argument that he made in defending why Bose was preferred under those circumstances. Unless this argument is understood with reference to his concern for the country as a whole, our assessment of Tagore's views shall be anything but logical.

---

[59] The argument is pursued in detail in my *Subhas Chandra Bose and Middle Class Radicalism in Bengal*.

[60] Tagore, 'To Subhas Chandra Bose', 19 August 1939, reproduced in Das, *The English Writings of Rabindranath Tagore*, Vol. 3, 717.

In the same appeal, he also coached the argument by highlighting that Bose was capable of leading the nation as well. Hence, he urged further that 'let the composite will of the nation ... mould you to the great responsibility that devolves upon such leadership [and] ... the whole nation shall find its self-expression in your person'.[61] Being aware that his appreciation of Bose who was also a regional leader was likely to be misunderstood, he thus added a disclaimer by categorically suggesting that

> Let no one misapprehend that in my provincial pride I want to separate Bengal from the rest of India or that I want to place anybody on a seat of rivalry with the Mahatma who has brought in a new age in the realm of politics and has thus made India's name famous in the comity of nations.[62]

The above statement is too clear to cause any confusion. Aware that it was the Mahatma who injected a new spirit of sacrifice for the nation and also his understanding of the nature of nationalist campaign in Bengal which was divisive and became politically mostly sterile with the alienation of the demographically preponderant Muslims, Tagore strove to build a bridge by projecting Subhas Chandra Bose as one of the politically effective leaders, not in opposition to Gandhi, but in consonance with him. Because he felt that the separation of Bengal from the rest of the country was politically suicidal, he appeared to have undertaken steps which, he thought, were appropriate to (a) awaken the Bengalis who, by resting on 'the unproductive luxuriance of an idle mind',[63] generally tended to not take responsibilities and (b) link the nationalist efforts in Bengal with what Gandhi had launched at the pan-Indian level for political freedom. The point is persuasively substantiated when Tagore unambivalently stated that

> My appeal is being made today because I want Bengal fully and substantially to cooperate with India and because I want this valuable cooperation to bear real fruit. I do not wish that a powerless

[61] Ibid., 717–718.
[62] Ibid., 718.
[63] Ibid., 717.

and weak Bengal should lag behind empty-handed while the other provinces bring their own offerings to the Motherland. Let Bengal's ... lamps of offering shine with her own true light.[64]

Tagore was thus a bridge between Bengal and the country as a whole because he strongly believed that since the separation was harmful it immediately needed to be meaningfully addressed to avoid further damage to the Congress endeavour for winning political freedom. While inaugurating the Mahajati Sadan which he christened as 'great hall of India', he reiterated the view that 'our strength will not lie in arrogant nationalism suspicious of friend and foe, [but] ... in Bengal's magnanimous heart of hospitality to which our humanity has found liberation ... in many-sided cooperation'.[65] Hence, it can also be argued that being aware of the potential that Bengal had, he insisted on linking the province with its all-India counterpart. This was the need of the hour which he adumbrated by saying that with the cooperation 'we shall come nearer to our united nationalism, never yielding to the egoistic vanity of isolation which hurts our inherent humanity'.[66] So, Tagore's views were not an outcome of his emotional attachment with Bengal, but one that was based on the bard's appropriate gauging of the prevalent politico-ideological scene especially after the shunting out of Subhas Chandra Bose from the Congress. His support for Bose was also tempered with his appreciation for Gandhi stating 'great as he is as a politician, as an organizer, as a leader of men, as a moral reformer, he is greater than all these as a man, because none of these aspects and activities limits his humanity'.[67] This was reiterated in his tribute to the Mahatma when he again admired him stating 'the influence which emanated from his personality was ineffable, like music, like beauty [since] ... its claim upon others was great because

---

[64] Ibid., 718–719.
[65] Rabindranath Tagore, 'Mahajati Sadan, 19 August 1939', reproduced in Ghosh, *The English Writings of Rabindranath Tagore*, Vol. 4, 606.
[66] Ibid., 607.
[67] Tagore, 'Gandhi the Man', reproduced in Ghosh, *The English Writings of Rabindranath Tagore*, Vol. 4, 458.

of its revelation of a spontaneous self-giving'.[68] Given the distinctive personality trait which made Gandhi a class by himself, Tagore also pondered on the politico-ideological foundation not only on which was the pan-Indian nationalist campaign organized and consolidated but also which led to India's political liberation in 1947. While characterizing the Gandhian mode of opposition as 'a new kind of political warfare',[69] the poet attributed the success of this battle to Gandhi's ability to generate 'the courage to accept suffering and not inflict',[70] which was the source of how it continued in adverse circumstances. It was further elaborated when he developed his point by saying that

> If a whole nation could be trained not to fear physical death, no power in the world could keep it in bondage. We yield to those who have physical power over us, not because of a difference in degree between our physical strength and theirs, but because of our own lack of moral courage. As long as people are afraid of physical suffering, machinery for intimidating them will always be invented. directly we are able to say we are no longer afraid of physical suffering or death, arms and armaments lose their significance. If such a faith in our spiritual strength can be inculcated, and ... a whole people can be brought to accept such an idea, that in itself would be permanent freedom. It is for this idea that he is struggling.[71]

Important here was Tagore's appreciation for Gandhi who inspired his followers for unconditional sacrifice for the cause of the nation. What helped the Mahatma to succeed was his ability to evolve politico-ideological preferences in which the disparate Indians found a voice, a powerful voice indeed which created 'sameness' and also instilled a sense of responsibility among the colonized Indians to battle for their political freedom. Tagore however went a step further for he also believed that Gandhi's ideological vision was likely to contribute to human emancipation from shackles of customary prejudices

---

[68] Tagore, 'A Tribute to Gandhi', 1939, reproduced in Das, *The English Writings of Rabindranath Tagore*, Vol. 3, 846.
[69] Tagore, 'Gandhi's Ideal', reproduced in Ghosh, *The English Writings of Rabindranath Tagore*, Vol. 4, 645.
[70] Ibid.
[71] Ibid., 645–646.

emanating from archaic social rules which were wrongly claimed to have been derived from the accepted religious texts. The argument is made at two levels: At the strategic level, it was an attempt to defend Gandhi's ideological design as internal to Indian society given the roots in indigenous philosophical discourses; the Mahatma simply reiterated those ideas which did not attract as much attention as they should have. It was possible for him to gather masses around him in his battle for liberation presumably because they found their voice in what the former had articulated. At the conceptual level, the courage to face even bullets, if it was necessary to fulfil the objective, was inculcated at a moment of India's nationalist struggle when none of the prevalent politico-ideological priorities was adequately inspirational to raise a voice in unison. Neither revolutionary nationalists, despite their genuine commitment to the nationalist cause, nor their *bete noire*, the Moderates, ever succeeded in galvanizing the masses for political liberation to the extent it was possible once Gandhi appeared on the scene.

In light of the above discussion, it can safely be argued that the Tagore–Gandhi interaction is both complementary and divergent in nature. The conceptual uniformity, as their approach to the idea of nationalism illustrates, was visible so long as they held similar politico-ideological views which however disappeared once they differed on fundamental grounds. Examples are plenty. The bard was vehemently opposed to Gandhi's support to *Varnashrama* as it helped the latter build a strong political platform supported by the caste Hindus. Similarly, Gandhi's explanation of the 1934 Bihar earthquake as nothing but God's caprice annoyed Tagore, since a deliberately spread superstitious belief and that too by the Mahatma, was likely to consolidate the forces supporting the archaic and also primordial values and mores. It was a battle between a rational mind drawing its sustenance from scientifically endorsed views and preferences that Tagore represented and a mind that privileged political gains over other considerations which Gandhi's views on the Bihar earthquake epitomized. The 1939–1940 exchange of views between Gandhi and the bard reveals that while the latter supported Bose wholeheartedly presumably because a politically expedient decision, despite being useful, was hardly morally justified as the former did not seem to have been scarcely rattled notwithstanding the strong opposition of an equally popular figure. Here is a pertinent question: Was Tagore persuaded by the political ideology that Bose held? Presumably not because the poet espoused non-violence, as his novel, *Rajarshi*, and plays like *Prayaschitta* (atonement) and *Visarjan* (sacrifice) illustrate; what may have governed Tagore's choice was the ill treatment that Bose was subject to despite having won the 1939 Congress presidential election. Therefore, it was neither parochial nor partisan since Tagore never expected Gandhi to stoop so low for fulfilling a narrow political aim. Furthermore, the poet had no doubt that given his youthful exuberance, Bose had the capacity to rouse the masses for the nationalist cause which should have been meaningfully utilized at a time when the Congress Party was in shambles. So, Tagore's intervention in this regard was directed to resensitize the mainstream nationalist leadership of its commitment to those moral values for which Gandhi stood out; it was also an endeavour to bring forward the youth to the nationalist campaign which appeared to have dwindled with the hegemonic grip of the well-established leaders of the Congress, including the Mahatma and his close associates.

Concluding Observations

Rabindranath differed from his grandfather and father while conceptualizing his distinctive politico-ideological priorities. Dwarkanath endeavoured to create an independent space by being involved in campaigns for social reforms and also by espousing the need for education cutting across social barriers. His role in seeking to spread education among women was noteworthy; with assistance from his British colleagues holding identical socio-economic and politico-ideological views based on their uncritical faith in the Enlightenment principles, the task was easier for him. Debendranath went a little further by sincerely following up what his father left unfinished. Striking for him was his serious effort in reinforcing the claim that India's ancient texts needed to be thoroughly grasped since they were also important sources of wisdom for humanity. In sum, the father–son duo pursued a similar path of social activities without being bothered much by the adverse impact that colonialism unleashed to consolidate its administration over the colonized. Perhaps, the historical experience of the erstwhile Mughal rule being ruthless and ideologically backward created a mindset which they unhesitatingly shared. With the consolidation of anti-British sentiments, India's political scene underwent radical changes which was manifested first in the campaign for revocation of Bengal partition during the period between 1905 and 1908 and later in the second decade of the 20th century once Gandhi rose to prominence as a pan-Indian leader. Rabindranath was raised and nurtured in an environment of massive social churning and significant politico-ideological metamorphosis. Unlike his forefathers, Tagore held views that he expressed in many of his deeds and creative texts which ran contrary to the rulers' desires and will. While being critical of the British rule, the bard also offered a scathing critique of the revolutionary nationalists for their anti-Muslim views which, he felt, were, instead of strengthening the nationalist campaign, clearly subversive of the selfless effort that they undertook to combat the alien administration. *Ghare-Baire* (1916) and *Char Adhyay* (four chapters) of 1934 are illustrated here. The dilemma of Nikhilesh in supporting Sandip in *Ghare-Baire* was Tagore's own dilemma; it was expected of an author who endorsed non-violence in *Rajarshi*, *Prayaschitta* and *Visarjan*. Similarly, the ruthlessness of Atin vis-à-vis Ela in *Char Adhyay* reinforced Tagore's condemnation of the violence as a method for liberating the country. His admiration for Gandhi was not only for the man and his simplicity but also for him championing non-violence for regenerating the nationalist fervour in a context when the political struggle against the British rule was confined particularly to the metropolis of Calcutta and Bombay; there were, of course, many regional campaigns against the British atrocities which however did not generally affect the pan-Indian colonial governance. So, the poet ushered in a new phase of history when the anti-British sentiments contributed to an organized anti-British offensive. It is true that he did not participate in the campaign against colonialism in the sense Gandhi or his colleagues did though, through his sharp critique of the British rule, helped prepare and consolidate a mindset which paved the way for an effective challenge to colonialism.

The ideological interaction between the Mahatma and Gurudev reveals interesting facets of India's nationalist offensive against the

British. For instance, both of them were critical of the idea of nationalism, as it was viewed in the Western prism because it tended to essentialize human identities which was simply inconceivable in India given the obvious disparate socio-economic and cultural character of her people. Nonetheless, nationalist sentiments acted instrumentally to bring them together which probably is the foundation of the claim that they also ideologically reinforced each other presumably because

> Both recognized the need for a "national" ideology of India as a means of cultural survival and both recognized that, for the same reason, India would either have to make a break with the post-medieval Western concept of nationalist or give them concept a new content.[72]

Hence, it can thus be also stated that, for both of them, nationalism meant patriotism which brought people together for a politico-ideological cause. Their ideas also coalesced at another level: Both Gandhi and Tagore strongly felt that unless the country was sensitive to her own cultural resources, patriotism remained vacuous which led them to accord importance to the little cultures of India while seeking to mobilize the masses for the political goal. Such an awareness not only was a source of pride but also created the feeling of oneness around their cultural identities. Here Gandhi played a critical role in refashioning the idea of nationalism which led Tagore to argue that the Mahatma's endeavour to 'become a major source of resistance to what [he] identified as the pathologies of nationalism'[73] and his firm views against the organized violence was associated with this conceptualization. Furthermore, instead of being persuaded by the Western theoretical approach to nationalism, they reinterpreted the idea as a substitute for patriotism. It was evident when in his 1904 tract, *Swadeshi Samaj*, Tagore insisted on organizing *melas* or fairs at regular intervals because it allowed people to closely interact with one another. This also confirms that Indian unity was a social fact and not merely a political agenda. There are two advantages on this conceptualization: On the one hand, coming together regardless of

[72] Nandy, *The Illegitimacy of Nationalism*, 2.
[73] Ibid., 77.

one's sociocultural location created an opportunity for building oneness which was required in the context of the anti-British struggle. The claim has, on the other hand, wider implications as the argument also provided persuasive inputs to justify that humanism was prior to nationalism that always divided humanity by compartmentalizing people around certain homogenizing categories. In their perception, patriotism was another description of nationalism because by privileging the notion of *Bharatchinta* (concern for India) or *Swadeshchita* (concern for one's own country),[74] both Gandhi and Tagore generated a new wave of thoughts which was 'national', but at the same time, created conditions for evolving concerns for humanity as a whole. The early nationalists, including Vidyasagar, Rammohun, Dwarkanath or any of their colleagues, initiated this trend by espousing humanism as prior to any other consideration. This tradition continued and fully unfolded in Gandhi's specific politico-ideological preference and with Rabindranath's persuasive claim for the goal in his various sociopolitical activities and creative writings.

Besides being supportive of the anti-British campaign, Rabindranath also evolved a blueprint for future India in his 1904 tract, *Swadeshi Samaj*, which was translated into a reality with the foundation of Visva-Bharati in 1921. Unlike his colleagues, he developed Visva-Bharati as a model of socio-economic regeneration by creatively blending the Eastern discourses with their Western counterparts. Furthermore, it was not just another experiment of education, but by espousing alternative modes of learning and pedagogy, he completed the task that Dwarkanath and Debendranath undertook in the past. Here Rabindranath appears to have amalgamated the ideas of his grandfather and father: While both Dwarkanath and Debendranath set the ball rolling for education in Bengal by establishing schools in collaboration with their like-minded compatriots, Rabindranath developed a model of education in which, besides the Western philosophical discourses, the ancient Indian texts, especially the Vedas and Vedantic texts, also received adequate attention. It was also noticeable

---

[74] The idea is taken from Aurobindo Poddar, 'Rabindranather Bharatchinta' (Rabindranath's Concern for India), *Calcutta Municipal Gazette*, Tagore Birth Centenary Number, 1961, 86–89.

that his hatred for English education, which transformed the Bengalis into a community of clerks for helping the British administration and commercial activities, led him to lay the foundation of a school of agriculture in Sriniketan since he believed that without strengthening the foundation, that was agriculture, India would continue to remain economically backward. It was therefore not a matter of accident that the bard sent his son, Rathindranath, to the United States to pursue a degree in agricultural sciences. A unique experiment, Sriniketan was a harbinger of a new era in India's journey towards being self-dependent in basic economic needs. So, unlike Dwarkanath and Debendranath, the poet stood out for his multifarious activities in which he acted politically by seeking to radically alter the prevalent power-equations between the colonizer and the colonized, besides among the colonized British subjects. Here, he was Gandhian at one level since his concern was also to bring about revealing political changes with the removal of the British rule; at another level, he was far ahead of the Mahatma simply because he evolved a model of socio-economic transformation and created conditions for its sustenance even after independence; he was thus a trailblazer who not only generated a new genre of thinking but also left for the posterity those set of ideas which are both axiomatic and transcendental.

Conclusion

I

The Tagores shaped India's sociocultural texture and evolved a unique politico-ideological voice which led to the conceptualization of equally unique sociocultural discourses. With the onset of colonialism in the wake of the East India Company rule, it was Dwarkanath who, along with his compatriot, Rammohun, created an ambience in which the Western mode of thinking was readily accepted as a means to combat the archaic and socially and culturally crippling practices. Their intervention ushered in an era of radical sociocultural metamorphosis. They not only contributed to the acceptance of newer ways of comprehending human existence but also helped build 'self-confidence' among the colonized. Besides establishing schools and colleges, the combined efforts of Rammohun and Dwarkanath instilled a sense of being capable of competing with the British even in trade and commerce. Their role was, in other words, critical to generating a zeal for change in adverse circumstances since there were many of his contemporaries who endeavoured hard to pull them down. Nonetheless, with their steadfast commitment to the cause, neither Rammohun nor his colleague, Dwarkanath, and his like-minded associates wavered while pursuing their sociocultural objectives. That their contribution was indispensable in fashioning a mindset appreciative of newer mores and values was uncritically admired when the contemporary press characterized their role as

> The pioneers of the progress ... [and] their career was the seed-time for the harvest which is ripening, and which posterity will reap. It was the time when there were laid the foundations on which a goodly (sic) superstructure is now being upreared. It was the time for planting the germs of that national life which is now developing itself. It was the time when social and moral agencies commenced to operate imperceptibly but infallibly for the improvement and

elevation of the condition of this country, even as islands and continents are upheaved slowly but surely by the subterranean forces in never-ceasing action.[1]

It is evident that well ahead of the rise of the Congress as a mainstream political platform, Dwarkanath and those who thought alike generated ideas in support of patriotic nationalism which also connotes that their concern was to make people aware of their distinctive sociocultural resources. As the available archival sources demonstrate, the tradition continued when Debendranath arrived on the political scene and he, like his father, also devoted his energy to some of the tasks that Dwarkanath left unfinished. For instance, similar to his father, Dwarkanath, he was keen to strengthen the indigenous education system and also created an ambience in which the study of ancient Hindu texts, especially Vedas and Vedantic text, was no longer as despised as in the past. This was a boost which led to an increasing scholarly interest in these relatively less discussed texts. While Debendranath appeared to have been indifferent to the political agenda that the nationalist forces pursued since his priority was diametrically opposite to what they represented. For him, unless India was socially regenerated, the idea of political liberation had no substance. The scene however had undergone a sea change, as the above discussion shows, when Rabindranath emerged on the scene. Along with his endeavour for spreading education and also for economically developing Indian villages, the bard also participated in the ongoing political struggle that the mainstream nationalists had launched. He not only wrote a strong critique of those who led the Swadeshi Movement but also uncritically supported Subhas Chandra Bose when he was ignominiously thrown out by the top Congress leadership at the behest of Gandhi. Despite being appreciative of Gandhi's non-violence, as his plays *Prayaschitta*, *Visarjan* and novel *Rajarshi* show, he did not go along with the Mahatma when, notwithstanding being victorious, Bose was forced to resign from the Congress. So, unlike Dwarkanath and Debendranath, the last of the Tagore patriarchs, Rabindranath, had explicitly stated his preference even at the cost of annoying the Mahatma whom he always held in high esteem.

[1] Banerjee, *The Life of Dwarkanath Tagore*, 5–6.

Instead of following the conventional biographical mould, the analysis of three Tagores as political actors, since their contribution in transforming the existing power-relationship in India was immense, helps us understand their role in the rapidly changing socio-economic and political contexts. In other words, by viewing their life and times contextually or by approaching the continuous unravelling of history of colonized India from their social, economic and cultural activities, it is an initiative to grasp British colonialism differently. An analytical scan of the onset of the British rule and its gradual unfolding in India reveals that with its beginning, it is claimed that Raj brought 'parts of an apolitical social order within the compass of politics at the end of the 18th century [which] initiated the first stage of India's politicization'.[2] This is one of the fundamental assumptions on which one is persuaded to argue that increasing politicization contributed to the efforts that were manifested in the sociopolitical activities that started with Rammohun and his successors, including the three Tagores. There is no denying that the indigenous elites endorsed the British rule not merely because it was a relief from the ruthless and communal Muslim rule but was also uncritically accepted because it supposedly drew its sustenance from the core values of the philosophy of Enlightenment. The idea gained acceptance because, as a historian argued, 'the Mughal king ... entered English discourse as a villain, a caricature, a king with ungoverned land ... and the Muslim rulers of Hindustan would become the proverbial "despots" of European Enlightenment'.[3] It was politically contrived to erase the particular history of Hindustan which did not receive support from the British government, for obvious reasons. With the acceptance of the 1835 Minute of Education, prepared by T. B. Macaulay, the process had begun. By dismissing all historical knowledge produced in India, Macaulay thus argued that

> When we pass from works of imagination to works in which facts are recorded and general principles investigated, the superiority of

[2] Nandy, 'The culture of Indian Politics', 58.
[3] Maman Ahmed Asif, *The Loss of Hindustan: The Invention of India* (Cambridge, MA: Harvard University Press, 2020), 33.

the European becomes absolutely immeasurable. It is, I believe, no exaggeration to say that all the historical information which has been collected from all the books written in the Sanscrit (sic) language is less valuable than what may be found in the most paltry abridgments used at preparatory schools in England.[4]

The aim was to separate India from the Hindustan that 'made the people of India remain in a state of the so-called primitivity, produced through subjugation by Muslims'.[5] The idea was reinforced rather unhesitatingly when it was further mentioned that the purpose of the British rule was to prepare the natives to appreciate and internalize the liberal values of the British Empire. It was thus emphasized that 'when we see the withering effects of the tyranny and capriciousness of a despot, [the natives] ... shall learn to estimate fully the value of constitutional liberalism'.[6] Although there was a powerful argument made by Firishta in his *Tarikh* adumbrating that Hindustan was 'a place that contains multitudes of faiths and politics [and] ... also a system of governance [that] appreciated social and cultural divergences'[7] which did not receive adequate attention from the Indian ideologues striving to redraw India's sociopolitical and cultural map in light of the derivative Enlightenment traditions that came piggyback with British colonialism. Explicit here are two fundamental points which are useful to understand and conceptualize how India's journey as a colony progressed; and also, how the indigenous public intellectuals redesigned their thought processes by absorbing what they learnt by being part of the Empire. First, it is not an accident of history that Rammohun accepted the received Western wisdom though he did not entirely neglect the indigenous intellectual traditions that the Arabic, Persian and Sanskrit texts contained. The tradition continued, but in a different form once Dwarkanath became

---

[4] G. M. Young, ed., 'Thomas Babington Macaulay', in *Macaulay: Prose and Poetry* (Cambridge, MA: Harvard University Press, 1952), 722.
[5] Asif, *The Loss of Hindustan*, 47.
[6] Henry Miers Elliot, *Bibliographical Index to the Histories of Muhammedan India*, Vol. 1 (Calcutta: Baptist Mission Press, 1849), xxvi, cited in ibid., 70.
[7] Asif, *The Loss of Hindustan*, 135.

a key figure in Bengal. While he remained a loyalist, he took ample care in fulfilling his social missions by opening schools and also by publishing in the vernacular his ideas in *Tattwabodhini Patrika*. It was certainly illustrative of an endeavour that gradually assumed massive proportions once Debendranath and his son Rabindranath arrived on the scene. Second, the 'native' intellectuals were also not completely blind to what they imbibed from the Western theoretical discourses; they simultaneously expressed their concern for reviving the indigenous intellectual discourses which the ancient texts, especially the Hindu texts, such as the Vedas and Vedantic texts, very persuasively established. It is also not a matter of surprise that Debendranath undertook the project of translating the Vedas by spending his own money which confirms that there had emerged a bunch of scholars and social reformers who, instead of completely rejecting the indigenous discourses, initiated an endeavour in which their keenness for reviving the rich intellectual traditions was evident. What Debendranath initiated by starting a Brahmo Vidyalaya in Santiniketan in 1866, where the study of the Vedas and Vedantic texts was mandatory, continued in Visva-Bharati which his son, Rabindranath, founded in 1921. Besides articulating an alternative pedagogy, Visva-Bharati became an alternative centre for academic learning where the students were taught to become a real human being and not merely an English-knowing clerk for the British offices, which was the sole objective of the colonial rule. Visva-Bharati was not just an academic institution but also represented a distinct politico-ideological design for human emancipation. Rabindranath was therefore the culmination of a process which his grandfather, Dwarkanath, had initiated along with his like-minded compatriots. Given the constraint of the historical context, Dwarkanath's language of protest was articulated differently from that of his son and later grandson, Rabindranath, though, broadly speaking, their concern remained the same. Their individual efforts thus can be said to have derived from a more or less identical mission of creating a new wave of thinking in which the indigenous sources of wisdom were equally appreciated along with their admiration for the derivative Western philosophical discourses.

II

The 19th-century Bengal witnessed fierce battles among various sociocultural traditions also upholding definite politico-ideological preferences. Broadly speaking, there were three institutionalized principal voices: the Dharma Sabha, espousing the orthodox Hindus, the Orientalists, led by the Asiatic Society of Bengal and their *bête-noire*, the Anglicists, and the Brahmo Sabha drawing ideological sustenance from the indigenous social reformers. While the main protagonist of Dharma Sabha was Radhakanta Deb who strongly believed in the retention of the prevalent sociocultural systems, the other forces, by being opposed to the orthodox views, were determined to generate views against Catholicism in Hinduism. Supported by the British government, the Orientalists and the Anglicists held the view that government intervention was required to civilize the barbarian Indians; the former was keen to dig out the indigenous sources of knowledge, while the latter was persuaded to believe that only through English education, the ideological aim of the British was likely to be fulfilled. The Brahmo Samaj, founded in 1828 with the initiative of the local Bengali elites, was a powerful voice against Hindu orthodoxy; the Samaj was initially an endeavour to derive its ideological sustenance from both the Western and indigenous discourses, based on both the core texts of Islam and Hinduism. Rammohun was one of them who always believed that ancient Hindu texts were as valuable as the Islamic texts in building persuasive explanatory moulds. Along with this, he also upheld the view that the core texts of the Enlightenment philosophy contained invaluable inputs to understand humanity and collective well-being. Being supporters of the prevalent sociocultural views governing humanity, the Dharma Sabha was generally opposed to attempts to threaten the status-quo. The Brahmo Samaj was perhaps one of those powerful endeavours that openly came out with a well-defined agenda for Bengal sociocultural milieu. It was a revolutionary voice which blossomed into a powerful campaign at the behest of Dwarkanath, Debendranath and Rabindranath of the Tagore family. There were, of course, different shades in their conceptual universe: Dwarkanath was in favour of combining the Western discourses with the indigenous sources of knowledge and wisdom since he strongly felt that the former contained ideas and schemes for rejuvenating the collective self of Bengal. Debendranath was different from his father, Dwarkanath, because he did not seem to have been persuaded by the argument that his father offered to highlight the relevance of the Western discourses for indigenous well-being. Instead, he drew attention to the ancient intellectual resources that led to the development of Hinduism as an all-pervasive religious faith. That the Brahmo Samaj gradually gained momentum in contemporary Bengal at the behest of the second of the Tagore patriarchs was also a testimony to the growing importance of neo-Hindu ideology because

> Neo-Hindu ideology provided the Bengali elite a new concept of their possible role as an elite independent of the British leading the rest of Bengali society whereas they had previously regarded British presence as necessary to safeguard their way of life. Neo-Hindu ideology thought in terms of independence and efforts to develop a broader base of political support to challenge British control.[8]

Implicit here are two fundamental arguments: On the one hand, an attempt is made here to show that being aided by the indigenous intellectual sources of knowledge, the local elites acquired strength to politically challenge the British government; the endeavour also represented a design of action, on the other hand, to assert their independence in thinking in support of a mode of assertion. The argument is partly correct and partly seems to be overstretched: Correct because the passion with which the neo-Hindu ideology was accepted by the Bengali elites shows that they were keen to evolve an independent mode of thinking; partly overstretched because, as history demonstrates, their attempts were directed to radically alter the prevalent sociocultural vision which drew sustenance on the archaic and also primordial values, justified in the name of Hinduism. A careful study of Brahmo Samaj and also the role of the Tagore patriarchs reveals that because they believed that so long as these prejudicial values remained

[8] Barbara Southard, *Neo-Hinduism and Militant Politics in Bengal, 1875–1910*, unpublished PhD dissertation (Manoa: University of Hawaii, 1971), 339, cited in Sen, *Hindu Revivalism in Bengal*, 16.

unchallenged their ideological aim remained elusive. As David Kopf argued persuasively,

> The objective of [the Brahmo Samaj] is to stress on harmonizing the basic social unit [which] was a nineteenth century puritanism that underlay the emphasis on the social good that is derived from sincerity, devotion, purity, forgiveness and gentleness and that castigated the social evils derived from their opposites.[9]

That the Brahmo Samaj was more a campaign for radical social changes was evident if one analytically scanned the set of activities that the Tagore patriarchs undertook along with their like-minded colleagues. So, the argument that it was also an endeavour to wrest political power does not seem to be persuasive, although there is no denying that the Brahmo Samaj campaign created an environment in which the colonized was made to believe that by giving up the age-old sociocultural prejudices segmenting one set of population from another was a source of their weakness. In that sense, it was a harbinger of a new set of ideas which was politico-ideologically articulated by the later nationalists.

The story of the Tagores also allows us to go back to the intellectual roots of the campaign with which they were associated to translate into practice what they so strongly felt. Two of the leading thinkers of the 19th century who appeared to have decisively influenced the organized campaigns against the sociocultural prejudices based on caste identities, in particular are the creative writer, Bankim Chandra Chattopadhyay (1838–1894), and the ascetic, Vivekananda (1863–1902).[10] Bankim's 1882 novel *Anandamath* articulated his responses, couched in his appreciation for the British rule and his hatred for the Muslim rule. Vivekananda took a different path since he believed that divisiveness among the Indians due particularly to caste and religion was an impediment towards their rise as a well-knit unit. Hence, his

---

[9] David Kopf, *The Brahmo Samaj and the Shaping of the Modern Mind* (New Delhi: Archives Publishers, 1988), 107.
[10] Amalesh Tripathy, *The Extremist Challenge* (Calcutta: Orient Longman, 1967).

advice was directed to generate concerted campaigns to get rid of these prejudices which was manifested when he said that

> I invite you to turn from a veneration of what is sterile and dead to what is full of life and promise. I invite you to turn from regretting over past mistakes to consolidating our present task. I urge you not to waste any more effort over retrieving obscure remedies but to join wholeheartedly in the newly founded national effort.[11]

This was a clarion call for those seeking to contribute to common wellbeing. Instead of focusing on the past failures, the ascetic Vivekananda endeavoured to revitalize the moribund 'nation' by striving to realize its own intellectual resources and also emotional strength. It was an attempt to generate love for the country and also its inhabitants irrespective of sociocultural differences. Interestingly, the idea was reverberated in what the British ruler, Curzon, who was instrumental in executing the first partition of Bengal in 1905, said in his convocation address to the students of University of Calcutta in 1905. He also urged the students to 'equip [themselves] with a genuine and manly love for [their] own people.... not the perfervid nationalism of the platform, but the self-sacrificing ardour of the true patriot'.[12] While pursuing the same argument, he further added that

> Learn that the true salvation of India will not come from without but must be created within. It will not be given to you by enactments of the British Parliament or of any Parliament at all. It will not be won by political controversy and most certainly it will not be won by rhetorics.[13]

What Vivekananda suggested was reinforced by Curzon, although the latter had a completely different ideological mission as a ruler in

---

[11] Vivekananda, *Hindudharma O Ramkrishna: Bani o Rachana*, cited in Sen, *Hindu Revivalism in Bengal*, 346.
[12] Curzon's speech at convocation of University of Calcutta, 11 February 1905, Lord Curzon speeches, Vol. IV, 1906, 83, cited in Argov, *Moderates and Extremists in the Indian Nationalist Movement*, 108.
[13] Ibid.

India. Nonetheless, by highlighting what was most appropriate under those circumstances, Curzon seemed to have expressed a common concern that the Bengali elites also evinced. It was not therefore surprising that Dwarkanath while venturing into the unknown world of trade and commerce insisted that the Bengali youths should come forward to join him since it was 'an opportunity for them to stand on their own and also to prove that Bengalis were equally equipped to efficiently handle business like their British counterparts'.[14] He also justified his claim by reiterating that 'with their intelligence they could easily compete with them'.[15] His son, Debendranath, reiterated the view by stressing on the importance of 'self-reliance, perseverance of effort and the utility of hard work'[16] because he believed that 'God has endowed man with wonderful faculties [which is required to be developed] by self-respect and self-improvement'.[17] In the case of the last of the Tagore patriarchs, Rabindranath, the idea was followed zealously since he also believed that unless a 'nation', in his parlance, Samaj, was self-reliant, no progress of the people was possible.

The discussion pursued so far makes three major arguments which merit further attention. First, it has been reinforced that the epistemic ideas that the three Tagores upheld while devising an alternative mode of thinking were both derivative and indigenous. As shown in the book, Dwarkanath was governed by a sense of propriety because he would 'follow the customs and traditions of his ancestors so long as they were not disgraceful or degrading to his self-respect'.[18] There was another aspect of his behaviour which was reflective of his loyalism to the Empire since 'much of what he did was done with an eye towards the reaction of the European community, for he craved their approval just as his orthodox kinsmen looked for approval to the Hindu caste

---

[14] Kshitindranath Tagore, *Dwarkanather Jiban* (in Bangla; Calcutta: Rabindra Bharati Vishwavidyalaya, 1969), 104.
[15] Blair Kling pursued this argument in his *Partner in Empire: Dwarkanath Tagore and the Age of Enterprise in Eastern India* (Berkeley, CA: University California Press, 1976), 25–28.
[16] Debendranath's statement is quoted by David Kopf in his *The Brahmo Samaj and the Shaping of the Modern Indian Mind*, 107.
[17] Ibid.
[18] Kling, *Partner in Empire*, 23.

leaders'.[19] What was true of Dwarkanath does not, of course, hold water vis-à-vis Debendranath and his son, Rabindranath, because, in the changed politico-ideological milieu, they devised their own design which did not seem to have been constructed by the considerations that Dwarkanath had. The second argument is related to the clamour for becoming self-dependent on the basis of the indigenous sociocultural and economic resources. It is true that the ideas that the Tagores developed in collaboration with their compatriots were a creative package based on their politico-ideological priorities. In view of the sources, both Western and indigenous, these ideas were hybrids which worked well to bring people together for a cause; they were presumably designed strategically to ward off the level that those who propounded them were not exactly loyalist nor clearly backward looking because the amalgamation of ideas had elements of both. This was probably one of the core reasons why the Brahmo Samaj, despite internecine conflicts among the colleagues, never deviated from the fundamental beliefs that led to its foundation in 1828. Finally, it is also evident that Tagores arrived on the scene when a new wave of thinking appreciative of the Hindu epics, Vedas and Vedantic texts, caught the attention of those who mattered in society. Critical here is the point that Tagores' well-argued challenge against Hindu Catholicism was readily accepted by a strongly committed contingent of their colleagues and co-workers which means that in view of their acceptance these sets of ideas contributed to the development of a widespread campaign against Hindu orthodoxy. In other words, led by the Tagores, a vigorous attempt was made to spread the view that sociocultural transformation was prior to the clamour for political freedom. Even Rabindranath who expressed his resentment against the British rule, sometimes openly and sometimes tacitly, also strongly felt that the struggle against artificial segmentation of humanity in India should precede demands for political freedom. As he argued, 'the country is inextricably linked to the people of the country, it is there that the most tragic estrangement is visible'[20]; instead of wasting time on blaming the government, he further added that 'we should endeavour to bring

---

[19] Ibid.
[20] Tagore, *Swadeshi Samaj*, 3.

people together by exploring how it is possible'.[21] Crucial here are two points critical to conceptualize the responses that Tagores articulated to express their politico-ideological preferences: On the one hand, it is evident that there were hardly serious differences of opinion among themselves in regard to the heartfelt desire to meaningfully attack the Hindu Catholicism which was, unanimously, a serious impediment towards realizing their goal for the collectivity; by deciding to create an institutionalized bond with the foundation of Brahmo Samaj, for instance, they also held, on the other hand, identical appreciation for an organized effort to combat the well-entrenched views in support of Hindu orthodoxy.

III

A careful dissection of the ideas of Tagores reveals that while pursuing their sociocultural goals they were championing a specific set of political goals. Implicit here is the fundamental idea that attempts at realizing sociocultural goals are embedded with an aim to alter the prevalent political relationships binding the different sets of people differently. In other words, noticeable social transformations invariably bring about shifts which may not always be visible in the prevalent power relationships, being engineered to justify a specific kind of inter-class networks. Critical here is the claim that social and political goals are indistinguishable or so closely well-knit that it is theoretically myopic to separate them. Having chosen to pursue the social goals, the indigenous elites seem to have made two interrelated points: On the one hand, they strongly felt that change in the social arena was critical to the rise and consolidation of a mindset which was supportive of libertarian views articulated by them. This was perhaps the reason why the early nationalists also endorsed the view that social reforms were prior to the political freedom, although by the late 19th century the nationalist like Bal Gangadhar Tilak (1856–1920) opposed the British legislation on the age of consent bill of 1891 because it invited the colonial regime to meddle in the nation's autonomous social domain. While characterizing the bill as 'an intervention in India's spiritual

[21] Ibid.

domain', Tilak argued that 'we would not like that the government should have anything to do with regulating our social customs or ways of living, even supposing that the act of government will be a very beneficial and suitable measure'.[22] The aim here was, as an analyst argues, 'to create a domain of sovereignty with colonial society [by the nationalists] well before it begins its political battle with the imperial power'.[23] What was paramount to the early nationalist responses was the unquestionable importance of social togetherness, and the British intervention was therefore injurious to the continuity of this social amity. Although Tilak's argument swayed many of the nationalists in the 20th century, the idea did not seem to be so appealing in the 19th century, as was evident in Dwarkanath's support to the abolition of sati by a legal enactment by the colonial power. Being a loyalist, his support to the British intervention in this regard did not seem to be a reflection of his commitment to the rescinding of a brutal social practice because he appeared to have been swayed as it was an official endorsement for its discontinuity. Nonetheless, there is no denying that the campaign for doing away with this custom would not have gained momentum had it not been raised by the 'native' social reformers. As is well known, Rammohun and Dwarkanath were the leading proponents who worked hard to build an opinion for its abdication despite the opposition of the orthodox Hindus, organized by the Dharma Sabha.

What is thus argued here is that social goal was integrally linked with political goal, although Tilak had a different take on this issue. Rabindranath, being supportive of building a well-knit society, however conceptualized the issue completely differently. In his perception, political goal was 'an essentially conflictual mode of being peculiar to the West and therefore foreign to the people committed to the primacy of the social goal'.[24] Critical to the rise of India as a well-knit multitude, the acceptance of diversity remained an integral feature to the

---

[22] Bal Gangadhar Tilak's commentary on the 1891 Age of Consent Bill was published in *Kesari* (21 March 1891), after it was enacted on 19 March 1891.
[23] Chatterjee, *The Nation and Its Fragments*, 6.
[24] Rabindranath Tagore, *Itihas* (in Bangla; Kolkata: Visva-Bharati, 2014), 10–11.

Indian mindset. It was well-elaborated when the poet argued further by saying that 'the ability to happily accept others as one's own despite stark sociocultural and political differences is a magical quality that helped India to readily embrace and internalize erstwhile unfamiliar values and practices'.[25] This is a perfectly conceptually defensible position, although it does not directly address the query that we made at the outset of this subsection, namely, whether social and political goals can hardly be separated given that they are interlocked. So, the Tagores, despite not being part of 'a conflictual mode of being', were very much involved in the political goal because their genuine concerns for meaningful social changes in Bengal had a serious impact on the prevalent power-relationships vertically dividing people around class, caste and clan axes. Dwarkanath was involved in social reforms presumably because his aspirations tallied with the ruler; Debendranath pursued the same aim with a specific ideological aim of championing a specific set of values which, he strongly felt, were of great importance to his modernizing zeal; Rabindranath followed the path with a clear difference with his predecessors because he accepted social reform for the rise and consolidation of well-knit multitude as a precursor to swaraj or political freedom. Despite having distinctive views, the three Tagores come together under one conceptual platform since they privileged social over political as one of the fundamental features of their views. In circumstances, when the Western discourses were presumed to have dominated their indigenous counterparts, it was not an insignificant conceptual design seeking to establish an alternative, a persuasive alternative indeed, despite challenges from multiple corners.

One of the intellectual sources of Tagores' conceptual insights was Upanishads which is characterized in contemporary analysis as an attempt by them 'to cast the problems of Indian political experience in terms that are distinctive of its own pre-modern, pre-colonial history'.[26] What was initiated by Debendranath with the foundation of Brahma Vidyalaya in 1881 was pursued further by his son, Rabindranath, with the establishment of Visva-Bharati in 1921 where

[25] Ibid., 13–14.
[26] Farah Godrej, *Cosmopolitan Political Thought: Method, Practice, Discipline* (New York, NY: Oxford University Press, 2011), 109.

he combined his concern for spiritualism with internationalism both in pedagogical and institutional structures of the institutions. The intellectual roots of Visva-Bharati can be traced back to Rabindranath's 1904 creative text, entitled *Swadeshi Samaj*, which was also a concerted effort to organize the villagers around what they felt appropriate for realizing the common goals and objectives. To bring them together and also to sustain their collective amity, it was required to develop a sense of being respectful to others despite being socioculturally different. We must note a caveat here since Rabindranath's appreciation of village life was based on his very unique experiences of a select set of Bengal villages. Nonetheless, he was keen to associate these villages around Visva-Bharati to evolve together by learning from each other. Gandhi also viewed the rise of India as a close-knit society with village as its centre. The argument led to a serious debate in the Constituent Assembly because the chairman of the Drafting Committee, B. R. Ambedkar, was hardly persuaded since he believed that villages were responsible for maintaining caste and the concomitant prejudices segregating one section of the villagers from another. Hence, being opposed to both Rabindranath and Gandhi, he, to defend the liberal conceptual foundation of the 1950 Constitution, thus forcefully argued that

> It is said that the new Constitution should have been drafted on the ancient Hindu model of a state and that instead of incorporating Western theories the new Constitution should have been raised and built upon village panchayats and district panchayats.... They just want India to contain many village governments. The love of the intellectual Indian for the village community is of course infinite if not pathetic.... I hold that the village republics have been the ruination of India. I am therefore surprised that those who condemn provincialism and communalism should come forward as champions of the village. What is the village but a sink of localism, a den of ignorance, narrow mindedness and communalism. [Hence,] I discarded the village and adopted the individual as its unit.[27]

---

[27] B. R. Ambedkar's statement in the Constituent Assembly, 4 November 1949, *The Constituent Assembly Debates*, Vol. VII (New Delhi: Lok Sabha Secretariat, 2003), 38–39.

Ambedkar's scathing critique of village-based Samaj was an outcome of his painful existential experiences by being born as a Dalit and also his exposure to the Enlightenment values by his teacher at Columbia University, John Dewey, which was reinforced during his doctoral studies at the London School of Economics.[28] There are reasons to believe that Rabindranath was aware of the consequences of the brutal caste division, especially in the villages. Nonetheless, as a constructivist, he preferred to devise a mechanism which, by injecting a sense of belongingness, was to create a platform for everybody irrespective of sociocultural schism to come together. This may sound simplistic since caste division was inherent in India. To translate his design into practice, he evolved various sets of activities which, with everybody's participation, neither were discriminatory nor upheld the caste-driven prejudicial practices; instead, it was a place where the villagers associated with the Samaj were equal to others. Visva-Bharati's Sriniketan campus epitomizes the system of practices that Rabindranath evolved by being intimately linked with this experiment. Here too, one sees a departure from what his grandfather, Dwarkanath, held, though his father, Debendranath, did not seem to be inclined in sustaining the caste division; otherwise, he would not have agreed to his son's suggestion to offer the seat of priest during the regular Brahmo prayers. Being grounded in the prevalent sociocultural reality, Rabindranath was also aware that sudden and also forcible changes were unlikely to create togetherness; instead, it would become a source of consternation in the villagers. Hence, he found it prudent to devise various schemes which ultimately led to fruition, as history witnesses.

The three Tagores represented a new wave of thinking and also practices. Despite being a loyalist, Dwarkanath initiated many unique sociocultural devices to bring people together which also demonstrated a vision for being independent of the colonized. His son, Debendranath, being committed to strengthen the spiritual foundation of humanity, reaffirmed his faith in the classical Hindu religious scriptures, especially Vedas and Upanishads. The trend that was visible when Dwarkanath undertook steps to design a new process

---

[28] I elaborated the argument in my *The Socio-political Ideas of B. R. Ambedkar: Liberal Constitutionalism in a Creative Mould* (Oxford: Routledge, 2019).

by being heavily drawn upon the ideas of his colleague, Rammohun, continued when his son emerged as the main proponent. A significant change took place when Rabindranath, following his father's footsteps, decided to undertake his own experiment on how to ensure human well-being away from Calcutta in Santiniketan. In his 1904 tract, *Swadeshi Samaj*, he developed a model by drawing upon his ideas which were both derivative and also indigenous. What was conceptually most innovative was his idea of Samaj as an alternative to nation that he had already elaborated in his 1916 lectures on nationalism. Given his appreciation for India's sociocultural diversity as integral to her existence long before the colonial rule, he was never persuaded to accept the European idea of nation presumably because it tended to essentialize human identity around some well-defined sociocultural axes. The argument sounds plausible which led one of the analysts to argue that for Rabindranath, Samaj provided 'a non-statist alternative to nation', one in consonance with his argument that the governing force of any collectivity ought to be spiritual, rather material.[29] Conceptually independent of the Europeanized idea of nation, given the obvious limitations, Samaj evolved in India as a time-tested mechanism presumably because it contained in itself the vision of a collectivity based on the internal sociocultural resources. In other words, the idea of Samaj as a mode of bringing diverse people together was thus hailed as congruous with the vision of India. It was articulated very succinctly by the bard when he stated that

> India has never had a real sense of nationalism. Even through from childhood I had been taught that idolatry of the Nation is almost better than reverence for God and humanity, I believe I have outgrown that teaching, and it is my conviction that my countrymen will truly gain their India by fighting against the education which teaches them that a country is greater than the ideals of humanity.[30]

Primary here was Rabindranath's concern for humanity. Since the idea of nation was at variance with humanity, the poet was thus persuaded

---

[29] Partha Chatterjee, *Lineages of Political Society: Studies in Postcolonial Democracy* (New York, NY: Columbia University Press, 2011), 107–109.
[30] Tagore, *Nationalism*, 64.

to reject it as completely unfit to explain the collectivity that India epitomized. Like his predecessors, who endeavoured hard to institutionalize the collectivity by creating Brahmo Samaj, for instance, the bard devoted his energy to strengthening the Samaj as he felt that unless this was done India's progress as a collectivity remained elusive. One must also emphasize here that Rabindranath was not a utopian thinker; he was a practitioner, which was reflected when he identified the impediments towards creating a collectivity comprising people with concerns for one another. It was expressed unambiguously when he further mentioned that

> The things we in India have to think of is ... to remove those social customs and ideals which have generated a want of self-respect and a complete dependence on those above us—a state of affairs which has been brought about entirely by the domination in India of caste system, and the blind and lazy habit of relying upon the authority of traditions that are incongruous anachronisms in the present age.[31]

With the above caustic remark, Rabindranath displayed his hatred for the caste system which, by sustaining the artificial segregation, helped build and continue a mindset in its support. Neither Dwarkanath nor Debendranath attacked caste system so bluntly; Debendranath, for instance, introduced various practices in Brahmo Samaj to develop a mindset among the members opposed to caste segregation, although he believed that 'the caste system in its original form is primarily a mode of differentiating people on the basis of their professional skills'.[32] With intellectual cues from his father, Rabindranath thus argued that India's

> Caste system is the outcome of the spirit of toleration. For India has all along been trying experiments in evolving a social unity within which all the different peoples could be held together, while fully the freedom of maintaining their own differences. The tie has been as loose as possible, yet as close as the circumstances permitted.[33]

[31] Ibid., 68–69.
[32] Chakrabarty, *Maharshi Debendranather Thakur*, 606.
[33] Tagore, *Nationalism*, 69.

Here, Rabindranath captured the trajectory of how the caste system was reduced to a form of social organization, the aim of which was to socially justify exploitation of human beings by their fellow counterparts given their separate caste identities. What was needed, in its place, was to evolve a self-sustaining Samaj by being sensitive to its members' needs and requirements irrespective of their caste affiliations. In pursuance his ideological goal, Rabindranath thus suggested that the social institutions that were complementary to

> His ideals ... have two objects: one is to regulate our passions and appetites for the harmonious development of man, and the other is to help him to cultivate disinterested love for his fellow creatures. Therefore, society is the expression of those moral and spiritual aspirations of man which belong to his higher nature.[34]

True to his commitment to the Upanishadic vision that also inspired his father, Debendranath, the bard also realized that the basis for the evolution of a healthy society was compassion for others, especially those who were in distress. Debendranath was introduced to this idea by Ramchandra Vidyabagish, while Rabindranath became privy to the claim by being close to his father. It will not be odd to also mention that by insisting on concerns for others as integral to humanity, Rabindranath also reiterated the spirit on which the Enlightenment philosophy was based.

As argued above, the bard designed his model of togetherness by being vehemently opposed to artificial caste segregation. His dance drama *Chandalika* (1938) is, for instance, a testimony to the claim. As one with tremendous foresight, it was easier for Rabindranath to understand that unless the caste division was done away with, India's political independence was likely to be a change of political guards with no substantial differences because, as he further elaborated that

> We must remember that whatever weaknesses we cherish in our society will become the source of danger in politics. The same inertia which leads us to our idolatry of dead forms in social institutions

[34] Ibid., 73.

will create in our politics prison-houses with immovable walls. The narrowness of sympathy which makes it possible for us to impose upon a considerable portion of humanity the galling yoke of inferiority will assert itself in our politics in creating the tyranny of injustice.[35]

Rabindranath pitched his argument at two levels: At a rather practical level, he put across the point that the age-old social prejudices continued to be a deterrent to the realization of the politico-ideological goals that the nationalists espoused. At a conceptual level, being exceedingly categorical, he thus argued that without completely uprooting the vicious caste system, our political aspirations could never be realized in their true spirit. Here, it is tempting to draw a parallel with what B. R. Ambedkar categorically stated in his last speech in the Constituent Assembly on 25 November 1949 where he condemned the caste system as anti-national since it was a constraint to the generation of a sense of 'fraternity or common brotherhood to all Indians, or, the idea of Indians being one people, an idea which gives unity and solidarity to social life'.[36] In the present circumstances, when caste order was well-entrenched, fraternity was neither instinctive to the Indians nor organic to their psyche. So, Ambedkar argued, so long as caste remained, the point about the inculcation of a sense of being one as a community seems fruitless. On the basis of this conceptualization, he further made a very perceptive theoretical formulation which was useful to comprehend Indian sociocultural reality. Since caste was divisive, it was 'anti-national [because] in the first place, they bring about separation in social life, and [second] because they generate jealousy and antipathy between caste and caste'.[37] Being an impediment to the building of a sense of fraternity, caste was, underlined Ambedkar, to be discarded to create and consolidate the sense of brotherhood. A careful reading of the ideas that Ambedkar articulated shows that he thought exactly the way Rabindranath built his conceptual model for 'nation' building. Like the bard, the chairman of the Drafting Committee

[35] Ibid., 75.
[36] B. R. Ambedkar's speech in the Constituent Assembly, 25 November 1949, *Constituent Assembly Debates*, Book No. 5, 979.
[37] Ibid., 980.

spoke in an identical language, although there was hardly a reference to the views that the former pursued while sharing the same concern with the latter. It was a confluence of thought that flourished presumably because they had identical concerns in this regard, although it was obvious that Rabindranath's model of *Swadeshi Samaj* in which villages formed the nucleus would have, under no circumstances, received Ambedkar's approbation in view of the powerful conceptual arguments that he put forward in support of his contention.

IV

A liberal humanist, Rabindranath always championed humanism despite challenges from the mainstream nationalists, including Gandhi. As he was convinced that nationalism and humanism were antithetical to each other, he sharpened his attack on attempts at conceptualizing India in the mould of a 'nation'. According to him, the *Swadeshi Samaj* was an articulation of a definite mode of realizing the core values of humanism which was 'stepped into the Brahmo tradition as central to the world view'[38] that three Tagores shared with one another. This was thus a wave of thought that conceptually bound three Tagores together. By being true to the tradition of universal humanism, Rabindranath thus argued that

> 'the problem of Europe is egocentric nationalism, a disease to be cured only by a universal ideal of humanity [and] ... it was the key role of the Brahma Samaj to help in saving the world from the madness of nationalism'.[39]

In pursuance of the sociocultural objectives that Rabindranath imbibed by being raised in a family that created a new genre of thinking by creatively blending the Western discourses with the indigenious counterparts. With Dwarkanath at the helm of affairs, the revolutionary

[38] Poulomi Saha, 'Bengal into a Nation: Tagore the Colonial Cosmopolitan?' *Journal of Modern Literature* 36, no. 2 (Winter, 2013): 19.
[39] Rabindranath Thakur, *Brahmo Samajer Sarkatha* (in Bangla; Fundamental Belief of Brahmo Samaj), 6, 7, 10, quoted in Kopf, *The Brahmo Samaj and the Shaping of the Modern Mind*, 301.

sociocultural goals of Rammohun blossomed. It was Debendranath who passed the baton to his son, Rabindranath, who, being born and nurtured in a different politico-ideological milieu, easily adopted a mode of communication which was neither exactly as that of a loyalist like his grandfather nor that of an extremely spiritualist social reformer like his father. By not really following their footsteps, Rabindranath evolved a unique mode of thinking, supplemented by concomitant practices which was complementary to his uncritical faith in universal humanism. It was therefore not surprising that being vehemently opposed to nationalism insisting on ideologically binding humanity by essentializing human identity, the bard set out a distinct mode of thinking when he categorically upheld the view that

> It is the continual and stupendous dead pressure of [the] inhuman upon the living human under which the modern world is groaning. Not merely the subject races, but you who live under the delusion that you are free, are every day sacrificing your freedom and humanity to this fetish of nationalism, living in the dense poisonous atmosphere of world-wide suspicion and greed and panic.[40]

Evident here is the argument in defence of the vacuous nature of freedom that one seemingly enjoyed in the modern world. Everybody was getting deceived with the rise of nationalism as a mechanism of bond among the people on the basis of their narrowly conceived identities undermining, at the same time, their existence as a part of wider humanity in which the concern of humanism reigned supreme. This created, according to the poet, two interrelated deficiencies in the very notion of nationalism: On the one hand, by arguing for the distinction between 'us' and 'they', the nationalist West devised and also consolidated a schism on the basis of a set of constructed criteria; so, freedom was thus articulated, on the other hand, differently by different sets of people. Not only did it cause and consolidate a permanent fissure in humanity but also the very conceptualization of nationalism was, according to Rabindranath, detrimental to his espoused ideal of universal humanism. What was most deceptive was the fact that although the West 'marches under the banner of freedom, the Nation of the

[40] Tagore, *Nationalism*, 15.

West forges its iron chains of organization which are most relentless and unbreakable that have ever been manufactured in the whole of man'.[41] Hence, the bard concludes that 'Nation is the greatest evil for the Nation [because] all its precautions are against it and any new birth of its fellow in the world is always followed in its mind by the dread of new peril'.[42] What was a source of consternation to the poet was the rise of nationalism as a deliberate design to permanently seal the natural blossoming of humanity because 'the truth is that the spirit of conflict and conquest is at the origin and in the centre of Western nationalism [and] its basis is not social organization, ... [but] has evolved a perfect organization of power, but not spiritual idealism'.[43] Basic to the argument was his unalloyed faith in universal humanism which was a casualty with the rise of nationalism as an endeavour to privilege one set of human beings over another. Here too, the idea does not seem to be exactly new since what Rabindranath expressed in clear terms was derivative of what his grandfather and father upheld while pursuing the same politico-ideological goals. As the sociocultural and political milieu was different when the bard rose to prominence, it was easier for him to sharply focus on how nationalism became a powerful ideological campaign against the instinctive sociocultural diversity among human beings and also an equally effective instrument of exploitation by one set of people against another.

V

Three Tagores is also an endorsement of the widely circulated Platonic dictum that every philosopher is a child of his time. It is partly true because the Tagore patriarchs represented both the concern and also limitations of the historical age in which they were nurtured. That they also surpassed some of the well-entrenched sociocultural values is illustrative of the claim that they were harbingers of change as well. In three specific ways, three Tagores were conceptually connected: (a) They never accepted the sociocultural limitations as axiomatic and hence

[41] Ibid., 14.
[42] Ibid., 17–18.
[43] Ibid., 12.

non-invincible; (b) they pursued their specific politico-ideological objectives in collaboration with those who felt alike which means that they realized that their individual efforts, however genuine they were, were not adequate to build and sustain an organized campaign in favour of what they deemed appropriate for fulfilling their goals; and (c) they became integrally connected with a mindset that evolved out of a sustained commitment of three generations of social reformers.

As shown in the book, Dwarkanath was inspired by his compatriot, Rammohun, who launched an effective campaign against those prejudicial and also brutal social practices. Accompanied by his zeal for social reform, he was also involved in the spreading of education and also undertook special initiatives to translate most of the important Hindu religious texts in English and vernacular. Given his untimely demise, it was Dwarkanath who shouldered the responsibility which was manifested in many of his activities so long as he remained in the reckoning in Calcutta's elite circles. His unconditional loyalty gave him dividends since, in many of the initiatives, he was aided by his British colleagues. In pursuance of the goals that his deceased colleague, Rammohun, set out for the posterity, the senior-most of the Tagore patriarchs devised new designs to sustain the campaign that gained momentum with the former at the helm of affairs. Like Rammohun, he also believed that the British rule unfolded new desires for change which 'are all beneficial [because] when you find', added Dwarkanath,

> The advanced section of the community throwing off the fetters of ignorance and superstition, asserting their rights, and vindicating their position, then you may be sure you have a people of whom you can confidently predict that the course before them is onward course.... Should the growing belief in higher things prove a living power instead of a dead petrification, we should then see India rising with the might of a giant, and assuming her proper position in the scale of nations.[44]

---

[44] Dwarkanath's statement, reproduced in Mittra, *Memoir of Dwarkanath Tagore*, 19.

True to his belief, Dwarkanath carried forward a campaign directed to translate what he strongly felt to accomplish the sociocultural goals against many odds. As an organization, the formation and also the consolidation of the Brahmo Samaj contributed to the sustenance of an endeavour that gradually gained momentum in support of the ideas that Rammohun initiated and Dwarkanath reinforced in unfavourable circumstances since 'he had to encounter prejudice at every step. Bigotry and superstition scowled upon every effort that he made to enlighten his countrymen. It was breaking in upon the system of the faith. It was against the way and manners of their fathers'.[45]

Dwarkanath stepped in an area of concern that did not seem to have received attention in the past presumably because of the threat of severe social backlash. It was to his credit that a group of socioculturally enlightened individuals zealously participated in the campaign that was directed to get rid of the well-entrenched retrogressive social systems and values. The task was relatively easier when Debendranath emerged on the scene presumably because (a) his father prepared the platform by bringing those together with identical sociocultural goals and (b) the past initiatives for generating interests in ancient Hindu religious scriptures fructified as the leading Bengali elites were drawn to them to ascertain whether what the Brahmo Samaj claimed in opposition to the orthodox Dharma Sabha was truly based on the holy texts. His effort in translating the *Ramayana, Mahabharata* and *Upanishads* was supported by his colleagues holding identical views which means that they were also keen to learn what these texts conveyed and how they contributed to the generation and dissemination of knowledge. Also, by founding Tattwabodhini Sabha in 1839 which was later merged with Brahmo Samaj in 1859, the second of the Tagore patriarchs revitalized the organizational strength of the campaign that started unfolding with Rammohun in the early part of the 19th century. Besides imitating his father's zeal for trade and commerce, Debendranath proved to be a true heir since he pursued those plans and programmes that Dwarkanath devised for ushering in an era of noticeable sociocultural changes. What needs to be highlighted is that like his father he also prepared

---

[45] Dr Thomas Dealtry's homage to Dwarkanath, 4 December 1846, reproduced in Mittra, *Memoir of Dwarkanath Tagore*, li.

his son who, being emotionally and also intellectually persuaded, firmly established the typical Brahma way of living a life with the foundation of Visva-Bharati in 1921.

Born and raised in a different socio-economic and political milieu, Rabindranath's approach to sociocultural and political issues was both similar at one level and completely different at another. Unlike his grandfather, he was not a loyalist per se; unlike his father, he was not, at all, indifferent to the ongoing nationalist struggle, first, at the behest of the revolutionary nationalists[46] and, later, Gandhi. As the novel, *Ghare-Baire* (1916), shows, Rabindranath was vehemently opposed to their political design to liberate India since it was neither socially inclusive nor based on concerns for bringing the socially disparate communities together for the cause. With Gandhi, he was both a critique and an admirer, as Chapter 6 underlines. As far as his approach to the British rule was concerned, he also held diametrically opposite views. At the beginning of literary career, he was clearly of the view that there were many aspects of British civilization which were worth imitating, though he expressed his resentment once innocent participants in a protest meeting were massacred in Jallianwala Bagh in 1919. That his assessment of the British rule had undergone a sea change was evident in his last public speech in 1941 which underlined that the ideal of civilization that unfolded in Britain influenced all of us. 'Born in that atmosphere, which was moreover coloured by our intuitive bias for literature', argued Rabindranath, 'I naturally set the English on the throne of my heart. Thus passed the first chapters of my life'.[47] Soon, the bard was disillusioned as the rulers undertook steps, contrary to what they propounded at the dawn of colonialism in India which was evident in his scathing critique of the colonial rule in India. According to him, 'then came the parting of ways accompanied with a painful feeling of disillusion which I began increasingly to discover how easily those who accepted the highest truths of civilization

---

[46] Peter Heehs dealt with the nature of the revolutionary nationalist campaign for India's freedom in his 'Bengali Religious Nationalism and Communalism', *International Journal of Hindu Studies* 1, no. 1 (April 1997): 117–139.

[47] Tagore, 'Crisis in Civilization', reproduced in Das, *The English Writings of Rabindranath Tagore*, Vol. III, 723.

disowned them with impunity whenever questions of national self-interest were involved'.[48]

Unlike Gandhi who, in his *Hind Swaraj* (1909), evolved a strong critique of industrial civilization that was possible by institutionalizing exploitation by the industrial Britain, Rabindranath developed his sharp critique of British colonialism on the basis of its denial of the fruits of industrialism to the colonized. He sharply made this point when he stated that 'the mastery over the machine, by which the British have consolidated their sovereignty over their vast Empire, has been kept a sealed book, to which due access has been denied to this hapless country'.[49] The bard's experience was different when he visited Japan because he saw with his 'own eyes the admirable use to which Japan has put in her own country [the machine-driven] progress'.[50] It was reinforced by his visit to Russia in 1930. The poet was enamoured by 'the unsparing energy with which Russia has tried to fight disease and illiteracy, and has succeeded in steadily liquidating ignorance and poverty, wiping off the humiliation from the face of a vast continent'.[51] What particularly pleased him was the success of the administration to completely wipe out the inter-community rivalry due to religious differences despite the fact that the country was religiously diverse. Appreciative of such an administrative feat, the poet thus claimed that it was 'a truly civilized administration [since] it is completely impartial while serving the common interests of the people'.[52] The same Rabindranath was however aghast when he found that the Russian administration was imposing a system of education to mould people to espouse one specific variety of ideological predilection. According to him, it was a serious defect which was manifested in the effort 'to turn their system of education into a mould, which was detrimental to the humanity because humanity cast in a mould cannot endure'.[53] While

---

[48] Ibid.
[49] Ibid.
[50] Ibid.
[51] Ibid.
[52] Ibid., 724.
[53] Rabindranath Tagore, 20 September 1930, reproduced in *Letters from Russia* (Kolkata: Visva-Bharati, 1984; reprint), 4.

elaborating his argument, he further mentioned that 'if the theory of education does not correspond with the law of living mind, either the mould will burst into pieces or man's mind will be paralyzed to death or man will be a mechanical doll'.[54]

Primary to the bard's concern was to contribute to the growth and consolidation of a civilization which was based on 'cooperation' and not 'exploitation', 'compassion' and not 'animosity'. He was a supporter of the Brahmo Samaj to the extent that it upheld universal humanism by nurturing those civilizational values that brought human beings together.[55] What was therefore critical to him was to generate a milieu in which, instead of nurturing enmity against other fellow human beings, one should devote oneself in cementing a bond given the fact that we all belonged to one race, that is, the race of humanity. Rabindranath was unable to comprehend why 'intellectual people drift into the disorder of barbarism in India'[56] when it was not difficult for the 200 nationalities of Russia to form a strong union.

Ideationally, the Tagores represented simultaneously a quest and also a conceptual design for addressing contemporary sociocultural issues and politico-ideological concerns. Instead of championing exclusively either the derivative or indigenous discourses, their voices were articulated on the basis of their own assessment of what they learnt as history unfolded. Despite being appreciative of Vedic cosmology, it will be conceptually myopic to argue that they privileged the Vedic texts over others while charting their mode of comprehending the prevalent socio-economic and politicocultural realities. They were open to the Western discourses which also confirms that they were also sensitive to the unique conceptual visions that had definite alien sociological roots. It is therefore conceptually perfect to recognize 'the synthetic capacities inherent within [them because] each of them incorporated elements of Vedic thought, Enlightenment thought as

---

[54] Ibid.
[55] David Kopf elaborates this argument in *The Brahmo Samaj and the Shaping of the Modern Indian Mind*, 302–304.
[56] Tagore, 'Crisis in Civilization', reproduced in Das, *The English Writings of Rabindranath Tagore*, Vol. III, 724.

well as non-classical folk knowledge into their ideas'.[57] What therefore emerged out of this creative blending were those normative insights which were not unique to their own spatiotemporal contexts, but an outcome of cross-cultural dialogues. So, the ideas of Dwarkanath, Debendranath and Rabindranath do not seem to be dissimilar since the conceptual ingredients on which they are based are clearly identical, although the texture differs presumably because of the variant contextual milieu in which they operated. The Tagores can thus fairly be said to have been one of those renaissance thinkers who, despite not being so vocal against the denial of rights and opportunities by the colonizers of the colonized, continued to remain active in articulating an independent voice that gradually assumed massive proportions in the processes of India's decolonization. On a surface reading, their exact responses might have lacked political connotations, although the models that the Tagores developed were of tremendous significance in spreading out and also consolidating a common concern for the enslaved 'nation'; it was a concern for coming together for a shared cause in opposition to myriad sociopolitical forces which were not exactly anti-British in character. This was where they not only succeeded but also raised the collective emotions high amid threatening circumstances which made them a class by themselves.

---

[57] Godrej, *Cosmopolitan Political Thought*, 17.

Select Bibliography

Bibliographical Note

Bibliography is integral to a book primarily because it contains intellectual resources in the form of monographs, essays and reports which are of great use for further research. It is not an exhaustive list of books and other resources, but it provides the future researchers with a list of some of the major works on a particular theme. There is a possibility of misunderstanding since a specific bibliography contains the resources according to the priorities of a specific author which may not be universally acceptable. What is meant to be argued is the possibility that under no circumstances a bibliography is acceptable to all, given the conceptual inclination of the author who prepares it. Nonetheless, it will be of help since it allows the researchers to locate some of the useful tracts representing an alternative and/or different point(s) of view. One should also appreciate the fact that a bibliography is always useful since it provides instantaneously a list which helps the researchers to begin the exercise at the first instance. There is no denying that a bibliography is of foremost importance for further research, and it thus constitutes an indispensable part of any creative work.

To not burden the readers and also future researchers with a long list of texts, I have decided to prepare as short a list as possible. Before the bibliography is presented, I would like to make two general observations. First, given the fact that *The Three Tagores, Dwarkanath, Debendranath and Rabindranath* draws on many vernacular texts, for obvious reasons, I translated them by keeping the spirit of the argument, instead of making a verbatim translation. As is well known, Tagores wrote extensively in Bangla and without consulting them no work shall be authentic which is why these sources are of immense value. Second, there are some tracts which, by being exhaustive in terms of information, are very useful to build the argument. Some of these texts are not easily available; I am fortunate that with support from Dr Nimai Saha, our librarian, I got them easily. For instance, for an analysis of the life and times of Dwarkanath, the texts by Kshitindranath Tagore, entitled *Dwarkanather Thakurer Jibani* (biography of Dwarkanath Tagore) and Kissory Chand Mittra's *Memoir of Dwarkanath Tagore*, published in 1870, were simply most precious in unearthing the complexities that the senior-most of the Tagore patriarchs' life represented. In a similar vein, the activities of Debendranath Tagore were well-articulated by him in his *Atmajibani* (autobiography) and also Ajit Kumar Chakrabarti's *Maharshi Debendranath Tagore*, which are also utilized in building the argument whenever necessary. Furthermore, the Rabindra Bhawan's archives also contain useful inputs which remained, so far, inaccessible to the outside world. In this book, I drew on them to comprehend the life of Debendranath as a zamindar before he became Maharshi. Besides *Rabindra Rachanabali* (collected works of Rabindranath), for the chapters on Rabindranath, I have also drawn on many other published books which are now out of print and also many letters which are in the possession of Rabindra Bhawan archives. I have also extensively utilized the collection of Rabindranath Tagore's written texts, published by Sahitya Akademi, entitled *The English Writings of Rabindranath Tagore* (four volumes). It would not have been possible to venture in such a terrain of Bengal's intellectual history that evolved around the Tagores without the support that I received from my colleagues in Visva-Bharati library and Rabindra Bhawan archives. It would not be an exaggeration to suggest that by supplying the relevant resources, my colleagues did not allow interruption to happen while being engaged in working on a very complex theme of Bengal's historical past.

I must also clarify why some of the texts are included in the bibliography and why some of them have been discarded, though they appear to be pertinent to other researchers. Here, what is critical is the goal of this project that focuses on how the Tagores shaped the cognitive-cum-epistemic identity of those involved in reinventing Bengal by creatively blending the derivative Western discourses with what they considered to be indigenous. In other words, it was an interesting juncture of Bengal's intellectual history when the Tagores appeared on the scene. Being a product of the ideas that unfolded with the rise of colonialism and also the indigenous endeavour towards rediscovering India's intellectual past, Dwarkanath saw the outside world in distinctive conceptual parameters. Despite being uncritically appreciative of the early colonialism, the senior-most of the Tagore patriarchs carved an independent space by being one of the prominent businessmen of the era. Debendranath also remained a distinct source of influence which unfolded with the strengthening of Brahmo Samaj and also the establishment of Brahmacharya Ashram in Santiniketan which blossomed into a full-fledged centre of learning and alternative pedagogy when his son, Rabindranath, spearheaded the campaign with the foundation of Visva-Bharati in 1921.

My purpose is not to narrate the history as is done above; my goal is to show the radical sociocultural metamorphosis in Bengal which was complemented with the rise and universal acceptance of compatible politico-ideological preferences. One notices a clear shift from what Dwarkanath held to what became Debendranath's priority. It is also visible that Debendranath did not seem to have been as politically active as his father because he was far more spiritualist in his day-to-day existence. With this serious endeavour, a new school of thought emerged to conceptually justify that one's spiritual root was as important as one's outer manifestation; in fact, the latter appeared hollow unless it was endorsed by the former. It was Debendranath who instilled this idea among his followers who generated a wave of thinking which did not receive adequate attention in the past. Many books have been written on Rabindranath's literary genius, very few on his sociopolitical ideas. The purpose of this bibliography is to include those texts that are directed to demonstrate that the bard had equally penned down his view on contemporary sociopolitical issues; he also raised his voice against the British when he disliked the way the government was functioning, although, unlike Gandhi, he was never an active participant in the anti-British campaign in the sense the Mahatma did. Nonetheless, he served the nation's cause in his own distinctive way. A careful analysis of how Visva-Bharati developed since the second decade of the 20th century reveals that Rabindranath's concern for the nation and his countrymen was qualitatively different from the conventional nationalists, for he believed that so long as socioculturally justified discriminatory and also prejudicial practices prevailed in India, political freedom could hardly be realized in its true spirit and texture. A proponent of a unique conceptual formulation, the bard was perhaps the most innovative thinker among his compatriots who held the views despite being vehemently opposed by the contrarians.

Select Bibliography

Anderson, Benedict. *Imagined Communities: Reflections on the Origin and Spread of Nationalism*. New York, NY: Verso, 1991.

Balagangadhara, S. N. *Reconceptualizing India Studies*. New Delhi: Oxford University Press, 2012.

Banerjee, Prathama. 'Between the Political and Non-political: The Vivekananda Moment and a Critique of the Social in Colonial Bengal, 1890s–1910s'. *Social History* 39, no. 3 (2014).

Banerjee, Sreenath. *The Life of Dwarkanath Tagore*. Calcutta: Manomohan Press, 1914.

Bera, Sadananda, and Narayanchandra Sau. *Rabindranath O Rajniti: Eekhan O Thakhan* (in Bangla). Kolkata: Kallol Prakashani, 2013.

Berlin, Isaiah. *The Sense of Reality: Studies in Ideas and Their History*. New York, NY: Farrar, Straus and Giroux, 1996.

Bhabha, Homi K. *The Location of Culture*. London and New York, NY: Routledge, 1994.

Bhattacharya, Raja. *Dwarkanath: A Prince in a Colonized Nation* (in Bangla). Kolkata: Patrabharati, 2020.

Bhattacharya, Sabyasachi. *The Mahatma and the Poet: Letter and Debates between Gandhi and Tagore, 1915–1941*, New Delhi: National Book Trust, 1997.

———. 'Antinomies of Nationalism and Rabindranath Tagore'. *Economic & Political Weekly* 51, no. 6 (February 2016).

Chakrabarty, Bidyut. *Social and Political Thought of Rabindranath Tagore*. New Delhi: SAGE Publications, 2020.

Chakrabarty, Dipesh. 'Friendships in the Shadow of Empire: Tagore's Reception in Chicago, circa, 1913–1932'. *Modern Asian Studies* 48, no. 5 (2014).

Chakraborti, Ranjit. *Dwarkanath Tagore: A Historical Evaluation* (in Bangla). Kolkata: Granthabitan, 1983.

Chatterjee, Kalyan. 'Gora: Tagore's Paradoxical Self'. *Indian Literature* 49, no. 3 (May–June 2005).

Chatterjee, Partha. *The Nation and Its Fragments: Colonial and Post-colonial Histories*, New Delhi: Oxford University Press, 1994.

———. 'The Fruits of Macaulay's Poison Tree'. In *The Present History of West Bengal*. New Delhi: Oxford University Press, 1997.
Chaudhuri, Rosinka. 'The Flute, Gerontion, and Subalternist Misreadings of Tagore'. *Social Text* 22, no. 1 (2004).
———. 'Hemchandra's Bharat Sangeet (1870) and the Politics of Poetry: A Prehistory of Hindu Nationalism in Bengal?' *Indian Economic and Social History Review* 42, no. 2 (2005).
Chaudhuri, Sukanta, ed. *The Cambridge Companion to Rabindranath Tagore*. Cambridge: Cambridge University Press, 2020.
Collins, Michael. *Empire, Nationalism and the Post-colonial World: Rabindranath Tagore's Writings on History, Politics and Society*. Oxford: Routledge, 2013.
Dasgupta, Subrata. *The Bengal Renaissance: Identity and Creativity—From Rammohun Roy to Rabindranath Tagore*. Ranikhet: Permanent Black, 2007.
Dasgupta, Uma. *Rabindranath Tagore: A Biography*. New Delhi: Oxford University Press, 2004.
Dutta, Krishna, and Andrew Robinson. *Rabindranath Tagore: The Myriad-minded Man*. New York, NY: St Martin's Press, 1995.
Dutta, Pradip Kumar. *Rabindranath Tagore's 'The Home and the World': A Critical Companion*. London: Anthem Press, 2004.
Elmhirst, Leonard K. *Rabindranath Tagore: Pioneers in Education*. London: John Murray, 1960.
———. *Poet and Plowman*. Kolkata: Visva-Bharati, 2008; reprint.
Fraser, Bashabi. *Rabindranath*. London: Reaktion Books, 2020.
Furrell, James W. *The Tagore Family: A Memoir*. New Delhi: Rupa, 2004.
Ghose, Benoy. *Iswar Chandra Vidyasagar*. New Delhi: Publication Division, Ministry of Information and Broadcasting, Government of India, 1971.
Ghosh, Murari. *Dwarkanath O Bharate Burjua Juger Udbodhon* (in Bangla). Kolkata: Progressive Publishers, 2000.
Ghosh, Sachindralal. *Raja Rammohun Roy: Pathmaker of Modern India*. New Delhi: National Council of Educational Research and Training, 1970.
Godrej, Farah. *Cosmopolitan Political Thought: Method, Practice, Discipline*. New York, NY: Oxford University Press, 2011.
Guha, Chinmoy, ed. *Bridging East & West: Rabindranath Tagore and Roman Rolland Correspondence (1919–1940)*. New Delhi: Oxford University Press, 2018.
Guha, Ranajit. *History at the Limit of World History*. New York, NY: Columbia University Press, 2002.
Hatcher, Brian A. 'Remembering Rammohan: An Essay on the (Re)emerging of Modern Hinduism'. *History of Religion* 46, no. 1 (August 2006).
———. *Vidyasagar: The Life and After-life of an Eminent India*. Oxford: Routledge, 2014.
———. *Idioms of Improvement: Vidyasagar and Cultural Encounter in Bengal*. New Delhi: Primus, 2020.

Hay, Stephen H. *Asian Ideas of East and West: Tagore and his Critics in Japan.* Cambridge, MA: Harvard University Press, 1970.
Hees, Peter. Bengal Religious Nationalism and Communalism. *International Journal of Hindu Studies* 1, no. 1 (April 1997).
Inden, Ronald. *Imagining India.* Oxford: Basil Blackwell, 1990.
Jones, Kenneth W. *Socio-religious Reform Movements in British India.* Cambridge: Cambridge University Press, 1994.
Kaviraj, Sudipta. 'Tagore and Transformation in the Ideals of Love'. In *Love in South Asia: A Cultural History*, edited by Francesca Orsini. Cambridge: Cambridge University Press, 2006.
Khilnani, Sunil. *The Idea of India.* London: Hamish Hamilton, 1997.
Kopf, David. *The Brahmo Samaj and the Shaping of the Modern Indian Mind.* New Delhi: Archives Publishers, 1988.
Kripalani, Krishna. *Dwarkanath Tagore: A Forgotten Pioneer.* New Delhi: National Book Trust, 1980.
———. *Rabindranath Tagore: A Biography.* New Delhi: UBS Publications, 2008; reprint.
Kumarappa, J. C. *Gandhian Economic Thought.* Bombay: Vora and Co., 1951.
Mahalanobis, Prasanta Chandra. *Prasange Rabindranath* (in Bangla). Kolkata: Mahalanobis Trust, 1985.
Mahalanobis, Prasanta. *Rabindranath* (in Bangla). Kolkata: Ananda, 2002.
Mehta, Uday Singh. *Liberalism and Empire: India in British Liberal Thought.* New Delhi: Oxford University Press, 1999.
Metcalf, Thomas R. *Ideologies of the Raj.* Cambridge: Cambridge University Press, 1998.
Mittra, Kissory Chand. *Dwarkanath Tagore* (Translated from English into Bangla). Kolkata: Sommodhi Publication, 1962.
Mukherjee, Kedar Nath. *Political Philosophy of Rabindranath Tagore.* New Delhi: S. Chand & Company, 1982.
Mukherjee, Subrata. *The Political Ideas of Rabindranath Tagore: Reflections of a Public Intellectual.* New Delhi: Rupa, 2020.
Mukhopadhyay, Amartya. *Politics, Society and Colonialism: An Alternative Understanding of Tagore's Responses.* Delhi: Foundation Books, 2010.
Nandy, Ashis. 'The Culture of Indian Politics: A Stock Taking'. *The Journal of Asian Studies* 30, no. 1 (November 1970).
———. *The Illegitimacy of Nationalism: Rabindranath Tagore and the Politics of Self.* New Delhi: Oxford University Press, 1994.
———. 'Nationalism: Genuine and Spurious: Mourning Two Early Postnationalist Strains'. *Economic & Political Weekly* 41, no. 38 (2006).
Naoroji, Dadabhai. *Poverty and Un-British Rule in India.* London: S. Sonnenschein, 1901.
Nehru, Jawaharlal. *An Autobiography.* London: John Lane the Bodley Head, 1941.
———. *The Discovery of India.* Delhi: Oxford University Press, 1989; reprint.

Neogy, Ajit K. *Santiniketan and Sriniketan.* New Delhi: National Book Trust, 2015; reprint.
O'Hanlon, Rosalind. *Caste, Conflict and Ideology: Mahatma Jotirao Phule and Low Caste Protest in Nineteenth-century Western India.* Cambridge: Cambridge University Press, 1985.
Omvedt, Gail. *Cultural Revolt in a Colonial Society: The Non-Brahmin Movement in Western India, 1873–1930.* Bombay: Scientific Socialist Educational Trust, 1976.
———. *Dalits and the Democratic Revolution: Dr Ambedkar and Dalit Movement in Colonial India.* New Delhi: SAGE Publications, 1994.
Palit, Debabrata. *Dwarkanath Tagore, 1794–1846* (in Bangla). Kolkata: Tagore Research Institute, 1995.
Parekh, Bhikhu. *Debating India: Essays on Indian Political Discourse.* New Delhi: Oxford University Press, 2015.
Petit, Philip. *Republicanism: A Theory of Freedom and Government.* Oxford: Oxford University Press, 1999.
Philips, Anne. *The Politics of Presence.* Oxford: Clarendon Press, 1995.
Poddar, Arabinda. *Tagore: The Political Personality.* Kolkata: Indiana, 2004.
Ray, Bhrati. 'New Woman in Rabindranath Tagore's Short Stories: An Interrogation of Laboratory'. *Asiatic* 4, no. 2 (December 2010).
Roy, Satyendranath. *Rabindranather Samajchinta* (in Bangla). Kolkata: Granthalaya, 1985.
Rudolph, Lloyd, and S. H. Rudolph. *The Realm of the Public Sphere: Identity and Policy.* New Delhi: Oxford University Press, 2008.
Saha, Poulomi. 'Singing Bengal into a Nation: Tagore the Colonial Cosmopolitan'. *Journal of Modern Literature* 36, no. 2 (Winter, 2013).
Sen, Amartya. 'Tagore and His India'. *New York Review of Books* 44, no. 12 (1997).
———. *Development as Freedom.* New Delhi: Oxford University Press, 1999.
———. *The Argumentative India: Writings on Indian History, Culture and Identity.* New York, NY: Picador, 2005.
———. *Identity and Violence: The Illusion of Destiny.* London: Allen Lane, 2006.
———. *The Idea of Justice.* New York, NY: Allen Lane, 2009.
Sen, Amiya P. *Hindu Revivalism in Bengal, 1872–1905: Some Essays in Interpretation.* Delhi: Oxford University Press, 1993.
Sen, Ashok. *Rajnitir Pathakrame Rabindrnath* (in Bangla). Kolkata: Visva-Bharati Granthana Vibhaga, 2004.
Sen, Sachin. *The Political Thought of Tagore.* Kolkata: General Printers and Publishers, 1947.
Sengupta, Kalyan. *The Philosophy of Rabindranath Tagore.* Burlington: Ashgate Publishing, 2005.
Seth, Sanjay. 'Rewriting Histories of Nationalism: The Politics of "Moderate Nationalism" in India, 1870–1905'. *American Historical Review* 104, no. 1 (February 1999).

Sinha, Dixit. *A Poet's Experiment in Rebuilding Samaj and Nation: Sriniketan's Rural Reconstruction Work, 1922–1960*. Bolpur: Birupjatio Sahitya Sammiloni, 2019.
Stokes, Eric. *The English Utilitarians and India*. Cambridge: Cambridge University Press, 1959.
Thompson, Edward. *Rabindranath Tagore: Poet and Dramatist*. London: Macmillan, 1926.
Thompson, E. P. *Introduction to Rabindranath Tagore's Nationalism*. New Delhi: Rupa & Co., 1992.
———. *Alien Homage: Edward Thompson and Rabindranath Tagore*. New York, NY: Oxford University Press, 1993.
Vajpeyi, Ananya. *Righteous Republic: The Political Foundation of Modern India*. Cambridge, MA: Harvard University Press, 2012.

About the Author

Bidyut Chakrabarty is Vice Chancellor of Visva-Bharati, Santiniketan, West Bengal, India. He was a professor in the Department of Political Science in University of Delhi till November 2018. He completed his PhD from London School of Economics and Political Science and has been associated with teaching and research for more than three decades. He has taught in several prestigious educational institutions, such as London School of Economics and Political Science, London, UK; Indian Institute of Management (IIM) Kolkata, India; Monash University, Australia; National University of Singapore, Singapore; University of Hamburg, Germany. He has authored several textbooks and academic books. Among his publications are *Public Administration: From Government to Governance* (2017), *Winning the Mandate: The Indian Experience* (2016), *Communism in India: Events, Processes and Ideologies* (2014), *Indian Politics and Society since Independence: Events, Processes and Ideology* (2008) and *The Governance Discourse: A Reader* (2008).

Index

Adi Brahmo Samaj see also Brahmo Samaj, 8
Adi Brahmo Samaj
  revival of *Tattwabodhini Patrika*, 8
Akshay Kumar Dutta
  belief in God, 148
  view on science subjects, 148
Anandamath, 12
Atmaparichay, 202
Atmiya Sabha, 58

B. R. Ambedkar
  condemned caste system, 311
Bal Gangadhar Tilak (1856–1920), 303
Bankim Chandra Chatterjee, 214
  revolutionary step, 214
Bankim Chandra Chattopadhyay, 12
Bengal Herald, 176
Bengal Provincial Congress Committee
  Pabna session, 228
Bengal
  19th century, 297
  Debendranath intellectual as watershed, 196
  role of landlord of Debendranath, 155
  transformation era, 155
Bharati
  published essay, 236
Bharattirtha, 230
Black Act, 66
book
  The Three Tagores, 35
  The Three Tagores, 1, 25, 37

books
  Atmaparichay, 202
  Char Adhyay, 206
  Jibansmriti, 202
  Swadeshi Samaj, 206
  Brahma Dharma, 11
  Brahmacharya Vidyalaya, 34
Brahmo Sabha
  founded by Rammohun and Dwarkanath, 122
Brahmo Samaj, 6, 156
  creating, 72
  established by Roy, 1828, 16
  failed somewhere, 157
  hope of detractors, 73
  more people joined, 7
  objective, 299
  platform to stay together, 162
  Rabindranath, 8
  revamped in 1882, 219
Brahmo School, 3
  establishment, 219
Brahmoism, 2
British expansionist policy, 134
Calcutta Courier
  initiatives regarding education, 146

Carr Company, 42
Carr, Tagore & Company, 85
caste, 311
Chandalika, 310
Charitrapuja, 225
Civil Disobedience Movement (1930–1932), 281

Debendranath Tagore, 1, 120

letter to Rajnarayan Basu, 191
accepted Vedas and *Upanishads*,
  176
balanced man, 163
battling against Hindu orthodoxy,
  161
Brahmo Samaj, creating, 72
close intimacy with Rammohun,
  129
colleagues, 7
continuity with Dwarkanath
  Tagore's socio-ideological
  ideas, 127
critical role as educationist, 154
designing new conceptual mould,
  189–196
Dwarkanath's regular interactions
  with British colleagues, 161
educationist, 146–155
effective landlord, 131–138
establishing Brahmo Vidyalaya in
  rural Bengal, 123
exposed to Western philosophical
  discourses, 163
Gandhi's contribution to social
  reform, 225
harbinger, 158
ill luck, 149
inspired by Rammohun thoughts,
  130
introduction of Vedantic wisdom,
  120
less interest in material possessions, 128
letter by father, 128
letter to Sharadaprasad, 131
like father, like son, 6
new responsibilities, 177
no dissociation with aspirational
  hankering, 157
oppose Hindu idolatry, 176
organizational endeavour, 138–146
part of sociocultural reforms, 200
patriot, undoubtedly, 156
political liberation, no place, 293
pragmatic, 181
radical transformation, 179
Rammohun's importance, 163
reiteration and recasting of socio-
  ideological preferences, 175
relation with Rammohun, 166
ruthlessness, 136
social rebel, 161
sociocultural milieu, 163–165
support for idol worship, 182
support to Vedas and Upanishads,
  183
well-decided path to follow, 162
deistic religious ideas
  Rammohun Roy, 5
Derozians, 130
Dharma Sabha, 11
drama
  Chandalika, 310
Dwarkanath Roy
  family environment, 41
Dwarkanath Tagore, 1
  adopted by, 47
  benevolent guardian, 51
  Brahmo Samaj, 316
  businessman, 88
  conceptualizing, 48–54
  contribution, social reformer and
    entrepreneur, 32
  different version, 79–80
  dramatic sociopolitical and cultural
    changes, 75
  educationist, 59–61
  eras of British colonialism, 11
  fallen Hindu, wife described, 74
  fierce campaign launched, 62
  followed path of Rammohun, 52
  full of thoughts, 52
  idea of universal brotherhood, 53
  international perspectives, 51
  introduce English education,
    15
  introduction to business, 80

Kshitindranath Tagore's description, 54
Landholders' Society establishment, 62
liberal, 48
man of organization, 61
patriot and a philanthropist, 53
perfect landlord, 47
praised by Thomas Turton, 49
reasons for success, 87
schools and colleges, 292
significant historical role, 40
social reformer, 54–59
speech on William Bentinck, 89
success story, 82–85
successful entrepreneur, 77–79
support from well-wishers, 47
together with Rammohun, 197
tough competitor, 47
true liberal and confirmed loyalist, 72
truthful and honest, 52
two important qualities, 55
viewed Company rule, 15

East India Company
Dwarkanath's presence, 292
education
Debendranath's contribution, 146

Gandhi, 37
Hind Swaraj, 318
Ghare-Baire
argument, 231
critique of Swadeshi Movement in Bengal (1905–1908), 232
organizational grip of Congress leadership, weakening, 282
Tagore's assessment of inner debates, 233
violence, 212
Gora
Hindu–Muslim amity, 252
Gurudev, 209

Hindu Hitarthi Vidyalaya
formation in 1846, 151
Hinduism, 129
Hitabrata, 235

India
economic transformations, 13
radical social changes, 13
socioculturally and in economic terms, 12
Tagores' contribution sociocultural texture, 292
Indian nationalism
ideological interaction between Gandhi and Gurudev, 288
political difference between Gandhi and Tagore, 278–287
two contrasting perspectives, 275–278
Isa-Upanishad
shloka, 180
translation in Bangla, 219
IshaUpanishad's, 2
Ishoponishad, 120
slokas, 120
Jeevan-Smriti, 224
Jibansmriti, 202
jotedar, 13

K. K. Mitra, 8
Keshab Chandra Sen, 191

mufassil towns, 63
Mukhojje-Barrujje, 237
Muktadhara
dialogues of *Dhananjoy Bairagi*, 212
Nababarsha, 222

neo-Hindu ideology, 298
Nirakar Brahma, 6, 10
Non-cooperation Campaign (1920–1922), 281
novel

Anandamath, 12, 299
Char Adhay, 206
Ghare-Baire, 204, 206, 317
Gora or 1934 *Char Adhay*, 206
Rajarshi, 256, 293
Rajarshi, 1887, 211

Palmer Company
  success story, 88
Patha Bhavana, 3
plays
  Prayaschitta, 211, 256, 293
  Tasher Desh, 278
  Visarjan, 256, 293
Prayaschitta, 256
  testimony to Tagore's emotional
    chords, 212
Presidency College
  establishment in 1855, 153

Rabindranath Tagore, 3, 5, 202, 209
  admirer and critic of Mahatma
    Gandhi, 252
  alternative centre in learning, 226
  argument, 312
  argument on Indian history, 224
  Atmaparichay, 202
  basic concerns to society, 239
  British rule in India, views, 257
  caste system, 310
  concern for humanity, 308
  confluence of thoughts, 209
  Constitution 1950, defend liberal
    conceptual, 306
  contemporary political, 34
  denial of fruits of industrialism,
    318
  departure from Europeanized
    thoughts, 222
  differed from grandfather and
    father, 287
  family background and society,
    218
  follower of Gandhi, 253–260
  foundational ideas, 227
  India's freedom environment, 251
  innovative and compassionate
    social designer, 224–229
  Jibansmriti, 202
  liberal humanist, 312
  memoirs, 213
  nurtured in politico-ideological
    environment, 236
  pirali brahmin, 217
  politico-ideological context,
    229–243
  socialcultural and political issues
    approach, 317
  spirit of rejection, condemning,
    215
  un-Gandhian perception, 260
  Upanishads, 204
  views on Bose, 280
  zamindar, 238
Rajnarayan Basu
  letter by Debendranath, 191
Ramaprasad Roy, 129
Ramchandra Vidyabagish, 120, 160
Ramlochon Tagore
  Dwarkanath Tagore, 47
Rammohun Roy, 1, 214
  relation with Debendranath, 166
  views on Bible, 10
  basis of conceptualization of new
    social morality, 169
  deistic religious ideas, 5
  Farquhar's argument on ideol-
    ogy, 5
  first Indian thinkers, 40
  food served, 129
  idea of God, 5
  idea of universal brotherhood, 53
  importance in Tagore family, 163
  influencer, 165
  inspired by Western discourses, 49
  reminding importance of sacrifice,
    169
  social reforms, 42

spiritual persuasion, 168
universalism, 191
Rathindranath Tagore
  status quo, argument, 221

Sambad Bhaskar
  appreciating initiatives by
    Debendranath, 151
Sati Regulation Act, 1829, 54
Sridhar Nayaratna, 7
Sulabh Samachar, 175
Sunset Law, 135
Swadeshi Movement
  source of inspiration, 235
  motion politico-ideological processes, 236
  three trends, 234
Swadeshi Samaj, 290, 308
  argument in, 226

Tagores
  powerful critique of Western
    philosophical, 4
Tattwabodhini Pathshala, 150
Tattwabodhini Patrika, 9, 41, 158
Tattwabodhini Sabha, 16, 146, 167, 181
  covenant, 184–189
  hierarchical social division, 168

reason of establishment, 176
The Bengal Herald, 41
three Tagores
  analysis, 294
  careful dissection of ideas, 303
  complementary points, 219
  eras of British colonialism in India, 11
  new wave of thinking, 307
  sources of conceptual insights, 305
  specific ways, conceptually connected, 314

Upanishads, 305

Vedas and Vedantic texts, 1
  Debendranath Tagore's perception, 3
Vedas
  translation in Bangla, 219
Visarjan, 256
Visva-Bharati, 3, 122, 175
  emergence, 34
  establishing, 210

zamindar
  Debendranath, 132
  letter of 4 June 1883, 135